INDUCTIVE
STUDY
of the book of
JEREMIAH

Preliminary Edition

William Carey Library INTERCULTURAL INTERTEXTS*

Principles of Church Growth
by Weld and McGavran
440 pp. $3.95

Inductive Study of the Book of Jeremiah
the Word of the Lord in a Time of Crisis
by F. Ross Kinsler
584 pp. $4.95

Inductive Study of the Book of Mark
the Gospel of Jesus Christ the Son of God
by F. Ross Kinsler
400 pp. $3.95

*An *Intertext*, as the term was originally coined in Latin America,
implies the following: it is a theological seminary textbook
designed for use with a single weekly seminar and more than usual
out-of-class study. It can be used with either residence or
extension programs. It is built specifically to fit into a larger
matrix, a complete curriculum of other books and courses. In
preliminary form it is reviewed by a large number of institutions
and denominations and is produced with joint use in mind. Thus
the three books mentioned above are (in Spanish) part of a whole
matrix of Intertexts under joint development by many schools of
many denominations for use in Spanish-speaking areas of the world.
The Spanish Intertext program has been called "the largest non-
governmental educational development project in the world today."

Now, however, schools in practically every other country of the
world have become interested in the use of this new type of text.
Rather than every area having to start from scratch, it has been
felt that the Spanish *Intertexts* can helpfully be brought into
English. Where English is a native tongue, they may be used
directly or with minor adaptation. In other language and culture
areas the English *Intercultural Intertext*--with strict observance
of the cautions mentioned in the *Publisher's Foreword*--can greatly
speed up the development of a whole new Intertext matrix carefully
elaborated within the new situation. Then we hope that other texts
beyond the three mentioned above will shortly be available. These
three in preliminary form will be revised and reissued again and
again and hopefully will profit from improvements suggested by
schools all over the world.

INDUCTIVE STUDY

of the book of

JEREMIAH

the Word of the Lord in a time of crisis

F. ROSS KINSLER

533 HERMOSA STREET • SOUTH PASADENA, CALIF. 91030

This is a limited, preliminary edition for purposes of study
and experimentation in residence and extension theological
seminaries. Editorial correspondence or requests for permission to translate and adapt should be directed to the
Presbyterian Seminary of Guatemala. A Spanish edition will
be available in 1973.

International Standard Book Number 0-87808-112-7
Library of Congress Catalogue Number 70-180707

Published and distributed by:

William Carey Library
533 Hermosa Street
South Pasadena, California   91030

and

The Presbyterian Seminary of Guatemala
Apartado 3
San Felipe, Reu.
Guatemala, C. A.

PRINTED IN THE UNITED STATES OF AMERICA

Preface

A preliminary edition of this book was published last year. I
would like to repeat here my deep appreciation for my colleagues on
the staff of the Seminario Evangelico Presbiteriano de Guatemala, whose
companionship has made extension theological education a joyful experience in Guatemala and whose dedication has made it a by-word in
Latin America!

Jose G. Carrera
James and Gennet Emery
Baudilio and Alma Recinos
Benjamin and Nelly Jacobs
Blanca Nieves Canos

This new edition is only a partial revision of the original, but
it does include many corrections and recommendations suggested by
Gennet Emery and Louise Jeter Walker, who have worked through the
entire course carefully. I wish to thank them for their patience
and wisdom and also for their enthusiastic encouragement.

More fundamental changes in the content and format of this textbook
will have to come later. I want to invite all who read it, especially
those who are involved in extension theological education, to send us
their criticisms and suggestions so that this textbook may become an
effective instrument "for the equipment of the saints for the work of
ministry."

F.R.K.

Publisher's Foreword

The publisher cannot be sure into whose hands a book may fall. Since this is a very unusual, preliminary edition of a book which is itself quite unusual, let the following comments be directed to several possible recipients:

1) *Pastors and Christian Education Directors in the United States.* This book has been sent to certain churches that have long standing interest in the expanding program and worldwide interest focussed upon the Evangelical Presbyterian Seminary in Guatemala. The assumption is that you will be fascinated to see an English version of one of the unique textbooks that are at the heart of this new program and that you will be willing to help us with this first, preliminary edition. The book was not designed with you or your church in mind (see #2), but we hope that you will be willing to help us in two ways:

a) By accepting and using this book with a choice few of your laymen (who may be interested in what is taught in seminary) you will help us pay for this first, limited edition.

b) You can help us iron out the remaining wrinkles in the wording and "programmed" structure. When a study group agrees that a particular question is not clear, the recorder for that group should make a note to be sent directly to the author: Dr. F. Ross Kinsler, Apartado 1881, Guatemala, C.A. Use a 17¢ stamp for a half-ounce (3 sheets) letter.

We hope you will feel the pulse of the overseas mission movement as you undertake this task with us. To that end we invite you to read what we have to say to the people for whom this special edition is primarily prepared.

2) *Those who are training men for the ministry.* This is not a laymen's course. It is a standard, credit-bearing seminary course currently being offered in the Evangelical Presbyterian Seminary of Guatemala. It is relatively simple in that it is a first-year course, and because it is designed for pastoral leaders of outstanding intelligence who nevertheless have not spent the first

third of their lives with books in classrooms. But it is not a
Bible Institute course in the sense that that might be taken to
mean it is designed for all laymen and young people of the church.
Some of the tough questions of Biblical scholarship are raised,
not to disturb the faith of laymen but to prepare the mature
Christian leader to deal with people who may already be disturbed
by their religion courses in college, or by other popular, secular
treatments of the Bible.

A second caution is necessary. It is true that this "intercultural" English edition was produced with other linguistic and
cultural areas in mind. The rapidly growing movement toward theological education by extension has created a great interest in high
quality textbook materials that have been developed especially for
such use. Since the movement began in Latin America, most of these
are in Spanish or Portuguese and are not directly useful in other
parts of the world. However, now that some of these are being
reworked in English, it is time to point out that "reworking" in
another language, not mere translation, is what is necessary.
Ordinary books may be of some value in simple translation, but not
books constructed along the lines of Programmed Instruction. A
straight translation will serve only as a basis for a trial with one
or two key students and must be reworked, question by question, in
the new language and in the new cultural context. Requests for
permission to use these materials in other languages must, therefore, be accompanied by a detailed description of the process of
adaptation. In no case will permission be given for a simple
translation.

Contents

Introduction

1. Preparing to do a Job.

One of the primary responsibilities of a church leader is to preach and teach from the Bible. This is a very important part of his ministry. It is also very complicated. To be successful he must develop a number of skills. He should establish a careful pattern of Bible study and exposition. These skills and habits will guide him every day in his:

1. Devotional reading and study.
2. Sermon preparation.
3. Lessons for Sunday school and other programs.
4. Formation of biblical theology.
5. Other special uses.

Not only does a pastor preach and teach from the Bible constantly. He should also train other leaders in the church in these same skills. And together with them he should help all the members to read and understand and share the Bible. This added responsibility underlines the fact that a pastor needs to know how to study and use the Bible.

The Inductive Study of Jeremiah, one of a series of Bible book studies, is an opportunity for you to prepare for these tasks. The book of Jeremiah will serve as a case study, an experiment. You will work with the text of Jeremiah itself. Through various exercises you will uncover its meaning. You will of course want to find out all you can about this particular book. But that is not your primary goal. Your main concern is to develop new skills in Bible study, skills that will serve you throughout your ministry, skills that will be applicable not only in your study of Jeremiah but also in your use of the other Old Testament prophets and even to some extent in your understanding of all the books of the Bible.

2. Some Prerequisites.

This course has been prepared especially for a certain group of people. It will be too difficult for some people, too simple for others. The following paragraphs should tell you if it is right for you.

We have aimed the manual at men and women who have read the Bible a great deal and who are serving in their churches as teachers and preachers and workers. It is for those who have a strong desire to study and use the Bible systematically and effectively.

Students who are starting out in this course should already be able to use the references in their Bibles and concordances. They should be familiar with the major periods, leaders, and literary groupings of the Old and New Testaments. They should be able to use an atlas and understand how to draw a map. They should be able to calculate periods of history from given points before and after the time of Christ. They should know how to recognize paragraphs and how to make a simple outline.

Many will have studied previously an introductory course on the Old Testament, but this is not absolutely necessary. Some will have gone through other inductive Bible courses. All should eventually take other inductive studies based on other parts of the Bible.

If you feel that you are not able to meet these prerequisites or that you are weak at some point, perhaps you should talk with your professor before beginning the course. He may recommend some further testing or preliminary study so that you will best profit from the course.

3. Our Objectives.

Before starting into the course itself let's set down clearly what we hope to achieve. We will define our objectives in terms of what you will be able to do, in terms of specific knowledge and skills you will be able to use in your ministry.

Someone has said that defining objectives is like looking at a road map before setting out on a trip. First you decide on your destination. There can be no doubt about that. And once you know where you are going you can find the best roads to get there. What follows is a description of our destination and some of the roads we will be using in this course. I think you will want to take the trip and I hope the route we have prepared will take you to your destination.

By the end of this course of study you will be able to write a summary of Jeremiah's personal experience, his message, and the political and religious conditions of his day. You will be able to recite the dates of the fall of Jerusalem, the destruction of Nineveh, and the Battle of Carchemish. Using the Bible alone you will be able to construct a chronological chart showing the length of Jeremiah's ministry, the exact periods of the kings of Judah at that time, and the relationship of Jeremiah and Judah to the conflicts of the great world empires of the time. You should be able to sketch a simple map of the Near East without the help of an atlas, showing the geographical position of Judah in these conflicts.

You should be able to recognize the main ideas as you read through the book of Jeremiah. You should be able to identify historical information and relate those passages to the important events and periods mentioned above. You should be able to give a clear explanation of the many literary figures and dramatizations that Jeremiah used. You should be able to locate in Jeremiah and elsewhere in the Bible information about the destruction of Jerusalem and the various deportations of the Jews. You should be able to explain the historical and theological significance of the fall of Jerusalem, the captivity, and the future hope as they are presented in Jeremiah. You should be able to interpret the experience of Jeremiah and his people (through exposition of relevant passages) and show the relevance of their experience for us today.

To these objectives we must add three more dimensions of your learning experience. Each of these is as important as all the previous objectives. In fact, each of the following objectives includes all the earlier objectives.

a. You should be able to explain how to discover the historical background of the book of Jeremiah, how to form paragraph titles, how to interpret literary figures and other passages.

b. You should be able to prepare lesson and sermon outlines based on passages of Jeremiah dealing with ethical teachings, religious problems, theological concepts and personal vocations.

c. You should be able to apply the skills you have learned in the study of Jeremiah to other prophetical books of the Old Testament.

I hope this rather long statement will help you define what you hope to accomplish and also inspire you to work to reach these objectives. The course is not easy, but the goals are worthwhile. And the experience can be not only useful but exciting.

These objectives tell you, also, what the final examination will be like. In fact, you can measure your own progress as you work through the course by referring back to this opening statement. And when you finish you can grade yourself and the course to see if it has achieved its purpose and enabled you to reach these objectives.

4. How to Study this Course.

The course is divided into 15 lessons, and it is planned on the basis of one lesson per week. If you add one week of orientation at the beginning and one week for the final review and exam, it will take a total of 17 weeks. Some professors and students may, of course, decide to go at a slower or at a faster rate.

Each lesson is divided into 5 sections, and you should be able to complete each section in about one hour. We recommend that you set aside an hour a day during the week. This will help you develop a habit of regular, daily study which you should maintain throughout your ministry. And it is probably the most effective way to study this course. In other words, don't try to do too much at once, and don't leave your week's assignment to the last minute.

The course has been set up especially for extension seminary programs in which the students meet with their professors once a week. It may, of course, be used in a night school or a residence seminary just as well. In any case, we believe it is best for you to study Jeremiah on your own and to have class time with a professor just once a week.

The weekly class session is very important. There you will be tested, perhaps every week or every other week, on the material you have been studying. You will discuss with the other students the concepts and methods of each lesson. And you will be asked to explain and apply these teachings to your own life and ministry. If you have any difficulties or doubts about your studies, your professor will help you find the answers.

Some people wonder why we have put the answers to most of the questions right
in the work book. They say it makes the work too easy; they say some students
will just copy the answers. It certainly is true that you could do that. No
one will check up on you. But this also means that the only one you can cheat
is yourself. If you just copy the answers, you probably won't learn what is
being taught. And you will probably fail the weekly quizzes and the final exam.

There is an important reason for including the answers in this workbook. As
you work through each section and each lesson, you need to know if you are on
the right track. If you make a mistake, you need to correct it before you go
on. Even if your answers are correct, you need to know that they are correct
so that you can go ahead confidently. Educators have showed us that we are
capable of learning mistakes just as we are capable of learning facts.

Actually the educators know very little about how learning takes place. But
recent experience with programmed instruction has given us some guidance in
the preparation of this course. As you study, you will be asked to use each
new piece of information and each new method immediately. And you will see
immediately whether you have used that information or technique correctly.
This procedure is based on the principles of programmed instruction.

Some people have other questions about this kind of instruction. They ask if
it is mechanical. They want to know if the program forces the student to give
only one answer to every question. They are afraid that programmed instruction
makes the student a slave of a predetermined process and mentality. You will
soon see that this course tries to do just the opposite. There are some skills
and there is some information that you will have to learn more or less mechani-
cally. But the course as a whole will develop your ability to think for yourself and to interpret the Bible for yourself. Keep this in mind as you compare
your answers with the information given in the work book.

In order to avoid seeing the answers given in the text use a piece of heavy
paper to cover the page. Read each question, slide the mask down to the next
sign in the margin (*), write in your answer, then slide the mask down further
and compare your answer with the answer given in the text. Do not expect to
have exactly the same wording in your answer, and do not change your answer
unless it has a different meaning. Be complete: generally the size of the
space indicates how long your answer should be. If you come to a question
that you do not understand at all, put a question mark in the margin and look
at the answer given in the text. Bring up any major problems in the next class
session.

Quite obviously you, the student, are the center of the learning process. This
special workbook has been prepared only to help you reach your objectives. In
these lessons I have tried to lay out series of steps which will enable you to
learn skills in Bible study and exposition. The real test of this learning
experience will be the application of these skills in your daily on-going ministry.

A final note for the student: Your only textbook in this course is the Bible.
For the sake of uniformity in the class use the Revised Standard Version. You
must also have access to a Bible dictionary, an atlas or maps of the Bible

lands, and a good concordance. You will also need an 8 1/2 by 11 inch looseleaf notebook.

A final note for the professor: I hope to prepare a Teacher's Guide with additional suggestions about the course, bibliographical references, sample quizzes
and examinations, etc. This guide may be requested at the following address:
Presbyterian Seminary of Guatemala, San Felipe Retalhuleu, Guatemala, C.A.
In order to keep track of this material send your request with the signature
of an official of your institution or church. And please take into account
that this kind of material is still in an experimental stage. We need your
criticisms and recommendations.

1

Beginning   Steps

How should I begin? That is perhaps the first question you should ask yourself as you start to study Jeremiah and you should ask yourself the same question as you approach other books of the Bible. It is a very important question. The way you begin may determine the results you will achieve. Many people never study the Bible seriously because they don't know how to get started. Many people who do study the Bible get confused because they have not asked this question or because they have assumed that any method is all right.

In this lesson you will learn how to begin an Inductive Bible Study. There are, of course, several very good study methods, and there are many different ways to begin. This manual does not attempt to teach one strict way or just one method. But there are certain things that all Bible students should do as they begin to study a book like Jeremiah.

When you finish this lesson you should be able to:

Write a definition of Inductive Bible Study.

List and explain three steps for beginning an Inductive Bible Study.

Note that in Lesson I you will only be introduced to the three steps for beginning an Inductive Bible Study. In Lessons II, III, and IV you will study each of these steps in greater detail.

A. How to Start an Inductive Bible Study

1. Inductive Bible Study is an approach to Bible study which begins with the Bible. This is a very simple explanation. Later we will try to give more complete explanations. But if someone asks you for a definition now, you can tell

him Inductive Bible Study is an approach to Bible study which _____

* _____. *

Begins with the Bible

2. Or if someone asks you what method you are using you can say: This approach

to Bible study is called _____.
*   *

Inductive Bible Study

3. Really, Inductive Bible Study is not a method. It is not a set of rules or techniques which you can learn and then apply to any part of the Bible. It is an approach. It is a way of going to the Bible, a way of looking at it, a way of learning from it. Inductive Bible Study uses many methods. But it only uses these methods after it has looked at the text to see what it says. It uses old methods and develops new methods as it finds what is in the Bible.

Inductive Bible Study begins with _____. It is an

_____ to Bible study. It is not a method but it uses

* _____.   *

the Bible   approach   many methods

4. You may think that all methods begin with the Bible. But many methods
really don't. For example, when a Sunday School teacher prepares his lesson,
he usually begins by reading his teacher's manual. The lessons in his manual
are based on the Bible. They have Bible references, and they usually give explanations about the Bible. They give the theme of the passage, its historical
background, an outline, and some applications.

This Sunday School teacher begins with (the Bible/someone else's interpretation of the Bible).

This method (should/should not) be called Inductive Bible Study. (Underline
correct answer.)
*   *

someone else's interpretation of the Bible   should not

5. Here are some more examples of Bible study which are not inductive. Many
preachers begin their sermon preparation by choosing a topic and looking in a
concordance to find several passages that mention that topic. Then they put
together the ideas they have on the subject. Others choose a passage and look
up explanations which have been written about the passage in other books called
commentaries. They study the passage itself, but usually follow what the commentaries say about it. Some preachers use only the passage itself. But instead of
studying it seriously to see what it has to say they use the ideas they already
have about the passage.

Explain why these examples are not Inductive Bible Study. _____

_____

* _____ *

They don't begin with the Bible. They begin with someone's ideas about the Bible.

6. Let's take one more example. Suppose you have been asked to lead an Inductive
Bible Study on Jeremiah. You want to teach your students about Jeremiah's personal experience, his message, and the political and religious conditions of
his day.

How will you teach them these things? _____

_____

* _____ *

Your answer should indicate that you will have the students go directly to the Bible or to the book of Jeremiah to find this information.

7. You probably have a pretty good idea now what we mean by Inductive Bible Study. And you probably have a good idea how we are going to begin our study

of Jeremiah. We are going to start with _____.

*   *

the book of Jeremiah itself, the Bible.

8. As we begin studying the book of Jeremiah, we have to know how to read it. In other words we can't just pick out any passage of Jeremiah and expect to understand it. Even if we go through the entire book from the beginning, we may not interpret correctly what we are reading.

We have to read and study the book of Jeremiah on its own terms. We have to see it as it really is. This is what we will try to do in the Inductive Study of Jeremiah. And this is what we should do in all Inductive Bible Study.

Complete the following definition. Inductive Bible Study is an approach to Bible

study in which we begin with the Bible and _____

_____.

*   *

study it on its own terms, see it as it really is.

9. We want to study the Bible on its own terms, see it as it really is. For example, it is quite obvious that the Bible is not one book but a collection of 66 books written at different times by many different authors.

The inductive approach therefore studies the Bible by _____

_____.

*   *

books, by looking at each book separately.

10. Let's look at some examples of how to study Jeremiah on its own terms. First, we need to know what kind of writing or literature it is, what kind of a book it is. It will be very easy to answer this question. And the answer will help us understand the book. For example, if it is law we will expect to find rules

for life and worship. If it is history, we will expect to find events and
leaders and periods of time. If it is a letter or epistle, we will look for
salutations and personal comments.

To study Jeremiah on its own terms we have to find out _____

* _____ *

what kind of book or literature or writing it is.

11. This is an important first step in Inductive Bible Study.

If we wish to study a book on its own terms we should _____

* _____ *

find out what kind of writing or book it is.

12. In order to understand Jeremiah we will also have to find out something
about its historical background. We need to know what time in history it is
talking about, what places and nations are involved, what events and circumstances are referred to. Only with this information will we be able to study
Jeremiah on its own terms and understand it.

Call this the second step in beginning an Inductive Bible Study. If we wish to

study a book on its own terms we should _____

* _____ *

find out something about its historical background.

13. Another important step in our study of Jeremiah has to do with the structure
of the book. The structure is the order or outline of a book. When an author
writes a book he usually has a few major ideas or events he wants to emphasize.
Or he wants to tell his readers how something happened. Or he is describing an
object. Usually the way he arranges or organizes his book is important. If we
want to read and understand the book we should try to discover its outline or
structure. This is another part of studying a book on its own terms. Of course
we have to be careful and find the author's structure and not make up our own.

A third step in Inductive Bible Study is _____

* _____ *

to look for the outline or structure of the book.

14. You are now ready to begin your study of Jeremiah. But first let's review what we have done so far.

Write a definition of Inductive Bible Study. Your definition should include

two basic ideas. _____

_____   _____

* _____. *

Inductive Bible Study is an approach to Bible study that <u>begins with the Bible</u> and <u>studies it on its own terms</u>. Be sure your definition includes the two under-lined ideas.

15. Now list the three beginning steps or ways in which we study a book of the Bible on its own terms.

a. _____

b. _____

c. _____

*

---

a. Find out what kind of writing it is.
b. Find out something about its historical background.
c. Look for the outline or structure of the book.

These are the three steps for beginning an Inductive Bible Study that you should be able to explain by the end of this lesson. In this lesson you will begin the study of Jeremiah using these three steps. Later, if asked, you should be ready to try out these same steps on another prophetical book.

You will notice that we shall find this information in the book of Jeremiah it-self. It would be much easier for me to tell you what kind of book Jeremiah is, what its historical background is, and what is its structure. But that would not help you find out how to do an Inductive Bible Study. Remember, we said that Inductive Bible Study begins with the Bible.

(Note: You have just finished Section A, which is calculated as one day's study assignment. Go on to Sections B, C, D, and E to complete Lesson I.)

B. What Kind of a Book is It?

Read through Jer. 1-6 rapidly and carefully. As you read keep in mind the three steps for beginning an Inductive Bible Study. Consider especially what kind of literature this book consists of. When you have finished reading, go on to the questions below. If the book of Jeremiah were not so long you should read all the way through it at this time.

1. No doubt you knew what kind of a book Jeremiah is before starting this course. It is one of the books of the Major Prophets of the Old Testament.

What kind of literature does the book of Jeremiah consist of?_____
*   *

prophecy

2. You probably also know that the basic meaning of the word "prophecy" is proclamation of God's word or God's will. Check this definition of prophecy by reading through Chapter I again and underlining all the phrases that say "the Lord said" or "the word of the Lord" or something like that.

How many times do these phrases appear in Jeremiah 1? _____
*   *

If you include the phrases "I command you" and "I will utter" you should have about 14.

3. Now glance at several other parts of Jeremiah at random to see if these phrases are repeated throughout the book.

It is obvious that they are repeated (never / often / constantly).
*   *

constantly

4. What is the basic meaning of the word prophecy? _____

_____

What evidence can you give to show that Jeremiah is a book of prophecy?_____
*   *
_____

Proclamation of God's will or God's word.
Throughout the book we find phrases like "the Lord said."

5. Perhaps we should mention that some people think that prophecy is foretelling events of future history. It is true that some prophecy has to do with God's will for the distant future.

Do you happen to remember what famous prophecy of Jeremiah was fulfilled in

Jesus Christ (Mark 14:24)? _____
*   *

Jer. 31:31-34, the prophecy about the new covenant.

6. But the major emphasis of the prophets was the challenge of God's word to His people for that particular time and for the <u>immediate</u> future. Jeremiah, like other prophets, spoke often of Israel's past and of the coming destruction. But his purpose was primarily to call His people to repentance right then.

So we should insist on our definition of prophecy as _____

* _____ . *

the proclamation of God's word or will.

7. As you read through Jer. 1 did you notice the passage where Jeremiah is

called a prophet? Copy the phrase here: _____

* _____ *

I appointed you a prophet to the nations.

8. This first chapter gives us a clear and exciting picture of what a prophet is.

Write down 2 or 3 phrases from this chapter that best express what a prophet is.

_____

_____

* _____ *

I like the phrases "Whatever I command you you shall speak" and "Behold, I have put my words in your mouth." Later in the book (Jer. 15:19) God says to Jeremiah, "You shall be as my mouth."

9. What is a prophet? _____

* _____ *

A prophet is a man who proclaims God's word or God's will.

10. In Jer. 1:1-2 you will find another reason for saying that the book of   is
Jeremiah is a book of prophecy.

Here it is stated that these are the words of_____, a man

to whom the word of_____came.

*   *

Jeremiah   the Lord

11. Since this is the opening statement or introduction of the book, it is
especially important. Here we see that the word of God came to Jeremiah and
that these prophecies of Jeremiah are recorded in this book.

We might say that the whole book consists of_____

_____.

the proclamation of the word of the Lord through Jeremiah, the prophecies of
Jeremiah.

12. We have mentioned 4 reasons for saying that the book of Jeremiah contains
prophecy.

See how many you can remember, then check the list below.

a. _____

b. _____

c. _____

d. _____

---

a. This book is included with the Major Prophets of the Old Testament.
b. Throughout it we find phrases like "the Lord said."
c. Jeremiah was a prophet.
d. The opening statement of the book says it is the word of the Lord through
   Jeremiah.

---

13. Since Jeremiah is a book of prophecy, you will expect to find in it _____

_____.

proclamations of God's will.

14. We have said that it is important for us to know what kind of writing Jeremiah contains. And we have said that this is an important beginning step in
Inductive Bible Study.

Explain why it is important to know what kind of writing Jeremiah contains.

_____

_____

_____

If we know what kind of a book it is, we will understand it better. We will
be able to study it on its own terms.

15. We have said that if we know what kind of book we are studying, we will understand it better. We have said that the book of Jeremiah is prophecy, which means proclamation of God's word. But is not all the Bible God's word? How then are prophetical books different from other kinds of books in the Bible? How shall we distinguish them from the rest of the Old Testament?

The books of the law (Genesis through Deuteronomy) tell how God established His people and how they were supposed to worship Him and live day by day. The historical books (Joshua through Esther) narrate how God's people obeyed and disobeyed God's will through different periods of their history. The poetical books (Job through Song of Solomon) give lyrical expression to the experiences and emotions of God's people.

The prophetical books are collections of the sayings and experiences of the prophets. And these sayings of the prophets are proclamations of God's word for His people at a particular time in history. They refer to the law and the history of God's people. But they do this primarily to remind the people of their sin and to call them to repentance. They refer to future events, as we have mentioned. But this is primarily to show the people the urgency of repentance and obedience at that particular moment.

What books of the Old Testament are God's word?_____

_____

How are the prophetical books different from the other books of the Old

Testament? _____

* _____ *

All the books of the Old Testament are God's word. The prophetical books consist of collections of the sayings of the prophets which are proclamations of God's word at a particular time.

16. Now you can see more clearly why it is important to know what kind of book Jeremiah is. Since we know it is prophecy, we know what type of literature it is. And we will be able to understand it better. We will be able to study it on its own terms.

And we have learned something else that will help us in our study of Jeremiah. We have said that prophecy is proclamation of God's will at a particular time in history. This leads us to the second step in beginning an inductive study which was mentioned earlier in this lesson. We should try to find out when Jeremiah prophesied and where he lived.

The second step in beginning an inductive study is _____

* _____ *

to find out something about the historical background of the book.

C. What is the Historical Background?

Read through Jer. 1-6 again; this time look for information about the historical background of the book. Notice any places and events and important
people who are mentioned. Put a mark in the margin beside these passages so
you can find them again easily. Here again it would be good to read through
the whole book, but that would take too much time.

1. We first asked the question, what kind of a book is Jeremiah? And we
found the answer easily. And we decided that the answer will help us to
understand Jeremiah, to study the book on its own terms.

Now we are asking, what is the historical background of Jeremiah? And you
will not have difficulty in finding the answer.

Why is it important to find out about the historical background of Jeremiah?

_____

* _____ *

It helps us understand the book. It helps us study the book on its own terms.

2. We know that Jeremiah is a book of prophecy and that prophecy is proclamation of God's will at a particular time and place. So it is very important
to learn when Jeremiah prophesied, to whom he preached God's word, and what
was happening in those days. You should find out how the people were living
and what were their major problems. All this information will help you understand Jeremiah's message. It will help you understand the book of Jeremiah.

Answer these questions as well as you can by looking over the passages you
checked as containing historical information.

a. When did Jeremiah prophesy? _____

_____

b. To whom did he preach? _____

c. What was happening at that time? _____

_____

_____

d. What major problem was Jeremiah dealing with? _____

* _____ *

a. From the 13th year of Josiah to the 11th year of Zedekiah.
b. To Judah (and to the nations).
c. Judah was being attacked. At the end of this period Jerusalem was destroyed and her people taken captive.
d. The people were living in idolatry and rebellion against God.

3. It doesn't matter if your answers to these questions were not exactly the
same as mine. We will study these items more carefully later. Right now we
want to emphasize the importance of finding out the historical background.

For example, we have noted that this was a time of rebellion against God
and a time of idolatry. So when Jeremiah speaks about "broken cisterns that

can hold no water" (Jer. 2:13) we know he is talking about _____

and when he says that his people has "played the harlot with many lovers"

(Jer. 3:1) he is talking about _____.
*   *

idolatry   idolatry

4. The great event at the end of this period was the destruction of Jerusalem
and the captivity of her people. We will study more about this event later.
However we can see already how important it was and we can see in Jer. 1-6
that the prophet knew what was going to happen and that he preached about it
often. And we can see how necessary it is for us to keep in mind this historical background as we read and interpret the words of Jeremiah.

When Jeremiah talks of a roaring lion (Jer. 2:15) he refers to _____

_____.

When he uses the example of a hot wind (Jer. 4:11-12) he refers to _____

*   *
_____.

the coming destruction   the coming destruction

5. You should find out as much as you can about the historical background as
you begin to study Jeremiah because this information will help you understand the book as you read it.

We asked four simple but important questions about the historical background
once. List them once again so that you will remember them. They are simple
questions that you would naturally ask about any prophetical book.

a. _____

b. _____

c. _____

d. _____
*   *

> a. When did Jeremiah prophesy?
> b. To whom did he preach?
> c. What was happening at that time?
> d. What problems was Jeremiah dealing with?

6. There is much more to learn about the historical background. Let's look
carefully at Jer. 1:1-3. Read this passage over two or three times and then

explain why the author begins his book this way. _____

_____

*   *

You should have said that the author wants to tell his readers the historical
context or background for his book. This passage does not contain prophecy. It
indicates when and where Jeremiah prophesied. We can say that it is an historical introduction to the book of Jeremiah.

7. As you study other prophetical books in the future you will want to discover the historical background of these books. One way to find this information is to look at the opening verses.

Check the following books to see if they contain introductions with historical
information. If they do, give the reference. If they don't, write "No."

Isaiah _____

Lamentations _____

Ezekiel _____

Daniel _____
*   *

Isaiah - Isa. 1:1
Lamentations - No
Ezekiel - Ezek. 1:1-3
Daniel - Dan. 1:1-7

8. Where are you likely to find historical information in the prophetical

books? _____
*   *

In the opening verses.

9. We have not yet mentioned all the information that the author gives us in Jer. 1:1-3. You should take advantage of all these details as you analyze the historical background of Jeremiah. For example, we noted previously that the phrases "the words of Jeremiah" and "to whom the word of the Lord came" tell us that this is a book of prophecy. They also indicate that Jeremiah is the author.

List other items of information that we have not yet mentioned from these verses.

a. _____

_____

b. _____

_____

c. _____

* _____ *

a. Jeremiah is the son of Hilkiah and his family was a family of priests.
b. They lived in Anathoth in the land of Benjamin.
c. Jeremiah prophesied during the reigns of Josiah, Jehoiakim and Zedekiah.

10. Later in the course we will make a more extensive study of the historical background of Jeremiah. You will learn how to use this information in a meaningful way and how to find more information. Now consider briefly the items we have just listed.

It is interesting to note, first, that Jeremiah belonged to a family of priests. We might assume that he and his relatives were in charge of the religious ceremonies and sacrifices of their country. This would be an important factor in the formation of Jeremiah. But we should check to make sure. If you have a large concordance, look under "Hilkiah." There you will see that the High Priest in Jerusalem at the time of King Josiah was a man

named Hilkiah. Was this Jeremiah's father? _____
* *

No. In the concordance, Hilkiah, the father of Jeremiah, is listed separately.

And the only reference for the father of Jeremiah is _____ .
* *

Jer. 1:1. Since we have no further information about Hilkiah, the father of Jeremiah, look up Anathoth in the concordance. Notice especially I Kings 2:26-27.

There we read that Abiathar, the High Priest at the time of David, was ex-

pelled by Solomon and sent to _____ 。

*   *

Anathoth。   So Jeremiah was a descendant of Abiathar。 His family was not in
charge of the sacrifices in Jerusalem at that time。

11。 Now consider the fact that Jeremiah grew up in Anathoth。 Look in a concordance, a Bible dictionary or an atlas until you find out where Anathoth is lo-

cated。 _____

*   _____   *

It was a town of the tribe of Benjamin located just a few miles northeast of
Jerusalem。

12。 Finally, we know that Jeremiah prophesied during the reigns of Josiah,
Jehoiakim and Zedekiah。 Even without a concordance you should know where
to look in the Bible for more information about these kings。 Use a concordance if necessary。

The reigns of these kings are described in the book of _____ and

in the book of _____ 。

*   *

2 Kings   2 Chronicles

13。 We will study these passages in another lesson。 Here it is important to
notice that there is more historical information in the Bible and that this
information may help us to understand the book of Jeremiah。

In order to find rapidly passages in the Bible on a particular subject you may

look in a _____ 。

*   *

concordance

14。 If you glance through the book of Jeremiah you will see that these kings
are mentioned several times。 These references are important and you will want
to use them later in your study of Jeremiah。

Another way to find out where these kings are mentioned in the book of Jeremiah

is _____ 。

*   *

To look in a concordance。 Only a large concordance will give these references。

15. Look over the passages in Jer. 1-6 which you marked as having historical information besides Jer. 1:1-3.

King Josiah is mentioned in _____.

*   *

Jer. 3:6   This tells us that Jer. 3:6-12 refers to the time of Josiah.

16. As we read through the book of Jeremiah we will be able to find out what

period of time some passages refer to by noticing _____

_____.

*   *

When they mention the kings of Judah.

17. You may have marked in Jer. 1-6 passages which mention Egypt and Assyria. These were great empires in Jeremiah's day and we will study more about them in the future.

When Jeremiah speaks of an enemy from the north, he may be referring to

(Egypt / Assyria). See an atlas if necessary.

*   *

Assyria

Jer. 1-6 also mentions other places in Palestine and further away. And there are many references to Judah's enemies. As we study these passages we will use this information also. Now it is time to review.

18. What is the second step in beginning an Inductive Study? _____

*   *

Find out something about the historical background.

19. Why is it important to study the historical background of a book? _____

*   *

It helps us understand the book and study it on its own terms.

20. Why is it especially important to study the historical background of

prophetical books? _____

*   *

Because prophecy is proclamation of God's will for a particular time and place.

21. List the 4 key historical questions we have used to find out the historical background of Jeremiah.

a. _____

b. _____

c. _____

d. _____
*   *

a. When did Jeremiah prophesy?
b. To whom did he preach?
c. What was happening at that time?
d. What problems was Jeremiah dealing with?

22. Do you know the answers to these 4 questions? If you have difficulty, go back to #2 of this section.

23. Where would you look first for historical information if you were going

to study another prophetical book? _____

* _____ *

Probably you should look first at the opening verses of that book.

24. In our study of the historical background of Jeremiah we have used primarily the Bible.

What other sources or tools have we used? _____

* _____ *

A concordance, an atlas, and perhaps a Bible dictionary.

25. Write down once again our definition of Inductive Bible Study. _____

_____

* _____ *

Inductive Bible Study is an approach to Bible study which begins with the Bible and studies the Bible on its own terms.

26. List the three steps for beginning an Inductive Bible Study.

a. _____

b. _____

c. _____

*   *

a. Find out what kind of book it is.
b. Find out something about its historical background.
c. Look for the outline or structure.

D. What is the Structure?

Read through Jer. 1-6 once again. This will be the third time in this lesson,
so you should be quite familiar with this part of Jeremiah. This time look
for the structure of the book. See if you can identify major sections or
divisions.

1. This is the third step for beginning an Inductive Study and often it is
the most difficult one. But it can be very important.

Why should we look for the structure? _____

* _____ *

It will help us understand the book, study the book on its own terms, see the
book as it really is.

2. There are several ways of thinking about the structure of a book. Some people use the example of a skeleton. As you know, the skeleton of an animal is
made up of all its bones. In a live animal you can't see the bones because
they are covered with flesh and skin and hair. But you can tell where the bones
are. And they are all tied together and joined to the back bone. The skeleton,
which is made up of all these bones, is what holds the animal together and
gives it shape and enables it to stand up.

See if you can explain what is the structure of a book, using the example of

the skeleton. _____

_____

_____

_____

_____

_____
_____

* _____ *

Here are some ideas you might have mentioned: Like the skeleton of an animal,
the structure of a book is made up of a number of pieces or divisions. These
divisions are hidden in the narrative of the book. But we can find them. And
we know that these divisions are tied together and form a central idea or
plot or story. This structure is what holds the book together, gives it meaning, and enables it to teach us something.

3. Another way of talking about the structure of a book is to use the idea of
a drawing or an outline. When an artist paints a person's picture, he usually
begins by making a drawing or a sketch. He draws a line to indicate the outside of the faces and the arms and legs and body. It all fits together to
make a figure. We call it an outline. Later, of course, the artist will fill
in the rest of the picture - all the details of the face and clothes, the
colors, and even the different shades and shadows. Finally the outline is all
covered up. It is hidden by the life-like picture that appears on the canvas.

But the outline or drawing is still there, underneath. And the outline is
very important because it gives the picture its shape and size.

Now explain what is the structure of a book, using this example of an artist's

drawing. _____

_____

_____

_____

_____

_____

_____

* _____ *

If you haven't yet tried to answer this question, please do so before going on
to #4. You may have a chance to give your explanation in class.

4. Let's list the characteristics of a book's structure that we have seen through these two examples.

> a. It is made up of several parts or divisions.
> b. These parts or divisions are hidden but we know they are there.
> c. They are tied together to form a central idea or plot or story.
> d. This is what holds the book together, gives it meaning, and enables it to teach us something.

Now state again why it is important to look for the structure or outline of a book as a beginning step in Inductive Bible Study. (You may give the answer we have used previously if you like, but it should be more meaningful

now). _____

_____

*   *

_____

We look for the structure of a book because it helps us understand the book, study the book on its own terms, see the book as it really is. (You can probably say this better in your own words.)

5. We have said that the structure of a book is hidden. Nowadays some books have structures that are not hidden. They begin with a table of contents, which gives the titles for the chapters and sometimes even for all the minor divisions in each chapter. And as you read through these books you can see the structure clearly because these chapter titles and division titles are included in the text.

The table of contents or outline of a book is like the _____ of

an animal or a _____for a painting.

*   *

skeleton   drawing or outline

6. When the books of the Bible were written their structures were hidden. As you know, they were not even divided into chapters and verses. And they did not have titles in the text or at the top of the page, as many of our Bibles do today. If your Bible has some titles, you may read them as you study Jeremiah. But remember that you are doing an Inductive Study and Inductive Bible Study begins with the original text of the Bible itself.

As we look for the structure of Jeremiah we should not base our outline on

the divisions of chapters and verses of our Bibles. Why? _____

Why should we not use the titles in our Bibles? _____

_____

Why should we not use the outlines which we find in commentaries and other

books? _____

_____

In answer to all three questions you can say that we want to begin with the
Bible itself and study it on its own terms. These divisions and titles were
not made by the original authors of the books of the Bible. They were added
later. They are other people's interpretations of the Bible.

7. In Inductive Bible Study we look for the structure of each book in the
text itself. Since this structure is hidden, it is sometimes hard to find.
There are, of course, different kinds of structure. And some books don't
really have a structure. Each book has to be studied on its own terms.

It is quite easy to find the structure of 1 and 2 Samuel, 1 and 2 Kings, and
1 and 2 Chronicles. As you glance through these books you see that they are
historical. The major divisions follow the lives of Samuel, Saul, David,
Solomon, and the other kings. The order is chronological (time).

In poetical books like Psalms and Proverbs the structure is much less important because these are collections of poems. All we can do is look for groups
of poems that seem to fit together around a particular theme.

Genesis tells the story of the great patriarchs. As you read through this
book, you see that it has several main divisions divided by genealogies.

Some of the prophetical books are collections of prophecies with very little
structure. Some have historical references which give them chronological
order. Others have groups of passages centered around different themes.

The books of the Bible have many different kinds of structure.

How can we find out what kind of structure a book has? _____

_____

By studying the book itself. We have to study each book on its own terms.

8. Let's see what we can find in Jeremiah. Did you find any clues to the
structure of Jeremiah as you read chapters 1-6? Are there enough historical
references to make a chronological outline? Does the author present a definite series of themes? How are Jeremiah's prophecies organized in this book?
These are the kinds of questions which should come to your mind.

One way to look for the structure is to analyze each paragraph, starting at the beginning of the book. Look for the main idea in the paragraph and any special clues (like historical information). Then as you go from one paragraph to another see if there is similarity or change. You may find several paragraphs in a row that have the same theme, followed by a change. That group of paragraphs could be a part of your skeleton or outline. You may find a definite change after just one paragraph. That could be another division or section of the book.

We already looked at Jer. 1:1-3. These three verses form a paragraph. They give the historical background of the book. And the following passage is very different.

Write a title for Jer. 1:1-3. _____
*   *

You might call this division "Historical Introduction" or just "Introduction." Since this paragraph introduces the whole book, it should be considered a major division in your outline.

9. Now read the rest of chapter 1.

a. What is the main idea in Jer. 1:4-10? _____

b. What is the main idea in Jer. 1:11-12? _____

_____

c. What is the main idea in Jer. 1:13-16? _____

_____

d. What is the main idea in Jer. 1:17-19? _____

* _____
                                                                     *

a. The call of Jeremiah.
b. The vision of the rod of almond.
c. The vision of the boiling pot.
d. God's promise to Jeremiah.
(Your answers will probably not be the same).

10. As you study these four paragraphs you begin to notice how they form a group. For example, in Jer. 1:11-12 God tells Jeremiah He will quickly perform His word. This follows nicely His call to Jeremiah in Jer. 1:4-10. Jer. 1:17-19 repeats some of the ideas of Jer. 1:4-10. Both passages deal with Jeremiah's call to be a prophet. And notice that in all four paragraphs God is speaking directly to Jeremiah. He is not giving him a message for the people.

Now look ahead at Jer. 2:1-3. Here the Lord speaks to Jeremiah, but He gives him a message for the people. And this paragraph doesn't have anything to do with Jeremiah's call. It is about Israel's election.

So it looks like Jer. 1:4-19 is another important division of the book of

Jeremiah. Write a title for this division. _____

* _____ *

Probably the best title is "The Call of Jeremiah."

11. In other lessons you will have an opportunity to work some more on the structure of the book of Jeremiah. This is a difficult job because the book is very loosely structured. But it is important to learn how to look for the structure of a book. Now let's review.

What is Inductive Bible Study? _____

_____

* _____ *

Inductive Bible Study is an approach to Bible study that begins with the Bible and studies the Bible on its own terms.

12. How do you begin an Inductive Study of a book of the Bible?

a. _____

b. _____

c. _____

* _____ *

a. Find out what kind of a book it is.
b. Find out something about its historical background.
c. Look for the structure or outline of the book.

13. Why do you look for the structure of a book? _____

_____

* _____ *

It helps you understand the book, study the book on its own terms, see it as it really is.

14. What is the structure of a book like? (Mention the two illustrations or examples we used above).

a. _____

b. _____
*   *

a. a skeleton
b. a drawing or outline

15. What are the characteristics of a book's structure?

a. _____

_____

b. _____

_____

c. _____

_____

d. _____

* _____ *

a. It is made up of several parts or divisions.
b. These parts or divisions are hidden but we know they are there.
c. They are tied together to form a central idea or plot or story.
d. The structure holds the book together, gives it meaning, and enables it to teach us something.

16. How can we find out what kind of structure a book of the Bible has? _____

* _____ *

By studying the book itself. We have to study each book on its own terms.

17. What are the first two divisions of the book of Jeremiah? (You may use your Bible to answer the question). Write the references and the titles.

        Reference   Title

a. _____   _____

b. _____   _____
*   *

a. Jer. 1:1-3   Introduction
b. Jer. 1:4-19   The Call of Jeremiah

E. Self-Test

At your next class session you may have a short test over what you have studied up to this point. Rather than leave you to worry about that possibility,
I have prepared a test that you can take and grade yourself. You can call it
a review, if you like, but it really is a test. You will be able to see how
well you have learned the material presented in this first lesson. If you
do well on this self-test, you should not worry at all about any test your
professor may give you. And if you do not do well on this self-test, you
may go back and study the points where you are weak.

The self-test is divided into two parts. You may use your Bible and a concordance for both parts, but do not refer back to the previous pages of this
lesson until you have finished the self-test. You may check your answers when
you have finished, by referring to the following pages. The best way to test
yourself is to take this self-test at least one day after you have finished
the previous sections of this lesson and without any review.

Part I

1. Write a definition of Inductive Bible Study. _____

_____

_____

2. List the three steps for beginning an Inductive Bible Study.

a. _____

b. _____

c. _____

3. Why are these three steps recommended for beginning an Inductive Study? ___

_____

_____

4. How should you find the information necessary for these three steps? _____

_____

5. What kind of a book is Jeremiah? _____

Give three reasons for saying so.

a. _____

b. _____

c. _____

6. What is prophecy? _____

_____

What kind of literature do we find in the prophetical books?_____

_____

_____

_____

7. What are some questions you should ask as you look for the historical background of a prophetical book like Jeremiah?

a. _____

b. _____

c. _____

d. _____

8. In an Inductive Study you should find the historical information in _____

_____

One of the best places to look for this information is in _____

_____

9. What was the most significant event that occurred during Jeremiah's ministry?

_____

What influence did this event have on his preaching? _____

_____

10. To whom did Jeremiah preach? _____

_____

What was the main problem he was dealing with? _____

11. The structure of a book is like a _____

or a _____ .

12. List the four characteristics of a book's structure.

a. _____

_____

b. _____

_____

c. _____

_____

d. _____

_____

13. How can we find out what kind of structure a book in the Bible has? _____

_____

14. Give the references and titles for the first two sections of Jeremiah.

      References   Title

a. _____   _____

b. _____   _____

Part II.

Show how you would begin an Inductive Study of the book of Haggai. List the steps you would take or the questions you would ask as well as the information you find in Haggai. Spend only about 30 minutes on this part of the self-test. Write your notes and your conclusions on this page and the following.

_____

_____

_____

_____

Answers to the Self-Test

Part I

Check your answers and take off two points for each mistake. Each space or point is worth two points.

1. Inductive Bible Study is <u>an approach to Bible Study that begins with the Bible and studies it on its own terms.</u>

2. The three steps for beginning an Inductive Bible Study are:

   a. Find out what kind of a book, writing, or literature you are studying.
   b. Find out something about its historical background.
   c. Look for the structure or outline of the book.

3. These three steps are recommended because they help us <u>to understand the book, to study it on its own terms, to see it as it really is.</u>

4. You should find this information <u>by studying the book itself.</u>

5. Jeremiah is <u>a book of prophecy.</u>

   Actually we found four reasons for saying so. You were asked to put down three of these.

   a. It is included with the Major Prophets of the Old Testament.
   b. Throughout it we find phrases like "the Lord said."
   c. Jeremiah was a prophet.
   d. The opening statement of the book says it is the word of the Lord through Jeremiah.

6. Prophecy is the <u>proclamation of God's word or God's will.</u>

   The prophetical books are <u>collections of the sayings of the prophets which are proclamations of God's word at a particular time in history.</u>

7. We asked four questions about the historical background of Jeremiah.

   a. When did he prophesy?
   b. To whom did he preach?
   c. What was happening at that time?
   d. What problem was he dealing with?

8. In an Inductive Study you should find the historical information <u>in the book itself.</u>

   In the prophetic books one of the best places to look for this information <u>is in the opening verses.</u>

9. The most significant event that occurred during Jeremiah's ministry was the destruction of Jerusalem and the captivity of its people.

   Jeremiah referred to the coming destruction frequently, and the threat of destruction made his message urgent.

10. Jeremiah preached to the people of Judah and the nations.

   The main problem he was dealing with was idolatry.

11. The structure of a book is like a skeleton or a drawing or outline.

12. A book's structure usually has these four characteristics:

   a. It is made up of several parts or divisions.
   b. These parts or divisions are hidden, but we know they are there.
   c. They are tied together to form a central idea or plot or story.
   d. This is what holds the book together, gives it meaning, and enables it to teach us something.

13. We should find out what kind of structure a book has by studying the book itself.

14. These are the first two sections or divisions of Jeremiah:

   a. Jer. 1:1-3   Introduction
   b. Jer. 1:4-19   The Call of Jeremiah

                         Part II

Your study of Haggai will not look exactly like mine, but you should have included the steps and the information I have listed below. Don't worry about the form or the order. Just see if your analysis includes these points. Take off four points for each of these points that is missing in your Inductive Study of Haggai.

1. What kind of a book is Haggai? Prophecy.

   How do we know it is prophecy?

   a. It is included with the Minor Prophets of the Old Testament.
   b. The contents are presented as "the word of the Lord."
   c. Haggai is called a prophet.
   d. The book begins as the word of the Lord by Haggai the prophet.

2. What is the historical background of Haggai?

   a. Haggai prophesied at the time of King Darius.
   b. He preached to Zerubbabel, the governor, and Joshua, the high priest, and to the Jews.

    c. The people had returned from exile and they were rebuilding Jerusalem.
    d. The main problem of Haggai was to get the people to rebuild the
       Temple.

3. What is the structure of Haggai?   The structure of the book seems to be
   divided into prophecies that Haggai received on specific dates as indicated in the text.

When you have finished checking your answers, add up the number of points
you lost in Part I and Part II and subtract that number from 100. The result
is your grade. You will probably get 90 points or more on this self-test. If
you get less than 70 points you should go back and study the lesson again at
the places where you are weakest.

2

The Call of Jeremiah

(Jeremiah 1:4-19)

In the previous lesson you covered a lot of ground very rapidly. And it was just the first lesson. You learned a definition of Inductive Bible Study, and you learned three steps for beginning an Inductive Study. We used the beginning steps in our study of the book of Jeremiah. Then you applied briefly the same method to the book of Haggai.

In this lesson you will follow up the first step of beginning an Inductive Bible Study. You will study carefully Jer. 1:4-19. You already know that Jeremiah is a book of prophecies. And you know that Jer. 1:4-19 describes the call of Jeremiah. This passage will be very helpful in revealing what is prophecy and what this book is about.

As you begin to study the book of Jeremiah you will appreciate its importance for your life and ministry. Someone has said that no other book in the Old Testament describes so vividly and intimately the experience of a man with God. And no period in the history of the Old Testament was more crucial for God's people than the period leading up to the fall of Jerusalem.

When you finish this lesson you should be able to:

Describe Jeremiah's call and interpret it in terms of God's servants today.

Explain the vision of the rod of almond and the vision of the boiling pot.

State Jeremiah's message and the nature of prophecy.

A. What is Prophecy?

Read and meditate over Jer. 1:4-19. Although these verses contain some figurative language, they are fairly easy to understand. And yet you should not quickly assume that you have grasped the full significance of these words.

Remember that Inductive Bible Study begins with the Bible and studies it on its own terms. We have identified Jeremiah as a book of prophecy, and we have defined the historical period in which Jeremiah prophesied. But we must be careful not to impose our ideas on his words. We must be careful to see what God's call meant to him.

1. We have defined prophecy as proclamation of God's word or God's will at a particular time in history. Let's see if we can understand how Jeremiah thought about prophecy.

Notice that there are three parts to this definition. Prophecy has to do with God's word. It is the proclamation of that word from God by a prophet. And it is given at a particular time. Show how Jeremiah thought about prophecy by answering the following questions, which are based on Jer. 1:4-19.

33

a. Did Jeremiah believe that his calling and his message were based on God's

word? _____

b. Did Jeremiah believe that he was called to proclaim God's word? _____

c. Did Jeremiah believe that the word of God which he heard and proclaimed

was for that particular moment in history? _____
*   *

a.b.c. Yes. It is quite clear in Jer. 1:4-19 that these three ideas are central to Jeremiah's concept of prophecy.

2. Consider first the phrase "God's word." What does it mean to talk about
God's word? What did it mean to Jeremiah? What does it mean to us? Although
we use the same expression today, it may mean something very different.

Jeremiah and the other Old Testament prophets had a profound sense of the
holiness and power of God. Their God was the God of Israel and also the Lord
over the nations. He had called His people to worship Him and serve Him, and
when His people disobeyed Him He sent judgment and destruction upon them.

Answer the following questions on the basis of Jer. 1:4-19.

a. What did God's holiness and power mean to Jeremiah personally? What did

God do to him? _____

_____

_____

b. What did God's holiness and power mean to the people of Jerusalem at the

time of Jeremiah? What did God do to them? _____

_____

_____

_____

a. God formed Jeremiah's life. He set him apart to be a prophet, and He
promised him He would protect him.

b. God sent judgment on His people because of their wickedness and idolatry.
He sent the nations of the north against Jerusalem.

3. Now consider what people think of God today. Ask yourself what you think of God's holiness and power.

a. What has God done in your life? _____

_____

_____

b. What has God done in the life of your church? _____

_____

* _____ *

a.b.Perhaps you have seen the holiness and power of God in your own life and in the life of your congregation. But it seems that few people today really believe, as Jeremiah believed, that their lives have been formed and consecrated by God to do His will. And few people believe that God determines the rise and fall of nations.

4. If we want to understand how Jeremiah thought about God we should first

of all intensify our concept of God's _____ and His _____.

* _____ *

holiness   power

5. We should have a greater concept than Jeremiah of God's holiness and power because we have received the Gospel of Jesus Christ. Jeremiah lived 600 years before the time of Christ, so he did not see the full revelation of God.

a. How were the power and holiness of God manifested in Jesus Christ? _____

_____

b. How do we experience that power and holiness in Jesus Christ? _____

_____

* _____ A

a. In His miracles, but especially in His death and resurrection, His victory over sin and death.

b. By faith we receive the resurrected Christ into our lives. God's Spirit dwells in us.

6. Now look at the second part of our definition of prophecy, proclamation.
What does it mean to talk about the proclamation of God's word? What did it
mean to Jeremiah? What does it mean to us? Here again we use the same language today, but we may not mean the same thing.

Jeremiah and the other prophets had a profound sense of the proclamation of
God's word. For one thing they really felt that what they were preaching or
proclaiming was God's word.

a. Count again how many times in Chapter I we find phrases like "the word

of the Lord" and "the Lord said." _____ You have already underlined

these phrases in your Bible.

b. Note again one or two phrases that say explicitly that the words that

Jeremiah prophesied were God's words. _____

* _____ *

a. 14
b. "Behold I have put my words in your mouth."

7. Of course we, too, talk about the Bible as God's word. And we say that
the preacher proclaims God's word when he preaches. But all too often we
read the Bible without paying attention. And many of the sermons that we hear
or preach make no difference in our lives. Jeremiah believed profoundly that

what he preached was _____. Do we believe the same about

most sermons now? Should we expect God to speak through us to the people?

*   *

God's word. These questions are for you to think about and pray about.

8. Here again we should have a greater concept than Jeremiah did. We know
Jesus Christ, the word of God incarnate. We really should know what God's
word to man is because we have received Christ into our lives.

What is the message of God's word as revealed in Jesus Christ? _____

_____

* _____ *

God's word is that He loves all men and gave His Son for their salvation.
This is the Gospel that we believe and preach. It can be stated in many
different ways.

9. Notice that Jeremiah's calling and his proclamation are intensely personal. In this first chapter and throughout the book God talks to Jeremiah as in a conversation.

Of course we don't know exactly what Jeremiah's experience was like. And
we won't necessarily have the same kind of experience.

But the word of God which we receive and which we proclaim must be _____.

*   *

Personal. We cannot depend on other men's experience of God's word and
preach other men's ideas.

10. Notice, too, that Jeremiah believed in the power of his message. God
said to Jeremiah that he had put His words in Jeremiah's mouth. And He
also said that He had set him over nations and kingdoms. He said that He
would utter His judgments against His people. And we know that Jerusalem
was destroyed in fulfillment of His word.

The prophets believed in the power of God's word to accomplish His will.
Like an arrow flies to its mark, driven by the force of the bow and the
skill of the archer, God's messages would find their mark and accomplish
His purpose in nations and individuals. Read Isaiah 55:10, 11.

a. In Jer. 1:10 God let Jeremiah know that His message of judgment against

the nations would be to _____

b. God's message of forgiveness and hope that Jeremiah was to proclaim would

be to _____

*

    a. pluck up and to break down, to destroy and to overthrow.
    b. build and to plant.

11. Do we really expect to see definite results when we preach God's word?
If not, our concept of the proclamation of God's word is weaker than Jeremiah's, although it should be stronger because of our experience of Christ.

a. Explain how our concept of the proclamation of God's word often seems

weaker than Jeremiah's. _____

_____

b. Explain why our concept should be greater than Jeremiah's. _____

_____

* _____ *

a. When we preach we don't always expect to see definite results. We need to recognize the power of God's word to accomplish His purpose.
b. We know that Christ dwells in us and that the Spirit of God operates through our preaching.

12. We have noted that Jeremiah had a profound concept of God's word and that he had a profound sense of the proclamation of God's word. The third part of our definition of prophecy says that it is God's word at a <u>particular time in history</u>.

This does not mean simply that it was given at a particular moment. It means that God spoke through the prophets definite messages for them and for their contemporaries. He revealed His will to them in their particular situations. We mentioned earlier that these prophecies sometimes referred to past history and included future promises. And they revealed timeless truths about God. But God's word was first and foremost a message for those who heard it for the first time.

a. What was God's message to Jeremiah in Jer. 1:4-10? _____

_____

b. Why did God give Jeremiah that message? _____

* _____ *

a. God told Jeremiah that He had called him to be His prophet to the nations.
b. He wanted Jeremiah to accept that call and serve Him.

13. In Jer. 1:13-16 we read of Jeremiah's vision of the boiling pot. This is a message to Jeremiah, but it reveals the message he is to proclaim to his people.

a. What was God's message to His people? _____

_____

_____

b. Why did God give them this message? _____

_____

*   _____   *

a. God told them that He was sending judgment upon them because of their
   sin and idolatry.
b. He wanted to warn them of this judgment so that they would repent of
   their sin and turn to Him.

14. Perhaps another weakness in our preaching is that we do not have a genuine sense of God's word for us here and now. We give expositions of the
Scriptures, which were written long ago. We tell of the experiences of the
early Christians. We explain the teachings of Jesus and Paul. We impart the
eternal truths of God. But we often fail to challenge our people with a
Gospel which will change their lives today.

a. Jeremiah's message focused on the (past / present / future).

b. Our message tends to focus on the (past / present / future).

*   *

a. Present
b. Past (This varies from one person to another, from one denomination to
   another, and from one country to another).

15. Write once again our definition of prophecy. It should carry more significance now that we have studied Jeremiah's concept of prophecy. And this

should help us to study the book of Jeremiah on its own terms. _____

_____

*   _____   *

Prophecy is the proclamation of God's word at a particular time in history.

16. List the three parts of this definition which we have discussed.

a. _____

b. _____

c. _____
*   *

a. Prophecy is God's word.
b. It is the proclamation of God's word.
c. It is the proclamation of God's word at a particular time in history.

17. Mention briefly how Jeremiah's concept of <u>God's word</u> was more profound

than ours. _____

_____

_____

* _____ *

Jeremiah had a profound concept of God's holiness and power. He really believed that the Lord had shaped his life and that He determined the life
of the nations.

18. Mention briefly how Jeremiah's concept of <u>proclamation</u> was more pro-

found than ours. _____

_____

_____

* _____ *

Jeremiah believed intensely that the words he preached were from God. He
believed that God had put the words in his mouth. And he believed that the
words he proclaimed would accomplish what they said.

19. Mention briefly how Jeremiah's concept of the immediate application of

his message was more profound than ours. _____

_____

_____

* _____ *

Jeremiah believed that God was speaking directly to him, calling him to be
a prophet and that He was speaking directly to His people, calling them to
repent of their evil and idolatry.

B. Jeremiah 1:4-10

As you study this passage in detail, try to put yourself in Jeremiah's position. Identify yourself with him at this great moment in his life when he
receives God's call to be a prophet. Try not only to understand the meaning
of these words but also to feel the significance of this experience.

Also keep in mind the relevance of Jeremiah's experience for us today. See
if his call is like God's call to His followers in the 20th century. Consider how you would use this passage for a sermon in your church.

1. At each stage of an Inductive Study you should ask yourself, How should
I study this passage? And the answer is always, Study the passage on its
own terms.

We have noted, for example, that the Bible is a collection of books. So it
should be studied book by book. Each book should be studied separately.

As we began our study of Jeremiah in the previous lesson we studied the
book itself to find out what kind of a book it is, what is its historical
background, and what structure it has.

As we focus our attention on Jer. 1:4-10 we should use the same inductive

principle which says _____

* _____. *

Begin with the Bible (or passage) and study it on its own terms.

2. As we look at Jer. 1:4-10 we see that it is a unit, so it is wise to
study these verses first as a whole.

How do we know that Jer. 1:4-10 is a unit? _____

* _____ *

It all fits together around one experience or one theme.

3. As we look at Jer. 1:4-10 we observe that it is a conversation between
the Lord and Jeremiah. We see that it includes not only the words of the
Lord and the words of Jeremiah as they speak to each other but also the words
of the author, for example, in v. 4. The author is, of course, Jeremiah, but
we should distinguish those places where he writes as author from the places
where he speaks in a conversation or sermon.

Go through Jer. 1:4-10 and write in the spaces below who is speaking or writing in each verse. There may be more than one indication for a verse.

a. v.4 ___the author_____   e. v.8 _____

b. v.5 _____   f. v.9 _____

c. v.6 _____   g. v.10 _____

d. v.7 _____
*   *

a. the author   e. the Lord
b. the Lord   f. the author, the Lord
c. the author, Jeremiah   g. the Lord
d. the author, the Lord

4. From this analysis we see that v.7 and 8 go together and v.9 and 10 go together.

Now study the different parts of the conversation or dialogue and write down briefly their significance. For example, v.4 simply introduces the passage. In v.5 the Lord calls Jeremiah.

Complete the following analysis.

a. v.4 ___Introduction_____

b. v.5 ___The Lord calls Jeremiah to be a prophet._____

c. v.6 _____

d. v.7-8 _____

e. v.9-10 _____
*   *

a. See above.
b. See above.
c. Jeremiah responds but hesitates.
d. The Lord repeats His call.
e. The Lord ordains Jeremiah as His prophet to the nations.

5. In Jer. 1:4-10 it is evident that the Lord is the principal actor. And Jeremiah receives the action. In fact it is rather striking the number of times these verses indicate that the Lord did something to Jeremiah.

List all the phrases in Jer. 1:4-10 that indicate that the Lord did something to Jeremiah. (Do not include phrases like "the Lord said to me.")

a. _____   f. _____

b. _____   g. _____

c. _____   h. _____

d. _____   i. _____

e. _____   j. _____
*   *

From this point on you will not always find an answer given to compare with what you have written.

6. Now we have a good idea of the passage as a whole, so we can go on to study it verse by verse in detail. But first review the steps we have taken so far. We have looked at Jer. 1:4-10 as a unit, and we have tried to study it on its own terms.

List the steps which we took as we studied Jer. 1:4-10 as a whole.

a. _____

b. _____

c. _____

a. We noted who is speaking in each verse.
b. We studied the significance of the different parts of the dialogue.
c. We listed all the things that the Lord did to Jeremiah.

7. Of course this is not the only way to study Jer. 1:4-10. But it is a useful way. It gives us a lot of information about the passage. And it is an inductive way. This information comes from the passage itself.

In Inductive Bible Study we look at a book as a whole (for example, the book of Jeremiah) or at a passage (for example, Jer. 1:4-10) or at a single verse (for example, Jer. 1:5). We should always begin with the text of the Bible and study it on its own terms.

a. Since Jer. 1:4-10 is clearly presented as a conversation, we studied _____

_____.

b. Once we had identified the different parts of the conversation or dialogue

we noted _____.

c. Finally, since the Lord is the principal actor in the passage and Jeremiah

the recipient we listed _____

_____.

a. Who is speaking in each verse.
b. The significance of the different parts of the dialogue.
c. All the things that the Lord did to Jeremiah.

8. In an Inductive Study each passage should be studied on its own terms. Since Jer. 1:4-10 is a conversation we analyze it as a conversation. Other passages in Jeremiah will not be conversations, so we will not analyze them as we did Jer. 1:4-10.

a. What is the basic principle we should always keep in mind as we study

a passage of the Bible? _____

_____

b. How do we know how to analyze a given passage? _____

* _____ *

a. We should always begin with the text itself and study it on its own terms.
b. We should look at the passage itself and analyze it according to what we
   find there.

9. Now let's begin our detailed study of Jer. 1:4-10 verse by verse. First
we looked at the passage as a whole. Now we will look at the different parts
that make up the whole. The first part is v. 4.

We have noted already that in v. 4 the word of the Lord came to _____

and that this verse is an _____ to Jer. 1:4-10.

* _____ *

the author (Jeremiah)   introduction

10. Although v. 4 is an introduction to the passage, we should not consider
these words unimportant. And although, as we have noted, phrases like "the
word of the Lord" are very common in Jeremiah, we should not overlook their
significance.

Write a brief paragraph on Jeremiah's concept of the word of God, including

some of the ideas presented in the previous section of this lesson. _____

_____

_____

_____

_____

* _____ *

Jeremiah had a profound sense of God's holiness and power. He really believed
that God moved men and nations by His word. And he believed intensely that God
spoke to him personally.

11. In Old Testament times a man's word was taken seriously, so seriously
that at times it could not be withdrawn. Remember how Jacob obtained his
father's blessing by fraud; even though Isaac was tricked into blessing
Jacob, once his word was given, he could not change it.

The word of the Lord was of course even more powerful. Whether He was calling a man to serve Him or sending His judgment on the nations, His word must
be fulfilled.

Write a brief paragraph from memory on what happened to Jonah when he tried

to escape God's call. _____

_____

_____

_____

*   *

God sent a storm and a great fish and brought Jonah back to land and sent him
to save the city of Nineveh.

12. So when Jeremiah heard the word of the Lord calling him to be a prophet,
he could not take it lightly.

You have noticed that v. 4 says "word of the Lord", not "word of God." We know,
however, that the author is referring to God. In the original Hebrew version of
this book the name Jehovah is used most frequently, and it has been translated
in this version as "the Lord."

In v. 4 Jeremiah refers to God as _____ which comes from

the Hebrew name _____

*   *

the Lord   Jehovah

13. Before leaving v. 4 consider its application for us today.

a. Does God speak to His people today? ____   _____

b. How does He speak to us? _____

_____

_____

c. Is He the same God who spoke to Jeremiah? _____

d. How should we respond to His word? _____

_____
*   *

a. Yes.
b. Through the Bible, through preaching and teaching, through prayer, through
   the church, through what happens in the world.
c. Yes.
d. With the same profound faith and obedience.

14. The most important verse in this passage is v. 5, which contains _____

_____.
*   *

God's call to Jeremiah.

15. In v.5 the Lord tells Jeremiah that He has done four important things to him.
List these four expressions and try to imagine what they meant to the young Jeremiah when he first heard them. (Do not fill in the spaces at the right.)

a. _____   _____

b. _____   _____

c. _____   _____

d. _____   _____

16. We do not have enough space here to consider fully these four concepts. You
can see that this verse by itself would be an excellent text for a sermon. In
the space to the right of each phrase above write the name of a doctrine or
experience that Christians believe in today similar to Jeremiah's experience.
*   *

The four answers need not be exactly the same as mine.
a. predestination
b. communion
c. sanctification
d. vocation

17. We could look at these concepts in many different ways and never exhaust
their meaning. These words must have been tremendously moving to Jeremiah when
he first heard them. They must have carried him through the many difficult
years of his ministry. And they sustained him in those terrible days of the
siege and fall of Jerusalem.

a. Comment on the meaning of the words "I formed you" for the young Jeremiah

at the moment of his call. _____

_____

b. Comment on the meaning of the words "I knew you" for Jeremiah year after
year as his family, the people, the priests, and even the kings of Judah
refused to accept his message, rejected him and mocked him, threw him in jail,

and threatened to kill him. _____

_____

_____

_____

c. Comment on the meaning of the words "I consecrated you" for Jeremiah. At
that time his people followed pagan religions, worshipped idols all over the
countryside, and even sacrificed babies to these false gods.

_____

_____

_____

_____

d. Comment on the meaning of the words "I appointed you a prophet to the nations"
for Jeremiah as he watched the movement of the great world empires of his day
and heard the noise of advancing invaders who would destroy his land.

_____

_____

_____

_____

*   *

a b c d. I hesitate to give you my interpretation of these phrases because I
want you to express your own thoughts. And our ideas may be different, Note
that Inductive Study includes the use of the imagination. You should try to
feel what Jeremiah felt and identify yourself with him in his experience.

18. In the previous section of this lesson we indicated that we as Christians
experience some of the same things that Jeremiah experienced and we said that
our understanding should be greater than his because we know Jesus Christ, who
is the fullness of God's revelation.

Interpret each of the four concepts in Jeremiah's call in terms of the
Christian's call to serve God in the 20th century.

a. "I formed you" _____

_____

_____

b. "I knew you" _____

_____

_____

c. "I consecrated you". _____

_____

_____

d. "I appointed you a prophet to the nations" _____

_____

* _____ *

a.b.c.d. Perhaps there will be time to discuss your answer at the next class
session.

19. Now consider Jeremiah's response to God's call in v. 6.

How would you describe Jeremiah's response? _____

_____

_____

* _____ *

You may at first think that Jeremiah is refusing to accept God's call. But
that is very unlikely. You may think that Jeremiah is overwhelmed and fright-
ened by the call. That is probably at least partly true. Or you may think
that Jeremiah felt he was too young and incapable of such a high calling. Certainly that would have been a natural and sincere response.

20. Remember that God's call to Jeremiah was something extraordinary that very
few men at that time experienced. There were other prophets in those days, but

most of them were false prophets. There were priests and nobles and kings
but most of them did not serve God truly. There were no doubt believers
among the people, but their faith was mostly limited to the traditions and
the sacrifices and feast days. Jeremiah was singled out by the Lord for a
unique mission at a very difficult time.

How do you think you would have responded if you had been in Jeremiah's

place? _____

* _____ *

Probably just like Jeremiah did.

21. What reason does Jeremiah give for not being a prophet? _____

   _____

* _____ *

Jeremiah said he was only a youth. Not only was this an overwhelming responsibility but Jeremiah was young and inexperienced. He said that he did not know
how to speak.

22. Do you see an application of v. 6 for us today? Isn't Jeremiah's response
something with which we can identify? Aren't there many people in our churches
who also feel unworthy and incapable of following God's call? And when we are
looking for people to take responsibilities in the church, don't we hear many
excuses like Jeremiah's?

How would you use v. 6 in a sermon? _____

   _____

   _____

* _____ *

You could show your people that the greatest men of God have felt the same way
they do. And this would help them respond as these great men responded - in
spite of their fears and inadequacy.

23. In v. 7-8 the Lord puts aside Jeremiah's excuse and his fears and repeats
His call. If you plan to use this passage in a sermon you should study this
part further. Note here that the Lord not only repeats His call but He adds
at least two new elements. What are they?

a. _____

b. _____

* _____ *

a. He says, "I command you." Now the call is an order.
b. He also says, "I am with you to deliver you." The call includes His promise
of God's presence and protection.

24. Finally, in v. 9-10 the Lord touches Jeremiah's mouth and puts His words
in Jeremiah's mouth. This is one of the most eloquent expressions of prophecy
in the Old Testament.

Write here the Lord's words to Jeremiah in v. 9. _____

_____. Remember these words as a state-

ment of Jeremiah's ordination to be a prophet.

God tells Jeremiah once again that he is to be a prophet to the nations, not
just to his small rural town of Anathoth, not just to the people of Jerusalem
and Judah, but to the nations of the world.

Who are God's prophets or ambassadors or apostles to the nations of the world

today? _____
*   *

Those who know Christ are called to be God's messengers in the world today.

25. Jeremiah's mission was two-fold. His message, as we shall see more fully
later, had two dimensions. See if you can figure out already what these two
dimensions were on the basis of v. 10.

a. What was he called to destroy? _____

_____

b. What was he called to build? _____

* _____ *

a. He announced God's judgment on the people's evil ways and idolatry.
b. He called his people to repent and return to the Lord.

26. As you review this brief study of Jer. 1:4-10, notice especially the
procedure we followed. Inductive Study is flexible because it always begins
with the text and studies each passage on its own terms.

Inductive Study is not rigid but _____ because it _____

* _____ . *

flexible   studies each passage on its own terms.

27. We studied Jer. 1:4-10 in two ways. First, since the passage is a unit, we

studied it as _____ . Then we studied the details of the pas-

sage _____ .

a whole   verse by verse

28. We used our imagination as we tried to understand what God's call to Jeremiah meant to him. We imagined what we would have felt if we had been in his
position, and we asked what these words must have meant to him in his day.
This, too, is a part of Inductive Bible Study.

In order to understand a passage on its own terms Inductive Study makes use of

our _____ .

imagination.

29. Finally, as we studied the different parts of this passage, we asked what
is the meaning or application of Jeremiah's experience for Christians of the
20th century. Since Jesus Christ, who lived on earth 600 years after Jeremiah,
is the full revelation of God's word, we said that Christians should have an
even greater understanding of God's call than did Jeremiah.

Inductive Study includes finding the _____

of a passage for Christians today. An Old Testament passage like Jer. 1:4-10

has even greater meaning for us because we know

* _____ . *

application or meaning   Jesus Christ, the full revelation

C. Jeremiah 1:11-19

Read over two or three times Jer. 1:11-19. We have already indicated that
these verses seem to accompany Jeremiah's call in Jer. 1:4-10. You will study
the significance of the different parts of this passage and their relationship to Jer. 1:4-10. You will try out several methods which are useful for
analyzing other passages like this.

1. As you read through Jer. 1:11-19 look for the major units or parts. Remember that the original text did not have paragraphs and verse divisions. So,
even if your Bible divides the text into paragraphs you may make your own
divisions as you study the passage on its own terms.

First Jeremiah sees two visions. Each of these visions forms a natural unit
in the text. Then follow words of exhortation and promise to Jeremiah.

Study Jer. 1:11-19 carefully to see where these divisions occur, then write
down the references for these three units.

a. _____

b. _____

c. _____

a. Jer. 1:11-12
b. Jer. 1:13-16
c. Jer. 1:17-19

2. Now consider what titles you will give to these small units. These titles
should represent the content of the paragraphs. They should be brief. And each
title should be different and distinctive.

One way to find appropriate titles is to choose four words or less from the
text itself. For example, Jer. 1:4-10 could have as its title, "I appointed
you prophet."

Select a title of four words or less for each of the following paragraphs from
the text itself.

a. Jer. 1:11-12. _____

b. Jer. 1:13-16. _____

c. Jer. 1:17-19. _____

Your titles do not have to be the same as mine. However, I will include
mine here so you can compare them with yours.
a. Jer. 1:11-12 A rod of almond.
b. Jer. 1:13-16 A boiling pot.
c. Jer. 1:17-19 Against the whole land.

3. The first of these units or paragraphs, Jer. 1:11-12, is short but it
requires some study. It apparently tells of a vision which Jeremiah saw.
And this vision takes the form of a symbol. Then the Lord Himself tells
Jeremiah the meaning or interpretation of the vision.

a. What words in Jer. 1:11-12 indicate that this was a vision? _____

_____

b. What is the symbol? _____

c. What is the meaning or interpretation of the symbol? _____

* _____ *

a. "What do you see?" "I see."
b. A rod of almond.
c. "I am watching over my word to perform it."

4. We shall see later that the book of Jeremiah contains many symbols or
literary figures. And you will study how to interpret them.

In Jer. 1:11-12 we are given both the symbol and the interpretation of the
symbol. In other cases we will have to figure out the interpretation for ourselves. Even in this case, however, we should try to understand the relationship between the figure and the interpretation or message.

There doesn't seem to be any obvious relationship between a stick of an almond tree and the fact that the Lord is watching over His word. So here we
have to turn to a Bible dictionary and the commentaries. There we learn
that the Hebrew word for almond means "early awake" and that the almond tree
is the first tree to blossom in the spring. There is then a very clear relationship between the symbol and the interpretation in Jer. 1:11-12.
Also there is a play on the words "almond" and "watching" in Hebrew.
a. What does the almond tree do? _____

b. What does the Lord do? _____
* *

a. Blossoms early.
b. Fulfills quickly His word.

5. We do not know whether Jeremiah saw the vision of the almond rod at the time he was called to be a prophet. But it does seem as if this vision was placed right after the call of Jeremiah in the book of Jeremiah for some reason.

a. According to Jer. 1:4-10 God told Jeremiah to _____ His word.

b. According to Jer. 1:11-12 God told Jeremiah He would _____

_____ His word.

*   *

a. Proclaim
b. Quickly fulfill

6. Jer. 1:13-16 is similar to Jer. 1:11-12, although its message is different.

a. Does Jer. 1:13-16 present a vision? _____

b. Is the vision symbolical? _____

c. Is the interpretation of the symbol given? _____

*   *

a. Yes.
b. Yes.
c. Yes.

7. What is the symbol in Jer. 1:13-16? _____

_____

What is the meaning or interpretation of the symbol? _____

_____

* _____ *

A boiling pot facing away from the north.
"Out of the north evil shall break forth upon all the inhabitants of the land."

8. In the case of the rod of almond it was difficult for us to see the relationship between the symbol and the interpretation because we are not familiar with the Hebrew language.

In the case of the boiling pot facing away from the north, we can easily see the relationship between the symbol and the interpretation. First notice the characteristics of the symbol.

List the two important characteristics of the pot.

a. _____.

b. __ _____ *

a. It is boiling.
b. It faces from the north.

9. Compare these two characteristics of the pot with the interpretation which is given in the text.

a. The boiling represents _____.

b. The north represents _____. *

a. Evil or destruction or the enemy invader.
b. The direction from which this evil will come.

10. The interpretation of the boiling pot in the text is unusually long and it includes some important information. List some of the important information you observe in v. 15-16.

a. _____,

b. _____,

c. _____. *

Perhaps the most important concepts are these:
a. The enemies from the north will be sent by the Lord.
b. They will attack all the cities of Judah, even Jerusalem itself.
c. They are being sent as God's judgment of His people's idolatry.

11. Again we may ask what is the relationship between the vision of the boiling pot and the call of Jeremiah. We do not know whether Jeremiah saw this vision at the time of his call, but it has been placed in the book of Jeremiah at this point. Here, for the first time, we see what is the message that Jeremiah is to proclaim.

a. According to Jer. 1:4-10 God told Jeremiah _____

_____

b. According to Jer. 1:11-12 God told Jeremiah _____

_____

c. According to Jer. 1:13-16 God told Jeremiah _____

* _____ *

a. to proclaim His word as a prophet
b. He would fulfill His word quickly
c. what message he should proclaim

12. Before we go on to the final part of this chapter, make a note of the way in which we studied the two visions or symbols. In both cases we followed the same three steps. List them here.

a. _____

b. _____

c. _____
*   *

a. We identified the object or symbol.
b. We looked for the interpretation of the symbol.
c. We analyzed the relationship between the symbol and the interpretation.

13. Jer. 1:17-19 does not contain a vision like the previous two units or paragraphs.

What is this passage about? _____

_____

_____

14. Jer. 1:17-19 goes directly back to the theme of Jeremiah's call. Several expressions of this paragraph seem to repeat ideas that are presented in Jer. 1:4-10. Make a careful comparison of the two passages in order to iden- tify these similarities.

Copy here the expressions from Jer. 1:4-10 and similar expressions from Jer. 1: 17-19 in pairs.

a. "Whatever I command you you shall speak."

a. "Say to them everything that I command you."

b. _____

b. _____

c. _____

c. _____

15. Although this paragraph does not present a vision like the previous two units, it does use figurative language.

List the three figures or symbols in v. 18.

a. _____ _____

b. _____

c. _____

What do these figures or symbols represent? _____

*   *

_____

They represent safety and strength.

16. As you read through a passage like Jer. 1:17-19 you should observe care-fully all the details of the passage. (We will not be able to look at all the details in Jer. 1:17-19 in this lesson). You should point out figurative expressions, as we have just done, and be sure you know what they mean. You should compare the passage with others, as we compared Jer. 1:17-19 with Jer. 1:4-10. You should find out what the central idea or message of the passage is.

Some simple recomendations for Inductive Study of a Bible passage are:

a. Observe carefully all the _____

b. If there are figurative expressions, make sure you know _____

_____

c. Compare the passage with _____

d. Find out what is the central _____ of the passage.
*   *

a. details of the passage
b. what they mean
c. other passages
d. idea or message

17. Sometimes you should ask why the passage says certain things.

For example, in v. 18-19 we read that the kings, princes, priests, and people of Judah will fight against Jeremiah. So we ask ourselves why they will fight against Jeremiah. The book contains much more information about this opposi-tion, so we will be able to answer this question better later. Even now, how-ever, we can ask and answer the following questions.

a. What was the spiritual condition of the people at this time, according

to Jer. 1:16? _____

_____

b. What was Jeremiah told to say to the people, according to Jer. 1:14-16?

_____

c. What would be the natural reaction of evil, rebellious people to Jeremiah's

message? _____
*   *

a. They had forsaken the Lord and were serving other Gods.
b. He was told to announce God's judgment against them.
c. They would be angered by Jeremiah's message.

18. Jer. 1:17-19 helps then to complete our understanding of Jeremiah's call
to be a prophet. In these verses the Lord repeats His call to Jeremiah. He
also tells Jeremiah of the danger and opposition he must face as a prophet.
And He promises Jeremiah that He will be with him and protect him.

a. The central idea in this passage is _____.

b. Other important ideas in the passage are _____

_____ and _____.
*   *

a. Jeremiah's call.
b. Danger and opposition   God's presence and protection

19. In review, let's list some of the steps or methods we have used in our
study of Jer. 1:11-19. You do not need to memorize these steps at this time.
But you should understand how to take these steps. As you gain more practice
in future lessons, you will become more skillful and more independent.

In our study of Jer. 1:11-19 we:
a. Defined the divisions or units of this passage.
b. Choose titles for these units using words from the text.
c. Noted the symbols, their interpretation, and the relationship between each
   symbol and its interpretation.
d. Observed other details in the passage and their significance.
e. Compared the different units to see their similarities.
f. Found the central idea or message in each paragraph.
g. Studied the relationship of these units to the previous passage, Jer. 1:4-10.

By using these methods you have been able to study Jer. 1:11-19 inductively.
At each step you began with the text and studied it on its own terms.

20. As a final review of Jer. 1:11-19, write down the reference for each
unit of this passage, a title of four words or less taken from the text,
and one or more of the main ideas in each unit. You may use your Bible,
but do not refer back to previous points in this lesson.

    Reference   Title   Main Idea

a. _____   _____   _____

b. _____   _____   _____

c. _____   _____   _____

If you have any doubts about your work, go back in the lesson and find what
you need.

D. Isaiah 6

In this section you will do a brief Inductive Study of the call of Isaiah
in Is. 6. This is a famous passage, and it will help you understand the concept of Old Testament prophecy. You will notice some similarities between
this passage and Jer. 1:4-19. And you will be able to follow the same steps
we used in our study of Jeremiah's call. In this case, however, you will be
expected to work more independently. Spend time working out your answers
before you compare them with mine. Read through the whole chapter now.

1. Notice first that this passage begins with an historical introduction.
Study Is. 6:1 and put down all the information you can find about the historical background of this passage. You may use a Bible dictionary.

_____

_____

_____

_____

_____

_____

Your answer should include these points:
a. This event took place in the year King Uzziah died. My Bible dictionary
   says that Uzziah reigned from 785-734, so the call of Isaiah took place
   in about 734.
b. Uzziah was King of Judah, so apparently Isaiah was called to be a prophet
   of Judah.
c. Isaiah was in the Temple when he saw a vision of the Lord and had this
   experience.

2. Now look at Is. 6 as a whole. See if it all belongs together as a unit.

Give your own analysis here. _____

_____

_____

_____

_____

* _____ *

Your answer should include these points:
a. Is. 6:1 introduces a specific event. The whole chapter tells about that
   event, the call of Isaiah.
b. Is. 6 is a conversation between the Lord and Isaiah. The whole chapter
   is tied together by that conversation.
c. Is. 7:1 introduces another event which took place at a different time.
   This sets off Chapter 6 as a separate unit.

3. Analyze the passage by identifying who is speaking in each part.

a. v. 1-2 _____   g. v. 8a _____

b. v. 3 _____   h. v. 8b _____

c. v. 4 _____   i. v. 9-10 _____

d. v. 5 _____   j. v. 11a _____

e. v. 6 _____   k. v. 11b-13 _____

f. v. 7 _____

4. Now write down the main idea of the following divisions of the passage.

a. v. 1 _____

b. v. 2-4 _____

c. v. 5 _____

d. v. 6-8a _____

e. v. 8b _____

f. v. 9-10 _____

g. v. 11a _____

h. v. 11b-13 _____
*   *

a. The historical introduction to the passage.
b. Isaiah sees a vision of the Lord in the Temple.
c. He confesses his uncleanness before the Lord.
d. He is cleansed and called.
e. He responds.
f. He is to speak to an unresponsive people.
g. Isaiah asks how long he is to preach to this people.
h. The Lord answers, until Judah is destroyed.

5. Now we will go through the passage verse by verse and point out some of the significant details. There is not enough time to make a complete study. We are primarily interested in finding out Isaiah's concept of his prophetic call and we want to gain practice in Inductive Study.

In our study of Jer. 1:4-10 we noted that Jeremiah had a profound sense of the Lord's power and holiness. What indication of the Lord's power do you find in

Is. 6:1? _____
*   *

He was sitting on a throne.

6. What indications of the Lord's power do you find in Is. 6:2-4? _____
* _____ *

The seraphim called Him "the Lord of hosts" and said "the whole earth is full of His glory," and the Temple shook.

7. What indications of the Lord's holiness do you find in v. 2-4? _____

* _____ *

The words of the seraphim: "Holy, holy, holy is the Lord of hosts."

8. What were the seraphim? _____

* _____ *

Consult your Bible dictionary if you have not already done so.

9. What indication of the Lord's power do we find in v. 5? _____

* _____ *

Isaiah feels almost terrified as he stands in the presence of God. He calls
Him "the King, the Lord of hosts."

10. What indication of the Lord's holiness do we find in v. 5? _____

* _____ *

Isaiah feels unclean and confesses his uncleanness as he stands in the presence
of the holy God.

11. This expression of inadequacy is somewhat similar to Jeremiah's response to

the Lord's call. What did Jeremiah say when he heard God's call? _____

* _____ *

See. Jer. 1:6.

12. In v. 6-8a two things happen to Isaiah. What are they?

a. _____

b. _____
*   *

a. He is cleansed as a burning coal touches his lips.
b. And he is called to be the Lord's messenger.

13. What happens to Jeremiah in Jer. 1:9-10

a. _____

b. _____
*   *

a. The Lord touches his mouth.
b. And He sets Jeremiah over the nations as His prophet.

14. In Is. 6:8b Isaiah responds to the Lord's call. He says, "Here I am! Send

me." Explain briefly the significance of those words. _____

_____

_____

*   *
_____

There are many ways of explaining these words. Be sure to refer to the prophet's
concept of God's holiness and power. Isaiah had experienced the awful power of
the Lord of hosts; he could not but submit himself to the Lord's call. He had
confessed his uncleanness and been cleansed; now he could serve the holy Lord
as His prophet.

15. In v. 9-10 Isaiah is commissioned as a prophet. This is a very difficult
passage. Study it and try to answer the following questions.

a. To what people is he sent? _____

b. What is his message to them? _____

_____

c. What response is he to expect from them? _____
*   *

a. Judah (See answer to #1 above.)
b. Although it appears to be a condemnation of the people, it contains a call
to repentance. Note the final words of v. 10.
c. Resistance or rejection.

16. Here again notice the similarity to Jeremiah's experience.

a. To whom was Jeremiah sent? _____

b. What was his message? _____

c. What response was he to expect? _____
*   *

a. Judah (and the nations)
b. It was a call to repentance and a warning of judgment. (Jer. 1:13-16)
c. They would all turn against him. (Jer. 1:17-19)

17. Isaiah asks how long he is to prophesy to this rebellious people in

v. 11a. What is the Lord's reply? _____
*   *

Until destruction overtakes the land.

18. If Isaiah began his ministry in 734 B.C., he could not have continued

prophesying until the final destruction in 587 B.C. Why?_____

_____.
*   *

  That is 147 years later.

19. Is. 6:11b-13 describes the coming judgment. State in your own words what

is to happen. _____

_____
*   *

You should have mentioned these two points:
a. The passage speaks of the complete destruction of Judah.
b. And it mentions a deportation or exile.

20. The language of destruction here is similar to many passages in Jeremiah.
What literary figure or vision from Jeremiah's call expresses the Lord's

coming judgment? _____
*   *

The boiling pot.

21. Jeremiah not only foresaw but also lived through the final destruction of
Jerusalem.

Although Isaiah could not have lived to see that day, he did witness several
invasions of Judah. The great world empire which invaded Judah at the time

of Isaiah was Assyria. The great world empire that invaded and destroyed J

Juday at the time of Jeremiah was_____

*   *

Babylonia

22. Consider now Isaiah's concept of prophecy in Is. 6 as a whole. First

write out our definition of prophecy. _____   _____

* _____   *

Prophecy is the proclamation of God's word at a particular time in history.

23. State what was Isaiah's concept of prophecy in these terms by referring
to specific phrases in Is. 6.

a. God's word: _____

_____

b. Proclamation of God's word: _____

_____

c. At a particular time in history: _____

* _____   *

a. Isaiah "heard the voice of the Lord." He believed that God Himself had
spoken to him, and he responded to that call.
b. The Lord told Isaiah "Go, and say to this people...." He believed that
God had given him a message which He would fulfill.
c. Isaiah experienced God's call to him personally "in the year that King
Uzziah died." And he was given a message for his people.

24. Summarize Isaiah's experience of the prophetic call in terms of God's

holiness and power. _____

_____

_____

_____

* _____   *

We have noticed several indications of God's power and holiness.
a. God's power: The Lord is seen sitting on a throne. He is called the Lord
of hosts. The whole earth is full of His glory. The Temple shook. And when
He called, Isaiah knew he must respond.
b. God's holiness: The seraphim proclaimed His holiness. And Isaiah confessed his own uncleanness before God, and he was cleansed.

25. List briefly (without references) the steps in Isaiah's call in Is. 6.

a. Introduction

b. Isaiah's vision of the Lord.

c. _____

d. _____

e. _____

f. _____

g. _____

26. List briefly the steps in Jeremiah's call in Jer. 1:5-10.

a. _____

b. _____

c. _____

d. _____

e. _____

E. Review

We began this lesson with the question, What is prophecy? And we tried to
find an answer to that question by looking at the call of Jeremiah. Then we
made a careful study of Jer. 1:4-19. First we analyzed Jer. 1:4-10, then we
looked at the rest of the chapter. And we noted that all these paragraphs
are tied together around the theme of Jeremiah's call to be a prophet to the
nations. Later we will prepare a sermon outline based on Jer. 1:4-10.

You should use your Bible as you answer the following questions. But do not
refer back to the lesson and do not look at the answers given below until
you have written your own answer. The purpose of this review is not to see
if you remember the answers we have already worked out, but to see if you
can look at the text and find its significance.

The techniques of Inductive Study which you have used in this lesson will
be analyzed more carefully in future lessons. You have been guided through
an Inductive Study of an important passage of Jeremiah. As a result of
this experience you should be able to describe and interpret Jeremiah's
call, explain the two visions in Jer. 1, and state what is prophecy and
what was Jeremiah's message.

1. The first two questions of this review go back to Lesson I.

What is Inductive Bible Study? _____

_____   _____

*   _____   *

Inductive Bible Study is an approach to the study of the Bible which begins
with the Bible itself and studies the Bible on its own terms.

2. What are three steps for beginning an Inductive Study of a book of the Bible?

a. _____

b. _____

c. _____
*   *

a. Find out what kind of a book it is.
b. Find out something about its historical background.
c. Look for the structure or outline.

3. Now let's review Lesson II. Remember that this lesson is closely related
to the first step in beginning our Inductive Study of Jeremiah.

Jeremiah is a book of prophecy. And your study in this lesson of Jer. 1:4-19
has increased your understanding of what prophecy is and what the book of
Jeremiah is about.

Write the definition of prophecy which has been presented in this lesson.

_____

*   _____   *

Prophecy is the proclamation of God's word at a particular time in history.

4. List the three essential parts of this definition.

a. _____

b. _____

c. _____
                                                                        *
*

a. Prophecy is <u>God's word</u>.
b. It is the <u>proclamation</u> of God's word.
c. It is the proclamation of God's word <u>at a particular time</u> in history.

5. Explain briefly how Jeremiah's concept of prophecy was more profound

than our concept of preaching. _____

_____

*
*   *

We noted that Jeremiah had a profound sense of God's holiness and power. He
really believed that God moved men and nations by His word. And he believed
intensely that God spoke to him personally.

6. We studied Jer. 1:4-10 in two ways. First, since the passage is a unit, we

studied it _____. Then we studied the details

of the passage _____.
*   *

as a whole   verse by verse

7. First we studied Jer. 1:4-10 as a whole. We observed that it is a conver-

sation between the Lord and Jeremiah, so we noted _____

_____.
*   *

who is speaking in each verse.

8. Then we studied the different parts of the dialogue and wrote down briefly
the significance of each part.

List the references for each part of the conversation and its significance.
You may look at the text.

a. v. 4   Introduction

b. _____   _____

c. _____   _____

d. _____   _____

e. _____   _____
*   *

a. v. 4 Introduction.
b. v. 5 The Lord calls Jeremiah to be a prophet.
c. v. 6 Jeremiah responds but hesitates.
d. v.7-8 The Lord repeats His call.
e. v.9-10 The Lord ordains Jeremiah as His prophet to the nations.

9. We observed that the Lord is the principal actor in Jer. 1:4-10. So we
listed all the phrases that indicate what the Lord did to

                                              _____.
*   *

Jeremiah.

10. Then we studied Jer. 1:4-10 verse by verse. That is, we studied the different parts of the passage. At each point we tried to see what we·could learn
from the text itself.

a. We noted that Inductive Study must be <u>flexible</u> because it _____

_____.

b. We recommended the use of our <u>imagination</u> so that we could _____

_____.

c. We considered the <u>application</u> of the text to us today through our know-

ledge of _____.
*   *

a. Studies each passage on its own terms.
b. Understand what these. words meant to Jeremiah and feel what he felt.
c. Jesus Christ, the full revelation of God's word.

11. Write a brief application of each part of Jer. 1:4-10 for us as Christians of the 20th century.

a. v. 4 _____

_____

_____

b. v. 5 _____

_____

_____

c. v. 6 _____

_____

_____

d. v. 7-8 _____

_____

_____

e. v. 9-10 _____

_____

* _____ *

You will probably have an opportunity to discuss your answer in class.

12. Now go on to Jer. 1:11-19. List the references for the three units of
this passage and write a title for each one. The purpose of this exercise is
not to see if you remember what you wrote previously when we analyzed this
passage. It is to see if you can look at the passage and find the divisions
and write titles easily.

a. _____   _____

b. _____   _____

c. _____   _____
*   *

If you want to check your answers here with your previous work, see C.2. Your
titles do not have to be the same however.

13. Why did we say that the rod of almond and the boiling pot are visions?

* _____ *

Because the text says that Jeremiah saw these symbols. A vision is something you see.

14. What three steps did we follow in our study of each of these visions?

a. _____

b. _____

c. _____
*   *

a. We identified the object or symbol.
b. We studied the interpretation of the symbol.
c. We analyzed the relationship between the symbol and the interpretation.

15. Explain the vision of the rod of almond using these three steps.

a. _____

b. _____

c. _____
*   *

a. The symbol is the rod of almond.
b. The interpretation is that the Lord will soon fulfill His word.
c. The almond tree awakes early in the spring and so the Lord will soon fulfill His word.

16. Explain the vision of the boiling pot using these three steps.

a. _____

b. _____

c. _____
*   *

a. The symbol is a pot which is boiling and which faces from the north.
b. The interpretation is that destruction is coming down from the north.
c. The boiling is like destruction and the north indicates the source or direction from which it comes.

17. Explain the symbols in Jer. 1:18 using the same three steps.

a. _____

b. _____

c. _____
*   *

a. The symbols are a fortified city, an iron pillar, and bronze walls.
b. The interpretation is that God is with Jeremiah to deliver him.
c. The symbols represent strength and safety, which is what the Lord
promises to Jeremiah in the face of his enemies.

18. In our study of Jer. 1:11-19 we used several methods or steps. Look at
the passage once again and see how many of these methods you can remember.
Think how you would do an Inductive Study of these paragraphs.

a. _____

b. _____

c. _____

d. _____

e. _____
*   *

You have not been asked to memorize a particular set of methods because the
Inductive approach is flexible and varies constantly as the text changes. Also
you have not been asked to memorize the steps used in this lesson because they
were just introduced to you. If, however, you wish to review the methods we
used in our study of Jer. 1:11-19, go back to C.19, where seven methods are
listed.

19. Now go back over the entire passage of this lesson, Jer. 1:4-19, and
state briefly in your own words the main ideas in each paragraph. Base this
summary on the Bible itself without referring to any helps. Some paragraphs
have more than one idea. Use complete sentences, not just titles.

a. v. 4-10 _____

_____

_____

_____

b. v. 11-12 _____

_____

_____

_____

c. v. 13-16 _____

_____

_____

_____

d. v. 17-19 _____

_____

_____

_____

*   *

See if you have included most of these ideas.
a. v. 4-10 The Lord calls Jeremiah. He hesitates. The Lord calls him again,
            ordains him, and sets him over the nations as His prophet.
b. v. 11-12 The Lord says He will soon fulfill His word.
c. v. 13-16 The Lord announces that He will send destruction on His people
            from the north as judgment on their wickedness and idolatry.
d. v. 17-19 The Lord repeats His call to Jeremiah. He points out the danger
            and opposition he will have to face but promises His presence
            and protection.

3

Historical Background

In Lesson I you were introduced to three steps for beginning an Inductive Bible Study. The second step is to find out about the historical background of the book. In Lesson III you will study the historical background of the book of Jeremiah.

You have already looked at some of the historical information that Jeremiah included in his book. And you know that this information is very important for our understanding of the book. In this lesson you will look for more historical information. You will learn how to use this information in your study of Jeremiah. And you will practice making maps and chronological charts.

Remember that your objective in this course is primarily to learn skills. You have to learn some information also. For example, in this lesson you will have to memorize the dates for the fall of Nineveh, the battle of Carchemish, and the destruction of Jerusalem. But it is far more important for you to learn how to find and use the historical background for Jeremiah.

By the end of this chapter you should be able to:
1. Locate the important historical information about Jeremiah's time in the Bible.
2. Draw a simple map of the area from memory showing the position of Judah in the struggle for world dominance between Assyria and Babylonia.
3. Prepare a chronological chart showing the ministry of Jeremiah, the reigns of the last five kings of Judah, and the dominant world empires of that period.
4. Give the dates for the fall of Nineveh, the battle of Carchemish, and the fall of Jerusalem.
5. Explain the importance of all this information for our understanding of Jeremiah's ministry.

A. The Kings of Judah

In this lesson you will use some methods that you probably have never tried before. And the process may seem complicated. But each step is a simple one which you can do easily if you follow carefully the path of investigation.

Once again note that Inductive Study begins with the Bible and studies it on its own terms. You will begin here with the brief historical introduction found in the book of Jeremiah itself. You will look up further information about the kings of Judah elsewhere in the Bible. And you will see why this information is so important for our understanding of Jeremiah's ministry and message.

1. One of the beginning steps in Inductive Bible Study is to find out about

the historical background. Why is this important? _____

_____

We have to know something about the historical background of a book in order
to study it on its own terms.

2. We noted earlier that it is especially important to study the historical
background of the prophetical books.

a. What is prophecy? _____

_____

b. Why is the historical background especially important in understanding

prophecy?_____ *
*

a. Prophecy is the proclamation of God's word at a particular time and place.
b. We can only understand prophecy if we know when and where it was given.

3. In Lesson I we used four important historical questions in our study of
Jeremiah. These are questions you will use as you study any prophetical book.
See if you can complete the following list of historical questions.

a. When did Jeremiah prophesy? _____

b. _____

c. _____

d. _____
*   *

b. To whom did he preach?
c. What was happening at that time?
d. What problems was Jeremiah dealing with?

4. Now answer these four questions. This is a review of the historical information we already have about Jeremiah. You may use your Bible.

a. _____

b. _____

c. _____

d. _____
*   *

a. Jeremiah prophesied from the 13th year of Josiah to the 11th year of
Zedekiah.
b. He preached to the people of Judah (and the nations).
c. These were the last years of Judah ending with the captivity of Jerusalem.
d. Jeremiah preached against the evil and idolatry of his people.

5. The destruction and captivity of Jerusalem was, we have noted, one of
the most important events in the history of the people of God in the Old
Testament. It stands at the end of Jeremiah's time but it casts a dark shad-
ow across his ministry. His preaching was an urgent call to repentance in
the face of this impending destruction. You can see in this case the importance of finding out the historical background of a book.

a. What was the most important historical event which occurred during Jere-

miah's ministry? _____

b. Why is this information important for our understanding of the book of Jere-

miah? _____

* _____ *

a. The destruction and captivity of Jerusalem.
b. Jeremiah's ministry was very much affected by the approaching destruction.

6. We have noted that Jeremiah preached against the evil and idolatry of his
people. Jer. 1:10 says the Lord set him over nations and kingdoms to destroy
and to build.

a. What was Jeremiah called to destroy? _____

b. What was he called to build? _____
* *

a. evil and idolatry
b. repentance and obedience

7. We also noted in Jer. 1:13-16 what was the message that Jeremiah received
concerning his people.

a. What was that message? _____

_____

b. How was that message fulfilled? _____

_____

a. That the Lord was sending destruction on all of Judah as judgment upon their wickedness and idolatry.
b. Jerusalem was finally destroyed and her people taken captive.

The historical information which we have just reviewed is essential to our understanding of the book of Jeremiah. We should keep in mind this historical background whenever we read a passage from this book.

Now we will see what further information we can find about Judah in the days of Jeremiah.

8. Jer. 1:1-3 is a very important passage because it introduces the book and because it gives us historical information about the book. This is our starting point.

a. Inductive Study begins with _____.

b. We should look for historical information first in _____.

c. Jer. 1:1-3 is very important because it _____

_____.
*   *

a. the Bible, the text itself.
b. the Bible, Jeremiah.
c. introduces the book and gives us historical information about the book.

9. Jer. 1:1-3 states that Jeremiah prophesied during the reigns of _____

_____. Where in the

Bible can we find a description of the reigns of these kings? _____

_____
*   *

Josiah, Jehoiakim, and Zedekiah   2 Kings and 2 Chronicles

10. Find the exact references in 2 Kings and 2 Chronicles for each king's reign. You do not have to read through all this material. Just glance through it to make sure you have the references right.

a. Josiah   _____   _____

b. Jehoiakim   _____   _____

c. Zedekiah   _____   _____

11. If you have put down the references correctly, you will notice that there is a gap between Josiah and Jehoiakim and another gap between Jehoiakim and

Zedekiah. That is, 2 Kings and 2 Chronicles include the reigns of two kings who are not mentioned in Jer. 1:1-3. This fact should raise in your mind the question, Why doesn't Jer. 1:1-3 include these other two kings? First, write down the names of these two kings and the references in 2 Kings and 2 Chronicles.

a. _____   _____

b. _____   _____

12. Now go through these passages again and look for useful information about the reigns of these five kings. It is important to know, for example, how long each king reigned, because this will tell us how long Jeremiah's ministry lasted. And it is important to know which kings were obedient to the Lord and which ones were evil. Once again you can find this information without reading through the passages. Just glance at the opening verses about each king. Complete the following chart. Do not fill in the last column yet.

	King	Character	Length of Reign	Dates
a.	Josiah	Did right	31 years	
b.				
c.				
d.				
e.				

*   *

You should not need to check your answers. But be sure you put down how many years each king reigned, not how old he was when he began to reign.

13. Notice especially the length of the reigns of Jehoahaz and Jehoiachin. See if you can answer now the following questions.

a. How many kings were there during the time of Jeremiah? _____

b. Why doesn't Jer: 1:1-3 mention two of these kings? _____

*   *

a. Five
b. Because they reigned such a short time.

14. Notice, too, how many of those kings did evil and disobeyed the Lord.
Consider the significance of that fact for Jeremiah's ministry. In those
days kings had great influence on the religious life of their people.

a. How many of the kings did evil and disobeyed the Lord? _____

b. What significance did their disobedience have for Jeremiah's ministry? ____

*   *
_____

a. Four
b. These kings led their people away from the Lord while Jeremiah was calling
them back to the Lord.

15. We know how long these kings reigned, so now we should be able to figure
out how long Jeremiah carried out his ministry. Read over Jer. 1:1-3 and note
exactly when Jeremiah began to prophesy and when he finished his ministry.

a. Jeremiah began to prophesy in the _____ year of _____.

b. He finished his ministry in the _____ year of _____.

16. Now use simple arithmetic to figure out how long Jeremiah's ministry was.

He prophesied for _____ years under King Josiah, _____ years under King

Jehoiakim, and _____ years under King Zedekiah. You can omit the other

two kings because their reigns were so short. Jeremiah prophesied altogether

_____ years.
*   *

These calculations are based on the information in Jer. 1:1-3. Later you will see
that Jeremiah's ministry continued for some time after the fall of Jerusalem.

17. The chart under #12 above has a column called "Dates". We should not only
know how long each king reigned but also what were the years of their reigns.
In order to figure that out we only need to know one historical date from
which to calculate. In this case the most important date is the destruction
of Jerusalem in 587 B.C.

You already know that Zedekiah was the last king of Judah and that his
eleven-year reign ended with the destruction of Jerusalem. If 587 B.C. was
the last year of his reign, then the first year of his reign must have been
598 B.C. That is, we have to figure backwards from the date we already
know. And since these are years Before Christ, the numbers get larger as
we go further back in time. 587 plus 11 is 598.

Put these dates in the proper space for Zedekiah in the chart under #12 above: 598 - 587 B.C. Then figure out the dates for all the other kings. Put just one date for Jehoiachin and one for Jehoahaz since they reigned just a few months.

18. Now figure out the period during which Jeremiah carried out his minis- try, using the chart at # 12. You should have indicated that Josiah reigned during the period 640-609 B.C. Since Jeremiah began to prophesy in the 13th

year of Josiah, we know he began in the year _____ B.C. And since his

ministry ended with the destruction of Jerusalem, we know it ended in the

year _____ B.C. Now subtract the year his ministry ended from the year

it began. Jeremiah prophesied for _____ years.

*   *

Check your last answer with your answer at #16 above where you figured out how many years Jeremiah prophesied.

It is important to understand how to make these calculations because you will have to figure out other dates soon. You should have come to the con- clusion at #16 and at #18 that Jeremiah prophesied for 40 years. If either answer was incorrect, go back over those points and work out the calcula- tions again on scratch paper until they come out right.

19. As you went through the passages in 2 Kings and 2 Chronicles, you noticed that they give long descriptions of the reign of Josiah. Josiah was a good king, as we have already noted. He tried to lead Judah back to the Lord. The major events of his reign are important for us because they occurred just before and during the time of Jeremiah, who was also calling Judah back to the Lord.

Look up the following events in 2 Kings and 2 Chronicles. Indicate what year of Josiah's reign they took place and what date. Remember that Josiah reigned from 640 - 609 B.C.

a. Josiah began to purge Judah of her idolatry in the _____ year of his

reign, which was _____ B.C.

b. He repaired the Temple, found the book of the law, reformed the religion,

and celebrated the passover in the _____ year of his reign, which was

_____ B.C.

*   *

a. 12th year   628 B.C.
b. 18th year   622 B.C.

20. Compare these dates with the dates for the ministry of Jeremiah. Jeremiah began his ministry just _____ year after Josiah began to purge Judah. And when the Temple was repaired, the law found, the true religion reestablished, and the passover celebrated, Jeremiah had already been preaching for

_____ years.

*   *

one   five

21. To appreciate the importance of Josiah's reforms we should note that the previous two kings, his father and grandfather, did great evil and abomination. List some of the terrible things they did, according to 2 Kings and 2 Chronicles.

a. _____

b. _____

c. _____

d. _____

22. The reforms of Josiah were a great change from the practices of Manasseh and Amon. So we should expect to find evidences of those reforms in the book of Jeremiah.

Nevertheless, we should also note at this point that the kings who followed Josiah did not follow his example but rebelled against the Lord and practiced idolatry.

For _____ years Jeremiah prophesied under a king who sought the Lord and

for _____ years he prophesied under evil kings.

*   *

18   22

23. Run through the passages in 2 Kings and 2 Chronicles once again and note two more kinds of information that may be useful. These passages tell us the relationship of each king to his predecessors. For example, Jehoahaz was the son of Josiah. At the same time note the other names for two of these kings.

		Relationships	Other Names
a.	Josiah		
b.	Jehoahaz		
c.	Jehoiakim		
d.	Jehoiachin		
e.	Zedekiah		

*   *

Jehoahaz, Jehoiakim, and Zedekiah were sons of Josiah. Jehoiachin was the son
of Jehoiakim. 2 Chronicles 36:10 calls Zedekiah the <u>brother</u> of Jehoiachin,
when really he was an uncle. The term <u>brother</u> was often used for the next of
kin or close relatives. See 2 Kings 23:31; 24:17, 18. Jehoiakim's other name
is Eliakim. Zedekiah's other name is Mattaniah.

24. The following list is a review of our investigation of the kings of
Judah. In this study we began with the Bible, and all of this information
except the date of the destruction of Jerusalem came from, the Bible itself.
We used many methods, including arithmetic, but these methods simply found
and used the information in the Bible. We studied the historical background
of Jeremiah inductively.

a. We located the passages in 2 Kings and 2 Chronicles that describe the
reigns of the kings of Judah at the time of Jeremiah.

b. We noted the character of these kings and the significance of this information for our understanding of Jeremiah's ministry.

c. We wrote down the length of their reigns and calculated the dates of
each, based on the date for the destruction of Jerusalem (587 B.C.).

d. We observed that Jer. 1:1-3 omits the names of two of these kings, and
we explained why they were omitted.

e. We calculated the dates for Jeremiah's ministry.

f. We noted the dates for Josiah's reforms and the importance of these reforms for Jeremiah's ministry.

g. We noted the family relationships of these kings and other names for
two of them.

Some of these steps are more important than others, but all of this information will be helpful as we study the book of Jeremiah. The only piece of
information which you should memorize is the date for the destruction of
Jerusalem. But you should be able to find out all of the rest of this infor-

mation on your own using just your Bible. And you should gradually become
accustomed to these steps in Inductive Bible Study so that you can make
this kind of an investigation without any guidance.

B. World Power Struggle

In the 20th century several great nations have tried to gain control over
their neighbors and to become world rulers. Even since the last world war
the two strongest countries have been competing for world leadership. This
is what has happened since the beginning of history. It was going on in the
time of Jeremiah.

As you studied about the kings of Judah in 2 Kings and 2 Chronicles, you
probably noted that the history of Judah was marked by several invasions
during the time of Jeremiah. We know that Jeremiah prophesied about an enemy
from the north and that he was called to be a prophet to the nations. We
have said that the most important event during Jeremiah's ministry was the
destruction and captivity of Jerusalem. So it is important for us to understand the world power struggle that was going on at that time.

1. In 2 Kings and 2 Chronicles we note that Egypt was one of the great
powers during the reigns of Josiah, Jehoahaz, and Jehoiakim. Write down
the most important facts about Egypt's interference in the life of Judah
during each reign.

a. Josiah _____

b. Jehoahaz _____

c. Jehoiakim _____

2. The Egyptians killed King Josiah at Megiddo. The people of Judah made
Jehoahaz, his son, king, but three months later the Egyptians took Jehoahaz
off the throne and carried him to Egypt, and put Jehoiakim, his brother, in
his place. Egypt ruled over Judah for a time and forced Judah to pay tribute.

The Battle of Megiddo took place in the year _____ B.C. between King

_____ of Judah and Pharoah _____ of Egypt. Who won the battle?

* _____ *

Check the date for the end of Josiah's reign in #A.12 above. The information
about the Battle of Megiddo is found in 2 Kings 23:29-30 and 2 Chron. 35:20-24.

3. It is interesting to note that Pharaoh Neco of Egypt was going up to the
Euphrates River to meet the king of Assyria. (2 K. 23:29, 2 Chron. 35:20) He
did not intend to attack Judah. He just wanted to go through Judah on his way
to the north.

So we should find out why Pharaoh Neco was going up to meet the king of Assyria. If you study your Bible dictionary and concordance you will see that Assyria was another great world power. But Assyria had already been defeated by Babylonia and Nineveh, the capital of Assyria, was destroyed in 612 B.C.

Now you can begin to understand the power struggle that was taking place in the time of Jeremiah. The three great empires were:

a. _____   b. _____   c. _____
*   *

Egypt, Assyria, Babylonia.

4. 2 Chron. 35:20 says that Pharaoh Neco of Egypt was going up to the north in order to fight at Carchemish. Jer. 46:2 tells us that Pharaoh did go up to Carchemish on the Euphrates and was defeated there. Look up these passages and answer the following questions.

a. The Battle of Carchemish took place in the _____ year of Jehoiakim,

which was the year _____ B.C. (See your chart at A. #12.)

b. Those who fought at Carchemish were king _____ of _____

and king _____ of _____.

5. We now have three important dates.

a. The fall of Nineveh (Assyria) took place in the year _____ B.C.

b. The battle of Megiddo (near Judah) took place in the year _____ B.C.

c. The battle of Carchemish (on the Euphrates) took place in the year _____ B.C.
*   *

a. 612 B.C.
b. 609 B.C.
c. 605 B.C.

6. We still have to clear up one point. In 2 K. 23:29 we read that Pharaoh Neco of Egypt went up to the Euphrates River to meet the king of Assyria. But in Jer. 46:2 we read that Pharaoh Neco fought against King Nebuchadrezzar of Babylonia. (Nebuchadrezzar is also spelled Nebuchadnezzar).

The explanation is quite simple. Assyria had already been defeated in 612 B.C. by Babylonia. So Babylonia was the new ruler of the world. But Egypt did not want to be ruled by Babylonia. In fact Egypt wanted to rule the world instead of Babylonia. So Pharaoh Neco of Egypt wanted to join with the remaining Assyrian forces and fight against Babylonia.

a. Assyria was a great world power until its capital was destroyed in

_____ B.C.

b. Babylonia became the leading world power in _____ B.C.

c. Egypt had a chance to become the leading world power after the defeat

of Assyria, but was itself defeated in _____ B.C.

*   *

a. 612 B.C.
b. 612 B.C.
c. 605 B.C.

7. Judah was, of course, a small nation in those days, not one of the great
world powers. So it had to suffer under the domination of the other leading
nations.

a. At the end of Josiah's reign Judah was defeated by _____.

b. King Jehoahaz was deposed by _____.

c. King Jehoiakim was put on the throne of Judah by _____ and

paid tribute during the first year of his reign.

*   *

a.b.c. Egypt, or Pharaoh Neco

8. Notice that the battle of Carchemish took place during the reign of
Jehoiakim. The results of this battle made a change in the life of Judah.

a. Jehoiakim reigned from _____ to _____ B.C. (See your chart at A.#12)

b. The battle of Carchemish took place in the year _____ B.C.

c. During the first part of Jehoiakim's reign Judah was subject to _____.

d. The battle of Carchemish was won by _____.

e. After the battle of Carchemish Judah was subject to _____.
                                                      (see 2.K. 24:1)

9. After the battle of Carchemish in 605 B.C. Babylonia continued for many
years as the leading world power. Judah came increasingly under the rule
of Babylonia. Study the reigns of Jehoiakim, Jehoiachin, and Zedekiah in
2 Kings and 2 Chronicles and note the influence of Babylonia over Judah.

a. What did Babylonia do to Judah during the reign of Jehoiakim? _____

_____

_____

b. What did Babylonià do to Judah during the reign of Jehoiachin? _____

_____

_____

c. What did Babylonia do to Judah during the reign of Zedekiah? _____

_____

_____

a. Nebuchadnezzar sent enemies against Jehoiakim and finally bound him to
take him to Babylon.
b. The Babylonians besieged Jerusalem and then carried off Jehoiachin and
the leading people of the city and the vessels of the Temple to Babylon.
c. Nebuchadnezzar besieged Jerusalem almost two years, then destroyed Jerusalem and the Temple and carried off Zedekiah blind and the people and the
remaining vessels of the Temple to Babylon.

10. Explain why Egypt no longer interfered in the life of Judah after the

battle of Carchemish. See 2 K. 24:7. _____

_____

Babylonia controlled all the area of the near east right up to Egypt's fron-
tier.

11. A great struggle for power was going on during the time of Jeremiah.
Assyria lost its place of dominance. Egypt made an attempt to gain world
rule and lost. And Babylonia came out on top.

Explain briefly the importance of these events on the life of the small

nation of Judah. _____

_____

_____

Judah suffered under the rule of Egypt for a time, then under the dominance of Babylonia. In other words, the leading powers ruled the smaller countries like Judah.

12. Jeremiah was a prophet of Judah in those terrible years. He was also the Lord's prophet to the nations. He called God's people to repentance and obedience, hoping that they could escape destruction. He counselled his people and their rulers about their political alliances. But as they continued in their evil ways, he had to announce God's judgment on them, and finally he saw Jerusalem destroyed, the Temple burned, and the people taken into exile.

Explain the importance of the historical background for our understanding

of the book of Jeremiah. _____

_____

_____

_____

* _____
                                                                          *

Obviously the historical background is essential for our understanding of Jeremiah. Only as we look at the history of Judah and the world power struggle of that period can we interpret Jeremiah's mission and message and see the book on its own terms.

13. You have just stated that the historical background is essential for our understanding of the book of Jeremiah. In order to see the importance of this historical information in the interpretation of the book of Jeremiah, consider briefly that part of the book which we have already studied.

a. Why was Jeremiah's call in Jer. 1:4-10 a fearful and an awesome responsi-

bility? _____

b. In Jer. 1:11-12 the Lord promised to fulfill soon His word. What was the

Lord about to do? _____

c. Who was the enemy from the north mentioned in Jer. 1:13-16? _____

_____ When did this destruction finally come to pass? _____

d. Why did the people and the priests and the princes and kings of Judah

oppose Jeremiah as Jer. 1:17-19 indicates? _____

* _____
                                                                          *

a. Because this was a period of great danger and tragedy, perhaps the most crucial in the history of Israel.
b. He was about to destroy Jerusalem and take her people captive.
c. Assyria or Babylonia, probably. In 587 B.C.
d. Because they rebelled against the Lord and did not want to accept His judgment.

14. So far we have said very little about the geography of the Near East. You should study the location of the three great empires which we have mentioned. And you should be able to explain where Judah was located. Not only was Judah one of many small nations who suffered these great empires. Judah was located on the main trade route between them. So whenever Assyria or Babylonia fought against Egypt, their armies went through Judah. And when Egypt wanted to attack Assyria or Babylonia, her armies had to go through Judah.

Explain the role of Judah in the world power struggle of Jeremiah's time.

_____

_____

* _____ *

Judah was a buffer state on the invasion route between the three major powers, Egypt, Assyria, and Babylonia.

15. Look at a map of the Near East and find these empires.

a. Egypt is located to the <u>southwest</u> of Judah.

b. Assyria (Nineveh) is located to the _____ of Judah.

c. Babylonia is located to the _____ of Judah.

* *

b. northeast
c. east

16. Since Babylonia is located to the east of Judah, we should explain why Jeremiah speaks of Babylonia as the enemy from the north. Directly to the east of Judah, between Judah and Babylonia, is the Arabian Desert.

How would Babylonia's armies get to Judah and Egypt? _____

_____

* _____ *

They would normally travel up the Euphrates River and down into Judah from
the north. Note, for example, that Egypt and Babylonia fought at Carchemish,
north of Judah, not at some point in the Arabian Desert.

17. We should perhaps mention that there was another natural barrier to the
west of Judah, the Mediterranean Sea. In fact Palestine has been described
as a land bridge between Egypt and Assyria or Babylonia.

Judah was a small nation between _____ on the east and

_____ on the west.

the Arabian Desert   the Mediterranean Sea

18. In summary, write a brief description of Judah's geographical position
in relation to the world power struggle at the time of Jeremiah. This is
an important question, one which you will have to answer on the final exam.
Your answer should mention the location of the three major powers, and the
two natural phenomena to the east and west of Judah.

_____

_____

_____

_____

_____

_____

Your answer should read something like this. At the time of Jeremiah Judah was
a small nation located between the Mediterranean Sea on the west and the Arabian Desert on the east. It was a land bridge or trade route between Egypt
to the southwest and Assyria and Babylonia to the northeast and east. The
power struggle between these three empires inevitably involved Judah.

19. In order to fix in your mind the geography of the Near East at the time
of Jeremiah, locate the following names on the accompanying map with the
help of an atlas.

Egypt	Euphrates River	Mediterranean Sea
Assyria (Nineveh)	Tigris River	Arabian Desert
Babylonia	Nile River	Carchemish
Judah (Jerusalem)	Jordan River	Megiddo

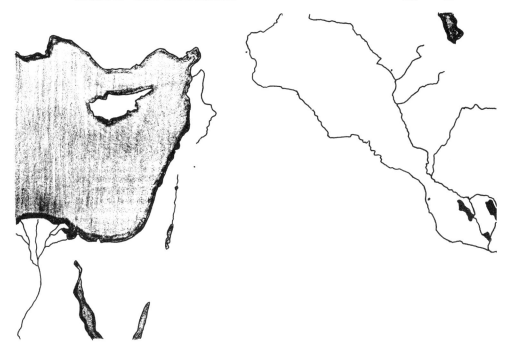

20. Now draw arrows along the invasion routes between the great powers.

a. Draw an arrow from Egypt through Megiddo to Carchemish.
b. Draw another arrow from Jerusalem to Megiddo.
c. Draw an arrow from Babylonia to Nineveh.
d. Draw another arrow from Babylonia to Carchemish.

21. Now add the dates for the following events. Just write each date on
the map after the name of the place where it occurred.

a. The fall of Nineveh - 612 B.C.
b. The battle of Megiddo - 609 B.C.
c. The battle of Carchemish - 605 B.C.
d. The destruction of Jerusalem - 587 B.C.

22. Be sure you understand the significance of these events and can explain
them.

a. Who defeated Nineveh and what is the significance of this event? _____

_____

_____

b. Who fought at Megiddo and who won? _____

c. Who fought at Carchemish and what is the significance of this event? _____

_____

_____

d. Who destroyed Jerusalem and what followed this event? _____

* _____ *

a. Babylonia destroyed Nineveh and took Assyria's place as the leading world
power.
b. Judah was defeated by Egypt at Megiddo.
c. Babylonia defeated Egypt at Carchemish and maintained its supremacy.
d. Babylonia destroyed Jerusalem and took her people into exile.

23. Practice drawing a simple map of the Near East like the one at #19 above.
Try it several times on scratch paper until you can do it from memory. Remember especially the location of the three empires and Judah. Put in the
arrows indicating the invasions and the dates indicating the important battles.
The map should help you remember the important facts about the power struggle
at the time of Jeremiah. And you will want to be able to sketch this map
without using an atlas when you are teaching a lesson or preaching a sermon.

After you have practiced drawing the map several times, draw it again on
page A.1 in the appendix. You will later use it in your Jeremiah notebook.

24. Review our investigation of the world power struggle at the time of Jeremiah. Do you think you can remember all of this information? Probably not.
No one could remember it very long. It really isn't necessary. But you should
be able to find out all of this information on your own, even five years from
now. How? Through Inductive Study. Just begin with the Bible, see what it
says, and figure out the significance of what it says. You only need as additional information the dates for the fall of Nineveh and the destruction of
Jerusalem and a simple map of the Near East.

Suppose you had lost all your notes from this course and had to prepare
a lesson on the world power struggle at the time of Jeremiah. What would
you do? List some of the steps and information you would use.

a. _____

_____

b. _____

_____

c. _____

_____

d. _____

_____

e. _____

*   _____   *

These are some of the steps we used. Your answer should include at least five
of them.
a. We used the dates for the five kings ending in 587 B.C.
b. We studied the information about Assyria, Egypt, and Babylonia in 2 Kings
and 2 Chronicles.
c. We noted that Babylonia defeated Nineveh in 612 B.C. and became the leading world power.
d. We noted that Pharaoh Neco of Egypt was on his way to Carchemish when he
killed King Josiah of Judah at Megiddo in 609 B.C. He also deposed Jehoahaz,
who reigned just three months, and put Jehoiakim in his place.
e. We noted that Pharaoh Neco went to the north to join up with the remaining
forces of Assyria against Babylonia (2 K. 23:29; 2 Chron. 35:20). But he was
defeated at Carchemish in 605 B.C. by King Nebuchadnezzar of Babylonia (Jer. 46:2).
f. We explained that Judah was dominated by Egypt until the battle of Carchemish, then Judah was dominated by Babylonia.
g. The Babylonians dominated Judah increasingly. They bound up King Jehoiakim,
carried King Jehoiachin and the leading citizens and the Temple vessels to
Babylonia, and finally destroyed Jerusalem in 587 B.C., taking her people
and King Zedekiah into exile.
h. Finally we made a map of the Near East, showing the location of the three
major powers and the position of Judah in the invasion route between them.

This may seem like a long process. But each step is a simple one if you know
where to find the information and how to use it. This information is very important for our understanding of the book of Jeremiah. And it shows us that
the study of Jeremiah is an exciting task.

C. Chronological Chart

You now have a considerable amount of historical information about the
time of Jeremiah. We have studied the history of the reigns of the five
kings of Judah in 2 Kings and 2 Chronicles. And we have analyzed the world
power struggle.

We have said that it is not necessary to memorize all this information.
That would be too difficult. All you need to do is to know how to find
the information when you need it.

Another problem may come to your mind as you look at all this historical
information. How can you see the significance of all these dates and names
and places? What relationships are there between these different pieces
of information? How can they be integrated into an intelligible picture
of the period? How can we add more information as we study the book of
Jeremiah without becoming confused?

At the end of the previous section of this lesson we drew a map of the
area to explain the world power struggle of the time of Jeremiah. This
helped you visualize much of the historical information you had studied
up to that point. With the help of that map you can easily see the significance of Judah's geographic position in middle of the conflicts between
the three great empires. And you can see the relationships between such
details as the fall of Nineveh, the battle of Megiddo, and the battle of
Carchemish.

In this section you will use another method called a chronological chart.
It is different from a map. But like a map it will help you visualize the
historical background of Jeremiah's ministry. You will be able to see clearly
the relationships between the different events of that period. You will
need a metric ruler to do some of the exercises in this section and the
following one.

1. A chronological chart is a time chart. The word chronological comes
from the Greek word "chronos", which means time.

A chronological chart is a _____ chart.

*   *

Time

2. The word "chart" sometimes means map. And the chronological chart we
are going to make is like a time map. In other words you will draw a
picture showing the history of the period of Jeremiah.

A chronological chart is like a _____.

*   *

Time map

3. A map is used to show the location of places in a geographical area. A chronological chart is used to show the location of events and periods on a time line.

A chronological chart is like a _____ which is

used to show the location of _____ _____ on a time

line.

*   *

time map   events and periods

4. Let's look at a sample chronological chart.

This chronological chart shows a time line from 1900 to 1980. It locates two periods on the time line, World War I and World War II. It also locates one event on the time line, the landing of the first man on the moon.

a. World War I took place between 1914 and 1918. World War II lasted from

_____ to _____.

b. The first men landed on the moon in _____.

*   *

a. 1939   1945
b. 1969

5. Now see if you can make a chronological chart of a person's life (real or imaginary). On the time line below, show the year he was born and several other important events; for example, the year of his graduation, the year of his marriage, etc. Just put events on the time line.

6. Now suppose the person died in 1970. Locate this event on your time line.
Then draw a line just below the time line from the year of the person's
birth to that of his death. This will show the period of his life. It
should look like the period of World War I or of World War II in the
earlier chronological chart, only much longer.

7. Maps can be made to cover large areas or small areas. In the same
way chronological charts can be made to cover long periods of time or
short periods of time. You could make a chronological chart showing
your schedule during one day. And you could make a chronological chart
showing the history of civilization.

Study the following chronological chart. Notice where we are in the
20th century A.D. Notice also how the numbers begin high, then go down
to zero, then go back up.

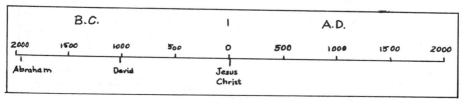

Locate on the time line the Protestant Reformation, 1517 A.D., and the
destruction of Jerusalem, 587 B.C.

8. The chronological chart you have just looked at shows the relationship
between events that occurred over a long period of time. But it would be
very difficult to put on that time line several events that occurred
within a short period of time. And it is hard to be exact. You probably
had a difficult time trying to decide just where to locate 587 B.C. and
1517 A.D. The year 587 B.C. should appear to the left of 500.

We want to make a chronological chart of the time of Jeremiah. Follow
carefully the instructions so that you will be able to reconstruct this
chronological chart by yourself.

First, write a definition of a chronological chart. _____

_____

* _____ *

A chronological chart is a time chart. It is like a time map. It is used to
locate events and periods on a time line.

9. The first step is to decide what period of time the chart should cover.
A chronological chart for the time of Jeremiah should cover the important
events we have studied:

The Fall of Nineveh in _____ B.C.

The Battle of Megiddo in _____ B.C.

The Battle of Carchemish in _____ B.C.

The Destruction of Jerusalem in _____ B.C.

You should know the dates by memory by now. 612, 609, 605, 587.

10. The chart should also cover the period of the five kings of Judah. List the five kings in order and give the dates for their reigns. You are not expected to remember these dates, but you should be able to figure them out rapidly by looking up in your Bible how long each king reigned. Figure out the year each king began and concluded his reign, using the date for the destruction of Jerusalem as your starting point.

	King	Year
a.		
b.		
c.		
d.		
e.		

11. Our chronological chart should cover the period of Jeremiah's ministry,

which lasted from _____ to _____ B.C. Once again figure out

the years by consulting your Bible and using the date of the destruction of

Jerusalem.

The last three questions are review questions, which will help you practice using the historical background of the book of Jeremiah. Also you will need to have this information at hand as you make your chronological chart.

12. We have now gathered the important international events, the reigns of the kings of Judah, and the ministry of Jeremiah. The earliest date in all this information is 640 B.C., the year Josiah began to reign. The latest date we have is 587 B.C., the year Zedekiah ended his reign and Jerusalem was destroyed and Jeremiah finished his ministry. So let's make our chronological chart to cover the period from 640 B.C. to 580 B.C.

The first step in making a chronological chart is to decide _____

* _____ *

What period of time it should cover.

13. How do you decide what period a chronological chart should cover? _____

* _____ *

Just look at all the information you want to include and make sure your chart
will cover all the dates.

14. The next step is to decide what scale or unit you will use. In the charts
at the beginning of this section each year is two millimeters and each centimeter is five years. Go back to #4 and #5 and measure the time lines with a
ruler.

Now look at the chart at #7 above and measure the time line. Each centimeter

represents _____ years.

*   *

250

15. The period of our chronological chart is from 640 B.C. to 580 B.C., or

_____ years.

*   *

60

16. Centimeters are easier to use than inches because they are divided in
tenths. If we used a scale of one centimeter to one year, our chart would

have to be _____ centimeters long.

*   *

60

17. This paper is too small for that scale. If we used a scale of one centimeter to two years, our chart would have to be _____ centimeters long. If we
used a scale of one centimeter to three years our chart would be _____
centimeters long.

*   *

30   20

18. These scales still will not fit in the space available. Try one centimeter for four years. With this scale our time line will be _____ centimeters long.

*   *

15

19. If one centimeter equals four years, then half a centimeter is _____
years and one/fourth of a centimeter is _____ years. Or, to say it the
other way, each year is _____ centimeter on the time line.

*   *

2   1   1/4

20. If one year is one/fourth centimeter and four years are one centimeter, then two years are _____ centimeters, and ten years are _____
centimeters.

*   *

1/2   2-1/2

If you do not yet understand how to do these calculations go back and
repeat #14-20. This is essential for making chronological charts.

21. On the following time line mark off ten year periods as we did on
the earlier charts. These dates are B.C., of course, so the numbers will
decrease rather than increase. But do not write B.C. because it takes up
too much space.

640   630

You should have 580 at the end of the line. There should be 2-1/2 centimeters between each mark of ten years.

22. On the same time line locate the fall of Nineveh, the battle of Megiddo,
the battle of Carchemish, and the destruction of Jerusalem. Be sure you locate each date exactly, counting one/fourth centimeter for each year. Put a
mark, write the date below, and below the date write the name of the event.

23. Now draw another chronological chart in the following box using the same scale and covering the same period of time. Mark off the ten year periods as you did before. Then indicate the periods of the reigns of the five kings of Judah. You listed the dates at #10 above. Remember that we show periods of time by drawing another line just below the time line and parallel to it. But first mark off the dates for the beginning and end of each reign. Then draw the other horizontal line. Finally write in the names of the kings.

24. Draw another chart in the following box showing the period of Jeremiah's

ministry. See Jer. 1:1-3. Jeremiah began to prophesy in the _____ year of

Josiah and finished his ministry in the _____ year of Zedekiah. Your

chart should show a double line from _____ B.C. to _____ B.C.

*   *

13th   11th   627   587

25. In the following sections of this lesson you will work some more on chronological charts for the time of Jeremiah. Be sure you understand what we are doing. Check your charts at #21-24 above by comparing them with the one below. If you have any difficulty, return to the beginning of this section and read over the explanations step by step until you are sure you understand.

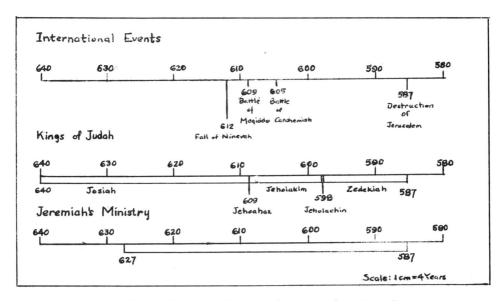

Now you can see how useful chronological charts can be. At a glance you can see how long Jeremiah's ministry lasted. You can see which kings were ruling Judah at that time. And you can see exactly when the important events of the world power struggle took place.

We have made three time lines. All of this information could be put on one time line, but it would be too crowded and confusing. So we have three lines which show the three different dimensions of the historical background of the book of Jeremiah. And these three lines are exactly parallel. For example, 587 B.C. on one line is exactly opposite 587 B.C. on the other two lines. So the information on the three time lines can be compared just as accurately as if it were all on one time line.

                    D. Chronological Chart

You now have two visual aids for explaining the historical background of the book of Jeremiah, a map and a chronological chart. The map shows the geographical position of Judah in the world power struggle of the period. And the chronological chart shows the period of Jeremiah's ministry in relation to the reigns of the last five kings of Judah and the major international events of that period.

In this section you will make another, larger chronological chart. You will use all the information which was included in the previous section,

and you will add further information. You will continue using this chronological chart throughout the course, adding information that appears in
the book of Jeremiah and interpreting different passages with the help of
the chronological chart.

Your professor may recommend that you make an even larger wall-size chronological chart for use in teaching classes on the book of Jeremiah. If you
have followed carefully the steps in this lesson, you should be able to
do so without any further guidance. And you should be able to draw a
chronological chart like the one at the end of the previous section on an
examination with just a ruler and your Bible.

Making chronological charts is a new experience for many students. And it
takes a lot of practice to learn this skill. For that reason you will now
repeat some of the work you did in the previous section. If you already
have some experience in making chronological charts and are certain that
you will have no difficulties you may skip this review and go on immediately to #12 below.

1. Without referring back to the previous section make a simple chronological chart for the period 640 to 580 B.C., showing the following events:
the fall of Nineveh, the battle of Megiddo, the battle of Carchemish, and
the destruction of Jerusalem. Use a scale of one centimeter to four years.

2. Now make another chronological chart showing the periods of the reigns
of the last five kings of Judah as follows:
    Josiah   640-609
    Jehoahaz   609
    Jehoiakim   609-598
    Jehoiachin   598
    Zedekiah   598-587

3. Make a third chronological chart showing the period during which Jeremiah carried out his prophetic ministry.

```

```

Now check your work by comparing it with the chronological chart at #C.25 above. If you still do not understand how to make these chronological charts please go back to the beginning of Section C.

4. Not only should you know how to make a chronological chart of the time of Jeremiah. You should also be able to explain to someone else how to make one. Review the steps we have followed.

Step 1: Decide what period of time the chart should cover.

How do you decide what period to include? _____

_____

Gather all the information that must be included with the corresponding dates. Then make sure your chart includes the earliest and latest dates.

5. Step 2: Decide what scale to use.

How do you decide what scale to use? _____

_____

Step 1 gives you the number of years to cover. Measure the space you have. Then figure out how many years each centimeter should represent so that the chart will fit in the space you have.

6. Step 3: Draw a time line.

How do you draw a time line? _____

_____

Just draw a straight line and mark off units of time - every ten years or every 100 years or every year - depending on the scale.

7. Step 4: Indicate the events on the time line.

How do you indicate the events? _____

* _____ *

Put a mark or a small line at the point when each event occurred. Write in
the date. And write the name of the event.

8. Step 5: Indicate the periods on the time line.

How do you indicate the periods? _____

_____

* _____ *

First mark off the dates for the beginning and end of each period. Then draw
a parallel horizontal line connecting the marks for the beginning and end of
each period.

9. Step 6: Use two or more time lines if there is too much information for one.

How do you use two or more time lines? _____

_____

* _____ *

Make the other time lines parallel to the first one. Each point in time on one
line should be exactly opposite to the same point in time on the other lines.

10. A chronological chart is a _____ chart. It is like a time map. It

shows the location of _____ and _____ on a time line.

* *

time   events   periods

11. See if you can remember the steps in making a chronological chart without
looking back. Then look back and check the ones you missed.

Step 1: _____

_____

Step 2: _____

_____

Step 3: _____

_____

Step 4: _____

_____

Step 5: _____

_____

Step 6: _____

_____

12. The rest of this section will be given over to the preparation of a
large chronological chart of the time of Jeremiah. You may use the page set
aside for this in the appendix, page A.2. You may also make another chart
on a large sheet of poster paper. Or your teacher may give you some other
instructions.

This chronological chart should have three time lines like the smaller chronological chart at the end of the previous section. Leave a lot of space between the lines so that you will be able to add more information later. Also,
use a scale for the time line that will give you as much space as possible.
For example, for your chronological chart on page A.2 of the appendix, turn
the page sideways and use a scale of one centimeter for three years. You
will later put this chronological chart and your map in a special Jeremiah
notebook.

Put a title above each of the three time lines as follows:
    International History
    Kings of Judah
    Jeremiah's Ministry

Include in your chronological chart all of the information we have put on
the previous charts. See. C.25 above. When you have finished, go on to #13
below.

13. In our study of the kings of Judah we noted several important events
for Josiah's reign. Study the passages in 2 Kings and 2 Chronicles and
find the dates for the following events.

a. Josiah began to purge Judah in the _____ year of his reign, in the

year _____ B.C.

b. Josiah repaired the Temple, found the Law, reformed the religion, and

celebrated the Passover in the _____ year of his reign, in the year ____ B.C.

c. Josiah fought against Pharaoh Neco at Megiddo in the _____ year of

his reign, in the year _____ B.C.

Write these three events on your chart as briefly as possible. For example, for a. put "Purged Judah." For b. just list the four items. For
c. put "Killed at Megiddo." These items go on the line, "Kings of Judah."

14. Put on your chart the following information about Jehoahaz. He was

deposed by _____ and taken captive to _____.

Just write on your chart "Taken captive to Egypt,"

15. Jehoiachin was deposed by _____ and taken captive to

_____ —.

Put on your chart "Taken captive to Babylonia."

16. Add to your chronological chart the important information about Zedekiah
in 2 Kings and 2 Chronicles.

a. Jerusalem was besieged in the year _____ B.C.

b. Zedekiah was blinded and taken captive to Babylonia in _____ B.C.

c. The Temple was burned, Jerusalem was destroyed, and her people taken captive

in _____ B.C.

You will probably have to use arrows to include all of this information.

17. Study Jer. 52:28-30. Nebuchadnezzar carried off the people of Judah in
three deportations. The first two deportations are mentioned in 2 Kings and
2 Chronicles although the dates are not exactly the same. Figure out the
dates for these three deportations and put them in your chronological chart
on the time line for International Events. Mark the three places, write in
the three dates, and draw three arrows to the indication "Deportations of
Jews to Babylonia." Nebuchadnezzar became King of Babylonia in the same
year as the battle of Carchemish, 605 B.C.

a. According to Jer. 52:28-30, Nebuchadnezzar carried away captives from

Judah for the first time in the _____ year of his reign, in the year

_____ B.C.

b. The second deportation occurred in the _____ year of his reign, in

the year _____ B.C.

c. The third deportation occurred in the _____ year of Nebuchadnezzar,

in the year _____ B.C.

a. 598   b. 587   c. 582

18. Now check these figures to see if they agree with the information you
already have in your chronological chart.

a. In the first deportation Nebuchadnezzar took King _____ of Judah

to Babylonia.

b. In the second deportation Nebuchadnezzar took King _____ to Babylon.

19. You already know one item from the book of Jeremiah, which you can put
on the time line for Jeremiah's ministry in your chronological chart. Jeremiah received his call at the beginning of his ministry. His ministry began

in the _____ year of Josiah, in the year _____ B.C. Write "His Call"

on your chart.

20. Answer the following questions by consulting your chronological chart.
You may also use your Bible but that probably won't be necessary. Notice
how useful the chronological chart can be. It will help you remember the
historical background of Jeremiah's time and see its significance.

a. Jeremiah began his ministry in the _____ year of Josiah, just _____

years after Josiah began to purge Judah.

b. King Josiah reigned for _____ years and sought to do the Lord's will.

In the _____ year of his reign he repaired the Temple and found the

books of the law.

c. King _____ of Judah was killed at the battle of Megiddo. His suc-

cessor, King _____, was carried off to Egypt just three

months later.

d. King Jehoiakim of Judah reigned for _____ years. During the first part of his reign Judah was subject to _____ and during the latter part

of his reign Judah was subject to _____.

e. The fall of Nineveh was followed by the battle of Megiddo just _____

years later. The battle of Megiddo was followed by the battle of Carchemish

just _____ years later.

f. The two countries that fought at Nineveh are _____ and

_____.

g. The two countries that fought at Megiddo are _____ and

_____.

h. The two countries that fought at Carchemish are _____ and

_____.

a. 13th   1   e. 3   4
b. 31   18th   f. Assyria   Babylonia
c. Josiah   Jehoahaz   g. Judah   Egypt
d. 11   Egypt   Babylonia   h. Babylonia Egypt

21. If someone asks you why you made a chronological chart of the time of

Jeremiah, how will you explain it to him? _____

_____

_____

_____

_____

_____

_____

_____

_____

_____

You should answer this question in your own way. But remember that this
chronological chart grew out of our Inductive Study of Jeremiah. Inductive
Study begins with the Bible and tries to see it on its own terms. And one
of the beginning steps for studying a book like Jeremiah is to find out
about the historical background of the book. This helps us to study the
book on its own terms. The chronological chart helps us to visualize the
historical background of Jeremiah. It is like a time map. It helps us to
see the relationships between all the pieces of historical information
which we have found.

The historical information in Jeremiah and 2 Kings and 2 Chronicles is
like a puzzle broken in a hundred pieces. It doesn't make much sense
until we put the pieces together and look at the whole picture. That is
what we have done by making a chronological chart of the period.

E. Review Exercises

In this lesson we have studied the historical background of the book of
Jeremiah. We have studied the historical background carefully and extensively, because it is so important for our understanding of the book of
Jeremiah. The book of Jeremiah is no longer, for us, a collection of ob-
scure prophecies with little meaning. Now we will see every passage of
Jeremiah in the light of Judah's great tragedy and in the light of a
world power struggle.

This has been a beginning step in the inductive study of Jeremiah. In this
case, we were able to find and use a large amount of historical information. So we took advantage of the material which we found. In the Inductive Study of other prophetical books there may be much less information.
And in the study of other non-prophetical books the historical background
may not be so important for our understanding of the text. In any case
this extended study of the historical background of Jeremiah should
show you the importance of trying to find out about the historical background of any book of the Bible.

It is interesting to note that Inductive Study does not just try to answer
a few questions, historical or otherwise. Rather it explores whatever the
text contains. Often this means that more and more information comes to
light as we investigate. So instead of just answering our original
questions we raise more and more questions. Our study leads us to more
study. And all of this leads to a greater understanding of the Bible on
its own terms. Perhaps one of the first requirements for a student of
the Bible should be curiosity.

The following review exercises will help you practise some of the skills
you have learned in this lesson. Work out these exercises using just
your Bible. After each exercise you will be referred back to the place
in the lesson where you can check your work. Review those points which
you find difficult.

1. List the four historical questions we asked about the book of Jeremiah
at the beginning of this lesson. These are simple questions that help
us to find the basic historical information about the book.

a. _____

b. _____

c. _____. _____

d. _____

*   *

See #A.3

2. Jeremiah prophesied from _____ B.C. to _____ B.C. Explain how to

to find these dates. You may use only the Bible. _____

_____

_____

_____

_____

_____

_____

This is not easy to explain. See #A.9, 12, 15, 16.

3. List the kings of Judah during the time of Jeremiah and give the dates
of their reigns, using your Bible.

a. _____   _____

b. _____   _____

c. _____   _____

d. _____   _____

e. _____   _____

*   *

See #A.12. You are not expected to memorize these dates, but you should be
able to figure them out rapidly using your Bible. Just start from the date
for the destruction of Jerusalem.

4. List the four important international events that occurred during Jeremiah's ministry with their dates.

a. _____   _____

b. _____   _____

c. _____   _____

d. _____   _____
*   *

These are dates that you should have memorized. See #B. 21 if you need to check your answer.

5. Explain the relationship between the first three of these events you have just listed. Name the nations which were involved and state why they

acted as they did. _____

_____

_____

_____

_____

_____

_____

_____

* _____ *

See #B. 6

6. On the following page draw a map of the Near East at the time of Jeremiah showing the location of the three major empires and Judah. Include on the map as much information as you need to explain the world power struggle.

*   *

See #B. 19 above. You should have included at least the following: Jerusalem, Megiddo, Carchemish, and Nineveh, with dates for the most important
events that occurred there; arrows showing the invasion routes between the
three great empires (Assyria, Babylonia, Egypt); and the location of Judah.

7. Write a brief statement of Judah's geographical position in relation to

the world power struggle at the time of Jeremiah. _____

_____

_____

_____

_____

* _____
                                                                     *

See #B. 18.

8. Explain what is a chronological chart. You may write a definition, say

what it is like, or describe how it is made. _____

_____

_____

_____

_____

_____

*   *

See #D. 10,11.

9. Chronological charts are visual aids that are very useful for understanding and explaining historical information. The two kinds of information that

are indicated on chronological charts are _____ and _____.

*   *

events   periods

10. Draw a chronological chart showing the four important international events you listed at #4 above.

*   *

See #C. 21,22.

11. Draw a chronological chart showing the period of Jeremiah's prophetic ministry in the following box. You now, of course, have to change the scale because the space is more limited.

*   *

If you have difficulty, go back and study sections C and D.

12. Reconstruct rapidly your chronological chart for the historical background of the book of Jeremiah. Use your Bible, but do not refer back to
the charts we made earlier. Include the major historical events, the kings
of Judah, and Jeremiah's ministry. You may refer to the dates of the kings
of Judah at #3 above. Include as much information as you can, but do not
spend more than fifteen minutes on this exercise.

*   *

If you have included the information found on the chronological chart at
#C. 25, that is sufficient.

13. Using your chronological chart, explain the significance of the battle
of Carchemish on King Jehoiakim. _____

_____

_____

_____

_____

_____

* _____ *

Jehoiakim was put on his throne by Pharaoh Neco of Egypt and paid tribute
to him for several years. Then Egypt was defeated by Babylonia at the battle of Carchemish. Thereafter Jehoiakim became increasingly subject to
Nebuchadnezzar of Babylonia. He was finally bound by Nebuchadnezzar, and
his successor, King Jehoiachin, was taken captive to Babylonia.

14. Almost all of the information we have used in this lesson has come
directly from the Bible. Make a list of the most important passages for
the historical background of the book of Jeremiah. You may include passages
from the book of Jeremiah itself which we have used as well as passages
from other books of the Old Testament.

a. _____   d. _____

b. _____   e. _____

* c. _____   *

The passages we have used are:
a. Jer. 1:1-3   d. 2 K. 23:1-25:30
b. Jer. 46:2   e. 2 Chron. 34:1-36;23
c. Jer. 52:28-30

15. You may have some uncertainty or some questions about some part of this
lesson. If so, it would be wise to clarify these points before going on. Make
a list of any specific problems you have had. Perhaps there will be an opportunity to discuss these points at your next class session.

a. _____

_____

b. _____

_____

c. _____

_____

d. _____

_____

e. _____

_____

4

Structure

The third step for beginning an Inductive Study of a book like Jeremiah is to look for the structure or outline. In Lesson I you had a brief introduction to this step. In Lesson IV you will study this step in greater detail.

Like the other two steps for beginning an Inductive Bible Study, this one can be very important for our understanding of the text. If we can find the structure of a book, we can see what the author was trying to communicate as he wrote the book. Out of all the details we can find what he considered to be the most important ideas. We can discover what his central message and purpose were. That is, we look for the structure of a book in order to study it on its own terms.

Sometimes this is a fairly easy task. At others it is difficult. Some books do not have a very clear structure. Some, such as Psalms and Proverbs, are collections of inspired messages in song and verse written by different people over a long period of time. There is no method that will tell us how to find the structure of all the books of the Bible. We just have to look at the book itself and see what we can find. As in all Inductive Study we must begin with the Bible.

In this lesson you will work toward the following objectives. You will learn how to:

Define what is the structure of a book.

List the different levels of structure.

Locate paragraphs, define their basic ideas, and write titles for them.

Find structural elements in Jeremiah 1 and 2.

A. What Is Structure?

When we look at a book like Jeremiah and try to find its structure, we begin by asking ourselves many questions. We need to know what is structure. We should have some idea of the kinds of structure to look for. We will have to look at the different levels of structure. And we will want to know what is the significance of the structural features we find.

In other words this can be very complicated. We shall soon see that it is very difficult to find an overall structure for the book of Jeremiah. Nevertheless, the basic inductive principle is still very simple. Just go to the text and see what you can find there. Try to see it as it really is.

1. Be sure you are clear about the reason for looking for the structure of Jeremiah or any other book. One of the beginning steps in Inductive Bible

Study is to look for the structure of the passage or book. Why? _____

_____

*   *
_____

In order to study the book on its own terms, to see it as it really is. That
is, the structure helps us to understand the book.

2. This is one of the beginning steps for Inductive Bible Study of a book
like Jeremiah. List all three steps for beginning an Inductive Bible Study.

a. _____

b. _____

c. _____
*   *

a. Find out what kind of a book it is.
b. Find out something about its historical background.
c. Look for the structure or outline of the book.

3. In Lesson I we suggested that the structure of a book is like the _____

_____ of an animal.
*   *

skeleton

4. We also suggested that the structure of a book is like a _____

or _____ for a painting.
*   *

drawing or outline

5. We said that a book's structure is like these two examples. Then we listed four characteristics of a book's structure. See if you can remember some
of them. Then look at the list below.

a. _____

b. _____

c. _____

d. _____

_____
*   *

a. It is made up of several parts or divisions.
b. These parts or divisions may be hidden, but we know they are there.
c. They are tied together to form a central idea or plot or story.
d. This is what holds the book together, gives it meaning, and enables it to teach us something.

6. Structure is organization. When we look for the structure of a book, we try to find out how the author organized the information as he wrote.

Another word for structure is _____.

*   *

organization

7. There are hundreds of different kinds of structure or organization all around us. For example, look at the structure of a bees' hive. There are many tiny carefully made sections where the honey is kept and the eggs are hatched. Not only is the hive a beautifully designed structure. The life of the bees is also very well organized. As many as 75,000 bees may live together. Some do one kind of work and others do other kinds of work. And there is a queen bee that lays all the eggs.

We can see structure or organization in the bees' _____ and in their

_____.

*   *

hive   life

8. Look at a tree. It has roots, a trunk, branches, and leaves. Each part has a special job to do.

These different parts make up the _____ of a tree.

*   *

structure or organization

9. Think of all the different kinds of structure or organization there are in a modern city. There are buildings - some for residences, some for offices, some for buying and selling, some for public services. There is a system of roads connecting all parts of the city. There is a system of telephones so well organized that each person can talk with all the other people in the city simply by dialing different numbers. Electricity and water are carried to all parts of the city. Every person in the city gets food to eat every day in the year. Newspapers, radio, and television keep everyone informed of the news. There are systems that collect taxes, dispose of garbage, transport people, put out fires, care for the sick, elect government officials, handle money, run industries.

To understand what is a city you have to look at all of its _____.

*   *

structures, organizations

10. Each one of these structures or organizations tells us something important about the life of that city. If we want to visit someone in that city,
all we need is his address and a road map. The map shows us how the roads
of the city are organized. We look up the address on the map, and we find
immediately how to get to our friend's house.

In order to find out where someone lives we have to understand the _____

system. And we have to know his _____ .

road   address

11. If we just want to talk with someone in the city, we can call him on
the telephone. We look up his telephone number in the telephone directory,
and dial his number and talk to him. Each telephone in the city has a different number.

Each telephone is part of a _____ .

system or organization

12. You have to understand how these systems work if you are going to live
in a city. For example, you can't call someone on the telephone if you just
have his address. And you can't find his house if you just have his telephone number. You can't buy vegetables at a bank. You can't use a television
set if you don't have electricity. And you can't wash your clothes if you
don't have water.

To live in a city you have to _____

_____ .

Understand how these systems work, how the city is organized

13. The same thing is true about the books of the Bible. In order to understand a book of the Bible you have to know _____

_____ .

How it is organized, what is its structure.

14. The books of the Bible have several different kinds of structure. We
mentioned some examples in Lesson I. We said that 1 and 2 Samuel, 1 and 2
Kings, and 1 and 2 Chronicles have two kinds of structure. They are organized
around the lives of important people - Samuel and the kings. And they are organized in chronological order.

Two kinds of organization are:

a. _____

b. _____
*   *

a. When a book is organized around the life of a person or several people we
say it is biographical.
b. chronological

15. We said that some of the poetical books of the Old Testament are collections of poems organized in groups around certain topics.

Another kind of structure is _____.
*   *

topical

16. One important factor in the structure of the book of Acts is geography.
In Acts 1:8 the author refers to Jesus' command to the apostles to be his
witnesses in Jerusalem, in all Judea, in Samaria, and to the end of the
earth. And as we read through the book we see how the apostles did carry
their witness to Jerusalem first, then to Judea and Samaria, and finally
to Rome.

Another kind of structure we find in books of the Bible is _____.
*   *

geographical

17. There are other kinds of structure in some parts of the Bible. For example we notice that many of the New Testament books are letters. They
have certain characteristics of letters of that period - salutations, personal greetings, etc.

Another kind of structure is _____.
*   *

We can call this kind of structure epistolary.

18. Of course a New Testament letter may have an epistolary structure and
also other kinds of structure too. For example Romans is a letter with the
usual characteristics of a letter at the beginning and at the end. But the
body of the letter has a very definite logical or theological structure.
It discusses the sinfulness of man and the righteousness of God in a carefully reasoned argument.

Another kind of structure is _____.
*   *

logical or theological

19. The Synoptic Gospels seem to have several different kinds of structure. The book of Mark, for example, seems to have a geographical structure. It presents Jesus' ministry in Galilee first, then his movement to Jerusalem, his ministry there, and finally the passion story. The structure of the book seems to be chronological, too, especially in the last division of the book where the story is told day by day. There are also biographical features in Mark's structure, because the whole book tells about Jesus Christ. There are certain topics that appear throughout the book and tell us something about its structure. And there is a logical or theological structure. Mark is a Gospel, a message about Jesus Christ, the son of God.

In other words as you study Mark you should look for five different kinds of structure at least. These are five of the kinds of structure which we have mentioned. List them here.

a. _____

b. _____

c. _____

d. _____

e. _____

*   *

a. geographical
b. chronological
c. biographical
d. topical
e. logical or theological

20. There are, of course, many other kinds of structure. You do not need to memorize all the different kinds. But you should know that there are many different kinds of structure. And you should know that one book may have several different kinds of structure. And you should know how to look for the structure of a book.

How should you look for the structure of Jeremiah in an Inductive Study? _____

*   _____   *

Go to the book itself. Inductive Bible Study always begins with the text and tries to see it on its own terms.

21. Later in this lesson we will look for the structure of the book of Jeremiah. We will look for the kinds of structure that have been mentioned. And we will look for other kinds. We will try to see what is in the text. And throughout this course we will continue to look for the structure or structures of the book of Jeremiah.

Why do we look for the structure? _____

* _____ *

In order to study the book on its own terms, to see it as it is, to understand what it has to say.

22. We need to find the structure of a book in order to understand it. Remember the example of a tree. You can't just study a leaf and understand what
a tree is. You have to see that the leaves are part of a whole structure
which is made up of roots, trunk, branches, and leaves.

And you can't explain where honey comes from just by looking at a beehive.
You have to study the structure of the hive and the functions of the different kinds of bees and the way they pick up nectar from flowers.

And you can't find someone's house in a city just because you have their
address. You have to look at a map, study the road system, and find the
right street.

In the same way you can't understand the book of Jeremiah just by studying

one passage or several separate passages. You have to _____

* _____ *

Study the structure of the book, see how it fits together.

23. The concept of structure is very important, and it is very difficult
to explain. That is why we have taken so much time trying to define it. And
we have explained it mainly by using illustrations. Let's write a definition of structure now using several of the ideas we have already mentioned.

> The structure of a book is its skeleton or outline. It is made
> up of several parts or divisions. These parts may be hidden,
> but we know they are there. They are tied together to form a
> central idea or plot or story. The structure holds the book
> together, gives it meaning, and enables it to teach us some-
> thing.

You can learn this definition if you remember that it is made up of two
examples and four characteristics. List the two examples first.

a. _____

b. _____

Now list the four characteristics of a structure as defined above.

a. _____

b. _____

c. _____

d. _____

24. We have indicated that the structure of some books of the Bible is very difficult to find. According to our definition of structure, the different parts or divisions may be hidden. In the following sections of this lesson you will look for indications of the structure of the book of Jeremiah. But don't be discouraged if you find this to be a difficult task. The structure of this book is difficult to find, even for the experts.

B. Levels of Structure

In this section we will look at some passages in Jeremiah and try to find some signs of structure. As we find elements of structure, we will try to point out their significance. We will look for structural elements at several different levels.

When we begin an Inductive Study, we often look for the overall structure of the book first. That is, we look for the main divisions. But the book of Jeremiah is rather long, so in this case we will begin with just a small part of the book, the first chapter. We have already studied this chapter in detail, and we have already noted some indications of structure.

1. Read over Jer. 1 and list the paragraphs.

a. _____

b. _____

c. _____

d. _____

e. _____
*   *

a. Jer. 1:1-3
b. Jer. 1:4-10
c. Jer. 1:11-12
d. Jer. 1:13-16   Some Bibles include Jer. 1:13-19 in one paragraph, but you
e. Jer. 1:17-19   will see that there are two paragraphs here.

2. Now study these paragraph divisions and see if you can explain why you divided the passage at these points. But first explain why you cannot just

use the chapter and verse divisions you find in your Bible. _____

* _____ *

Because the chapter and verse divisions were not made by the original writer. They were added to the text much later.

3. Many Bibles also have paragraph divisions. They mark the beginning of each paragraph by an indentation. Generally we will use those divisions. But we don't need to. At Jer. 1:13-19 we made an extra paragraph division.

Explain why we do not always follow the paragraph divisions found in our

Bibles. _____
*   *

These divisions, too, were added much later. They were not made by the author.

4. Now look at Jer. 1:1-3. We have said that this is a unit and that it is different from the following verses.

a. What is the central idea of Jer. 1:1-3? _____

_____

b Why do we say that Jer. 1:1-3 is a unit or paragraph? _____

_____

c. In what way is Jer. 1:1-3 separate or different from the following verses?

* _____ *

a. It is a historical introduction to the book.
b. It all fits together as a historical introduction.
c. The following verses do not have historical information.

5. Now look at Jer. 1:4-10.

a. What is the central idea of this paragraph? _____

_____

b. Why do we say that it is a unit? _____

_____

c. In what way is it separate from the preceding and following verses? _____

＊ _____ ＊

a. Jeremiah's call to be a prophet.
b. It all fits as part of one conversation or experience.
c. The previous verses contain historical information. The following verses contain a vision.

6. Now look at Jer. 1:11-12.

a. What is the central idea? _____

_____

b. Why do we say that it is a unit? _____

_____

c. In what way is it separate from the preceding and following verses? _____

＊ _____ ＊

a. The vision of the rod of almond. God will perform His word quickly.
b. It is all tied together around the vision.
c. The previous verses contain Jeremiah's call, and the succeeding verses contain another vision.

7. Now look at Jer. 1:13-16.

a. What is the central idea? _____

_____

b. Why do we say that it is a unit? _____

_____

c. In what way is this passage separate or different from the previous and

following verses? _____

＊ _____ ＊

a. The vision of the boiling pot. Destruction from the north.
b. It all ties together around the vision.
c. The previous verses contain another vision. The following verses present a different idea or topic.

8. Now look at Jer. 1:17-19.

a. What is the central idea? _____

_____

b. Why do we say that it is a unit? _____

_____

c. In what way is this passage separate or different from the previous and

following verses? _____

*   _____   *

a. The Lord's call and promise to Jeremiah.
b. It all fits together around this topic and experience.
c. The previous verses contain a vision and the following verses are unrelated.

9. Now notice what we have done. We have analyzed the text paragraph by paragraph. This is one of the kinds or levels of structure. We could go through
the whole book of Jeremiah and study each unit at this level.

One level of organization or structure is the _____ level.
*   *

paragraph

10. As we looked at each paragraph we asked three questions. These questions
were really inductive questions because they helped us study the text on its
own terms. List the questions here.

a. _____

b. _____

c. _____
*   *

a. What is the central idea?
b. Why do we say it is a unit?
c. In what way is it separate or different from the verses that precede and
follow it?

11. If we went through the whole book of Jeremiah this way, we would have a
long chain of small units. We would know what is the central idea of each
of these many units, and this would give us an understanding of what the
book is about. But there are so many of these units that we might not have

a clear concept of the author's main idea and purpose. We might just have a long list of many different ideas.

The paragraphs of a book are one level of its structure. In order to get a clear idea of the author's main idea and purpose we need to look at other

_____ of its structure.

*   *

levels

12. Once we have a long list of paragraphs, we can begin to compare the central idea in each one. Perhaps several paragraphs in a row have the same central idea or similar ones. We may group them together and call this a section of the book. Then we should state what is the central idea of the whole section. If we could group all the paragraphs of the book in several sections, this would be another level of structure. By looking at the central idea of all the sections of the book we would have a good indication of the author's message.

The two levels of structure we have mentioned are _____ and

*   *

paragraphs   sections

13. Of course there may be many other ways to group several paragraphs together. Sometimes they have the same central idea. Sometimes they take place in the same geographical area or in the same period of time. Sometimes there is a special characteristic or a special phrase that ties them together.

As you study the structure of a book you should look for paragraph-units

and you should look for sections, which are groups of _____.

*   *

paragraphs

14. Look at Jeremiah 1 and see if you can find a group of paragraphs. Earlier in the course we did make some suggestions about grouping the paragraphs of this chapter.

a. List the paragraphs of Jeremiah 1 that you think fit together around one

central idea. _____

b. What is the central idea of this group of paragraphs? _____

*   *

a. We suggested earlier that Jer. 1:4-10, 11-12, 13-16, and 17-19 all belong together as a group.
b. The central idea of this group of paragraphs is the call of Jeremiah.

15. It looks like Jer. 1:4-19 forms a section of the book of Jeremiah.
Write down once again the central idea of each of the paragraphs in this
section to show that they fit together.

a. Jer. 1:4-10   _____

b. Jer. 1:11-12   _____

c. Jer. 1:13-16   _____

d. Jer. 1:17-19   _____
*   *

You may compare what you wrote down for each paragraph with #5-8 above.

16. Note that these are separate paragraphs and that they are related to
each other. Jer. 1:4-10 and Jer. 1:17-19 refer directly to Jeremiah's call
to be a prophet. They even use some of the same phrases. And Jer. 1:11-12
and Jer. 1:13-16 complete the picture of Jeremiah's call. Jer. 1:11-12
shows that God's word will soon be fulfilled, and Jer. 1:13-16 shows what
God's message is. In all four paragraphs the Lord speaks directly to Jeremiah, not to the people or the nations.

Write a title for Jer. 1:4-19. _____
*   *

The title which we have used for this section is "The Call of Jeremiah."

17. Jer. 1:4-19 is a section of the book of Jeremiah. These four paragraphs
belong together because they all have something to do with Jeremiah's call.

We should also look for other special characteristics of this section of
the book. For example we have already put this passage on our chronological
chart.

a. What is the date of this passage on your chronological chart? _____

b. How did you know what date this passage refers to? _____

_____

*   *

a. 627 B.C.

b. We assumed that Jeremiah received his call at the beginning of his ministry. And we know that Jeremiah began to prophesy in the 13th year of Josiah,
according to Jer. 1:2.

18. We have already noted another special characteristic of this section.
In all of these paragraphs, Jer. 1:4-19, the Lord is speaking directly to
Jeremiah.

a. Who is speaking in Jer. 1:1-3? _____ To whom? _____

b. Who is speaking in Jer. 2:1-3? _____ To whom? _____

a. The author   the reader
b. The Lord   Jerusalem (The Lord speaks to Jeremiah but His message
                           is for Jerusalem).

19. We should also ask what is the significance of this section of the book
of Jeremiah. We know that it is made up of four paragraphs grouped around
the central idea of Jeremiah's call. We have dated this section at the beginning of Jeremiah's ministry, 627 B.C. And we have noted that in this section
the Lord speaks directly to Jeremiah. Now we should see if this section has
some special importance.

a. What special significance do you see in this section, Jer. 1:4-19? _____

_____

b. Why do you think the author put this section at the beginning of his book?

_____

_____

a. This section gives us the basis for all of Jeremiah's prophecies; his call.

b. Since this section gives us the basis of Jeremiah's prophecies, the best
place for it is the beginning of the book.

20. Not all the sections of the book of Jeremiah will have a special significance. But we should study each section this way in order to find the structure of the book.

Now let's list the steps we have followed.

```
1. We located the paragraphs and noted the central idea in
   each one.
2. We grouped the paragraphs that have the same or similar
   ideas, forming a section.
3. We looked for special characteristics of the section.
4. We asked what is the special significance of this section
   in the structure of the book.
```

Be sure you understand these steps, because you will be using them throughout your study of Jeremiah.

So far we have been dealing with two levels of structure. We call the units

of the lower level _____ and the units of the upper

level _____.
*   *

paragraphs   sections

21. Jer. 1:1-3 is a special case. As we have noted earlier in the course,
this passage serves as an introduction to the book of Jeremiah. It is short
enough to be a paragraph. It is set off by itself, so it can't be grouped
with other paragraphs. And yet it is more important than just a paragraph
or a section. It introduces the whole book. It gives the historical background for all of the sections and paragraphs of the book.

Nevertheless, we can use the steps we have just listed above.

a. What is the central idea of this paragraph? _____

_____

b. Can we group this paragraph with others that follow it?

c. What special characteristics does it have? _____

_____

d. What is its special significance in the structure of the book? _____

_____

a. It contains historical information.
b. No.
c. In this passage the author gives the historical background for the whole
book of Jeremiah.
d. It serves as an introduction to the book of Jeremiah.

22. We have considered two levels of the structure of Jeremiah: paragraphs
and sections. And we have considered Jer. 1:1-3 as a special case.

There are also units of structure which are smaller than paragraphs. Remember,
for example, that we found several parts or units in the paragraph Jer. 1:4-10.
First we noticed that Jer. 1:4-10 is a conversation between the Lord and Jeremiah. Then we identified the different parts of the conversation, according
to the person who was speaking. Finally we put down the central idea of each

part. Study Jer. 1:4-10 again briefly and put down the significance of each
part.

a. v. 4   Introduction _____

b. v. 5   _____

c. v. 6   _____

d. v. 7-8   _____

e. v. 9-10   _____

a. Introduction
b. The Lord calls Jeremiah to be a prophet.
c. Jeremiah responds but hesitates.
d. The Lord repeats His call.
e. The Lord ordains Jeremiah as His prophet to the nations.

23. As we studied Jer. 1:4-10, we considered each one of these smaller units.
But within these units we found even smaller ones. For example, we noted
that v. 5 has four important phrases. Each one of these merits special study.
We have mentioned these levels:

> 1. Words
> 2. Phrases
> 3. Sentences
> 4. Paragraphs
> 5. Sections

24. Later we shall try to find larger units of the book of Jeremiah. These
units will group several sections together. And we shall call these larger
units divisions. When you reach this level of a book's structure you should
know what are the author's most important ideas.

List again the different levels of structure.

> 1. _____
> 2. _____
> 3. _____
> 4. _____
> 5. _____
> 6. _____

25. This may seem like a very complicated process. Actually we can figure out most of the structure, for example words and phrases, without even thinking about it. We look at these levels as we read and study a passage in detail. The more difficult part is to figure out the three upper levels of structure. These are the ones we are working on specifically in this lesson. List the three highest levels of structure here.

a. _____

b. _____

c. _____

   *

a. Paragraphs
b. Sections
c. Divisions

26. Since we are talking about higher and lower levels perhaps we should have a diagram and put the paragraphs at the bottom. Each level is made up of several units. These units fit together in groups to form larger, higher units.

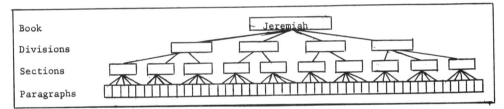

Book

Divisions

Sections

Paragraphs

27. Or think of the example of the skeleton. You can study the bones of the fingers. Then you can see how these fingers form the hand. Then you see how the hands belong to the arms. And finally you can see the whole skeleton. And when you see the whole skeleton you understand how the fingers work. And you see the importance of each bone in the hand in relation to the whole structure.

Compare the different levels of the structure of a book with the levels of structure of a skeleton.

a. Fingers   paragraphs _____

b. Hands   _____

c. Arms   _____

d. Skeleton   _____

   *

a. Paragraphs
b. Sections
c. Divisions
d. Book

Note: Imagine what would happen if someone broke up a skeleton and threw
all the bones in a pile. You wouldn't have any idea what the animal was
supposed to look like. But that is how some people study the Bible. Or
imagine all the bones laid out in a line, one after the other. That wouldn't
make sense either. But that is how some Bible courses treat the Bible. It's
only when you see how the pieces fit together that you understand a skeleton or a book.

28. Consider the tree illustration again. If you study just a leaf you won't
understand what a tree is. Even if you study all the leaves of a tree you
won't know what a tree is. You have to see how the leaves grow out of the
branches, how the branches are joined to the trunk, and how the trunk is
held up by the roots.

How is the structure of a book like a tree? _____

_____

* _____ *

The paragraphs fit together to form sections, the sections form divisions,
and the divisions make the book. You have to see how the parts fit together.

29. Let's try putting the information we have about Jeremiah's structure
into the form of an outline. This outline will be like the one you used
for your sermon outline in Lesson II. We only have enough information to
start the outline, but this is what it would look like.

THE BOOK OF JEREMIAH

```
Jer. 1:1-3  -  Introduction
I. Jer. 1:4 --              Early Prophecies
   A. Jer. 1:4-19             The Call of Jeremiah
      1. Jer. 1:4-10            I appointed you prophet
      2. Jer. 1:11-12           A rod of almond
      3. Jer. 1:13-16           A boiling pot
      4. Jer. 1:17-19           Gird up your loins
```

According to this outline I. is a division. A. is a _____.

1, 2, 3 and 4 are _____.

* *

section   paragraphs

Note that the reference at I. is not complete. That is because we have not
gone far enough into Jeremiah to see where this division ends.

30. There are many different ways of looking for the structure of a book.
And there are many different ways of writing it down. And there are many
different kinds of structure. And the structure is more important in some
books than in others. And the structure is clearer and more complete in
some books than in others.

The important thing to remember is the inductive approach. Go to the text
to find whatever you can. Begin with the Bible.

The third step in beginning an inductive study is to look for the structure. This is a beginning step because we try at the beginning to figure
out how the book is put together. And it is something we continue to look
for throughout our study of the book. As we come to each passage we will
consider the details (words, phrases, sentences) that make up each paragraph. And we will try to see how the paragraphs fit together to form
sections. And we will look for the larger divisions until we see how the
whole book fits together.

a. What is the purpose of studying the structure at any or all of these

levels? _____

_____

b. List the six levels of structure we have mentioned.

1. _____   4. _____

2. _____   5. _____

3. _____   6. _____
*   *

a. The purpose of studying the structure is to find the meaning of the text,
to see it on its own terms.
b. 1. words   4. paragraphs
    2. phrases   5. sections
    3. sentences   6. divisions

Really what we are studying here is the nature of language. When we talk
or write we don't just use words at random. We organize our words into
phrases and our phrases into sentences. And when we want to write or say
something important, we usually organize our sentences into paragraphs
and our paragraphs into sections. And if we want to write a book, we will
probably organize our sections into divisions or chapters.

C. Paragraphs

In this section you will work on paragraphs. This is perhaps the most important level of structure. Usually you will study the Bible by paragraphs. You will study words and phrases and sentences within the paragraph structure, that is, paragraph by paragraph. And only as you analyze the most important ideas in the paragraphs will you be able to discover the sections and divisions of the book.

You will learn how to recognize paragraphs units and how to write titles for these paragraphs based on the text. The best way to do this is by having lots of practice. So you will work through chapters 1 and 2 of Jeremiah, locating the paragraph units and writing titles for all of these paragraphs. As you continue working through the book of Jeremiah, you will want to keep on studying the paragraph units and writing titles. And as you study other books of the Bible you will want to study the paragraphs in a similar way.

1. We have already located the paragraphs in chapter 1.

Write the references for these paragraph units.

a. _____

b. _____

c. _____

d. _____

e. _____

*   *

a. Jer. 1:1-3
b. Jer. 1:4-10
c. Jer. 1:11-12
d. Jer. 1:13-16
e. Jer. 1:17-19

2. In general these paragraph units which we have indicated coincide with the paragraphs marked in the text (RSV). In the text the paragraphs are indicated by an indentation at the beginning. Check your Bible to see if there is an indentation at the beginning of each paragraph. Write "yes" or "no" after the following references.

a. Jer. 1:1   _____

b. Jer. 1:4   _____

c. Jer. 1:11   _____

d. Jer. 1:13 _____

e. Jer. 1:17 _____
*   *

If your text is like mine you have an indentation at all of these verses
except 1:17. Jer. 1:1 has a special form because it is the beginning of
the book, but we can say it has an indentation.

3. In the text (RSV) each paragraph is set off by an _____

at the beginning.
*   *

indentation

4. But in an Inductive Study you do not have to follow the paragraph indica-

tions given in the text. Why? _____

_____

* _____ *

Because they were not there in the original text. In other words in inductive study we begin with the original text. So we may ignore paragraph divisions, which are a modern addition to the text. And we may ignore verse
divisions and chapter divisions for the same reasons.

5. The text (RSV) indicates that Jer. 1:13-19 is one paragraph. We have
divided it into two paragraphs: Jer. 1:13-16, 17-19. Do you remember why?

Look at the text and explain why. _____

_____

_____

* _____ *

Jer. 1:13-16 presents the vision of the boiling pot. It is a complete unit
including the symbol of the pot and the interpretation of the symbol. Jer.1:17-19
presents God's call to Jeremiah. It is a different idea and should be separated.

6. A paragraph is a unit which is made up of one or more sentences. It generally contains one basic idea. Written paragraphs are usually set off at
the beginning by an indentation.

Go back over the paragraphs in Chapter 1 and write down the basic idea in each one. You will see that they <u>are</u> units because each one <u>does</u> have a central idea.

a. Jer. 1:1-3   _____

b. Jer. 1:4-10   _____

c. Jer. 1:11-12   _____

d. Jer. 1:13-16   _____

e. Jer. 1:17-19   _____

*   *

We already wrote down the basic idea of each paragraph at B.15 above. Compare the analysis you made here with the previous one.

7. One reason for studying the basic idea in a passage is to locate the paragraphs. When an author finishes discussing one idea and goes on to

another, he usually begins a new _____.

*   *

paragraph

8. A paragraph usually contains _____ basic idea.

*   *

one

9. A group of sentences that deal with one basic idea is called a _____.

*   *

paragraph

10. In Jer. 1:1-3, for example, we read about the historical background of the book of Jeremiah. We know this paragraph ends at verse 3 because

* _____.   *

We find another idea in the following verses which is altogether different.

11. In Jer. 1:4-10 we find several different ideas. But there is one basic idea which includes all the others, God's call to Jeremiah. Jer. 1:11-12 presents another new idea. Jer. 1:13-16 presents another one. Jer. 1:17-19 goes back to the basic idea of Jeremiah's call.

A paragraph is usually a group of _____ that are joined to-

*

gether by _____.

*

sentences   one basic idea

12. Read through Chapter 2 and look for the paragraph divisions. If your
Bible has paragraph indications (indentations and/or spacing), you may
take advantage of them, but you should be ready to change them if you
can think of better paragraph divisions. In any case go quickly through
this chapter and write down the references for each paragraph.

a. ___Jer. 2:1-3_____   e. _____

b. _____   f. _____

c. _____   g. _____

d. _____

13. Remember that your paragraph divisions do not have to be the same as
the ones in the text, and they do not have to be the same as the ones
your professor has. But they should be meaningful units.

In order to coordinate our study we will use arbitrarily the same paragraph divisions for the following exercises. Try to identify the main idea
in each paragraph listed. You are not being asked for a title here, just
the main idea of each paragraph.

a. Jer. 2:1-3   _____

b. Jer. 2:4-8   _____

c. Jer. 2:9-13   _____

d. Jer. 2:14-19   _____

e. Jer. 2:20-25   _____

f. Jer. 2:26-32   _____

g. Jer. 2:33-37   _____

*   *

Once again you should not expect to have the same answers as anyone else,
but you may want to compare your work with the following.
a. Jer. 2:1-3   Israel belonged to the Lord as a bride.
b. Jer. 2:4-8   Israel, including her leaders, was unfaithful to the Lord.
c. Jer. 2:9-13   Israel not only left her Lord but followed after other gods.
d. Jer. 2:14-19   Israel will be punished for her apostasy.

e. Jer. 2:20-25   Israel has degenerated as a harlot or as a wild ass in
                   heat.
f. Jer. 2:26-32   Israel shall be shamed; she has rebelled.
g. Jer. 2:33-37   Israel shall be shamed; she is shameless.

14. Read over once again the above analysis of the seven paragraphs in Jer. 2
and see if they all contain similar or related ideas. If we should find a
major change in theme, we might want to divide these paragraphs into two
or more sections.

Do you think these paragraphs fit together or should they be divided into

more than one section? _____

*   *

It seems to me that they belong together. They all deal directly with Israel's relationship to the Lord and her apostasy.

15. These seven paragraphs all present the same basic concept of Israel's
special relationship with God and her apostasy. But they do not all say
exactly the same thing. They bring out different aspects of the main subject. We can reduce the main ideas to three:

> 1. Israel's special relationship to the Lord.
> 2. Israel's unfaithfulness.
> 3. Israel's judgment.

Check over the seven paragraphs again and note down which of these three
basic ideas appears in each paragraph. Some paragraphs may contain more
than one.

a. Jer. 2:1-3   Israel's special relationship to the Lord _____

b. Jer. 2:4-8   _____

c. Jer. 2:9-13   _____

d. Jer. 2:14-19   _____

e. Jer. 2:20-25   _____

f. Jer. 2:26-32   _____

g. Jer. 2:33-37   _____

*   *

Jer. 2:1-3 speaks only of Israel's betrothal to the Lord and says nothing
about her unfaithfulness or judgment. Jer. 2:4-8 speaks of Israel's special
relationship to the Lord and of her unfaithfulness, but it does not mention
judgment. Jer. 2:9-13 describes primarily Israel's unfaithfulness. Jer. 2:14-19

speaks of Israel's unfaithfulness and her judgment. Jer. 2:20-25 deals with Israel's unfaithfulness. Jer 2:26-32 and Jer. 2:33-37 present Israel's unfaithfulness and judgment.

16. Notice once again that these seven paragraphs belong together because they all have the same basic ideas. Even the three different ideas we have mentioned belong together logically. Because Israel has a very special relationship to the Lord (like a wife), her unfaithfulness is a terrible thing (like an unfaithful wife), and she deserves judgment.

This is what it means to look for the structure of a book or part of a book.

We group together passages which have _____.
*   *

The same basic idea.

17. In our study of Jer. 2 we first defined the paragraph units. Then we

looked for _____ in each paragraph.
*   *

the basic idea

18. We decided that these seven paragraphs belong together because _____

* _____.
                                                                           *

They all have the same basic idea.

19. This is one way to look for the structure of a book. You read through it. You analyze the basic idea in each paragraph. You group together the paragraphs that seem to have the same basic ideas in sections. And then you group together the sections that have the same general ideas. This is called topical structure.

But we said previously that books can be structured or organized not only by topics or ideas but also by:

```
1. _____

2. _____

3. _____

4. _____
```
*   *

geography, chronology, biography, logic or theology

20. We found in Jer. 2 a _____ unity or structure.

*   *

topical

21. As we analyzed the basic idea in each paragraph of Jer. 2 and found
that all seven paragraphs have the same basic ideas, we learned a lot
about Jeremiah's message. We already have a good impression of what his
book is about. And if we go through the entire book this way, we will
know a great deal about it.

Now state again why we study the structure of a book like Jeremiah. _____

_____

*
_____   *

We study the structure in order to see it as it is, in order to know what
it's message is, in order to understand what it really says.

You can see how important it is to study the structure of a book. And you
can see that this is not an easy task. It takes time and careful thinking.
But just remember how many times you have read through Jer. 2 without
having a clear, concise idea of its message. Now you know exactly what
Jeremiah was saying in these paragraphs. And you can continue through the
book making this kind of analysis.

22. There is another important step. We have said that the seven paragraphs
of Jer. 2 belong together. But we have not defined the beginning and the
end of this section of the book. There may be other paragraphs that belong
to it.

a. Do any of the paragraphs of Jer. 1 belong in this section? _____

b. Why? _____
*   *

a. No.
b. They don't have the same basic ideas.

23. Now look at Jer. 3.

a. Would you include any of these paragraphs in the same section as the

paragraphs of Jer. 2? _____

b. Why? _____
*   *

It seems to me that this section continues into Jer. 3 because these paragraphs have the same basic ideas.

24. Write a title for this section of Jeremiah's book. You do not have to
use words from the text, but your title should be very brief.

* _____ *

A suggestion: "Israel's Apostasy."
Note that we do not yet know where this section ends.

D. Paragraph Titles

In this section you will practice writing paragraph titles. There are several ways of doing this, but you will just use one technique here. Analyzing
the basic ideas in the paragraphs of a book and writing titles for each
paragraph can be very helpful in your study of the structure of that book.

You may remember that in Lesson II we chose titles for the paragraphs of
Jer. 1. We will go over those paragraphs again picking out appropriate
titles using just four words or less from the text itself. At the same time
we will define carefully how to write paragraph titles. Finally, you will
choose titles for the paragraphs in Jer. 2.

1. Jer. 1:1-3 is a very special passage, as we have noted already. It is a
paragraph, but it is also the historical introduction to the whole book of
Jeremiah. So we really don't need to give it any other title. But let's see
if we can find a title in the words of the text.

Someone might choose "The words of Jeremiah" as a title for Jer. 1:1-3.
This sounds all right at first because these words at the beginning of the
book tell who is the author. But this title is not representative. It does
not tell us what is the content of the paragraph.

What does the paragraph contain? _____

* _____ *

Historical information about the book of Jeremiah.

2. A title should represent ____   _____ of the paragraph.

*   *

the content

3. Someone might choose "The word of the Lord" as a title for Jer. 1:1-3.
But this title is not distinctive. We have already noticed that this phrase

"the word of the Lord," is repeated again and again in the book of Jeremiah. If we use this phrase, we will not be able to distinguish this paragraph from many other paragraphs. And we will not remember what the paragraph contains just by reading this title.

A title should _____ the paragraph from other paragraphs.

*   *

distinguish

4. Someone might choose the title "Jeremiah son of Hilkiah." This phrase
indicates something about the historical background presented in this
paragraph. But it is not the most <u>important</u> information in the paragraph.

A title should refer to the _____ information or

idea in the paragraph.

*   *

most important

5. There are several things to keep in mind as you choose paragraph titles.
Remember at least these three characteristics. Paragraph titles should be:

> 1. Representative
> 2. Distinctive
> 3. Important

6. What title, then, shall we use for Jer. 1:1-3? Try this one: "Josiah,
Jehoiakim, Zedekiah."

a. Does this title represent the historical content of the paragraph? _____

b. Does it distinguish this paragraph from others? _____

c. Does it bring out the most important information of the paragraph? _____

*   *

I think I would answer all three questions "yes." Notice that this title
uses just three words and that the three words have been taken from the
text itself. And when you look over your list of paragraphs for the book
of Jeremiah years from now, you will remember exactly what this paragraph contains just by reading this title.

7. Go on to Jer. 1:4-10. First state what is the basic idea or content of

this paragraph. _____

*   *

The call of Jeremiah to be a prophet.

8. Now write a title for this paragraph using four words or less from the

text itself. _____

Ask yourself the same three questions about your title.

a. Is it representative? _____

b. Is it distinctive? _____

c. Is it important? _____

*   *

There are several good titles for this paragraph, for example:
       "I appointed you prophet."   "My words your mouth."
       "Prophet to the nations."   "Set over nations."
All of these phrases tell us that this paragraph talks about Jeremiah's
call to be a prophet.

9. Now write titles for the other paragraphs of Jer. 1.

a. Jer. 1:11-12 _____

b. Jer. 1:13-16 _____

c. Jer. 1:17-19 _____
*   *

From now on you will have to write and evaluate your own paragraph titles.
The titles we suggested in Lesson II are:
a. A rod of almond.
b. A boiling pot.
c. Against the whole land.

When a paragraph centers around a literary figure like Jer. 1:11-12 and
Jer. 1:13-16, it is often best just to mention that figure in your title.
This makes your title very distinctive as well as representative and im-
portant.

10. Now list once again the three characteristics of paragraph titles as
we have been writing them.

a. _____

b. _____

c. _____
*   *

a. They should represent the content of the paragraph.
b. They should distinguish the paragraph from other paragraphs.
c. They should refer to the most important information or ideas of the paragraph.

11. Of course we have said also that the titles should be made up of four words or less and that these words should be taken from the text itself.

How is this system of writing paragraph titles inductive? _____

* _____ *

It is inductive because it begins with the text and uses just words from the text.

12. Before going on to Jer. 2, perhaps we should give some reasons for writing paragraph titles. Now that you have written titles for several paragraphs you can see how useful it can be.

Writing titles for paragraphs is one way of summarizing the basic ideas of a passage. For example, if you want to state briefly what is the content of Jer. 1 you can study each paragraph, find the basic information or idea of each one, and write a title for each paragraph which will summarize its content.

A paragraph title is a _____ of its content.
*   *

summary or brief statement

13. As you work through passages like Jer. 1 and 2, writing titles helps you find the structure of those passages. As you work through an entire book in this way, you will be able to find the structure of that book.

a. Paragraph titles tell you _____

b. The structure of a book tells you _____
*   *

a. What is the content of those paragraphs or of the passage.
b. What is the content or message of the book.

14. We have said that a paragraph title is a summary of the content of that paragraph.

In a similar way an outline of a book is a _____.
*   *

Summary of the content of the book

15. One way to make an outline of a book is to write down titles for all the paragraphs of that book. But some books have hundreds of paragraphs. For example, the book of Jeremiah has more than 250 paragraphs. So you will want to do more than just write titles for all the paragraphs of the book of Jeremiah. You will look for groups of paragraphs which will form sections. And perhaps the sections can be grouped into divisions. When your outline is reduced to five or ten divisions, you can see at a glance what is the content of the book of Jeremiah.

The first step in making an outline of the book of Jeremiah is _____

* _____ *

To write titles for all the paragraphs.

16. The main reason for writing paragraph titles is to find the structure of a given passage and of the book as a whole. The structure is a summary of the main ideas.

a. The main idea of a paragraph can be written down as a_____.

b. The paragraph titles can be listed in the_____.
* of the book.   *

a. title or paragraph title
b. outline or structure or summary

17. The main reason for writing paragraph titles is _____

* _____ *

To find the structure of a passage and of the book.

18. Another reason for writing paragraph titles is to help us review the book and to find specific passages. Years after completing your list of paragraph titles you can read it over and remember much about the content of the book. And when you want to use an important passage from Jeremiah for a sermon, you will probably be able to find it simply by looking at your paragraph titles.

The second reason for writing paragraph titles is

* _____ *

To help us review the book and to find specific passages.

19. As a review, write down once again our definition of structure. _____

_____

_____

_____

* _____ *

The structure of a book is its skeleton or outline. It is made up of several parts or divisions. These parts may be hidden, but we know they are there. They are tied together to form a central idea or plot or story. The structure holds the book together, gives it meaning, and enables it to teach us something.

20. Now go on to Jer. 2 and write paragraph titles for all the paragraphs, using the method we have been studying.

a. Each title should be made up of _____ words.

b. These words must be taken from _____.
*   *

a. four or less
b. the text

21. The paragraph titles should have the following characteristics:

a. _____

b. _____

c. _____
*   *

a. They should be representative.
b. They should be distinctive.
c. They should be important.

22. As you write the titles for Jer. 2, you should read each paragraph carefully, identify the main idea, then choose the words from the text which are most appropriate. You have already identified the main idea of each paragraph at #C. 13 above. Write down here just the titles.

a. Jer. 2:1-3   _____

b. Jer. 2:4-8   _____

c. Jer. 2:9-13   _____

d. Jer. 2:14-19   _____

e. Jer. 2:20-25   _____

f. Jer. 2:26-32   _____

g. Jer. 2:33-37   _____
*   *

You should be ready to present and explain these titles at your next class
session. And you should be ready to go on through the book of Jeremiah
writing paragraph titles in this way.

E. Outline

In this last section of Lesson IV you will review briefly what you have
studied. Then you will fill in the outline sheets with the material you
have already gathered in your study of Jer. 1 and 2.

You should now be able to:
      * Define what is the structure of a book.
      * List the different levels of structure.
      * Locate paragraphs, define their basic ideas, and write titles for
        them.
      * Find structural elements in Jer. 1 and 2.

These are the objectives which we set down at the beginning of this lesson.
The following review questions should help you see whether you have reached
these objectives.

1. List the three major steps for beginning an Inductive Study of a book
like Jeremiah.

   a. _____

   b. _____

   c. _____
*   *

a. Find out what kind of a book it is.
b. Study its historical background.
c. Look for its structure.

2. Define the word 'structure' as we have been using it. _____

_____

_____

_____

* _____ *

See D.19 above.

3. List the six different levels of strucutre.

a.   Words _____

b. _____

c. _____

d. _____

e. _____

* f. _____ *

a. Words
b. Phrases
c. Sentences
d. Paragraphs
e. Sections
f. Divisions.

4. What is a paragraph? _____

* _____ *

A paragraph is a unit of one or more sentences grouped around one main idea.

5. What is a section? _____

* _____ *

A section is a group of paragraphs with the same basic idea.

6. We have studied Jer. 1 and 2 by looking for the main ideas or topics.
But we have said that passages and books can be organized not only by topics
but also by:

a. _____

b. _____

c. _____

d. _____

*   *

geography, chronology (time sequence), biography, logic or theology

7. After finding the main idea of each paragraph in Jer. 1 and 2, we prepared titles for each one. These titles are made up of four words or less
taken from the text iself. And they have three characteristics:

a. _____

b. _____

c. _____

*   *

a. They are representative. They represent the content of the paragraph.
b. They are distinctive. They distinguish each paragraph from others.
c. They are important. They refer to the most important information or
idea of each paragraph.

8. Paragraph titles summarize the content of the paragraphs of a book. We

call the summary of a book an _____.

*   *

outline

9. We gave two reasons for writing paragraph titles.

a. _____

b. _____

*   *

a. To find the structure of a passage or a book.
b. To help us review the book and to find specific passages.

10. Paragraphs are the most important units in the structure of a book. As
we study the most important ideas in the paragraphs, we can group them in

_____ and we can group the latter in _____.

*   *

sections   divisions

11. A _____ is a brief summary of the con-

tent of a paragraph. An _____ is a brief summary of the

content of a book.

*   *

paragraph title   outline

12. We prepare outlines of passages and of the whole book for the same reasons that we write paragraphs. Give two reasons for making outlines.

a. _____

b. _____

*   *

a. In order to find the structure of the passage or book.
b. To help us review and to find specific passages.

13. A third important reason for preparing outlines is to see the relationships between the different parts. Each passage is important for what it
tells us. But it is also important for what it tells us about other passages.

a. What happens if we separate all the bones of a skeleton? _____

_____

b. What happens if we study each paragraph of a book by itself only? _____

*   *
_____

a. We can't see what the animal looks like.
b. We can't see what is the message of the book.

14. Why do we study the structure of a book like Jeremiah? _____

_____

*   *
_____

In order to see it as it really is, to understand its message, to deal with
it on its own terms, to see how all the parts fit together.

15. The structure of a book is like:

a. _____

b. _____
*   *

a. The skeleton of an animal.
b. The outline of a book.

16. The structure of a book, like a skeleton, has these characteristics:

a. _____

b. _____

c. _____

d. _____
*   *

a. It is made up of several parts or divisions.
b. These may be hidden, but we know they are there.
c. The different parts are tied together to form a central idea or plot or
story.
d. They are what hold the book together, give it meaning, and enable it to
teach us something.

17. We have just said that one reason for studying the structure of a book
is to show relationships between different parts. A passage may be important for what it tells us about other passages.

Explain the significance of Jer. 1:1-3. _____

_____

_____

_____

It is a historical introduction to the book of Jeremiah. In other words it
tells us when and where all these things happened. It is the background for
all the other paragraphs and sections and divisions of the book.

10. Jer. 1:4-10 is made up of four paragraphs. Why did we group these para-

graphs in one section? _____

_____

They all seem to fit together around the topic of Jeremiah's call to be a
prophet.

19. What title did we give to Jer. 1:4-19? _____
*   *

The Call of Jeremiah.

20. What is the special significance of this section in relation to the

rest of the book? _____

* _____
*   *

It tells us about Jeremiah's call, which was the foundation of his entire
ministry.

21. Jer. 2 is made up of seven paragraphs. Why did we group these para-

graphs together? _____

* _____
*   *

They all deal with the same topic, Israel's apostasy.

22. What title did we give to Jer. 2? _____
*   *

Israel's apostasy.

23. We said that this section does not end at the end of chapter 2. Why?

   _____

* _____
*   *

Because the following paragraphs in Jer. 3 continue on the same topic.

24. Now put together your analysis of Jer. 1 and 2. First use the tradition-
al form for writing outlines. Use the information you have already gathered
at D.8, 9, 22 above.

The outline begins on the next page so that you may see it in its entirety.

Jer. 1:1-3 Introduction

I. Jer. 1:4-

A. Jer. 1:4-19 The Call of Jeremiah

1. _____

2. _____

3. _____

4. _____

B. _____

1. _____

2. _____

3. _____

4. _____

5. _____

6. _____

7. _____

25. Now turn to the outline in the appendix and begin to fill it in. Write in the paragraph titles you have just put down. Write in also the main idea for each paragraph. You will find this information at C.6, 13 above. You can check your work at the next class session. Keep adding to this outline as you work through the book of Jeremiah in this course and in the future.

In order to direct your study and coordinate the class, I have listed the paragraph references for the book of Jeremiah. In a sense this is arbitrary. You should define your own paragraph divisions. But we need to have a common set of paragraph divisions as we work through this course together.

5

Israel's Apostasy
(Jeremiah 2:1-4:4)

The first four lessons of this course gave you a general understanding of Inductive Bible Study and showed you how to begin an Inductive Study. You learned these principles and methods as you studied the text of the book of Jeremiah. So you have already made an intensive study of the first chapter, and you have begun to look at the second chapter.

In Lesson V you will make a careful study of Jer. 2:1-4:4. As you analyze Jeremiah's message in this passage you will develop your skills in Inductive Bible Study, and as you develop your skills you will be able better to analyze Jeremiah's message.

When you finish this lesson you should be able to:

Write a summary of Jeremiah's message to his people.

Interpret (and explain how to interpret) the principal literary

figures in this passage and elsewhere in the book.

Explain many other details found in this passage.

A. Outline

Before going into the details of Jer. 2:1-4:4, complete your outline for Jer. 3:1-4:4. Turn to the outline sheets in the appendix. Read through Jer. 3:1-4:4 and write down what is the main idea of each paragraph. At the same time write a title for each paragraph, using four words or less from the text itself.

You will notice that Jeremiah is dealing with his people's apostasy in Jer. 3:1-4:4, as in Jer. 2. But an important new note is added to his message. Be sure you know what that new element is. We shall look at it later in this lesson.

Do not go on to Section B until you have completed this assignment. This background study is necessary, and it will give you further practice in analyzing paragraphs and in writing paragraph titles.

B. Literary Figures

One of the interesting things about Jeremiah is his use of literary figures. These figures communicate his message with great incisiveness and even drama. And he uses them frequently. So it is important for you to learn how to interpret these literary figures. And you should be able to explain to others how to interpret them.

1. What is Inductive Bible Study? _____

_____

* _____ *

Inductive Bible Study is an approach to Bible study which begins with the
Bible and studies it on its own terms.

2. On the one hand this is a very simple principle. We study the Bible itself for ourselves and not someone else's explanation of the Bible. We try
to see what it is and what it says. For example, we see that it is a collection of 66 books written by different authors at different times.

So we must study the Bible _____.
*   *

By books. Each book separately.

3. As we study a book like Jeremiah we want to understand what it is and
what it says.

So we begin by taking at least three important steps.

a. _____

b. _____

c. _____
*   *

a. See what kind of book it is.
b. Find out about its historical background.
c. Look for its structure.

4. We use the same inductive approach as we study a section of the book, a
paragraph, or even a sentence, a phrase, or a word.

We try to _____.
*   *

See what it is and what it says.

5. As you read through Jer. 2:1-4:4, for example, you notice that there are
many places where the writer uses symbols or pictures or literary figures.
Sometimes it is very clear what he means. Other times it is not so clear.
Sometimes he explains the meaning of the figure. Other times he doesn't.

In Inductive Bible Study we look at these literary figures and try to _____

* ——°
                                                                              *

See what they are and what they say.

6. Look first at some figures that we have already analyzed in Jer. 1.

a. What is the figure in Jer. 1:11-12? _____

b. What does it mean? _____
*
                                                                              *

a. A rod of almond.
b. The Lord will soon fulfill His word.

7. This example is really a vision, something which Jeremiah saw, apparently.
But the rod of almond which he saw was a symbol or a figure. The symbol or
figure itself is unimportant. We need to find out what it represents.

a. The first step in interpreting a literary figure is to identify the
object.

b. The second step is to find out what the object _____°
*
                                                                              *

represents or means.

8. In Jer. 1:11-12 the Lord has an important message for Jeremiah. That
message really has nothing to do with a rod of almond. It is really about
His word. The rod of almond is only a symbol of God's word in this passage.

a. The object is _____°

b. The object represents _____°
*
                                                                              *

a. A rod of almond.
b. God's word.

9. Why does the Lord compare His word with a rod of almond? Because the
almond tree has a special characteristic. We noted in Lesson II that the
almond tree was known as the "early-awake tree" because it was the first
to bud in the spring. It is essential for us to notice that special characteristic for our interpretation of the figure.

a. The first step in interpreting a literary figure is _____

——°

b. The second step is _____.

c. The third step is to note the special characteristic or characteristics of the object.

*   *

a. Identify the object.
b. Find out what it represents.

10. In Jer. 1:11-12 the message or interpretation of the figure is given. But even if it were not given in the text we would be able to find out the meaning of the figure after taking the three steps just mentioned. We would say: just as the almond rod buds early, so the Lord will early (or soon) carry out His word. The fourth and final step in interpreting a figure is to define its message.

Repeat now the steps we have taken in our interpretation of Jer. 1:11-12.

a. What is the object? _____

b. What does it represent? _____

c. What is the special characteristic of the object? _____

d. What is the message of the figure? _____

*   _____   *

a. A rod of almond.
b. The word of the Lord.
c. It buds early.
d. The Lord will soon fulfill His word.

11. Now analyze the figure in Jer. 1:13-16. Note that the object in this case has two special characteristics. As in the previous case the interpretation or message of the figure is given.

a. What is the object? _____

b. What does it represent? _____

c. What are the special characteristics of the object? _____

   _____

d. What is the message of the figure? _____

*   _____   *

a. A pot.
b. God's judgment or the enemy.
c. It is boiling, and it faces from the north.
d. God is sending destruction on His people from the north.

12. One way to remember these four steps in interpreting literary figures is to make a diagram like the one below. You can use the same four questions and put the answers in the same four squares.

a. What is the object?	b. What does it represent?
c. What are the special charac- teristics?	d. What is the message?

You will notice that there is a logical progression through these four steps. And there are direct relationships between them. Add to the diagram an arrow from box a. to box b., another from a. to c., another from b. to d., and another from c. to d. These arrows show the relationships between the steps in interpreting a literary figure. You do not need to put these arrows in your diagrams in the future however.

13. In order to see how the diagram works, fill in the following one with our interpretation of Jer. 1:11-12.

14. Do the same with our interpretation of Jer. 1:13-16.

15. These two examples are fairly simple, and the interpretation of both these figures is given in the text. Some figures are more complicated, and sometimes no interpretation is given in the text. In Jer. 1:18 the Lord uses three figures at the same time. Apparently all three have more or less the same meaning, so you can interpret all three figures at the same time. Use the same simple diagram and give your interpretation of these figures..

a. What are the figures? A fortified city, an iron pillar, bronze walls.	b. What do they represent? Jeremiah
c. What is their special character- istic? Strength, safety, defense	d. What is the message? The Lord will enable Jere- miah to withstand all opposition.

16. A more complicated figure is found in Jer. 2:13. It is really a com- bination of two figures. And these two figures are not similar but con- trasting. We mentioned this passage in Lesson I and said that it speaks about Israel's idolatry. Study the figure carefully and give your inter- pretation in two parallel diagrams.

a. What is the ob- ject? The fountain.		a. What is the ob- ject? Cisterns	

a. What is the object?	b. What does it represent?	a. What are the objects?	b. What do they represent?
The fountain	The Lord	Cisterns	Idols
c. What is its special characteristic?	d. What is the message?	c. What is their special characteristic?	d. What is the message?
Gives abundant, living waters.	The Lord is the source of Israel's life.	Are broken and hold no water.	Israel has turned to useless idols.

17. In this case the meaning of the two figures is quite clear, and the interpretation is given in the text. We should perhaps go one step further, though, and ask what is the purpose of the passage. Why does the Lord through Jeremiah give this message?

a. Does He want to show Israel what evil they have committed? _____

b. Does He want to show them the folly of their idolatry? _____

c. Is He calling them back to Him in obedience? _____

You may want to answer all three questions "yes." At least the first two should be answered "yes." In any case you should not just make a mechanical interpretation of the literary figures. Try to see what they are and what they say. Look for the message of each figure in the context of Jeremiah's ministry.

18. Read through Jer. 2:1-4:4 and underline all the major literary figures. Then make a list here of the figures you have underlined. Just put down the objects.

a. _____   e. _____   i. _____

b. _____   f. _____   j. _____

c. _____   g. _____   k. _____

d. _____   h. _____   l. _____

I count at least 20 important figures in this passage. You should have no trouble finding twelve.

C. Literary Figures

We have not yet made a definition of what a literary figure is. And we have not listed the different kinds of literary figures. Perhaps this is not necessary. You will probably learn these definitions in another course. The important thing here is to be able to interpret literary figures when you find them. Inductive Bible Study is not concerned with technical terms and theories about the Bible but with the practical problems of how to understand the Bible on its own terms.

In the previous section you learned a simple way of interpreting literary figures. In this section you will use the same method. We noted that some figures are simple and others are more complicated. In the case of the rod of almond (Jer. 1:11-12) there is one object with one special characteristic. In the case of the boiling pot (Jer. 1:13-16) there is one object with two special characteristics. In the case of Jer. 1:18 there are three objects, but they are similar and have the same characteristics. In the case of the fountains and the cisterns (Jer. 2:13) there are two objects with contrasting characteristics. In all of these examples which we have studied so far, the same basic method can be applied. But in each case the figure should be studied carefully.

1. What are the four steps in interpreting a literary figure?

a. _____

b. _____

c. _____

d. _____

*   *

You should be able to give these four steps as statements. But if you put them in question form, that is all right.

```
a. Identify the object
b. Find out what it represents.
c. Note the special characteristic of the object.
d. Define the message of the figure.
```

2. As a review, draw a diagram for interpreting literary figures and write in the four questions in the proper places. Be sure to number (a,b,c,d) them.

*   *

See B. 12 above if you need to check your answer.

3. The figure of the bride in Jer. 2:1-3 is very interesting. It is used again and again in the book of Jeremiah, and it is used by other prophets too.

Note three important characteristics of the bride mentioned in Jer. 2:1-3.

a. _____

b. _____

c. _____
*   *

Love and devotion, obedience, holiness.

4. Now fill in the diagram for this literary figure. It is no longer necessary to write the questions. Just write the appropriate information in each box.

*   *

A bride	Israel or Jerusalem or Judah
Love and devotion, obedience, holiness	Israel once served the Lord in love, obedience, and holiness.

5. Analyze the figure of the lions in Jer. 2:15.

*   *

The lions	Israel's enemies
Roared	Israel's enemies have destroyed or will destroy her cities.

6. The paragraph Jer. 2:20-25 has a whole series of figures. List them here.

a. _____   d. _____

b. _____   e. _____

c. _____   f. _____

a. The yoke   d. The stain
b. A harlot   e. A camel
c. A choice vine   f. A wild ass.

The figure of the harlot is used frequently by Jeremiah and will be considered later.

7. Analyze the figure of the yoke. Note that there is a contrast between what the yoke does and what Israel does.

The yoke	The covenant between Israel and the Lord.
It binds together the two oxen.	Israel, in contrast, has thrown off her covenant and will not serve the Lord.

8. Analyze the figure of a choice vine. Note once again that there is a contrast in the application of this figure.

A choice vine	Israel
Planted of pure seed, it becomes a choice vine.	Especially chosen by God • Israel has behaved not as a chosen people but as a degenerate people.

9. Analyze the figure of the stain. Here again a contrast is implied.

The stain	Israel's guilt
It cannot be washed out with soap and lye.	Israel's guilt is so ingrained that it cannot easily be removed.

10. The figure of a young female camel is similar to the figure of a wild ass in heat. Analyze the latter here.

A wild ass	Israel
When in heat, the wild ass shamelessly seeks males.	Apostate Israel shamelessly seeks after other gods.

11. Analyze the figure of the thief in Jer. 2:26.

A thief	Israel
When caught stealing, he is ashamed.	Israel will be judged and her enemies will defeat her; then she will be shamed.

12. The most poignant figure in the paragraph, Jer. 2:26-32 is the figure
of the bride. In Jer. 2:1-3 Jeremiah uses the figure of the bride, but
here he uses a different characteristic of the bride.

Analyze the figure of a bride in Jer. 2:32.

A bride	Israel
She never forgets her wedding orna-ments and attire.	Israel, in contrast, has forgot-ten her covenant with the Lord.

13. The figure of the harlot is mentioned in Jer. 2:20, as we have noted,
and it is presented in Jer. 2:33-37. It is repeated even stronger in
Jer. 3:1-5. Analyze the figure of the harlot in Jer. 3:1-5.

The harlot	Israel
Is not one man's wife but shame-lessly seeks many lovers.	Israel is not faithful to her Lord but shamelessly goes after other gods.

14. You have now had a considerable amount of practice interpreting literary figures. If you still are uncertain how to do this, go back and review this section and the previous one. On the next test you will have to
analyze new figures without any assistance.

15. List once again the four steps in interpreting literary figures.

a. _____

b. _____

c. _____

d. _____

a. Identify the object.
b. Find out what it represents.
c. Note the special characteristic or characteristics of the object.
d. Define the message of the figure.

16. Now let's see if we can write a tentative definition of a literary figure using these four steps.

> A literary figure is the use of an object to represent some-
> thing else because the object has some special characteristic
> or characteristics which illustrate a message about the other
> thing.

That definition is rather awkward. Let's change the order and state it again.

> A literary figure is the use of an object with some special
> characteristic or characteristics to communicate a message
> about something else.

You can memorize this definition easily if you just remember that it is
based on the four steps we have used in interpreting literary figures.

17. As was stated at the beginning of this section, our main concern is to
be able to identify and interpret literary figures. Read over the definition of a literary figure and explain how you can recognize or identify one
when you are reading the Bible.

_____

_____

_____

_____

Your answer may include the four steps we have been using. At least you should
have said that you can recognize a literary figure when one object is used
to represent something else.

18. Literary figures play an important role in Jer. 2:1-4:4. They express
the essence of Jeremiah's message. In order to take advantage of our analysis of these figures, make a summary of our interpretations using the following chart. Just write in the message (Step 4) of each figure. You may
copy the material presented previously. The analysis of the fountain and
the cisterns is found at B.16 above.

a.	A bride	Israel once served the Lord in love, obe-dience, and holiness.
b.	The fountain and cisterns	
c.	The lions	
d.	The yoke	
e.	A choice vine	
f.	The stain	
g.	A wild ass	
h.	A thief	
i.	A bride	
j.	The harlot	

A final note on literary figures: We have not included in this lesson a
technical analysis of the different types of literary figures used in the
Bible. Your professor may give you additional material on this subject
or refer you to a book on hermeneutics. But it is not essential for your
study of the book of Jeremiah. The most important task is to recognize and
interpret accurately these figures. And this is what you have learned in
this lesson.

D. Jeremiah's Message

In an Inductive Study of a passage like Jer. 2:1-4:4, the main purpose is to discover what the text says, what is its message. In this lesson you have spent a large amount of time analyzing literary figures because Jeremiah used many literary figures to communicate his message in this passage. You have stated in your outline what is the main idea of each paragraph in this passage, and you have written titles for all of these paragraphs. All this work helps you understand what was Jeremiah's message to his people.

There are many details in Jer. 2:1-4:4 which we have not yet considered. Ideally, you should now go through this passage paragraph by paragraph and study all the information they contain. We will only have time here to look briefly at a few of these paragraphs, then try to give a summary of Jeremiah's message in these "Early Prophecies."

You will notice that we ask many different kinds of questions as we go through Jer. 2:1-4:4. In a sense we are just asking one question: What does it mean? But as we find many different kinds and pieces of information we have to 'ask different kinds of questions. This is how Inductive Study works.

1. Read through Jer. 2:1-3. Then write down the information we already have.

a. The main idea of this paragraph is _____

_____.(See your outline.)

b. Your title for this paragraph is _____.

c. The message of the figure of a bride is _____

_____. (See C.18 above.)

2. Now note any details in this paragraph that we have not yet considered or that we should study further. Many questions should come to your mind, such as the following.

a. Who is speaking? _____

b. To whom? _____

c. What event or period of time does he refer to? _____

_____

a. Jeremiah is telling what the Lord told him to proclaim.
b. To Jerusalem or to the people of Judah.
c. He refers to the time when the Lord made a covenant with Israel and led her in the wilderness of Sinai.

3. This paragraph refers to an historic event of singular importance. The covenant of Sinai was the foundation of Israel's existence as a people. Explain the following phrases:

a. "Your love as a bride" _____

_____

b. "You followed me in the wilderness" _____

_____

c. "Israel was holy to the Lord" _____

_____

d. "All who ate of it became guilty" _____

* _____ ж

a. At Sinai Israel committed herself to the Lord to be His people.
b. For 40 years Israel followed the Lord in the wilderness of Sinai.
c. Israel was to have no other gods but the Lord.
d. Israel's enemies were destroyed by the Lord. It was a grave thing to attack His people.

4. There is an important theological concept in the clause, "Israel was holy to the Lord." Many people think that holiness is a quality or a virtue. They think it means to be pure, pious, religious, perfect, etc. But we can see here that holiness is primarily a matter of relationship "to the Lord."

a. What is a wife's responsibility to her husband? _____

_____

b. What do we call a married woman who gives herself to other men? _____

_____

c. What was Israel's responsibility to the Lord? _____

_____

d. What do we call Israel's unfaithfulness? _____

* ж

a. She must give herself only to her husband.
b. Adultress.
c. She was to worship and serve the Lord only.
d. Apostasy or idolatry.

5. At Sinai Israel made a covenant with the Lord, who had delivered her from Egypt. This covenant was like a marriage commitment, and the Ten Commandments were like marriage vows.

Which one of the Ten Commandments (Exodus 20) states most clearly that

"Israel was holy to the Lord?" Quote it here. _____

* _____ ,

Exod. 20:3: "You shall have no other gods before me."

6. Remember that holiness is primarily a matter of relationship. Of course this relationship with the Lord should result in certain qualities, purity, etc. But these qualities only have real significance if they are based on this relationship.

This teaching can be applied to the Christian.

a. What is the believer's relationship to Christ? _____

_____

b. How does he follow Christ in the wilderness? _____

_____

c. Explain how the Christian is holy to the Lord. _____

_____

* _____ ,

a. He commits himself to Christ, to love and serve Him.
b. He becomes a disciple of Christ and follows His leading in his daily life.
c. He must worship and serve only Christ and not let other things gain his absolute allegiance.

7. In Jer. 2:4-8 we find again the basic concept of the covenant, which is prevalent throughout the book of Jeremiah. But the emphasis is on something which the previous paragraph does not mention explicitly.

a. Which verse refers most clearly to the covenant? _____

b. What new idea is emphasized in Jer. 2:4-8? _____

* _____ ,

a. Jer. 2:6
b. Israel's apostasy or unfaithfulness.

8. Refer to your outline and answer the following.

a. What is the main idea of this paragraph? _____

_____

b. What is your title for this paragraph? _____

9. Although Jer. 2:4-8 does not mention the Sinai Covenant explicitly, it does mention three important things that the Lord did for His people which are related to Sinai. List them.

a. _____

b. _____

c. _____

a. "Brought us up from the land of Egypt."
b. "Led us in the wilderness."
c. "Brought you into a plentiful land."

10. In Jer. 2:9-13 we find another exposition of Israel's apostasy. Refer to your outline and answer the following:

a. What is the main idea of this paragraph? _____

_____

b. What is your title for this paragraph? _____

c. What is the message of the figure of the fountain and the cisterns? _____

_____

_____

11. The Lord has a contention, a complaint, a charge against His people in

Jer. 2:9-11. What is that charge? _____

_____

They have been unfaithful to Him and gone after other gods.

12. The Lord makes an interesting comparison between the nations' faithfulness and Israel's apostasy.

a. What kind of gods do the other nations have? _____

b. Are they faithful to their gods? _____

c. What kind of God does Israel have? _____

_____

d. Is Israel faithful to her God? _____

*   *

a. False gods that are no gods.
b. Yes.
c. The true God who is her glory.
d. No.

13. Jer. 2:10 mentions Cyprus and Kedar. Look up these names in your atlas
or Bible dictionary and try to find where they are located. Then try to
figure out why they are mentioned here.

a. Cyprus is located to the _____ of Jerusalem.

b. Kedar is located to the _____ of Jerusalem.

*   *

a. Northwest
b. East

14. Why does this passage mention Cyprus and Kedar? _____

_____

* _____
*   *

They represent two directions or extremes, as we would say from East to West
or from North to South. They are mentioned to dramatize the fact that no
other nation is unfaithful as Israel.

15. Jer. 2:14-19 presents not only Israel's apostasy but also her judgment.

a. What is the main idea of this paragraph, according to your outline? _____

_____

b. What is your title for this paragraph? _____

c. What is the message of the figure of the lions? _____

_____

16. You should explain v. 16.

a. Where are Memphis and Tahpanhes located? _____

_____

b. Who are "the men of Memphis and Tahpanhes?" _____

*   _____   *

You should have found these names in your atlas or Bible dictionary. They
are cities of Egypt.

17. This verse says that the Egyptians have broken the crown of Israel's
head. This obviously refers to an historical event. Remember what happened

in 609. Now explain what this verse means. _____

*   _____   *

Pharaoh Neco came up to Megiddo and killed King Josiah of Judah.

18. In v. 18 we find two phrases which should be explained: "to drink the
waters of the Nile" and "to drink the waters of the Euphrates." Here again
we should remember the historical background of the book of Jeremiah and
the world power struggle that was going on at that time.

a. What were the three great world empires? _____

_____

b. What was Judah's geographical position in the world power struggle? _____

_____

*   _____   *

a. Assyria, Egypt, Babylonia.
b. Judah was located on the invasion route between Egypt and the other two
empires.

19. We studied this situation in Lesson III. You may want to refer back
to the simple map showing the world power struggle at Lesson III, B, 19.

When Judah was afraid of being swalloed up by the growing Babylonian em-

pire, she turned for help to _____.
*   *

Egypt and, apparently, Assyria.

20. Now you should be able to explain v. 18.

a. In this verse the Nile represents _____°

b. The Euphrates represents _____°

c. What does it mean "to drink the waters of the Nile" and "to drink the

waters of the Euphrates?" _____

* _____ *

a. Egypt
b. Assyria
c. Judah went to Egypt and Assyria for help.

21. This was the natural thing for a small nation to do in such a situation.

But Jeremiah calls this apostasy. Why? _____

_____

_____

* _____ *

Israel was the Lord's own people. He had liberated her from Egypt and He
had defended her from her enemies. She should have continued trusting in
the Lord. These alliances with other nations were an act of unfaithfulness
in the political sphere, just as the adoption of other gods was an act of
unfaithfulness in the religious sphere.

22. Unfortunately there is no more time now to continue through the remaining paragraphs of Jer. 2:1-4:4 and study all the information they contain.
You should someday complete this study on your own.

We should mention here one or two more details. Jer. 3:6 refers to King
Josiah. As we noted in Lesson I, this reference helps us identify this
paragraph, Jer. 3:6-10, and perhaps this group of paragraphs, Jer. 2:1-4:4,
with the period of Josiah's reign.

a. Josiah reigned from _____ to _____ B.C.

b. Jeremiah prophesied from _____ to _____ B.C.   *

*

If you do not remember these dates, refer back to Lesson III, A. 12, 18.

23. Another important detail should be clarified. We have used many times the name Israel in this lesson. But in fact the only nation that existed in the time of Jeremiah was Judah.

Israel was destroyed in the year 722 B.C., that is,_____

years before Jeremiah began his ministry.

*

95

24. So when Israel is mentioned in the book of Jeremiah it refers to the original United Kingdom of Israel or the former Northern Kingdom that was destroyed in 722 B.C., and sometimes it refers to the remaining tribe of Judah in a general sense.

Figure out which of these three meanings for the name Israel is intended in the following passages.

a. Jer. 2:3   _____

b. Jer. 2:4   _____

c. Jer. 2:14   _____

d. Jer. 3:6-10 _____
*   *

a. The original United Kingdom.
b. Judah
c. Judah
d. The former Northern Kingdom.

25. Finally, summarize Jeremiah's message in Jer. 2:1-4:4. Read over your outline, especially the main idea for each one of these paragraphs. In Lesson IV we analyzed the paragraphs of Jer. 2 and concluded that all speak primarily about:

a. Israel's special relationship to the Lord._____

b. _____

c. _____
*   *

b. Israel's unfaithfulness.
c. Israel's judgment.

26. In Lesson V you analyzed the main ideas of the remaining paragraphs. You should have noticed another important, recurring idea in Jer. 3:1-4:4. In these paragraphs the Lord not only recalls Israel's election but exposes her apostasy and speaks of judgment.

The new idea is _____.
*   *

Israel's call to repentance.

27. This call to repentance is especially evident in the repeated use of
the word "return." Glance through Jer. 3:1-4:4 once again rapidly and
underline the word "return" each time it appears.

List the specific verses that use the word "return."

a. _____   b. _____   c. _____

d. _____   e. _____   f. _____

Jer. 3:1, 7, 10, 12, 14, 22; 4:1

28. The idea of repentance is expressed, of course, not just by the word
"return." It is also presented very effectively in Jeremiah's literary
figures.

Analyze the figure of the fallow ground in Jer. 4:3.

The fallow ground	Israel
Needs to be broken up so that crops may grow in it.	Israel needs to be softened so that she may bring forth truth, justice, uprightness.

29. Analyze the figure of circumcision in Jer. 4:4.

A man is circumcised.	Israel should repent.
By removing the foreskin.	By removing the hardness of her heart.

30. Now list the complete summary of Jeremiah's message to his apostate people. Use the three points we found in Jer. 2 plus the viewpoint we found in Jer. 3:1-4:4.

a. _____

b. _____

c. _____

d. _____

*   *

> a. Israel's special relationship to the Lord.
> b. Israel's unfaithfulness to the Lord.
> c. Israel's judgment.
> d. Israel's call to repentance.

You can easily learn these four points because each one is related to the others. Israel was called to be a special people to the Lord. But she has become unfaithful, apostate, idolatrous. So the Lord will send judgment and destruction upon her. But He still calls her to repent and return to Him.

These four points are so interrelated that it is almost impossible to separate them. For example, when the Lord reminds Israel of her covenant with Him, it is because she has forgotten or broken that covenant. And when He accuses her of unfaithfulness and warns her of coming destruction, it is because He wants her to repent and return to Him.

This summary of Jeremiah's message is very important. But you will have to study other sections of the book of Jeremiah to see if he used the same message throughout his ministry. We have studied Jer. 2:1-4:4 inductively. You will have to go on and study the rest of the book inductively before you can give a complete statement of Jeremiah's message.

This summary shows why we have chosen the title, "Israel's Apostasy," for Jer. 2:1-4:4.

E. Self-Test (Jeremiah 4:5-31)

My main objective in this course is to help you learn how to do an Inductive Bible Study. I certainly hope that you learn something about the book
of Jeremiah and that you gain a deep appreciation of the prophet Jeremiah.
But I am primarily interested in your ability to continue studying the different books of the Bible, including Jeremiah, inductively.

The only way to see if you can do an Inductive Bible Study by yourself is
to try. So this last section of Lesson V is a test based on Jer. 4:5-31,
a passage which we have not yet studied together. You will be asked to
make an Inductive Study of this passage and answer several questions. Then
you will be able to check your answers. So it is a self-test. If you cannot
do this Inductive Study, then you should go back over the parts of this lesson, or previous lessons, that you did not understand. If you have just
been copying answers and memorizing them, you will probably fail this self-
test.

In your next class session you will probably be given another test over
another passage that you have not yet studied. So it is important to test
yourself right now and see if you have learned how to do Inductive Bible
Study.

1. Read Jer. 4:5-8 carefully.

a. What is the main idea of this paragraph? _____

_____

b. What title do you give to this paragraph? _____

_____

Put this information in your outline of the book of Jeremiah.

2. Explain in your own words the situation described in this paragraph. _____

_____

_____

_____

3. Explain the phrase "from the north." _____

_____

_____

_____

4. Explain the phrase "gird you with sackcloth." You may use your Bible

dictionary. _____

_____

_____

5. Study Jer. 4:9-10.

a. What is the main idea of the paragraph? _____

_____

_____

b. Write a title for it. _____

Put this information in your outline.

6. List the leaders of the people who are mentioned here.

a. _____   c. _____

b. _____   d. _____

7. Explain why they shall be appalled and astounded at what is to happen.

_____

_____

_____

8. What seems to be Jeremiah's attitude? _____

_____

9. Read Jer. 4:11-18.

a. What is the main idea of this paragraph? _____

_____

_____

b. Give it a title. _____

Put this information in our outline.

10. Analyze the figure of a hot wind.

11. Explain v. 14. _____

_____

_____

_____

12. Analyze carefully the reference to Dan and Mount Ephraim in v. 15. Explain why these two places are mentioned. You may consult your atlas and

Bible dictionary. _____

_____

_____

_____

_____

_____

13. An interesting detail about the enemy attack is mentioned in v. 16, 17.

What is it? _____

_____

14. Read Jer. 4:19-22.

a. What is the main idea of this paragraph? _____

_____

_____

b. Write a title. _____

Put this information in your outline.

15. This paragraph expresses a tremendous emotional feeling. Explain this feeling in your own words. _____

_____

_____

16. Read Jer. 4:23-28.

a. What is the main idea in this paragraph? _____

_____

_____

b. Write a title. _____

Put this information in your outline.

17. In v. 23-26 Jeremiah describes not just the cities but other objects too. List the objects and his description of them.

	Object	Description
a.		
b.		
c.		
d.		
e.		
f.		
g.		
h.		

18. Explain why Jeremiah describes all these objects. Do you think that the heavens were really darkened and that the mountains really gushed?

_____

_____

_____

_____

19. This paragraph, Jer. 4:23-28 speaks almost entirely of destruction.
But there is a note of hope. Copy the words that seem to offer some hope

for Judah. _____

20. Read Jer. 4:29-31.

a. What is the main idea of this passage? _____

_____

_____

b. Write a title. _____

21. Study v. 30 carefully.

Who is the "desolate one?" _____

This desolate one is described as a _____

Who are the "lovers"? _____

_____

22. Analyze the figure of a woman in travail.

23. Explain how to interpret a literary figure. _____

_____

_____

_____   _____

_____

24. How would you make a summary of the message of Jer. 4:5-31? _____

_____

_____

25. Make a summary statement of Jeremiah's message in Jer. 4:5-31. _____

_____

_____

Confirmation

Read over the following to check your Self-Test. Some of these points do
not require an exact answer. But if you have missed some be sure to find
out why. If you want to grade yourself, take off four points for each
wrong answer.

1. a. This is an urgent warning that the enemy is coming.
   b. A possible title is "Blow the trumpet" or "Flee for safety" or "Evil
      from the North."

2. You should have pointed out the urgency of Jeremiah's warning. Phrases
like "blow the trumpet," "go into the fortified cities,""raise the standard"
indicate that the enemy was on the march and that Judah must prepare for
battle.

3. We know that Babylonia attacked Judah from the north several times during Jeremiah's ministry and that Babylonia finally destroyed Jerusalem
in 587 B.C. In this passage Jeremiah points to that destruction.

4. Putting on sackcloth was a sign of mourning in case of death, defeat,
or other calamities. It was also used to express repentance for sin. Here
Judah is called to   mourn   because the Lord is against His people
and unless they repent their defeat is sure.

5. a. The leaders will be completely surprised by the coming destruction.
   b. A possible title: "Appalled and Astounded."

6. a. King   c. Priests
   b. Princes   d. Prophets

7. As we shall see more clearly later in the book of Jeremiah, the leaders
of Judah were convinced that the Lord would deliver His people. They did
not believe Jeremiah's repeated warning of destruction. And they did not
change their evil ways.

8. It seems as if Jeremiah accuses the Lord of deceiving His people.

9. a. God's judgment comes as destruction upon Jerusalem.
   b. A possible title: "A hot wind."

10.

A hot wind	God's judgment or the enemy.
It is so strong it destroys.	It comes to destroy.

11. Jer. 4:14 is a call to repentance. This shows that even as the Lord declared His judgment on His people He called them to repentance. If they would turn from their evil ways they might escape the coming destruction.

12. This is a difficult question because Dan refers to two locations, one west of Jerusalem, the other to the far north. Ephraim was located just north of Jerusalem. If you use your imagination you can find a special significance in this reference. A voice comes first from Dan (in the far north), then from Ephraim (just north of Jerusalem) announcing the ominous advance of the enemy. Probably the second location of Dan is meant here.

13. The cities were to be besieged by the enemy. This was a common form of warfare in those days. As we know, Jerusalem itself suffered under siege for two years before it was destroyed in 587 B.C.

14. a. Jeremiah suffers anguish as he contemplates the destruction of his people.
    b. A possible title: "My anguish, my anguish!"

15. Jeremiah must have had a great love for his people. As he watched the enemy destroy the cities he must have felt profound desperation.

16. a. All nature reflects the destruction of Judah.
    b. A possible title: "Earth waste and void."

17.

a.	The earth	was waste and void
b.	The heavens	had no light
c.	The mountains	were quaking
d.	All the hills	moved to and fro
e.	Man	there was none
f.	The birds	had fled
g.	The fruitful land	was a desert
h.	All the cities	were laid in ruins

18. You should have stated that this is figurative language. The only part that is literally true is the statement that the cities were laid in ruins. The earth was not really waste and void; the heavens were not completely darkened, and the mountains probably did not quake. But this description gives the destruction of Judah a transcendent, cosmic significance.

19. "Yet I will not make a full end."

20. a. The cities of Judah flee from advancing destruction.
    b. A possible title: "A woman in travail."

21. The desolate one is probably <u>Jerusalem</u>. Jeremiah says in v. 29 that all the cities are forsaken. Jerusalem was the last to fall. Yet even in the face of impending destruction, Jerusalem flirted with <u>other religions and other political alliances</u> as a <u>harlot</u>.

22.

A woman in travail	Jerusalem
Cries in anguish	Gasps before her murderers

23. You should have put down the four steps in interpreting literary figures.
a. Identify the object.
b. Find out what it represents.
c. Note the special characteristic or characteristics of the object.
d. Define the message of the figure.

24. You could review or list the main ideas in all the paragraphs of this passage. You have already made a list in your outline. Review it, if you have not already done so.

25. In Jer. 4:5-31 Jeremiah's message is almost entirely one of impending destruction.

6

The Enemy from the North and the Enemy from Within

(Jeremiah 4:5-6:30)

In your Self-Test at the end of Lesson V, you studied Jer. 4:5-31. In Lesson VI you will study in detail Jer. 5 and 6. This will give you more practice doing Inductive Study at the paragraph level, that is, paragraph by paragraph. Then you will consider Jer. 4:5-6:30 as a whole and look for indications of a broader structure in Jer. 2-6. In other words you will try to determine how to group these paragraphs in sections and larger divisions.

We began our study of Jer. 2:1-4:4 by looking for overall structure first. Then we studied the details of the passage paragraph by paragraph. This time we will study first the details of Jer. 4:5-6:30 paragraph by paragraph. Then we will look for the overall structure. Both approaches are inductive. In fact the two approaches should be used reciprocally, if not simultaneously.

As always, try to understand what the text has to say. Ask questions constantly. Look for the meaning of Jeremiah's message in his own historical context. As you study, think about how to interpret the Bible on its own terms. Learn how to study the Bible inductively.

Your specific objectives in this lesson are to:

Define Jeremiah's message in Jer. 4:5-6:30.

Explain many of the details in this passage.

Learn what kinds of questions to ask in Inductive Study.

Find indications of overall structure in Jer. 2-6.

A. Jeremiah 5.

In this section I will ask the questions, as I have done previously. You are to answer the questions as usual. But, even more important, notice how I ask the questions and what kinds of questions. In the following section you will ask the questions as well as answer them.

1. Read Jer. 5:1-3.

a. What is the main idea of this paragraph? _____

_____

b. Write a title. _____

Put this information in your outline.

*   *

a. In the face of judgment, Jerusalem refuses to repent.
b. A possible title: "Faces harder than rock."

2. Explain the argument or reasoning of v. 1. _____

* _____ *

Jerusalem might be pardoned if she had even one just citizen. Apparently
there was none.

3. What particular sin is singled out in this paragraph? _____

*   *

falsehood

4. Explain the argument of v. 3. _____

_____

* _____ *

The Lord has punished His people, but they still refuse to repent. They are
stubborn.

5. Analyze the figure of rock.

*   *

Rock	The people of Jerusalem.
Is very hard.	Are even harder of heart: they will not repent.

6. Read Jer. 5:4-5.

a. The main idea: _____

_____

b. A title: _____

*   *

a. From poor to great, all have broken away from the Lord's will.
b. A possible title: "The poor, the great."

7. Explain the argument of this paragraph in your own words. _____

_____

_____

It is understandable that the ignorant poor should leave the way of the Lord,
but the leaders are just as bad.

8. Who are "the great" mentioned here? _____

_____

_____

Jeremiah was probably referring to the priests, the prophets, the princes,
and the king. In other words he was talking about the leaders.

9. Mention another passage which we have studied where Jeremiah accuses the

leaders of the people specifically. _____
*

Jer. 2:8 and 4:9 are two examples.

10. Read Jer. 5:6.

a. The idea: _____

_____

b. Title: _____
*

Be sure you always fill in your outline with this information.
a. Because of their apostasies, they shall be destroyed.
b. A possible title: "Lion, wolf, leopard."

11. Analyze the three literary figures of v. 6 together.

*   *

| A lion, a wolf, a leopard | Judah's enemy |
| Destroy. | Will destroy her. |

12. Jeremiah says that their transgressions are many and great. What were

their sins? Mention three different kinds. _____

_____

_____

* _____ *

We know that they were guilty of flagrant idolatry, false political alliances, falsehood. Perhaps their greatest sin was their refusal to heed Jeremiah's message and repent.

13. Read. Jer. 5:7-9.

a. The main idea: _____

_____

b. Title: _____
*   *

a. Their apostasy is infamous, like lusty stallions.
b. "Well-fed lusty stallions."

14. Analyze the literary figure in v. 7.

Your children	People of Judah
Committed adultery, trooped to the houses of harlots.	Committed idolatry, worshipping other gods.

Note the difference between this figure and the figure of the harlot. In the figure of the harlot, Judah is like an immoral woman who makes love to many men. In Jer. 5:7 Judah is compared to a man who goes to houses of prostitution. In both cases the message is the same: Judah is committing idolatry with other gods. But check your analysis to see that it is correct.

15. The figure in v. 8 is one of the strongest expressions in the book of Jeremiah. Analyze it.

*   *

Well-fed lusty stallions.	Judah
Each neighing for his neighbor's wife.	Goes running after the gods of the other nations.

16. Read Jer. 5:10-13.

a. The main idea: _____

_____

b. Title: _____

*   *

a. Faithless Judah does not believe the Lord will judge her.
b. A possible title: "No evil will come."

17. As you read through this paragraph, you should have noticed a phrase that we have seen once before that has a special significance. Write it down

here. _____

*   *

"But make not a full end."

18. Now find the place where this phrase is repeated in a slightly differ-

ent form. _____
*   *

Jer. 4:27.

19. In the future be on the lookout for this phrase, because it may be an
indication of the overall structure. Also, underline this phrase in the
text (Jer. 4:27 and Jer. 5:10) so that you can find these references easily.

20. You may have noticed that the theme of this paragraph is similar to the
theme of another paragraph in this chapter. It is a theme of foolish, stubborn refusal to turn to the Lord. Note the reference of the other paragraph

here. _____
*   *

In Jer. 5:1-3 Judah refuses to repent even in the face of the Lord's judgment. In Jer. 5:11-13 Judah denies that the Lord will judge her.

21. Read Jer. 5:14-17.

a. The main idea: _____

_____

b. A title: _____
*   *

a. Because of their stubbornness, they shall be destroyed by a foreign nation.
b. A possible title: "A nation from afar."

22. Analyze the figure of a fire in v. 14.

*   *

A fire	The Lord's word in Jeremiah's mouth.
Burns up wood.	Shall devour the people of Judah.

23. This is a striking and terrible presentation of Jeremiah's ministry as the Lord's prophet. Remember what we said in Lesson II about the nature of prophecy. The prophet not only proclaimed the will of the Lord. As he proclaimed God's will he was instrumental in bringing it to pass. Find the

words in Jeremiah's call that express this concept most clearly. _____

_____

* _____ *

Jer. 1:10. Jeremiah was called "to pluck up and to break down, to destroy and to overthrow, to build and to plant."

24. Express in your own words what you think Jeremiah felt about this calling described in Jer. 5:14. _____

_____

* _____ *

You have to use your own imagination. To me, it must have been an awfully painful experience. Remember that Jeremiah loved his people. He struggled with them for 40 years, proclaiming God's word and calling them to repentance. But they would not repent, so he had to announce God's judgment upon them.

25. What is the "nation from afar?" _____
*   *

Babylonia was the nation which finally came and destroyed Judah, including Jerusalem.

26. Read Jer. 5:18-19.

a. The main idea: _____

_____

b. A title: _____
*   *

a. Because of his apostasy, Judah shall serve strangers.
b. A possible title: "You shall serve strangers."

27. Here again we find a peculiar phrase we have noticed twice before in this section.

a. The phrase: _____

Lesson VI: THE ENEMY FROM THE NORTH AND THE
ENEMY FROM WITHIN (JEREMIAH 4:5-6:30)

b. The previous references: _____

*   *

a. "I will not make a full end of you." (Underline the phrase in your text)
b. Jer. 4:27, 5:10.

28. This short paragraph also contains an important prophecy which we have

not yet found in Jeremiah. Express it in your own words. _____

_____

_____

This is a clear prophecy of the coming exile. The people of Judah would be
taken to a foreign land to serve a foreign people.

29. Read Jer. 5:20-29.

a. The main idea: _____

_____

b. A title: _____
*   *

a. They are not held back by God's will; they have gone away and practiced
evil.
b. A possible title: "Houses full of treachery."

30. One of the most eloquent literary figures in all of Jeremiah's prophecies
is found in v. 22-23. Analyze it.

* | | |*

The sea	The people of Judah
Is bound by the shore and cannot pass over it.	Should be bound by God's will, but they have broken it and gone away.

31. In v. 26-28 the Lord accuses His people of several specific sins. Some of the language is figurative, and it is hard to tell exactly what it means. See if you can list three specific evils.

a. _____

b. _____

c. _____

a. They become rich and great through treachery (fraud).
b. They exploit the fatherless.
c. They do not defend the rights of the poor.

32. Do God's people practice these evils today? _____ How? _____

_____

_____

_____

Certainly many Christians today become rich through dishonest business, exploit the helpless, and fail to defend the rights of the poor. These are among the most common sins of our time.

33. Do Christians today generally recognize and repent of these sins? _____
    Explain.

_____

I don't think so. We usually think we are all right as long as we go to church, pray, and "keep" the Ten Commandments. We don't really think that we are responsible for the injustices of our society. And we don't think these sins are as serious as idolatry, adultery, murder, and stealing.

34. In v. 29 the Lord asks two questions.

a. What is the obvious answer to these questions? _____

b. How did the Lord punish Judah? _____

c. Should the Lord punish us, if we practice the same evils? _____

a. Yes.
b. He destroyed Judah and exiled her people.
c. Yes.

35. Read <u>Jer. 5:30-31</u>.

a. The main idea: _____

_____   _____

b. A title: _____   *
*

a. The prophets, priests, and people all are guilty.
b. A possible title: "Prophets, priests, people."

36. Jeremiah calls this situation "an appalling and horrible thing." Who

was guilty of this terrible situation? _____

*   _____   *

The prophets, the priests, and the people themselves were all guilty.

37. In our own time we have known of false religious teachers and false political leaders and false economic leaders who mislead the people. And terrible evil has been committed in the 20th Century, as great as in any period

of human history. Who is guilty of all this evil? _____

*   _____   *

The leaders and the people. As long as the people are willing to go along
with their leaders and take advantage of the situation for personal gain,
they are guilty.

38. Without looking back over the previous questions, make a list of some
of the steps we have used in our analysis of each paragraph of Jer. 5. You
should look at the text and think of the kinds of questions we have been
asking.

a. _____

b. _____

c. _____

d. _____

e. _____

f. _____

g. _____
*   *

Here are some of the steps we have used.
a. Read the paragraph.
b. Define the main idea of the paragraph.
c. Write a title using four words or less from the text itself.
d. Analyze the literary figures.
e. Explain the reasoning or argument.
f. Explain any unusual or difficult details.
g. Notice references to the historical context.
h. Enumerate series of details.
i. Relate the passage to Jeremiah's message as a whole and to his ministry.
j. Relate the passage to our own day and to our own experience.
k. Notice recurrent phrases and ideas. Find parallel passages.

39. You are not expected to memorize these questions. And you should not approach each passage with a pre-determined set of questions. But as you read the text you should know what kinds of questions to ask. In other words the questions arise from the text itself.

Repeat here our definition of Inductive Bible Study. As we go on in the course we will continue to use the same definition, but the concept should

become more and more significant and more and more practical. _____

_____

_____

* _____ *

Inductive Bible Study is an approach to Bible study that begins with the Bible and studies it on its own terms.

                          B. Jeremiah 6.

This section is really another Self-Test. But it is more difficult and more important than the one you did at the end of Lesson V. This time you are asked to do an Inductive Study of Jer. 6 entirely on your own. Instead of just answering questions, you will have to write the questions yourself, and answer them.

Remember that from the beginning your primary objective has been to learn how to study the Bible inductively. This means that you have to learn to study the Bible on your own, independently, without my help. So it is important for you now to practice the skills you have been learning and apply them on your own. In all of these lessons you should be developing your own approach to the study of the Bible, an approach you can use after this course is over.

Work through Jer. 6 paragraph by paragraph as we did with Jer. 5. Write down your instructions and questions as if you were preparing a course or

a lesson. Put down your answers and also fill in your outline. This process
will help you study the text carefully. It will help you preserve the results of your investigation. And it will help you see if you can really
study the text inductively by yourself.

In Section C of this lesson you will work through the material I have prepared on this same chapter. You do not need to change your material, unless
you feel you have left out something important or made a wrong interpretation. But you should be able to evaluate your work as you compare it with
mine.

This is an important step to take. Make the most of it. Do not look at Section C until you have completed your own study of Jer. 6. There is no sub-
stitute for your own independent practice.

Jer. 6:1-5. _____

_____

_____

_____

_____

_____

_____

_____

_____

_____

_____

_____

_____

_____

_____

_____

Jer. 6:6-8. _____

Jer. 6:9-15. _____

_____

_____

_____

_____

_____

_____

_____

_____

_____

_____

_____

_____

_____

_____

_____

_____

_____

_____

_____

_____

_____

_____

_____

Jer. 6:16-21.

Lesson VI: THE ENEMY FROM THE NORTH AND THE
                                        ENEMY FROM WITHIN (JEREMIAH 4:5-6:30)

Jer. 6:22-26. _____

_____

_____

_____

_____

_____

_____

_____

_____

_____

_____

_____

_____

_____

_____

_____

_____

_____

_____

_____

_____

_____

_____

Jer. 6:27-30. _____

Lesson VI: THE ENEMY FROM THE NORTH AND THE
                                  ENEMY FROM WITHIN (JEREMIAH 4:5-6:30)
                              C. Jeremiah 6

It should be very easy now for you to work through my Inductive Study of
Jer. 6. As you answer the questions on each paragraph, however, go back to
Section B and see if you have considered the same points. No doubt your
questions are written in a different manner, which is fine. Perhaps you
have asked some questions which I haven't thought of, which is fine, too.
But notice, also, if you have left out some important aspect of the interpretation of the passage. Mark these questions by putting an X in the margin.

1. Read Jer. 6:1-5.

a. What is the main idea of this paragraph? _____

_____

b. Write a title for this paragraph. _____
*   *
Be sure to put this information in your outline.
a. Jeremiah announces the approach of the enemy.
b. A possible title: "Trumpet in Tekoa."

2. Several times now Jeremiah has mentioned the blowing of a trumpet. What

does that mean here? _____

_____

It is quite obviously to sound the alarm, to announce the arrival of the
enemy so that the people will be prepared or flee.

3. You should try to find out where Tekoa and Bethhaccherem are located, because this will indicate how close the enemy is coming.

a. Tekoa is located _____

_____.

b. Bethhaccherem is located _____.
*   *
You should have looked up these names in a Bible dictionary or atlas.
a. 6 miles south of Bethlehem, 11 miles south of Jerusalem.(16 km.)
b. About 4 1/2 miles west of Jerusalem. (7 1/2 km.)

4. Earlier in this same verse Jeremiah tells the people of Benjamin to flee

also. Where is Benjamin located? _____

_____

This tribe was located just north of Jerusalem.

5. Now summarize the position of the enemy at the time Jeremiah pronounced

these words. _____

* _____ *

Apparently they were on all sides of Jerusalem and very close.

6. This analysis is confirmed by v. 3. Explain the figurative language by
identifying the following:

a. "The shepherds" represent _____.

b. "Their flocks" are _____.

c. "They shall pitch their tents around her" means _____

* _____. *

a. Enemy generals or rulers.
b. Their armies.
c. They shall set up a siege around Jerusalem.

7. Who is "the daughter of Zion" in v. 2? (Use your Bible dictionary.)_____

* _____ *

This expression refers to Jerusalem.

8. Identify who are speaking in v. 4-5.

a. "Prepare war against her...." _____

b. "Woe to us...." _____

c. "Up, and let us attack...." _____
* *

a. The enemy.
b. The people of Jerusalem.
c. The enemy.

9. Underline the phrase "for evil looms out of the north" in v.1. Perhaps
you remember seeing that phrase earlier in Jer. 4. Find it and underline it.

Write down the reference here. _____
* *

Lesson VI: THE ENEMY FROM THE NORTH AND THE
ENEMY FROM WITHIN (JEREMIAH 4:5-6:30)

Jer. 4:6

10. This may be a key phrase in the overall structure, so keep it in mind
as you study further.

You may want to mark another passage in Jer. 4 that indicates that an enemy
comes from the north. Jeremiah speaks of the warning cry from Dan and from

*   Mount Ephraim. Put down this reference too. _____
                                                                              *

Jer. 4:15

11. We know that King Nebuchadnezzar's armies came down from the north and
laid siege to Jerusalem at least two times during Jeremiah's ministry. These
events are described in three different books of the Old Testament.

a. _____

b. _____

*   c. _____
                                                                              *

a. 2 Kings
b. 2 Chronicles
c. Jeremiah (especially Jer. 52.)

12. Check these passages and your Chronological Chart, and write down the
dates for these two sieges.

a. _____

*   b. _____
                                                                              *

a. 598 B.C.
b. 589-587 B.C.

13. Read Jer. 6:6-8.

a. The main idea: _____

_____

b. A title: _____

Remember that your paragraph titles should be made up of four words or less,
and these words should be taken from the text of that paragraph.
*   *

a. Wicked Jerusalem must be punished; she will be sieged.
b. A possible title: "A Siege against Jerusalem."

14. It is interesting to note that Jeremiah, as the Lord's mouthpiece, speaks here of two kinds of evil and violence. What are they?

a. _____

b. _____

*   *

a. The enemy which attacks the city from the outside.
b. The wickedness which springs up within the city.

15. These two kinds of evil are separate and very different. But there is an important relationship between them. We will study this relationship further in the following section of this lesson. See if you can explain the relationship between the enemy on the outside and the enemy on the inside of

Jerusalem. _____

_____

* _____ *

The Lord is sending the enemy on the outside as punishment for Jerusalem's evil on the inside.

16. A direct application of this concept can be a dangerous thing. But give

your own idea of what it means to us today. _____

_____

_____

* _____ *

It may be that God will send us some punishment or testing in our lives because we have disobeyed Him. At least this is a concept that we should study further, as we go through Jeremiah.

17. Read Jer. 6:9-15.

a. The main idea: _____

_____

b. A title: _____
*   *

a. The Lord's wrath will be poured out on all the people for their wickedness.
b. A possible title: "Glean thoroughly."

18. Analyze the figure of a grape-gatherer.

*   *

A grape-gatherer.	The enemy.
Passes his hand over the branches a second time to glean the remaining fruit.	Will come against Judah and take or destroy those who remain in Judah.

19. As in other paragraphs we see here Judah's stubborn refusal to hear the word of the Lord and repent of her sins. List two passages in Jer. 5 that emphasize this same theme.

a. _____

b. _____

*   *

Jer. 5:1-3, 20-29.

20. In many passages of Jeremiah it is difficult to distinguish who is speaking, the Lord or Jeremiah himself. Read through Jer. 6:9-15 again and identify who is speaking in each verse.

a. v. 9 _____   e. v. 13 _____

b. v. 10 _____   f. v. 14 _____

c. v. 11 _____   g. v. 15 _____

d. v. 12 _____

*   *

a. v. 9   The Lord   e. v. 13 The Lord
b. v. 10 Jeremiah   f. v. 14 The Lord
c. v. 11 Jeremiah, the Lord   g. v. 15 The Lord
d. v. 12 The Lord

21. In v. 10 and the first half of v. 11 Jeremiah expresses something about his role as a prophet. It was a weary task. And then the Lord tells him to

pour out His wrath on His people. Here the concept of the prophet is not just to proclaim God's will but to be His instrument in carrying it out. We have already noted this concept in two other passages. List them here.

a. _____   b. _____
*   *

Jer. 1:10, 5:14

22. According to v. 11-12, who shall suffer from the Lord's wrath? _____

_____

* _____ *

The children, the young men, both husband and wife, the old, the inhabi-tants.

23. Why does the Lord mention all of these? _____

* _____ *

This is a poetic or dramatic way of saying that all the people will suffer.

24. What is their sin, according to v. 13? _____
*   *

Unjust gain

25. Is this sin common today, even among Christians? _____
*   *

I think it probably is.

26. What is the sin of the prophets, according to v. 14? _____

* _____ *

They preach peace, when there is imminent danger of war and destruction.

27. Reread Jer. 5:30-31 about the false prophets, Then ask yourself, why

did the prophets preach peace at a time like that? _____

* _____ *

Probably they preached peace because that was what the people wanted to hear.

28. Can you think of a parallel situation today? _____

_____

_____

Certainly many preachers preach what the people want to hear and are afraid
to offend them, for example, by pointing out their sins.

29. Read Jer. 6:16-21.

a. The main idea: _____

_____

b. A title: _____
*   *

a. They have refused His way, His warning, His law; He shall reject their
sacrifices and punish them.
b. A possible title: "Have not given heed."

30. List the things that they have rejected.

a. _____   c. _____

b. _____   d. _____
*   *

a. The good way.   c. The Lord's words.
b. The sound of the trumpet.   d. His law.

31. Apparently, according to v. 20, the people continued to offer incense

and sacrifice. Explain why the Lord rejects them. _____

_____

_____

These outward acts of worship were only a false pretense. We know that the
people were worshipping other gods and disobeying God's will.

32. Can you see a modern application of this concept? _____

_____

_____

_____

No doubt many Christians who attend worship on Sunday morning fail to live
according to God's will during the week. Perhaps we are all guilty of this
to some extent. Certainly we should know that our worship is not acceptable
to the Lord unless we sincerely try to follow His commands.

33. Read Jer. 6:22-26.

a. The main idea: _____

_____

b. A title: _____
*   *

a. A great nation comes suddenly from the north to destroy Jerusalem.
b. A possible title: "Suddenly the Destroyer."

34. You probably noted immediately the reference to the enemy from the north.
Underline it in the text and list it here with the other references we have
noted previously in Jer. 4:5-6:30.

a. _____   c. _____

b. _____   d. _____
*   *

Jer. 4:6, 15; 6:1, 22

35. List the characteristics of the enemy from the north in v. 22-23.

a. _____   d. _____

b. _____   e. _____

c. _____   f. _____
*   *

They come from the north; they are a great nation; they use bow and spear;
they are cruel; they are many, for they sound like a roaring sea; they ride
on horses.

36. Notice how Jeremiah describes the reaction of the people as they face
destruction. Many paragraphs that we have studied speak of this destruction.
But each description is different. Really Jeremiah was amazingly gifted, for
he was able to repeat the same themes over and over with great variety of
expression. Underline the most dramatic words in v. 24-26.
*   *

The ones I have underlined are: "helpless," "anguish," "pain," "travail,"
"terror," "mourning," "bitter lamentation."

37. Read Jer. 6:27-30.

a. The main idea: _____

_____

b. A title: _____
*   *

a. Consumed by a refining fire, they are still stubbornly rebellious.
b. A possible title: "Assayer and Tester."

38. Analyze the figure of a refining fire.

*   *

A refining fire	Jeremiah proclaims God's judgment.
Burns out the impurities and leaves the pure metal.	But Judah refuses to be purified.

39. This is a terrible picture. Even when they experience God's judgment,
they refuse to repent. List four passages in Jer. 5-6, including this one,
that emphasize Judah's stubbornness in the face of judgment.

a. _____   c. _____

b. _____   d. _____
*   *

Jer. 5:1-3, 20-29, 6:9-15, 27-30

40. Who is the assayer in v. 27? _____
*   *

Jeremiah

41. What does the assayer do? _____

_____

He weighs and tests metals, throwing out the dross.

42. Once again we see that Jeremiah has a terrible role to play as the Lord's prophet to a rebellious people. As we have noted previously in this section, he not only announces the Lord's word, he carries it out. List the four references to this concept of Jeremiah's role and indicate what Jeremiah is called to do in each case.

a. Jer. 1:10 _____

b. _____ _____

c. _____ _____

d. _____ _____

*   *

a. Jer. 1:10 He is to pluck up, break down, destroy, overthrow, build, plant.
b. Jer. 5:14 He is to burn up the people with the Lord's word.
c. Jer. 6:11 He is to pour out the Lord's wrath on all the people.
d. Jer. 6:27 He is to assay them with a refining fire.

D. Structure

In this section you will study structural elements in Jer. 2-6. This is a large amount of material, but you have already studied most of it in detail.

The most important tool for this study is your outline. So it is absolutely necessary that you have it complete through Jer. 6. If you have not written in the main idea and a title for each paragraph, do so now.

Remember that it is very difficult to find any overall structure in the book of Jeremiah. Do not expect to divide up the whole book into divisions and sections easily. In the whole course we will only be able to work out some of the structure.

Remember, too, that our purpose is not just to figure out the structure of the book of Jeremiah. Our main objective is to learn how to analyze the structure of any book.

1. First, it would be a good idea to remind yourself what is the structure

of a book. Write out the complete definition we used in Lesson IV. _____

_____

_____

_____

_____

_____

_____

* _____ *

The structure of a book is its skeleton or outline. It is made up of several
parts or divisions. These parts may be hidden, but we know they are there.
They are tied together to form a central idea or plot or story. The structure holds the book together, gives it meaning, and enables it to teach us
something.

2. This definition, as we have pointed out, contains two examples and four
characteristics. List the two examples first.

a. _____

b. _____

Now list the four characteristics.

a. _____

b. _____

c. _____

* d. _____ *

a. The structure is like a skeleton.
b. Or it is like an outline.

a. It is made up of several parts or divisions.
b. These parts may be hidden, but we know they are there.
c. They are tied together to form a central idea or plot or story.
d. The structure holds the book together, gives it meaning, and enables it
to teach us something.

3. There are several different levels of structure, as we studied in Lesson
IV. Even words are put together in grammatical and logical structures to
form phrases. List six different levels of structure.

a. words _____   d. _____

b. _____   e. _____

* c. _____   f. _____ *

a. Words   d. Paragraphs
b. Phrases   e. Sections
c. Sentences   f. Divisions

4. In Lesson V and Lesson VI we have studied mostly words, phrases, sentences, and paragraphs. Now we will see if we can group the paragraphs of Jer.2-6

into _____.

*   *

sections

5. We have said that it is very important to find the structure of a book. We have said that one of the beginning steps in Inductive Bible Study is to

look for the structure of the book. Why do we look for the structure? _____

———— —— ———

* ———— —— *

In order to see the book as it really is, to study it on its own terms.

6. We study the words and phrases and sentences in a paragraph in order to understand the message of that paragraph. We study the different paragraphs,

sections, and divisions of a book in order to understand the _____

of that book.

*   *

message

7. Note that the analysis of paragraphs is very important. But it is not enough. In Jeremiah, as we pointed out earlier, there are more than 250 paragraphs. If you analyze all those paragraphs you will have a pretty good idea of the content of the book. But you need to see how those small units fit together in sections and divisions.

Remember the example of an animal skeleton. What happens if you just look

at the individual bones? _____

* ———— —————————— —— *

You can't see what kind of an animal it is, what it looks like, what its shape and height is.

8. What happens if you just look at the individual paragraphs of a book? _____

*

You can't see what is the structure of the book, its overall message, its
plot or central idea or argument.

9. You study the structure of the book in order to see the message of the
book as a whole. You also study the structure in order to see the significance of an individual passage.

For example, we noted that Jer. 1:1-3 contains historical information. This
historical information contributes to our understanding of the whole book
of Jeremiah. And we realize that this passage is the introduction to the
book, part of the overall structure of the book. So it is very important
for us to investigate the meaning of all its details.

Finally, you study the structure of a book in order to see the relationships
between passages. For example, we found in Jer. 2:1-3 the concept of Israel's
special relationship with the Lord. And we noted that this concept is basic
to the following passages which speak of Israel's unfaithfulness and judgment.

In conclusion, structure is important for three specific reasons:

> 1. In order to see the message of the book as a whole.
> 2. In order to see the significance of individual pas-
>   sages.
> 3. In order to see the relationships between passages.

10. Perhaps the most important way to look for structure is to identify the
main idea in each paragraph, then group together the paragraphs that have
more or less the same basic idea.

Jer. 1:1-3 belongs by itself. Why? _____

_____

*

It contains a historical introduction to the book. The following paragraphs
don't have the same basic idea. In fact they are altogether different in
content.

11. Jer. 1:4-19 forms a section. Why? _____

_____

*

Because this is a group of paragraphs that presents the call of Jeremiah.
The previous paragraph and the following paragraphs deal with different
topics.

12. What is the title of Jer. 1:4-19? _____
*   *

The Call of Jeremiah

13. When we studied Jer. 2:1-4:4 we decided that all these paragraphs be-

long in the same section. Why? _____

* _____ *

They all deal with the problem of Israel's apostasy.

14. What is the topic we suggested for Jer. 2:1-4:4? _____
*   *

Israel's Apostasy

15. This general topic of Israel's Apostasy has several basic ideas which
we also summarized in Lesson V. List these ideas.

a.   Israel's special relationship with the Lord. _____

b. _____

c. _____

d. _____
*   *

b. Israel's unfaithfulness to the Lord.
c. Israel's judgment.
d. Israel's call to repentance.

15. We have not yet explained why this section ends at Jer. 4:4. Study your
analysis of the paragraphs in Jer. 4:5-6:30 and see if you see any major
change in topic. We know that the four basic ideas listed above are repeated
throughout Jer. 2:1-4:4. Indicate which of these ideas are present in

Jer. 4:5-6:30. _____

_____

_____

* _____ *

Lesson VI: THE ENEMY FROM THE NORTH AND THE
                                ENEMY FROM WITHIN (JEREMIAH 4:5-6:30)
In a sense these same themes continue through Jer. 4-6. But you will notice
that beginning at Jer. 4:5 the only explicit themes are Israel's (Judah's)
unfaithfulness and judgment. In fact, most of Jer. 4:5-6:30 talks of destruction.

16. Note especially the use of the word "return." You have underlined the
word in your Bible several times in Jer. 3:1-4:4. Does it appear at all

after Jer. 4:5? _____
*   *

No

17. In order to make use of this observation, write the word "return" in
the column marked "Special Details" at each paragraph where it appears.

18. We have called the section Jer. 4:5-6:30 "The Enemy from the North and
the Enemy from Within." And you have underlined in your text four references
to the enemy from the north.

Which paragraph contains the first reference to the enemy from the north?

* _____
*   *

Jer. 4:5-8

19. Write in this information in the column marked "Special Details." Put
"from the north" at Jer. 4:5-8; 6:1-5, 22-26. And put "from Dan" at Jer. 4:
11-18.

20. We have, then, made another section from Jer. 4:5 to 6:30. In the following lesson we will discuss Jer. 7 and find out why it does not belong
in the same section with Jer. 4:5-6:30.

Why do we group together the paragraphs of Jer. 4:5-6:30? _____

* _____
*   *

They all deal with the topic of destruction, that is, Judah's apostasy and
judgment.

21. We should explain further the title, "The Enemy from the North and the
Enemy from Within."

a. What was the enemy from the north? _____

_____

_____

b. What was the enemy from within? _____

* _____ *

a. The enemy from the north was the Babylonian army which came and entered
Jerusalem in 598 and destroyed it in 587.
b. The enemy from within was Judah's stubborn rebellion against the Lord,
her apostasy.

22. There is, as we have noted already, a direct relationship between the
enemy from the north and the enemy from within. Explain that relationship.

_____

_____

* _____ *

Because of the evil practices within Judah, the Lord sent His judgment on
her in the form of the Babylonian army. In other words the second comes as
a result of the first.

23. Put in your outline of the book of Jeremiah the two sections we have
just defined with their titles.

a. Draw a dark line between Jer. 4:1-4 and 4:5-8 (like the one between
Jer. 1:1-3 and 1:4-10).
b. Make a bracket to unite Jer. 2:1-4:4 and write in the title "Israel's
Apostasy" in the column marked "Sections," (like the title "Call of Jeremiah).
c. Make a bracket to unite Jer. 4:5-6:30 and write in the title "Enemy from
the NOrth and Enemy from Within."

24. Something further should be said about structure. We have grouped together the paragraphs of Jer. 2-6 into two sections because of their topics.
In other words the paragraphs of Jer. 2:1-4:4 seem to belong together because they have the same topic, Israel's apostasy. And the paragraphs of
Jer. 4:5-6:30 seem to belong together because they have the same topic,
The Enemy from the North and the Enemy from Within. This is called topical
structure.

But remember that there are other kinds of organization or structure. Paragraphs may be put in chronological order. They may be grouped together because they happen in the same geographical area, etc.

List the different kinds of structure which were mentioned in Lesson IV.

a. _topical_____   d. _____

b. _____   e. _____

c. _____

*   *

Geographical, chronological, biographical, logical or theological

25. Other questions which should have occurred to you by now are these.
When were all these prophecies actually given? How were these prophecies
collected and written down? Is each paragraph a separate speech of Jeremiah? Did he himself write them down in this order in his book?

Fortunately, the book of Jeremiah itself tells us a great deal about how
these prophecies were collected and written down. So we will try to answer
some of these in a later lesson.

For the moment, just consider Jer. 2-6 as collections of Jeremiah's prophecies, probably from different periods of his long ministry.

                              E. Jeremiah's Message

The study of structure is not an end in itself. It helps us understand the
overall message of a book. It helps us see the significance of a passage.
And it helps us see relationships between passages.

In this section you will study Jeremiah's message. We have already summarized his message in Jer. 2:1-4:4 and in Jer. 4:5-6:30. But much more can be
said about it. We have used the structure to find the central ideas of Jeremiah's message. We will use other details which we have observed in our
study of the paragraphs. We will concentrate here primarily on Jer. 4:5-6:30.

1. We have noted that the dominant note in Jer. 4:5-6:30 is judgment or destruction. In order to appreciate the strength of this theme read through
the passage again and pick out some of the phrases that describe specifically this destruction. (Do not include descriptions of the enemy because
we will study that separately.) Just copy brief phrases. Perhaps you will
want to underline these phrases in the text first, using a special color.

a. great destruction   h. _____

b. your land a waste   i. _____

c. _____   j. _____

d. _____   k. _____

e. _____   l. _____

f. _____   m. _____

g. _____   n. _____

2. This language is certainly dramatic and highly figurative. We can conclude that this is no small enemy attack. Describe in your own words the

extent of the destruction _____

*   *

Apparently it will be complete. All the cities will be destroyed and the
land will be left desolate.

3. Now go through Jer. 4:5-6:30 and find descriptions of the enemy. Underline these phrases in the text, if you like, using a different color. Then
copy some of the key phrases. Make two lists: one, simple descriptions of
the enemy; the other, figurative descriptions of the enemy.

Simple Descriptions	Figurative Descriptions
a. _____	a. _____
b. _____	b. _____
c. _____	c. _____
d. _____	d. _____
e. _____	e. _____
f. _____	f. _____
g. _____	g. _____
h. _____	h. _____
i. _____	i. _____
j. _____	j. _____

4. Once again we can see that Jeremiah's language is often figurative and
dramatic. But he does give us important information about the enemy. He
tells us, for example, several specific details about the enemy's military
equipment and tactics.

Summarize these details. _____

_____

_____

*   *

The enemy use chariots and horses. They have archers. They use swords and
spears. They ride horses. They besiege the cities using trees and a siege
mound.

5. We know, of course, from secular history and from the Bible that Judah
was destroyed by an enemy who came down from the north and besieged her

cities. When did the final siege take place? _____
*   *

589-587 B.C.

6. Where is this event described in the Old Testament, besides Jeremiah?

* _____ *

In 2 Kings and 2 Chronicles.

7. Give the exact references for the description of the siege and fall of
Jerusalem.

a. 2 Kings _____

b. 2 Chronicles _____
*   *

2 Kings 25:1-21, 2 Chron. 36:17-21

8. Study these passages and give a summary of what happened. _____

_____

_____

_____

_____

_____

* _____ *

The Babylonians laid siege of Jerusalem for a year and a half, then they
breached the walls, killed and scattered the army of Judah, burned the Temple, the Palace, and all the city, broke down the city walls, killed Zedekiah's sons, blinded him, and took him prisoner to Babylon, carried off the
treasures of the Temple, and exiled all the people except a few wine dres-
sers and plowmen.

9. This was indeed a terrible event in the history of God's people. Jeremiah's description in Jer. 4:5-6:30 really isn't exaggerated. Jerusalem
was utterly destroyed and abandoned and the whole land laid waste.

But how could this happen to the people of God? Jeremiah declares time and again that the Lord himself sent this terrible destruction on His people. Not only did He allow it to happen; He caused it to happen. This concept is even more shocking than the fact of the destruction.

Find some phrases in Jer. 4:5-6:30 that state explicitly that the Lord himself sent this destruction upon Judah. You can mark your text with another color, then copy the phrases here.

a. I bring evil from the north   g. _____

b. _____   h. _____

c. _____   i. _____

d. _____   j. _____

e. _____   k. _____

f. _____   l. _____

10. We know, of course, that the Lord had ample reason to judge His people. He loved her; He had established her as a nation; He had sought to keep His covenant with her. But His people was unfaithful to Him.

We have noted three different kinds of sin practiced by the people of Judah. List them.

a. _____

b. _____

*
c. _____   *

a. Idolatry - the worship of other gods.
b. False political alliances - not trusting in the Lord.
c. Immoral practices - dishonesty, fraud, unconcern for the fatherless and the needy, unjust gain.

11. Go through Jer. 4:5-6:30 and note the reasons for the Lord's punishment. This is another theme which is repeated several times in this section. The Lord judged His people with terrible destruction because of her terrible apostasy. Underline or mark the reasons given in the text and list them here.

a.   Because she has rebelled against me. _____

b. _____

c. _____

d. _____

e. _____

f. _____

g. _____

h. _____

i. _____

*
j. _____   *

There are more references than you have room for. Here are some of them.
b. Your ways and your doings have brought this upon you.
c. For my people are foolish....skilled in doing evil.
d. Because their transgressions are many, their apostasies are great.
e. Your children have forsaken me, and have sworn by those who are no gods.
f. For the house of Israel and the house of Judah have been utterly faithless to me.
g. Because they have spoken this word.
h. As you have forsaken me and served foreign gods.
i. But this people has a stubborn and a rebellious heart.
j. Your sins have kept good from you.
k. This is the city which must be punished; there is nothing but oppression
within her.
l. The word of the Lord is to them an object of scorn...Therefore....
m. For from the least to the greatest of them every one is greedy for unjust gain.
n. They were not at all ashamed....Therefore....

12. Not only was Judah unfaithful to her Lord. She was stubbornly rebellious. She refused to hear His word and heed His warnings. She would not repent even in the face of judgment.

We have noted already that several paragraphs emphasize Judah's stubbornness. List the references for some of those paragraphs. (See C. 39 above)

a. _____   c. _____

b. _____   d. _____

13. This brings us to another important question. What did Jeremiah feel
about what was happening? He must have loved his people. But they did not
give heed to his message. Try to put yourself in his place and write an

analysis of his position. _____

_____

_____   _____

_____

* _____ *

Jeremiah loved his people. He called them urgently, even desperately, to repent before it was too late. But no one responded, and terrible destruction
came upon them. Jeremiah must have suffered tremendous anguioh.

14. Remember that Jeremiah, as the Lord's prophet, was called upon not only
to announce the coming destruction. According to the Old Testament concept
of prophecy, he was actually the instrument of God's wrath upon Judah.
Cite three passages in Jer. 4:5-6:30 that describe Jeremiah's role in these
terms.

a. _____ b. _____ c. _____
*   *

Jer. 5:14; 6:11; 6:27

15. What verses in Jer. 4:5-6:30 express most vividly Jeremiah's anguish

in the face of disaster? _____
*   *

Jer. 4:19-21. Note the tremendous feeling of these words. Perhaps you would
like to memorize this poem. Later we will study passages which reveal even
more Jeremiah's feelings about his people, about his own ministry, and about
the Lord's judgment.

16. Review the steps we have just taken in this section. We have gone through
Jer. 4:5-6:30 several times in order to note Jeremiah's use of certain topics.

What are the main topics we have investigated in Jer. 4:5-6:30?

a. _____

b. _____

c. _____

d. _____
*   *

a. The destruction that comes down from the north.
b. The Lord's role in sending the destruction.
c. The reasons why the Lord sent the destruction: Judah's sins.
d. Jeremiah's role as the Lord's prophet.

17. Most of the material in Jer. 4:5-6:30 is included in these four topics.
If you have underlined these materials in the text, using different colors,
you have marked most of the verses at least partly.

Lesson VI: THE ENEMY FROM THE NORTH AND THE
                              ENEMY FROM WITHIN (JEREMIAH 4:5-6:30)

Explain how you could apply this method in future study of the Bible. _____

_____

*   _____   *

You can look for the main ideas or topics and underline all the passages
that deal with the same topic one color.

18. This kind of investigation helps us find and understand the message of
a section and of the book. What is the title for Jer. 4:5-6:30?

*   _____   *

The Enemy from the North and the Enemy from Within.

19. Earlier in this lesson we pointed out some steps in analyzing paragraphs. See how many of those steps you can remember now. The important
thing is to study the text inductively. It is not necessary to memorize
these steps.

a. _____

b. _____

c. _____

d. _____

e. _____

f. _____

*   *

Go back to A.38, where eleven steps are listed.

20. There is some similarity between our analysis of paragraphs and our
analysis of larger passages and our analysis of a whole book. In all three
cases we have to study the text on its own terms.

a. A paragraph is _____

_____.

b. A section is _____

_____

c. A book is _____

a. One or more sentences with one central idea.
b. A group of paragraphs with the same basic ideas.
c. A group of writings with a central idea, plot, or story.

21. At each of these levels we study the structure of the text in order to

understand _____.

The message

22. At several points in our study of Jer. 4:5-6:30 we have noted an important application of the text for us today. Consider this section as a whole.

a. Is there a modern parallel to the enemy from the north? If so, what is

it? _____

_____

b. Is there a modern parallel to the enemy from within? If so, what is it?

_____

a. There are a number of external threats to our existence: thermonuclear
war, pollution, overpopulation, etc.
b. Our lives are constantly threatened by our own sins: materialism (a kind
of idolatry), unconcern for the oppressed and the needy, dishonesty, false
dependence on our own resources, etc.

23. Think, also, of Jeremiah's role as a prophet in those terrible last
years before 587 B.C. Who is called to fulfill a similar role in our time

of crisis today? _____

Aren't all those who know the Lord called to be His messengers?

24. What message are we called to proclaim? _____

We, like Jeremiah, are to call men to repent of their evil ways and to turn
to the Lord and be saved.

7

The Temple Sermon

(Jeremiah 7:1-8:3, Chap. 26)

In this lesson you will study two separate passages, Jer. 7:1-8:3 and Jer. 26. You will consider both of these passages together because they are, apparently, closely related. As in Lesson V and Lesson VI, you will study the details of each paragraph and the overall structure and message.

Your objectives are to:

Describe the relationship between Jer. 7:1-8:3 and Jer. 26.

Explain the details and summarize the content of these two passages.

Define Jeremiah's message with regard to the Temple and pagan worship.

A. Outline

Often the best way to begin an Inductive Study of a passage is to analyze the paragraphs as we have been doing. Your assignment in this section, therefore, is to define the main idea and write a title for each of the paragraphs in Jer. 7:1-8:3 and Jer. 26. As you do so, underline any details which you consider to be specially significant. And you may want to include some of these details in your outline as well as the main ideas and titles.

In particular be on the lookout for clues to the relationship between Jer. 7:1-8:3 and Jer. 26. There are at least two important links, which we shall discuss below. But do not go on to this discussion until you have completed your outline over these two passages.

1. Read through your outline analysis of Jer. 7:1-8:3. Write a summary of the content of this passage. _____

_____

*   *

The Lord calls Judah to repent of her evil ways, especially her idolatry, and warns her of terrible destruction.

2. Read through your outline analysis of Jer. 26. Write a summary of the content of this passage. _____

_____

_____

*   *

231

Jeremiah calls the people to repent and warns of destruction. His life is threatened by priests and prophets and people, but he is spared.

3. Notice the kind of material in Jer. 7:1-8:3.

a. Is it primarily prophecy or description of an event? _____

b. Does it appear to be a collection of short prophecies (as in Jer. 2-6)

or a single sermon? _____
*   *

a. It is primarily prophecy.
b. This question will require further study. It does appear, however, that the passage is not a collection of short prophecies but a sermon.

4. Now turn again to Jer. 26.

What kind of material do you find in this passage? _____

* _____
*   *

It is a narrative description of an event in the life of Jeremiah.

5. Now make a comparison between the two passages - first, with regard to Jeremiah's message.

a. Is the content of Jeremiah's message similar or different? _____

b. In what way is his message similar or different in the two passages? _____

* _____
*   *

a. It is similar.
b. In both cases he calls the people to repentance and warns of destruction.

6. Now compare the kind of material in Jer. 7:1-8:3 and Jer. 26.

a. Is the kind of material in the two passages similar or different? _____

_____

b. In what way is it similar or different? _____

* _____
*   *

a. It is different.
b. Jer. 7:1-8:3 is primarily prophecy, and Jer. 26 is primarily narrative.

7. Now consider the specific details you have underlined in the two passages
or included in your outline. You have probably found the two significant
links between these two passages. If not, look them over once again. One
link has to do with the context or the occasion of these passages. The other
is a distinctive note in Jeremiah's message in both passages. Write down
these two links.

a. _____

_____

b. _____

_____
*   *

a. In both cases Jeremiah is commanded to give this message at the entrance
to the Temple.
b. In both cases Jeremiah's message warns that the Temple will be destroyed
like Shiloh was destroyed.

8. Perhaps it is not possible to prove whether these two passages refer to
the same occasion. Perhaps it is not too important to find out. But is is
an interesting question. And in some cases it is very important to figure
out the relationships between different passages.

Consider the first link. Both passages refer to a message that Jeremiah
proclaimed at the entrance to the Temple.

a. Do you think that Jeremiah preached at the entrance to the Temple only

one time during his 40-year ministry? _____

b. Look up "Temple" and "House of the Lord" in a large concordance. Is there

any indication that Jeremiah preached at the Temple on more than one occasion?

_____

_____

c. Do you think that this link is sufficient to establish that Jer. 7:1-8:3

and Jer. 26 refer to the same occasion? Give your reasons. _____

_____

_____
*   *

a. I think Jeremiah must have preached at the Temple many times.
b. There are many references to the "House of the Lord" in Jeremiah. And

some passages, for example Jer. 19:14, state that Jeremiah prophesied at
the Temple.
c. This link by itself is not sufficient to establish that Jer. 7:1-8:3
and Jer. 26 refer to the same occasion.

9. Now consider the other link. In both passages Jeremiah's message warns
that the Temple will be destroyed like Shiloh. Follow the same reasoning

we used with the first link and write down your conclusions. _____

_____

_____

_____

_____

* _____ *

Your answer should include these three points:
a. It is not likely that Jeremiah would use a particular expression like
this over and over.
b. The concordance shows that Shiloh is mentioned four times in Jeremiah
with reference to the destruction of the Temple, all four times in these
two passages. It is only mentioned one other time in the whole book.
c. This link, together with the other link, is a strong argument for stating that Jer. 7:1-8:3 and Jer. 26 refer to the same occasion.

10. Be sure you include in your outline some reference to these two links.
For example, you may want to write in the column for Special Details the
words "Gate of the Lord's house" at Jer. 7:1-4 and "Court of the Lord's
house" at Jer. 26:1-6. And you may have mentioned Shiloh in your titles
for Jer. 7:8-15 and Jer. 26:1-6.

                        B. Jeremiah 7:1-8:3

As you work through this section, keep in mind the basic principle of Inductive Bible Study. As you answer the following questions, notice what kinds
of questions are being asked and why they are being asked. In the long run
these exercises will be useful for you only if you understand them as expressions of the inductive principle and learn to apply the inductive approach on your own.

1. Read over Jer. 7:1-4.

a. What is the main idea of the paragraph? _____

_____

b. What is your title? _____

You may copy this information from your outline.

2. Sometimes we don't realize the significance of the details of the text.
The significance may be obvious, or it may be hidden. One detail of obvious
significance in this paragraph is the fact that Jeremiah stood at the gate
of the Temple to deliver this message.

What is the significance of this fact? _____

*   _____   *

He preached to the public at a very prominent place.

3. A detail of less obvious significance is the reference to Jeremiah's
audience. Notice to whom Jeremiah addresses himself in Jer. 7:2 and notice
the parallel phrase in Jer. 26:2. Copy both phrases here.

a. _____

b. _____
*   *

a. Jer. 7:2 "All you men of Judah who enter these gates to worship the Lord."
b. Jer. 26:2 "All the cities of Judah which come to worship in the house of
the Lord."

4. Apparently this was a special occasion, a day on which Jeremiah could
speak to men from all over Judah. On what days did the people come from all

over Judah to worship at the Temple? _____
*   *

On the feast days.

5. If Jeremiah did in fact speak to the multitude on a feast day, it was a
very serious matter. As we have noted already, he made serious accusations
against his people. And his warnings were equally serious.

Look for further evidence that this was a special occasion.

Who, specifically, heard Jeremiah's Temple Sermon, according to Jer. 26? _____

*   _____   *

The priests, the prophets, and all the people. Jer. 26:7.

6. Another piece of information in Jer. 7:2 and Jer. 26:2 is very significant.

Why had these people come up to the Temple? _____

To worship the Lord.

7. This information helps us understand Jeremiah's situation. He declared
the word of the Lord to people who worshipped the Lord. But we also know
from this same passage and from many other passages that these people also
worshipped other gods.

a. Explain how Jeremiah's task was made easier by the fact that his people

did worship the Lord. _____

_____

_____

b. Explain how Jeremiah's task was made more difficult by the fact that his

people worshipped the Lord. _____

_____

_____

a. Since they did worship the Lord, they recognized the God of Jeremiah's
prophecy and His authority over their lives.
b. Since they worshipped the Lord, as well as other gods, they could say
that they were fulfilling His demands. They had compromised their allegiance to the Lord, and they were immunized against His full demands.

8. Think about this situation and compare it to our situation today. What

parallel do you see in our churches? _____

_____

_____

It seems to me that our situation is very similar. Our people do not practice pagan religions, but they do serve the gods of our society - money,
social position, education, etc. And they worship God on Sunday. And the
fact that they worship God is both an advantage and a disadvantage for the
preacher. He can speak God's word to them directly because they recognize
His authority in their lives. But their allegiance is compromised by their

other goals, and they are immunized against His complete demands.

9. In v. 3 Jeremiah calls on his people to amend their ways. Which para-

graphs of Jer. 7:1-8:3 describe their evil ways? _____
*   *

All of them.

10. In our previous study we have mentioned three different kinds of sin
which Judah practiced at the time of Jeremiah. List them.

a. _____

b. _____

c. _____
*   *

a. Idolatry.
b. Immoral social practices.
c. False political alliances.

11. Which of these kinds of sin are mentioned in Jer. 7:1-8:3? _____

* _____ *

Idolatry and immoral social practices.

12. Which of these kinds of sin are practiced by Christians today? _____

* _____ *

Idolatry and social evils are the most obvious. But perhaps we are also
guilty of false alliances with national and political structures.

13. V. 4 contains a very interesting concept. Apparently the people were
accustomed to chanting or repeating the phrase "the Temple of the Lord."
Consider carefully the situation and the context of this passage. Then ex-

plain why they repeated this phrase. _____

_____

* _____ *

Note that Jeremiah says "Do not <u>trust</u> in these deceptive words." Apparently
they believed that the Temple gave them protection. By repeating this phrase
they felt that they were safe from their enemies. The Lord would not allow

Jerusalem to be taken because He dwelt in the Temple. Remember this as you study v. 14.

14. The Temple was a fetish to the people of Jerusalem. It was a superstition. They believed it had power to protect them. But they did not obey the Lord.

Here again we see a close parallel to our situation today. List some fetishes or superstitions or deceptive practices among the members of our churches.

_____

_____

_____

_____

* _____ *

Some people today wear a cross on a chain or carry a New Testament as protection or good luck. Others believe that God will bless them if they say their prayers or attend church or read their Bible every day. These practices are not evil in themselves. But if we trust in these things rather than trusting in the Lord, we are deceived. And if we carry out these religious practices and do not obey God's commands, then we are fooling ourselves.

15. Read Jer. 7:5-7.

a. The main idea: _____

_____

b. Your title: _____

16. List the sins that are mentioned in this paragraph.

a. _____

b. _____

c. _____

* *

a. Oppress the alien, the fatherless, and the widow.
b. Shed innocent blood.
c. Go after other gods.

17. In Jer. 7:1-4 and 5-7 Jeremiah's message has a clear purpose. What is

it? _____

*   *

He is calling the people to repent, to return to the Lord, and to be saved.

18. What is the key phrase that expresses his purpose in both paragraphs? ____

_____

What phrase in Jer. 26 expresses the same idea? _____

*   *
_____

"Amend your ways and your doings."
"Every one turn from his evil way."

19. Ask yourself whether our preaching today has a clear and direct purpose
as did Jeremiah's preaching. We have said that people in our churches are
guilty of the same evils that plagued the people of Judah in Jeremiah's day.
So we should call them to repentance as he did. Give your own evaluation of

the purpose of preaching in our churches today. _____

_____

_____

_____

_____

20. Read Jer. 7:8-15.

a. Main idea: _____

_____

b. Title: _____

21. List the specific sins in this paragraph.

a. _____   d. _____

b. _____   e. _____

*   *
c. _____

Steal, murder, commit adultery, swear falsely, worship other gods.

22. Notice that the people of Judah were breaking several of the Ten Commandments, the most important law of the Old Testament. Turn to Exod. 20 and list briefly the Ten Commandments. Then check (✓) the ones Jeremiah mentions here as having been broken.

a. _____

b. _____

c. _____

d. _____

e. _____

f. _____

g. _____

h. _____

i. _____

* j. _____ *

Jeremiah mentions specifically the First, Third, Sixth, Seventh, Eighth, and Ninth Commandments and by implication the Second.

23. Study v. 10 carefully and explain it. _____

_____

* _____ *

You should have pointed out that this is the same concept we analyzed in Jer. 7:1-4. The people not only do evil but also continue worshipping the Lord. And they expect to be protected by the Lord.

24. What did the people put their confidence in, according to v. 10? _____

* _____ *

The Temple. They said "We are delivered." This is a confirmation of our interpretation of v. 4.

25. The phrase "a den of robbers" in v. 11 has become famous because of its use in the New Testament. Find the New Testament reference.

* _____ *

Mt. 21:13 / Mk. 11:17 / Lk. 19:46

26. The sense of this phrase in Jer. 7:11 is, however, slightly different
from its use in the New Testament.

Study Jer. 7:8-11 very carefully. Then analyze Jeremiah's use of the figure
of a den of robbers.

A robbers'den.	The Temple
Is where the robbers run to hide between crimes.	Is where the people run for protection between evil deeds.

27. Now turn to the New Testament use of this figure and explain how Jesus
used it. (Mt. 21:13; Mk. 11:17; Lk. 19:46)

A robbers' den.	The Temple
Is where they do their evil business and keep their loot.	Has been turned into a place of evil business.

Jesus' use of the figure is significantly different from Jeremiah's. This
is an indication that in Inductive Bible Study you should not only compare
similar and related passages but also study each passage carefully on its
own terms.

28. The most important detail in the paragraph Jer. 7:8-15 is the reference
to Shiloh. Investigate this name on your own and explain why Jeremiah used

it in this passage. _____

_____   _____

_____

_____   _____

_____   _____

* _____ *

Do not go on to the following questions until you have made a serious attempt to explain Jeremiah's reference to Shiloh. This is a difficult assignment but you can handle it on your own.

29. One procedure for figuring out the meaning of this reference is as follows:
First, notice what Jeremiah says about Shiloh. This will tell you what to
look for. Jeremiah mentions two things:

a. _____

b. _____
* *

a. The Lord dwelt there.
b. The Lord did something to Shiloh.

30. Second, look up in a concordance and in a Bible dictionary to find out
more about Shiloh.

a. When did the Lord dwell there? _____

_____

b. What happened to Shiloh? _____

_____

* _____ *

a. When the Israelites conquered the Promised Land, Joshua set up the Taber-
nacle at Shiloh.
b. According to 1 Sam. 4, the Israelites took the Ark of the Covenant out from Shiloh
against the Philistines, but they were defeated and 30,000 died.

31. There is a very important parallel between what happened at Shiloh in
1 Sam. 4 and what happened at Jerusalem in 587. Explain this parallel.

_____

_____

* _____ *

The Israelites believed that the Ark of the Covenant would save them, but
they were defeated (1 Sam. 4). The people of Judah believed that the Temple
would save them, but they were defeated in 587.

32. Read Jer. 7:16-20.

a. The main idea: _____

_____

b. A title: _____

33. As you study a passage, you should always keep in mind who is speaking
and to whom he is speaking.

a. Who is speaking in Jer. 7:16-20? _____

b. To whom? _____

*   *

a. The Lord
b. To Jeremiah

34. In this paragraph the Lord tells Jeremiah not to pray for his people
any more. This is a terrible commandment. Think what it meant for:

a. The Lord: _____

b. Jeremiah: _____

c. Judah: _____

*   *

a. The Lord was determined to punish Judah. It was useless to intercede for
her.
b. Jeremiah could no longer hope for deliverance for his people.
c. Judah was now sentenced to inevitable destruction.

35. Another interpretation of v. 16 is possible. Perhaps the Lord used this
expression to shock the people. He had pleaded with them year after year
with no response. They were accustomed to His pleas for repentance. Now He
speaks to them as if the door were already closed. According to this interpretation, what is the meaning of v. 16 for:

a. The Lord: _____

b. Jeremiah: _____

c. Judah: _____

*   *

a. The Lord has lost patience with Judah. They must respond now or suffer.
b. Jeremiah must announce for the last time that they will be punished if
they do not repent.
c. Judah must respond now for the Lord's wrath is about to strike.

36. What sin is pointed out in Jer. 7:16-20? _____

*   *

Idolatry

37. Read Jer. 7:21-26.

a. Main idea: _____

_____

b. A title: _____

38. In this paragraph the Lord, speaking to his people through Jeremiah,
seems to reject the sacrificial system. What does the Lord want from His

people? _____

* _____ *

Obedience to His commandments.

39. Apparently the Lord rejects burnt offerings and sacrifices altogether.
And yet there may be another interpretation of His words.

Remember the matter of the Temple, which we have just studied in Jer. 7:1-4
and 8-15.

a. What was the people's attitude toward the Temple? _____

_____

b. Was the Lord opposed to this attitude? _____

c. Did the Lord reject the Temple or worship in the Temple as such? _____

*   *

a. They used it as a fetish for their protection, but they were not obedient
to the Lord.
b. Yes.
c. No.

40. Now use this same reasoning to explain God's attitude toward sacrifices.

_____

_____

_____

_____

*   *

Your answer should include these points:
a. The people used the sacrifices as a fetish for their protection, but
they were not obedient to the Lord.
b. The Lord rejected this attitude.
c. But He did not necessarily reject the sacrificial system as such.

41. There is another problem in this paragraph. The Lord says that He did
not command the Israelites to offer sacrifices when He brought them out of
Egypt. Go back to the book of Exodus and see what the Lord told them.

What did the Lord command them, according to Exod. 13-14? _____

_____

*   *

He commanded them to remember their deliverance from Egypt by celebrating
each year the Feast of Unleavened Bread and the Passover with a sacrificial
lamb and by offering their first-born animals.

42. This problem is at least partially resolved if we accept the interpretation of #39 above. Certainly the Lord did not want His people to practice
a mere form of religion when He brought them out of Egypt. Why did He order

them to offer sacrifices? _____

_____

*   *

To remember that the Lord had delivered them and that they must obey Him.
He did not command them to trust in sacrifices as a fetish.

43. Read Jer. 7:27-29.

a. Main idea: _____

_____

b. Title: _____

44. Often you can find the meaning of a figure or a strange practice simply by reading the context.

What is the meaning of the expression in v. 29, "Cut off your hair and

cast it away?" _____
*   *

The context shows that it is a sign of lamentation.

45. Read Jer. 7:30-34.

a. Main idea: _____

_____

b. Title: _____

46. In this paragraph the Lord attacks their idolatrous practices. List three specific practices mentioned here.

a. _____

b. _____

c. _____
*   *

a. Apparently they set up pagan images in the Temple.
b. They built pagan altars at Topheth.
c. They even offered their children in sacrifice to these pagan gods.

47. These were an abomination to the Lord. We shudder at the thought of human sacrifice. And these were the chosen people of God.

Just as they committed terrible, evil deeds, so the Lord warned them of terrible judgment. List three specific results of this judgment.

a. _____

b. _____

c. _____
*   *

a. There will be great slaughter so that there is no room to bury all the bodies.
b. All the cities, including Jerusalem, will be silent.
c. The land will become a waste.

48. Locate the places named in this paragraph.

a. Topheth: _____

b. Valley of the Son of Hinnom: _____

They are both located on the south side of Jerusalem. The high place of Topheth is in the Valley of the Son of Hinnom.

49. Read Jer. 8:1-3.

a. Main idea: _____

_____

b. Title: _____

50. What terrible judgment is declared in this paragraph? _____

_____

_____

The bones of all Jerusalem, including the great, shall be desecrated and left out in the open.

51. There is a note of cynicism or irony in this judgment. It is a tragic recompense for their apostasy.

a. Whom had they wrongly worshipped? _____

_____

b. Before whom were their bones desecrated? _____

_____

a. The sun and the moon and all the host of heaven.
b. The sun and the moon and all the host of heaven.

52. We have not yet defined the limits of this section of Jeremiah. We have arbitrarily taken Jer. 7:1-8:3 as the object of study.

First, reflect on the study you have just made of these paragraphs to see if they belong together as a group or a section. Note and write down specific links between these paragraphs. Some have been mentioned already; others have not.

a. _____

_____

_____

b. _____

_____

_____

c. _____

_____

_____

d. _____

_____

_____

* _____ *

a. Both Jer. 7:1-4 and 5-7 use the expressions "Amend your ways and your
doings" and "I will let you dwell in this place."
b. The concept of false trust in the Temple is present in Jer. 7:1-4 and
8-15.
c. The concept of false trust in sacrifices in Jer. 7:21-26 is similar to
the concept of false trust in the Temple in 1-4 and 5-7.
d. The phrase is repeated in Jer. 7:8-15 and 21-26 and a variation in 27-29.
e. Idolatry is condemned in most of these paragraphs. The phrase "go after
other gods" is repeated in Jer. 7:5-7 and 8-15. Idolatrous practices are
described in Jer. 7:16-20, 30-34, and 8:1-3.

You probably did not find all the same links between these paragraphs. Perhaps you found some that I missed. The important thing is to sharpen your
observation and your imagination so that you can discover these kinds of
links between paragraphs.

53. We cannot say for sure that all of Jer. 7:1-8:3 was a single sermon.
Nevertheless this passage does show a unity.

Now we must indicate the limits of this section of the book.

a. Study the last verses of Jer. 6 and the first verses of Jer. 7 and indi-

cate why this is a dividing line. _____

_____

b. Study the verses following Jer. 8:1-3 and indicate why this is a dividing

line. _____

_____

_____

*   _____   *

a. The main ideas in the paragraphs of Jer. 6 are different from those of
Jer. 7. And Jer. 7:1-2 clearly introduces a new section.
b. The paragraphs following Jer. 8:1-3 are different in content. They are a
collection of different prophecies.

54. Mark off Jer. 7:1-8:3 in your outline.

a. Draw a dark line between Jer. 6:27-30 and Jer. 7:1-4 and another one
between Jer. 8:1-3 and Jer. 8:4-7.
b. Put a bracket around Jer. 7:1-8:3 and write "Temple Sermon" in the column for sections.

C. Jeremiah 26

Your assignment in this section is to do an Inductive Study of Jer. 26 on
your own. Study the passage paragraph by paragraph first. Then analyze the
overall structure and message. You may repeat some of the questions we used
in the previous section and also make comparisons between Jer. 26 and
Jer. 7:1-8:3.

Once again, let me point out the importance of practicing Inductive Bible
Study independently. You need to do this on your own in order to test your
ability and to gain confidence in Inductive Bible Study. You may never study
another course like this on the Old Testament prophets. So you need to
learn to study them on your own throughout your ministry.

On the following pages write down the key questions on each paragraph and
the answers to those questions. This will help you think through the steps
of investigation and interpretation of the text. It will also provide you
with the kind of material which you can use in a Bible class or Sunday
School class.

Jer. 26:1-6 _____

_____

_____

_____

_____

_____

_____

_____

_____

_____

_____

_____

_____

_____

_____

_____

_____

_____

_____

_____

_____

_____

_____

Jer. 26:7-9 _____

_____

_____

_____

_____

_____

_____

_____

_____

_____

_____

_____

Jer. 26:10-11 _____

_____

_____

_____

_____

_____

_____

_____

_____

_____

_____

Jer. 26:12-15 _____

_____

_____

_____

_____

_____

_____

_____

_____

_____

_____

Jer. 26:16-19 _____

_____

_____

_____

_____

_____

_____

_____

_____

_____

_____

_____

Jer. 26:20-23 _____

_____

_____

_____

_____

_____

_____

_____

_____

_____

_____

_____

Jer. 26:24 _____

_____

_____

_____

_____

_____

_____

_____

_____

_____

_____

Structure and Message _____

_____

_____

_____

_____

_____

_____

_____

_____

_____

_____

_____

_____

_____

_____

_____

_____

_____

_____

_____

_____

_____

_____

_____

_____

D. Jeremiah 26

Since you have already made an independent study of Jer. 26, this assignment will be quite simple. Work through the following questions rapidly.
But as you do so, compare your own questions with mine. Mark with an X any
points which you have overlooked. You do not have to ask the same questions,
but you should cover most of these points in some way. When you have finished
this section, note the number of points that you did not include in your own
Inductive Study of Jer. 26. If you omitted many of these points, this means
that you should be more careful and complete in the future. You have probably included some points which I have omitted. You may want to mark these
points in your Inductive Study of Jer. 26 and bring them up for discussion
in class.

1. Read <u>Jer. 26:1-6.</u>

a. What is the main idea of this paragraph? _____

_____

b. Choose a title of four words or less from the text itself. _____

*   *

a. The Lord threatens to destroy the Temple if they do not repent.
b. "This House Like Shiloh."

2. According to the information in this paragraph, when did Jeremiah preach

his Temple Sermon? _____
*   *

In the beginning of the reign of Jehoiakim.

3. If we assume that this means the first year of Jehoiakim, what year did

Jeremiah preach the Temple Sermon? _____ Consult your Chronological

Chart.
*   *

609 B.C.

4. Remember the historical events of this period.

a. What important battle took place in 609 B.C.? _____

b. What happened at that battle? _____

*   _____ _____   *

c. How did Jehoiakim become king of Judah? _____

* —— *

a. The Battle of Megiddo.
b. The Egyptians defeated Judah and King Josiah was killed.
c. He was put on the throne in place of his brother by Pharaoh Neco.

5. As we look at the Temple Sermon in the light of the historical background
of the book of Jeremiah, an interesting question comes to mind. Follow the
reasoning in these questions as you answer them. Consult 2 Kings and 2 Chron.
and use your concordance.

a. Was Josiah a good king or a bad king? _____

b. What was his attitude toward his people's apostasy? _____

_____

c. What did he do about the pagan worship in Judah? _____

_____

d. What did he do specifically to the high place of Topheth in the Valley

of the Sons of Hinnom? _____

e. Was Jehoiakim a good king or an evil one? _____

f. When did he begin his reign over Judah? _____

g. When did Jeremiah preach this sermon? _____

h. What evils did Jeremiah preach against in this sermon (Jer. 7:1-8:3)? _____

_____

i. What was going on at Topheth at the time Jeremiah preached this sermon? ___

* —— *

a. Good.
b. He tried to turn the people back to the Lord.
c. He purged Judah of its idolatrous practices.
d. He defiled it. (2 Kings 23:10)
e. Evil
f. 609 B.C.
g. 609 B.C.
h. Idolatry and injustice.
i. Apparently they were again practicing pagan worship (Jer. 7:31).

6. Jer. 26:1-7 contains the summary of a message which Jeremiah preached. Repeat here the arguments for saying that this is the same sermon which we find in Jer. 7:1-8:3.

a. _____

_____

b. _____

*   *

a. Both passages state that they were messages delivered at the entrance to the Temple.
b. Both contain a warning that the Temple will be made like Shiloh, which is a specific phrase repeated nowhere else.

7. Note two other significant similarities between Jer. 26:1-6 and Jer. 7:1-4.

a. _____

b. _____

*   *

There are at least three significant similarities.
a. Jeremiah speaks to men from all over Judah who have come to worship.
b. He calls them to repent and turn from their evil ways.
c. The Lord says He will withhold His judgment if they do repent.

8. On what occasion did Jeremiah preach this sermon? _____

*   *

We have noted that it was probably a feast day when people gathered at the Temple from all the cities of Judah.

9. What significance do you find in the fact that they had come to worship in the Temple?

a. _____

b. _____

*   *

See B. 7 above.

10. Notice that the Lord tells Jeremiah to speak "all the words that I command" and "do not hold back a word."

What is the significance of these expressions? _____

_____

* _____ *

They suggest that the message he was to give was very serious or harsh or
even dangerous and that Jeremiah might be tempted to soften it or leave
something out.

11. Do you think Jeremiah did in fact speak all that he was commanded to

speak? _____ What was the result according to Jer. 26? _____

* _____ *

Yes
They became angry and wanted to kill him.

12. Do we need to be reminded also in our preaching to speak all the words

that the Lord commands us? _____ Why? _____

* _____ *

I certainly think so, because we are tempted to withhold words of judgment
that might offend people or put us in danger of losing our jobs.

13. Explain the clause "I will make this house like Shiloh." _____

_____

_____

* _____ *

We studied this in B. 30, 31 above.

14. Read Jer. 26:7-9.

a. Main idea: _____

_____

b. Title: _____
*   *

a. The priests, prophets, and people threaten Jeremiah's life.
b. "Priests, Prophets, People"

15. Who heard Jeremiah's Temple Sermon? _____

* _____ *

The priests, prophets, and all the people.

16. What was their apparently unanimous reaction? _____

* _____ *

They became angry and wanted to kill Jeremiah.

17. What response had Jeremiah wanted them to give to his words? _____

* _____ *

To repent and turn from their evil ways.

18. Why did they respond so violently? Give a carefully reasoned explanation.

_____

_____

_____

* _____ *

Here are some reasons. You should have mentioned at least the third one.
a. They were offended because he accused them of evil doings.
b. They did not want to change their sinful ways.
c. They were threatened by his reference to the destruction of the Temple,
which they believed would protect them.

19. What happens today if a preacher offends his congregation? _____

_____

_____

* _____ *

This varies from one place to another. In many places they simply stop going
to hear him. In some places they stop giving their offerings. They may ask
him to leave or tell him to change his sermons.

We should note here that Jeremiah offended his people at the Lord's command. There are preachers who offend their congregations because of a lack of understanding of the Lord's message or of the people's needs or of their own role.

20. Read Jer. 26:10-11.

Main idea: _____

_____

Title: _____

*   *

a. The princes come up to hear the case.
b. "Princes of Judah."

21. Apparently Jeremiah is now being put on trial for his life. The next three paragraphs are the record of his trial.

a. Who are the judges? _____

b. Who are the prosecutors? _____

c. Who is the accused? _____

d. What is the charge? _____

e. What is the evidence? _____

f. What is the recommended sentence? _____

*   *

a. The princes.
b. The priests and the prophets.
c. Jeremiah.
d. He prophesied against the city.
e. All the people heard his sermon.
f. Death.

22. Once again we may ask why the priests and the prophets took such strong action against Jeremiah and how they could ask for the death penalty before the court of princes.

a. What did the Temple mean to them? _____

_____

b. What did Jeremiah say about the Temple? _____

_____

c. Would this be interpreted as false prophecy? _____ If so, what was

the penalty in those days for false prophecy (Deut. 18:20)? _____

a. To them the Temple signified God's eternal protection and presence.
b. He warned that it would be destroyed, that God would abandon it.
c. Yes, it could have been interpreted by them as false prophecy, which
merited the death penalty in those days.

23. Read Jer. 26:12-15.

a. Main idea: _____

_____

b. Title: _____

a. Jeremiah says the Lord sent him to speak thus.
b. "The Lord Sent Me."

24. Here Jeremiah makes his defense. He has only one argument. What is it?

_____

That the Lord sent him with the message he gave.

25. Remember that Jeremiah was on trial for his life. Remember, too, that
the Lord had told him to speak all that He commanded.

a. Who was against him? _____

b. What was the king's attitude toward idolatry? _____

_____

c. Did Jeremiah soften his message or leave anything out? _____

d. Did he try to avoid the accusation they made against him? _____

e. What does this show us about Jeremiah's character? _____

_____

This is a remarkable scene. The priests and the prophets and the people
were against Jeremiah. The king himself was a wicked king and encouraged
pagan idolatry. Yet Jeremiah repeated clearly and completely the message
the Lord had given him. He did not try to avoid their accusations. He was
a valiant, committed man.

26. List the main points of Jeremiah's message in v. 12-13.

a. _____

b. _____

c. _____

d. _____
*   *

a. The Lord has sent me.
b. To prophesy against this house (the Temple) and this city.
c. Amend your ways and obey the Lord.
d. So that the Lord will repent of the evil he has pronounced against you.

27. Now compare this list with Jeremiah's message in Jer. 26:1-6. Indicate

by letter the points which are found there. _____
*   *

a, b, c, d.

28. Underline in your text the words, "The Lord sent me." They appear in

this paragraph _____ times.
*   *

two

29. Read Jer. 26:16-19.

a. Main idea: _____

_____

b. Title: _____
*   *

a. The princes and certain elders defend Jeremiah.
b. "Micah Prophesied."

30. What argument did the princes and the people use in favor of Jeremiah?

_____

_____

They said that Jeremiah had spoken what the Lord told him to say and should
not be punished for that.

31. What argument did the elders use in favor of Jeremiah? _____

_____

* _____ *

They remembered the case of Micah as a precedent. He had done the same as
Jeremiah and he was not condemned.

32. What was the verdict of the court according to these arguments? _____

* _____ *

Not guilty.

33. Where in the Bible do we find the prophecies of Micah of Moresheth?

_____ Where do we find the words of Micah quoted by the

elders? _____
*   *

In the book of Micah.   Micah 3:12

34. Read Jer. 26:20-23.

a. Main idea: _____

_____

b. Title: _____
*   *
.— - -
a. The case of Uriah.
b. "Uriah Fled."

35. Consider the nature of this paragraph in relation to the rest of Jer. 26.

a. How does Uriah's case help the argument for Jeremiah? _____

b. How could it be used against Jeremiah? _____

*   *
a. It confirms Jeremiah's message--both Micah and Uriah had prophesied the
   same things against Jerusalem in the name of the Lord.

b. Uriah's execution was a precedent to execute Jeremiah for treason.

36. What promise must have come to Jeremiah's mind as his life hung in the
balance during the trial? _____

*   *
God's promise in Jer. 1:17-19 at the time of his commission. Read it.

37. What happened to Uriah is an interesting contrast to Jeremiah's experience. Notice the parallel between the two cases.

a. What did <u>Uriah</u> prophesy? _____

b. What was the reaction of the leaders? _____

c. What did he do when he was threatened? _____

d. What happened to him? _____

e. What did <u>Jeremiah</u> prophesy? _____

f. What was the reaction of the leaders? _____

g. What did he do when he was threatened? _____

h. What happened to him? _____
*   *

Uriah prophesied against Jerusalem. The leaders sought to kill him. He fled.
And he was killed.
Jeremiah prophesied against Jerusalem. The leaders sought to kill him. He
held his ground. And he was vindicated.

38. Does this mean that if we do not run from danger we will be vindicated,

like Jeremiah? _____

*   *
_____

Not necessarily. You should be careful of this kind of simplified application of Bible interpretation. Remember that many Christians have been un-
justly persecuted and killed.

39. Read <u>Jer. 26:24</u>.

a. Main idea: _____

_____

b. Title: _____
*   *

a. Jeremiah was saved by Ahikam.
b. "Ahikam with Jeremiah."

40. The dramatic episode of the Temple Sermon ends with this brief but significant note. Apparently the trial of Jeremiah was not decided until Ahikam the son of Shaphan intervened on his behalf.

Find out what you can about this man. _____

_____

_____

* _____ *

Check your concordance and Bible dictionary, if you have not done so already.

41. Now consider Jer. 26 as a whole. First, explain why the paragraphs of

Jer. 26 belong together. _____

* _____ *

They all deal with the same theme, the Temple Sermon and the trial of Jeremiah.

42. Now explain why Jer. 26 stands apart from the surrounding material as

a separate section of the book of Jeremiah. _____

_____

_____

_____

* _____ *

You should have pointed out the following:
a. Jer. 26:1 begins a section; it is an introduction setting of Jer. 26
from the previous chapter.
b. Jer. 27:1 begins another section; it is another introduction setting
off Jer. 27 from Jer. 26.

43. Apparently these chapters relate incidents from the life of Jeremiah.
Each incident has a brief introduction telling when it took place.

a. Jer. 25 took place in the year _____ B.C.

b. Jer. 26 took place in the year _____ B.C.

c. Jer. 27 took place in the year _____ B.C.

*   *

You should have been able to find this information easily on your Chronological Chart: a. 605   b. 609   c. 598

44. This information gives us an important clue to the overall structure
of the book of Jeremiah. Later when we study this part of the book we will
have to investigate this line further. Explain what this clue is.

_____

_____

_____

* _____ *

You should have noted the following:
a. These sections of the book tell incidents from the life of Jeremiah.
b. They are set off by brief introductions telling when they took place.
c. They are not in chronological order.

45. The structure of this part of the book of Jeremiah is different, then,
from the structure in Jer. 2-6.

a. Jer. 2-6 contains _____.

b. How is this material organized? _____

c. Jer. 26, 27, etc. contains _____.

d. How is this material organized? _____

* _____ *

a. Collections of prophecies.
b. By topics or themes.
c. Incidents from the life of Jeremiah.
d. By brief introductions which identify when they took place. Non-chrono-
logical order.

46. Finally, write a summary of Jer. 26. Just write one sentence for each
paragraph. But write your analysis as a drama. Each paragraph represents a
scene.

"The Temple Sermon Episode"

a. Jer. 26:1-6   _____

b. Jer. 26:7-9   _____

c. Jer. 26:10-11 _____

d. Jer. 26:12-15 _____

e. Jer. 26:16-19 _____

f. Jer. 26:20-23 _____

g. Jer. 26:24   _____

This and other passages from Jeremiah could be used as plays for the Sunday
School, the youth program, and the congregation.

47. Put on your Chronological Chart a reference to the Temple Sermon. Use
the line for Jeremiah's ministry.

a. At 609 draw a small vertical line.
b. Below the line write "Temple Sermon."
c. Below the title put the references: Jer. 7:1-8:3, Jer. 26.

                        E. Test (Micah 6:1-8)

Your primary objective in this course is to learn how to study the Old Testament prophets inductively. You have been studying primarily Jeremiah. But
it is important to see if you can apply the inductive approach to the other
prophetical books.

In this section you will test your ability to study inductively a passage
from another Old Testament prophet. You will carry out this study entirely
on your own, although you should follow the steps and methods we have been
using in our study of Jeremiah.

The passage is Micah 6:1-8. It is brief, so you should be able to work out
your Inductive Study in four or five pages. It is a very famous passage,
so you will want to use it in your preaching. Be sure to put down all the
significant steps you take as well as the results of your investigation.
See if you can complete this assignment in one hour.

This is a test. You may be asked to turn in your work. Or you may be given
a quiz over this passage. The important thing is to see if you can do Inductive Bible Study on your own. Use notebook paper.

8

Sermon Outline

Preparing sermon outlines is one of the most frequent tasks you have to perform if you are a leader in the church. And, it is one of your most important responsibilities.

The book of Jeremiah contains many excellent texts for sermons. The more you study this book, the more you will want to preach from it. And Inductive Bible Study provides you with the materials for sermon preparation.

Therefore we will give some time in this course to the preparation of sermon outlines based on the Inductive Study of Jeremiah. In this lesson you will prepare several outlines based on passages in Jeremiah that we have already studied. As you work through the rest of this course you will want to identify other passages for sermon outlines. And in the future you will want to continue your Inductive Study of Jeremiah so that you can prepare other sermons based on this book. This will be one of the biggest rewards you gain from this course.

This is not, however, a course in homiletics. So we will not make an extensive study of sermon preparation here. We will suggest some simple steps in preparing a sermon outline based on Inductive Bible Study.

Your objectives in this lesson are to:

Follow a simple procedure for sermon outline preparation.

Write sermon outlines based on four passages of Jeremiah.

Practice using sermon outline forms.

Start a file or a notebook of sermon outlines using these forms.

A. Jeremiah 1:4-10

There are several steps in preparing a sermon outline. These steps can be defined in different ways. And they do not need to follow the same order all the time.

In this section you will prepare a sermon outline based on Jer. 1:4-10, a passage which we have already studied in detail. You will go through several steps in order to prepare this outline. In this way you will begin to learn the steps for sermon outline preparation. In other words, you will learn by doing.

1. The first step in sermon preparation is to choose a text. You may be studying through a book like Jeremiah. And you may want to find an appropriate message from that book for a sermon. Or, as you work through the book you may want to mark a number of passages for use later on.

You may be concerned about certain specific needs that arise in your congregation. And you may want to find passages that will help you respond to
those needs in your preaching.

The first step in sermon preparation is _____.

*   *

to choose a text

2. There are at least three things to look for as you choose a text.

> 1. It should have an important application to the life of your
>   congregation.
> 2. It should be interesting.
> 3. It should be a manageable unit.

As you choose a text for a sermon you will want to see if it has three general characteristics. Consider Jeremiah 1:1-3, for example, and see if it
would be useful as a sermon text.

a. Does Jer. 1:1-3 have some practical lessons for the members of your con-

gregation? _____

b. Is it interesting? _____

c. Could you handle it in the 20 minutes of a sermon? _____

*   *

a. I don't see any application or lesson.
b. It is interesting for the study of Jeremiah, but as a text for a sermon
it might be very uninteresting.
c. The passage is not very long, but it would be difficult to handle without rather long explanations.

3. Now look at Jer. 1:4-10 and see if it would be useful as a sermon text.

a. Is it applicable to the life of your congregation? _____

b. Is it interesting? _____

c. Is it a manageable unit? _____

*   *

a.b.c. I would answer all three questions "Yes." This passage contains a
very important lesson for Christians today. It is very interesting, even
dramatic. And it could be handled in a sermon, although it might not be
easy to cover all the information in the passage.

4. The second step in the preparation of a sermon outline is to state the
purpose of your sermon. A sermon should do something for the congregation.
It may teach them a doctrine or a lesson on how to live, challenge them to

repent of sin and accept Christ, encourage them in times of difficulty, etc.
You should prepare each sermon with a definite purpose in mind.

a. The first step in sermon preparation is _____.

b. The second step is _____.

*   *

a. To choose a text.
b. To state the purpose of your sermon.

5. The purpose for your sermon should have these three characteristics.

> 1. It should be similar to the purpose expressed in the text.
> 2. It should be personal.
> 3. It should be clear and definite.

In Inductive Bible Study we always try to study the text on its own terms.
The purpose for a sermon should, therefore, be similar to the purpose expressed in the text. If the passage tells the story of Paul's conversion,
your purpose may be to invite others to be converted. If it is one of Jesus'
teachings on discipleship, your purpose may be to teach your members how to
be true disciples.

What is God's purpose in Jer. 1:4-10? _____

* _____ *

God's purpose is to call Jeremiah to be His prophet to the nations.

6. The purpose of a sermon should also have something to do with the lives
of the people who hear it. It should be personal. For example, if you preach
about the call of Jeremiah you should find some definite application of that
experience for your audience. They should know what it means for their own
lives.

What challenge does Jer. 1:4-10 have for the members of your congregation?

_____

* _____ *

You may find in this passage a challenge to your members to be God's witnesses in the world today. Or you may prefer to use the passage as a challenge
to certain individuals to go into the ministry, to become pastors and evan-
gelists.

7. Finally, the purpose of a sermon should be clear and definite. Our preaching is very often general and vague. We talk about the doctrines of the Bible,
the Christian faith, the Gospel. We give people a sense of challenge or inspi-

ration. But too often our efforts are lost because we do not bring our people to decision and action. At the end of a sermon each person should know
what to do in response to what you have said.

After hearing your sermon on Jer. 1:4-10 what should your members do? _____

_____

*   _____   *

If your purpose is to challenge the members to be God's witnesses, then after hearing your sermon they should decide to be God's witnesses and begin
to witness. If your purpose is to present the call for pastors and evange-
lists, then those who feel called should decide to enter the ministry and
begin to prepare themselves.

8. Write down the purpose for your sermon based on Jer. 1:4-10. Be sure your
purpose is similar to the purpose expressed in the text, personal and clear

and definite. _____

_____

_____

9. The third step in the preparation of a sermon outline is to write a summary of the content of the passage. This means that you should study the
passage inductively and underline all the main ideas. Then write out a brief
resumé of these ideas. This is not the outline for the sermon, but it will
help you later in the preparation of an outline.

Since we have already made an Inductive Study of Jer. 1:4-10, we have already looked at the major ideas in this passage. Write them down here verse
by verse.

a. v. 4   Introduction _____

b. v. 5   _____

c. v. 6   _____

d. v. 7-8   _____

e. v. 9-10   _____

If you would like to check your analysis, go back to Lesson II, B, 4 above.

10. This list of major ideas verse by verse will serve as your summary of
the passage. A summary should have these qualities.

> 1. It should be complete.
> 2. It should be in order.
> 3. It should be brief.

Is your summary complete, in order, and brief? _____

11. <u>The fourth step in the preparation of a sermon outline is to give your</u> <u>sermon a title.</u> Many preachers do not give titles to their sermons. But titles can be very useful. They arouse interest in the sermon, especially if
they are announced in advance. And you as a preacher will want your people
to look forward to your sermons with interest and expectation.

What is the purpose of sermon titles? _____

To arouse interest in the sermon.

12. A sermon title should have these characteristics.

> 1. It should represent the content of the sermon.
> 2. It should be attractive.
> 3. It should be concise.

It may take some practice before you are able to find sermon titles that
are representative, attractive, and concise. Work at it, but don't use too
much time looking for catchy phrases.

One source of sermon titles is the text itself. For example, in Jer. 1:4-10,
we could use one of these phrases: "I Appointed You," or "I Send You" or "My
Words in Your Mouth" or "Set over Nations."

Pick one of these phrases or another one for the title of your sermon. _____

_____

13. Before we go on to the next step, list the four steps in preparing a
sermon outline that we have mentioned so far.

a. _____

b. _____

c. _____

d. _____

a. Choose a text.
b. State the purpose of your sermon.
c. Write a summary of the content of the passage.
d. Give the sermon a title.

14. <u>The fifth step is to make the outline itself</u>. This is usually the hard-
est part. But if you have gone through the other steps carefully, much of
the work is done already. It is especially important to keep in mind the
purpose of the sermon. The summary may provide you with an outline, although
you may have to omit some of the ideas presented in the text because the
time for a sermon is very short.

The fifth step in preparing a sermon outline is _____.
*   *

To make the outline itself.

15. There are many different kinds of sermon outlines. But we cannot study
them here. If you have made an Inductive Study of the passage you can usually base your outline on the text. Just follow the main ideas of the passage verse by verse. These become the main points in your outline.

According to our analysis, Jer. 1:4-10 is divided into _____ parts. But the

first one is an introduction so we can omit it. Then our outline will have

just _____main points.
*   *

five   four

16. List the four main points of your outline. Use the same points as you
used in #9 above, omitting the first one. You may also omit the references.
Write the main points without using Jeremiah's name.

I.   _____

II.   _____

III. _____

IV.   _____
*   *

Your outline should read something like this.
I.   The Lord Calls a Man.
II. He Responds, Hesitating.
III. The Lord Repeats His Call.
IV. The Ordination of the Prophet.

17. A sermon not only presents the content of a Bible passage. It also in-
terprets the meaning of the passage for us today. Both aspects can appear
in your outline. One way to complete your outline is to put two sub-points
under each main point. Let the first sub-point in each case refer to Jeremiah, and the other sub-point refer to ourselves.

Complete the following outline, using the system we have just described. The main points are the ones you have just written above.

Be sure each sub-point A refers to Jeremiah and each sub-point B refers to us today. If your purpose is to challenge the members of your church to be God's witnesses in the world today, then make this clear in your outline. If your purpose is to present the call to the ministry, make this clear. (You wrote your statement of purpose in #8 above.)

I. The Lord Calls a Man

    A. The Call of Jeremiah

    B. Our Call to be God's Witnesses (or, The Call to the Ministry)

II. _____

    A. _____

    B. _____

III. _____

    A. _____

    B. _____

IV. _____

    A. _____

    B. _____

18. Remember that the sermon outline is not the same thing as the outline of the text. It may not even follow the same order as the outline of the text. But it should be an exposition of the text.

The important thing is to have some kind of order. When you study a text like Jer. 10:1-16 you find that there is a lot of repetition in the text. But you can gather all of the ideas in the text under two main points, "The False Gods" and "The True God." These two main points do not follow the order of the text, but they are a true expression of the message of the text.

Express in your own words what a sermon outline should have.

    1. _____

    2. _____

    3. _____

I think a sermon outline should have these qualities:

> 1. It should have some kind of order.
> 2. It should express the content of the text.
> 3. It should apply that message to our lives.

19. <u>The sixth and final step in the preparation of a sermon outline is to write out the introduction and conclusion of the sermon.</u> It is a good idea to write out in greater detail these two points in your outline because you want to be very careful what you say at the beginning and at the end of your sermon.

One striking way to begin a sermon based on Jer. 1:4-10 is to mention the critical times in which Jeremiah lived and to state the great significance of the fact that the Lord's word came to Jeremiah calling him to be His prophet to the nations. Then it is easy to draw a parallel to our own critical times and to ask whom does God call to be His prophets to the nations today.

In the conclusion you should present the challenge of your sermon directly to the congregation. As we have noted earlier, you may challenge them to be the Lord's witnesses in today's world. Or you may ask who will respond to the call to the ministry.

There are, of course, many other ways of writing introductions and conclusions. Sometimes an illustration is very useful because it is interesting and dramatizes the purpose of the sermon. Sometimes an example or an immediate application of the content of the sermon helps the people see what it can mean in their lives. Or perhaps a quotation or a poem will provide an incisive statement of your message.

Try to put down three qualities that introductions and conclusions should have.

1. _____

2. _____

3. _____

*   *

I would say that sermon introductions and conclusions should have these qualities:

> 1. They should arouse interest in the topic of the sermon.
> 2. They should focus attention on the purpose of the sermon.
> 3. They should relate the sermon to the lives of the listeners.

20. The sixth and final step in the preparation of a sermon outline is _____

* _____. *

To write the introduction and conclusion.

21. Write a brief introduction for your sermon based on Jer. 1:4-10. _____

_____

_____

_____

_____

_____

_____

22. Write a brief conclusion. _____

_____

_____

_____

_____

_____

23. List the six steps in the preparation of a sermon outline which we have suggested.

a. _____

b. _____

c. _____

d. _____

e. _____

f. _____

24. In the Appendix (page A.4) find the sermon outline for Jer. 1:4-10.
It includes the six steps which you have studied. (Also look at page A.3
which reviews the six steps for you). Fill in the form with the material
you have prepared for a sermon based on Jer. 1:4-10. Just go back to #8, 9,
12, 17, 20 and 21 and copy what you have already written in the spaces pro-
vided in the form.

B. Jeremiah 2:12-13

In this section you will prepare another sermon outline based on another
passage which you have already analyzed. This time you will be able to go
through the steps for outline preparation with fewer explanations. And as
you gain more practice, you will find that the procedure we have suggested
is very easy to follow and very useful for your ministry.

1. <u>The first step is to choose a text.</u> The text I have chosen is Jer. 2:12-
13. Read it over and see if it has the qualities of a good sermon text.

a. Does it have an important application to the life of your congregation?

_____

b. Is it interesting? _____

c. Is it a manageable unit? _____

2. How would you apply this text to the life of your congregation? _____

_____

_____

_____

_____

* _____ *

You will have to answer this question on your own. I don't know your congregation. But let me ask you one or two suggestions. Isn't it true that
most Christians are tempted to turn to worldly concerns for their deepest
satisfactions in life? Aren't we all caught up by economic and social pres-
sures to the extent that our faith is only a small part of our life? Do we
really believe that God is the fountain of living water and that these
other concerns are only empty cisterns?

I think idolatry is very much present among the people of God today. And
our people need to be reminded of the futility of these broken cisterns
and of the abundance of God's living waters.

3. The second step is to state the purpose of your sermon. Think over the message of Jeremiah's literary figure, and state what will be the purpose

of your sermon. _____

_____

* _____ *

My statement would be something like what I wrote for #2 above. This sermon should remind the people of the futility of looking to worldly concerns for their satisfaction in life. It should call them back to the living God.

4. Check your statement of purpose to see if it has the characteristics we have recommended.

a. Is it similar to the purpose expressed in the text? _____

b. Is it personal? _____

c. Is it clear and definite? _____

5. Perhaps you are uncertain about your statement of purpose. Take each one of the questions in #4 separately. Is the purpose of your sermon similar to the purpose expressed in the text? In order to answer this question you have to find out what was the original purpose of the text. Why did the

Lord speak these words through Jeremiah to the people of Judah? _____

_____

* _____ *

In order to show them the futility of their apostasy and to turn them back to Himself. In other words it is a call to repentance.

6. If necessary restate the purpose of your sermon so it is more closely

related to Jeremiah's purpose. _____

_____

_____

7. The second question regarding purpose is: Is it personal? Think for a moment about the people in your congregation. Go over in your mind some of the names and faces. And ask yourself what are the ideals, the ambitions, the goals that dominate their lives. Is the Lord God really their only God? What other gods do they have?

List some broken cisterns (idols) that these people might be tempted to

trust in. _____

_____

_____

8. The third question about your purpose is: Is it clear and definite? Be
sure your listeners know what you mean. Be sure you know what you are talking about. In other words state your purpose in specific terms.

Ask yourself, "What are the gods I am tempted to serve in my daily life?"
Did you answer #7 in specific terms? Or did you write in broad generali- ?
zations? Some people worship and dedicate their lives to social and economic advantages. Specifically we might mention job security, salary increase, material possessions, status in the community, etc.

Write down once again the specific idols that tend to dominate the lives

of the people in your congregation. _____

_____

_____

9. Now try stating what your listeners should do in response to your sermon.
This may be difficult to say in specific terms. Jeremiah could tell his people to abandon their images and worship the Lord only. Our people have more
subtle idols. They have made idols out of things that are essential to their
lives: family, home, job. And our society constantly builds up idols for
us: youth, physical attractiveness, material possessions.

What should your listeners do about these idols? _____

_____

_____

_____

_____

*   *

They cannot abandon family, house, job, or material possessions. But they
can examine their lives, find out what things have become idols, confess
their apostasy, and put all these things in God's hands. Instead of pursu-
ing these goals selfishly they can use these things to serve God and neigh-
bor. Rather than worship these gods that do not satisfy they can worship
the true God and find real peace and love and meaning in life.

10. Restate the purpose of your sermon in final form taking into account

#3-9. _____

_____

_____

11. The third step is to write a summary of the content of the passage. First
you should study the passage. We have already studied Jer. 2:12-13 in a
previous lesson. But repeat your analysis of the literary figure in v. 13.

Remember that this is a combination of two figures, the fountain and the
cisterns. Check your analysis with Lesson V. B, 16.

12. Write a summary of Jer. 2:12-13. _____

_____

_____

* _____ *

You should have divided the text into three points:
a. This is an appalling situation.
b. The Lord's people have forsaken Him.
c. And they have made their own gods.

13. Check your summary by answering these questions.

a. Is it complete? _____

b. Is it in order? _____

c. Is it brief? _____

14. The outline or summary I have written at #10 has three points. But it
has really just two main points. What are they?

a. _____

b. _____
*   *

Leave out the first point listed at #10 above because it is only an introduction to the two main ideas. When you write your summary of the text on
the sermon outline form you should include all three points. But when you
make your sermon outline you may leave out the first point.

15. <u>The fourth step is to give your sermon a title</u>. Read over the text and
see if you can find a phrase that might make a good title for your sermon.

* _____   *

I like the phrase "Broken Cisterns."

16. Now see if you can make up a better title using your own words. _____

* _____   *

Here is a title which merely changes the wording of the text: "They Don't
Hold Water." Another possibility: "The Case of the Broken Cisterns."

17. Check each of the titles you have just written down.

a. Does it represent the content of the sermon? _____

b. Is it attractive? _____

c. Is it concise? _____

"Concise" means terse, succinct, laconic, pithy. Your title should say a
lot in a very few words.

18. Now decide which title from all those mentioned best suits your sermon.

_____

19. <u>The fifth step is to make the outline itself</u>. Write out your sermon outline. Use the two main points from your summary of the content of the passage as the two main points of your outline. Then add two sub-divisions for
each of the main points, one for Jeremiah's time and the other for your
situation.

I. _____

   A. _____

   B. _____

II. _____

    A. _____

    B. _____

Your outline should look something like this:
I. God's People Have Forsaken Him, the Fountain of Living Water
    A. In Jeremiah's Time
    B. In Our Time
II. They Have Hewed Out Broken Cisterns That Hold No Water
    A. In Jeremiah's Time
    B. In Our Time

20. Check over your outline to see if it has the characteristics we have
recommended.

a. Does it have some kind of order? _____

b. Does it express the message of the text? _____

c. Does it apply that message to our lives? _____

21. The sixth step is to write out the introduction and conclusion of the
sermon. This is the final step. You have a clear and definite purpose in
mind. You have studied the text. You have worked out your sermon outline.
Now decide how you will introduce your sermon and how you will conclude it.

First, write out a brief introduction. _____

_____

_____   _____

_____

_____

_____

_____

Here is a sample. You should not use my introduction. But it may give you
some ideas for another sermon introduction.

The Prophet Jeremiah faced a terrible situation. His people, the people of
God, had fallen into idolatry. They were worshipping pagan idols. So he
spoke these words: Jer. 2:12-13. Perhaps it is time for you and me to take
stock of our lives, to see what are our primary goals and ideas, and to root
out the pagan gods of our day.

22. Now write out a brief conclusion. _____

_____

_____

_____

_____

_____

* _____ *

Here again is a sample.

What a foolish thing it would be to try to find water in broken, man-made
cisterns when a natural artesian well is available. What a foolish thing
it was to worship pagan idols when the Lord God had established a covenant with His people. What a foolish thing it is to give your life to the
pursuit of social prestige or financial security, when God Himself calls
you to His service. In these final moments look within and look to Him.
Turn to the fountain of living waters.

23. Check over your introduction and conclusion to see if they have the following qualities.

a. Do they arouse interest in the topic of the sermon? _____

b. Do they focus attention on the purpose of the sermon? _____

c. Do they relate the sermon to the lives of the listeners? _____

24. Now fill out the sermon outline form for Jer. 2:12-13 (page A.5 of the
Appendix) with the information you have just prepared. Copy the material
at #10, 12, 18, 19, 21, 22. Some of this material, particularly the introduction and conclusion, may have to be shortened in order to fit on the
form.

C. Jeremiah 5:22-23

Now you are ready to prepare a sermon outline on your own. All you need to
do is go through the steps we have been using. In the Appendix you will
find "Steps for Preparing Sermon Outlines" (page A.3). It lists the questions you should ask yourself at each step.

The text for this sermon outline is similar to the one we have just used.
It contains an interesting literary figure. And it is a passage that we
studied in an earlier lesson. In your interpretation of Jer. 5:22-23 you

should take into account v. 24-29. Note that the main idea of this passage
is different from the main idea of Jer. 2:12-13. If you want to review your
previous study of Jer. 5:20-29 see Lesson VI, A, 29-34.

Use notebook paper. Go through the steps for preparing the sermon outline.
Then fill in the sermon outline form for Jer. 5:22-23 on page A.6 of the
Appendix as you did for Jer. 1:4-10 and Jer. 2:12-13.

You may be asked to turn in this sermon outline or discuss it at your next
class session.

D. Jeremiah 26 and 7:1-8:3

This time we will take a different kind of passage and go through the steps
for preparing a sermon outline. We just studied Jer. 26 and Jer. 7:1-8:3, so
we are familiar with the content of the text. And we have noted some important applications of these passages for our own situation.

1. The first step is to choose a text. We want a text that has certain
characteristics. What are they?

a. _____

b. _____

c. _____

*   *

See the page entitled "Steps for Preparing Sermon Outlines" on page A.3
of the Appendix.

2. Which of these three characteristics seems to be lacking in the texts we

have chosen for this sermon? _____

*   *

They don't seem to be a manageable unit. They are much too long.

3. First, see if these passages have an important application to the life

of your congregation. What application do you see? _____

_____

_____

_____

*   *

It seems to me that we today need to hear Jeremiah's warning. Our people
worship the Lord in our churches on Sunday but do not obey His commandments during the week.

4. Second, see if the passages we have chosen are interesting. Give your

evaluation. _____

_____

* _____ *

I think that these passages are very interesting, even dramatic. They describe an exciting episode in the life of Jeremiah. They tell how he was
put on trial for his life, because he preached God's word.

5. Third, see if these passages are a manageable unit. We have already said
that Jer. 26 and 7:1-8:3 are much too long. So we will have to find a way
to shorten the text. One way to shorten the text is to find the essential
elements.

One essential element is Jeremiah's condemnation of the popular concept of

the Temple. What paragraphs present this element? _____

*   *

Jer. 7:1-4 and 8-15. We should probably include all of Jer. 7:1-15.

6. Another essential element is the dramatic story of Jeremiah's trial. What

paragraphs present this element? _____

*   *

All of Jer. 26, with the possible exception of Jer. 26:20-23.

7. We have now narrowed our text down to Jer. 7:1-15 and Jer. 26:1-19, 24.
This is much shorter than what we started with. But it is still very long.
We could not cover all the ideas in all these paragraphs in a sermon.

One way to handle a long text like this is to concentrate on just one part
of it. In this case, for example, we can use Jer. 26 as background.

Our primary text, then, will be _____.

*   *

Jer. 7:1-15.

8. The second step is to state the purpose of your sermon. What characteristics should your statement of purpose have?

a. _____

b. _____

c. _____

*   *

See the page entitled "Steps for Preparing Sermon Outlines." (Page A.3 of
the Appendix)

9. State the purpose of Jeremiah's Temple Sermon. _____

_____

_____

_____

* _____ *

His purpose was to call his people to repentance and obedience. More specifically he wanted to expose their false pretense of worship and their false
confidence in the Temple. He wanted to show them that God demanded their
allegiance and obedience, not a form of religious piety.

10. Now state the purpose of your sermon based on Jer. 26 and 7:1-15.

_____

_____

_____

* _____ *

Your purpose should be based on Jeremiah's purpose. But it should be stated
in terms of your congregation. It should be personal, clear, and definite.
What do you want to tell them to do?

11. The third step is to write a summary of the content of the passage. What
characteristics should this summary have?

a. _____

b. _____

c. _____

* _____ *

See the "Steps for Preparing Sermon Outlines."

12. Write a summary of the main ideas in Jer. 7:1-4 and 8-15. Make it as
brief as you can, but put down more than one statement for each paragraph.

Be sure to include the references to the Temple. _____

_____

_____

_____

_____

_____

_____

_____

13. A summary of Jer. 26:1-19, 24 would be too long to include in your sermon outline form. In any case you only want to use this passage as background for your sermon. And you already have a summary of what happened in

Jer. 26:1-19, 24. Where is this summary? _____

* _____ *

In your outline of the book of Jeremiah. The titles and main ideas of the
paragraphs give a good summary of Jeremiah's sermon and trial. When you
write sermon outlines based on this book in the future, be sure to look
at your outline first. And if you have not yet done so, fill in the main
idea and a title for each paragraph.

14. The fourth step is to give your sermon a title. What characteristics
should a sermon title have?

a. _____

b. _____

c. _____

15. Write a title for your sermon. _____

_____

16. The fifth step is to make the outline itself. You may want to tell the
story of Jer. 26:1-19, 24 as the first main point of your sermon. Or you
may want to do this in the introduction. The other main points based on
Jer. 7:1-15 should, however, deal with the concept of Temple worship. The
points in your outline do not have to be in the same order as the text. And
you may include ideas that are not mentioned in the text but are implied
by the text. For example, consider what was the original purpose of the
Temple. Be sure to include in your outline an application of the main points
to the people in your congregation.

_____

_____

_____

_____

_____

_____

_____

_____

_____

*   *
_____

Your outline should probably include these three points, although you may
have them in a different order. Or you may use these ideas in a different
way.
a. The true purpose of the Temple (the covenant).
b. The false use of the Temple (apostasy).
c. The warning about the Temple (Shiloh).
Each of these points has an interesting and important application to our
churches today.

17. The sixth step is to write out the introduction and conclusion of the
sermon. What characteristics should the introduction and conclusion have?

a. _____

b. _____

c. _____

18. Write out an introduction for your sermon. You will want to relate
Jeremiah's Temple Sermon to your church. But you do not need to compare
the Temple with our church buildings. As have noted already, this passage
deals with worship. It gives us an insight into the nature of true reli-

gion. _____

_____

_____

_____

---

19. Write out a conclusion for your sermon. Remember that Jeremiah had a
very definite purpose for his sermon and that you have written out a specific purpose for your sermon. Your conclusion should call the people to a

definite, specific response. _____

---

20. Now fill in the sermon outline form for Jer. 7:1-15 on page A.7 in the
Appendix. You may just copy the points you have worked out in this section.
Or you may want to make some changes.

E. Conclusion

You have worked hard in this lesson. You have prepared four sermon outlines
based on four passages from the book of Jeremiah. Therefore this last section will be very brief. But if you have not completed any of the other
sections of this lesson, you should go back and do so now.

Start a looseleaf notebook of sermon outlines based on the book of Jeremiah.
You can begin with the four outlines you prepared in this lesson. And include "Steps for Preparing Sermon Outlines" in your notebook. (Pages A.3
to A.7 in your Appendix) You will be asked to prepare more outlines later
in the course. And you will want to have these outlines accessible for
preaching. You may be asked to turn in your notebook at the next class
session and at the end of the course. Prepare additional sermon outline
forms as you need them in the future.

Include in your notebook some of the other materials you have prepared in
this course:

    a. Political Map of the Time of Jeremiah.
    b. Chronological Chart of the Time of Jeremiah.
    c. Outline of the Book of Jeremiah.

These materials will be useful when you want to preach a sermon or teach
a lesson based on Jeremiah. They are found in the appendix to this book.
Include also studies you are asked to do in future lessons.

Let me make one more clarification about the Steps for Preparing Sermon
Outlines and the sermon outline form. You are not required to memorize the
steps we have suggested in this lesson. And you do not have to learn the
three characteristics for each step. But you should be able to use these
steps and the sermon outline form. And you should be systematic in your
sermon preparation.

In this lesson you have learned a simple system for preparing sermon outlines. There are, of course, many other ways of preparing sermon outlines.
And I hope you will develop your own system using the steps that are most
effective for you. Perhaps you will some day want to develop a new list
of Steps for Preparing Sermon Outlines to replace the one we have used in
this lesson. And you may want to work out new sermon outline forms.

Whenever you prepare a sermon outline you should remember the inductive
principles. Begin with the Bible and study it on its own terms. Don't just
copy someone else's outline or use someone else's interpretation of the
text. And don't force the text to fit your system of sermon outline preparation. Make your system fit the text. And make your outlines be a true
analysis of the ideas presented in the text.

9

Jeremiah's Acted Parables

One of the fascinating aspects of Jeremiah's ministry is his use of acted
parables. We have studied Jeremiah's use of literary figures, which made his
message so clear and powerful. Now we will study three passages in which he
dramatizes his message through symbolic action.

Your objectives in this lesson are to:

Interpret three of Jeremiah's acted parables.

Prepare a sermon outline based on Jer. 13:1-11.

Summarize Jeremiah's message in these acted parables.

Test your ability to study independently.

A. The Linen Waistcloth Episode (Jeremiah 13:1-11)

In this section you will make an Inductive Study of Jer. 13:1-11. In the
following section you will prepare a sermon outline based on this passage.
So it is doubly important for you to study this passage carefully.

1. Read through Jer. 13:1-7.

a. What is the main idea of this paragraph? _____

_____

b. Choose a title for the paragraph, using four words or less from the text.

_____

Put this information in your outline of the book of Jeremiah.

2. Read Jer. 13:8-11.

a. Main idea: _____

_____

b. A title: _____

Put this information in your outline.

3. Explain why these two paragraphs belong together. _____

* _____ *

They both deal with the story about the linen waistcloth

4. Compare Jer. 13:1-11 with the paragraphs that come before this passage and with the paragraphs that follow it. Explain why Jer. 13:1-11 forms a

unit or section of the book of Jeremiah. _____

_____

*   *
_____

The previous and following paragraphs do not deal with the story of the linen waistcloth. So Jer. 13:1-11 can be considered a separate unit or section. Mark it off in your outline of the book of Jeremiah with the title "Linen Waistcloth."

5. Read through Jer. 13:1-11 two or three more times and try to figure out what is the meaning. It is evident that this is a kind of figure or parable. The linen waistcloth represents something. Make an analysis, first, of the new linen waistcloth, using a diagram like we have done in our interpretation of literary figures.

*   *

The new linen waistcloth	Represents Judah.
It clings to the loins of the man who wears it.	So Judah was called to cling to the Lord as his people.

6. Now make an analysis of the waistcloth which is hidden in the rock by the Euphrates.

*   *

The hidden waistcloth becomes soiled, good for nothing. So Judah has abandoned her Lord and become apostate, good for nothing.

7. Now write a summary of the Lord's message in Jer. 13:1-11. _____

_____

_____

_____

8. Compare the Lord's message in Jer. 13:1-11 with His message in Jer. 2-6.
Remember our analysis and summary of Jeremiah's message in Jer. 2:1-4:4 and
Jer. 4:5-6:3.

Would you say that it is the same basic message? _____   *

*

It is the same basic message.

9. See if you can remember the summary of Jeremiah's message in Jer. 2:1-4:5.
If you cannot remember the four points, turn back to Lesson V, D, 30.

a. _____

b. _____

c. _____

d. _____

10. Now consider Jer. 13:1-11 and indicate which of these four points are

either stated or implied in this passage. _____

_____

_____

_____

*   *

It seems to me that all four points are included here, at least by implication.
a. The new linen waistcloth represents Judah's special relationship to the
Lord.
b. The waistcloth hidden in the rock represents Judah's unfaithfulness or
apostasy.
c. The spoiled waistcloth represents judgment or destruction.
d. And apparently this story about the waistcloth is a call to repentance.

11. It is not always easy to figure out the purpose of Jeremiah's messages.
Often, as in Jer. 7:1-8:3 and Ch. 26, he calls his people to repentance.

In other passages he merely points out their apostasy or announces the coming destruction. But even in these cases the underlying purpose is probably
to call them back to the Lord. What is the purpose of Jeremiah's message

in Jer. 13:1-11? _____

*   _____ *

He is probably calling them to repent and cling to the Lord as the waistcloth is intended to cling to the loins of a man.

12. What was Judah supposed to be, according to Jer. 13:1-11? _____

    _____

*   _____ *

According to Jer. 13:11 Judah was intended to be:
a. the Lord's people   c. a praise to Him
b. the bearer of His name   d. His glory among the nations

13. What had Judah become, according to Jer. 13:11?_____

*   _____ *

Judah had become apostate, according to Jer. 13:10, going after other gods
to serve them and worship them.

14. Interpret the meaning of Jer. 13:1-11 for us today.

a. The new linen waistcloth: _____

    _____

b. The waistcloth hidden in the rock: _____

*   _____ *

a. We, too, have been called by God to cling to Him and follow Him and worship Him and serve Him.
b. If we are unfaithful to God and follow the gods of our society, our lives
can be ruined and become useless.
15. If you preach a sermon based on Jer. 13:1-11, what will be your purpose?

    _____

*   _____ *

Your general purpose will be, I suppose, to call your people back to the
Lord, to repent and follow Him. You should indicate, however, what they
need to turn from specifically.

16. Consider now some of the details in Jer. 13:1-7. We have indicated that
this is an acted parable. How do we know that this story was something that

Jeremiah __did__ and not just something he __saw__ or __imagined__? _____

_____

*   _____   *

The passage says that Jeremiah bought a waistcloth and put it on, etc. His
message doesn't make much sense without the action itself. Only if the people saw him, could they understand what he said.

17. There are differences of opinion about the details of Jeremiah's action.
Some people think Jeremiah made two round trips to the Euphrates River.
Others believe that he went to the Euphrates valley and stayed there about
seven years before returning to Jerusalem. Others point out that the translators may have made a mistake in the name of the place.

a. Where is the Euphrates River?_____

b. How far from Jerusalem is it?_____

c. How far would Jeremiah travel in two round trips?_____

*
a. In Mesopotamia.   *
b. About 350 miles or 560 kilometers.
c. About 1400 miles.

18. The name Perath in the original Hebrew of this passage can be translated
either Parah or Euphrates. Both names are spelled the same in Hebrew. Parah
was a small town about three miles northeast of Anathoth in the rocky valley
of the Wady Fara. See Joshua 18:23. Considering the distance to the Euphrates,
many scholars believe this passage refers to Parah. There Jeremiah's people
could watch him act out God's message in the parable.

Jeremiah very likely took the linen waistcloth to _____   _____

and not to _____
*   *

Parah   the Euphrates River

19. What happened to the linen waistcloth? Try to imagine a damp riverbank
and explain what it would do to a fine piece of linen over a period of

time. _____

* _____ *

It probably got moldy and rotted. Perhaps insects and worms got into it, and
it may have been covered with silt.

20. Read over Jer. 13:8-11. There are not many details in this paragraph
that need explanation. Explain the relationship between Jer. 13:1-7 and

Jer. 13:8-11. _____

_____

* _____ *

We have pointed out previously that both these paragraphs deal with the story.
You should have added here that Jer. 13:8-11 gives the interpretation of
Jer. 13:1-7.

21. In v. 9 and 10 the Lord describes His people's sin. Give four different
words to summarize their nature.

a. _____   c. _____

b. _____   d. _____
*   *

Here are some words that come out of the text: proud, evil, stubborn, and
idolatrous.

22. We have studied several passages which speak of Judah's stubbornness.
To Jeremiah the people seemed to be not only apostate but stubborn and foolish and persistent in their sinfulness. Find at least two paragraphs that

mention Judah's stubbornness. _____

* _____ *

See Lesson VI, E, 12.

23. Who was intended to be the Lord's waistcloth, according to v. 11? _____

* _____ *

Israel and Judah.

24. Israel and Judah betrayed their Lord and became useless.

a. Israel was destroyed in _____ B.C.

b. Judah was destroyed in _____ B.C.

*   *

a. 722   b. 587

25. We have said that Jer. 13:1-11 is an acted parable. Explain what is a

parable. _____

_____

_____

*   *

Look in your dictionary or in your Bible dictionary for this definition.

26. Explain what is an acted parable. _____

_____

_____

*   *

An acted parable is one which is acted out or dramatized. Jeremiah demon-
strated his message by symbolic action. He illustrated his message not just
by literary figures but also by acted parables.

B. Sermon Outline (Jeremiah 13:1-11)

Your assignment in this section is to prepare a sermon outline based on
Jer. 13:1-11. Since you have already made an Inductive Study of this passage, this should be fairly easy.

Work out your sermon outline on scratch paper. Follow the steps we have
been using for sermon outline preparation. Then fill in the sermon outline
form for Jer. 13:1-11 on page A.8 in the Appendix. Put it in your notebook.
You may call your sermon, "The Linen Waistcloth Episode."

C. The Broken Flask Episode (Jeremiah 19-20)

In this section we will study another of Jeremiah's acted parables. Jer. 19-20 tells not only what Jeremiah did and the message he proclaimed but also the reaction this acted parable caused. It is another exciting event in the life of Jeremiah.

1. As a first step in your Inductive Study of Jer. 19-20, fill in your outline for these seven paragraphs. Write in the main idea of each paragraph and a title for each paragraph. This is an important step in your analysis of the paragraphs. Look, also, for relationships between the paragraphs.

2. As you read through Jer. 19 you probably noticed that Jeremiah's action is only briefly mentioned. In fact the passage only gives the Lord's command to buy the flask and to break the flask. Most of the passage contains Jeremiah's message.

a. Give the reference for Jeremiah's action: _____

b. Give the reference for Jeremiah's message: _____
*   *

a. Jer. 19:1-2, 10, 14
b. Jer. 19:3-9, 11-13, 15

3. The acted parable has a very clear, simple meaning. Give your analysis in the following diagram.

The earthen flask	Judah
Is irreparably smashed.	Will be utterly destroyed

4. As you read through Jer. 20, you probably noticed a change between v. 1-6 and 7-18.

a. What does Jer. 20:1-6 contain? _____

_____

b. What does Jer. 20:7-18 contain? _____

* _____ *

a. Jer. 20:1-6 tells of Jeremiah's encounter with Pashhur the priest.
b. Jer. 20:7-18 is a soliloquy of Jeremiah, who is contemplating his own
tragic state.

5. How much of Jer. 20 is directly related to the story of the broken flask?

* _____ *

Just Jer. 20:1-6. Apparently Pashhur reacted to Jeremiah's message of destruction when he repeated it in the Temple.

6. What did Pashhur do to Jeremiah? _____

_____

Why did he react so violently to Jeremiah's message? _____

* _____ *

Pashhur beat Jeremiah and put him in the stocks. He was obviously angry because Jeremiah had prophesied against Jerusalem and Judah.

7. Remember that in those days there was a serious concept of prophecy. If
a prophet of the Lord announced the destruction of Jerusalem, what did this

mean? _____

* _____ *

It meant that Jerusalem must be destroyed. The words themselves carried
the power of God to fulfill His will.

8. Jeremiah's action must have made this message even more threatening. He
took the earthen flask and threw it down and smashed it.

a. Explain this as a symbolic action: _____

_____

b. Explain it as a prophetic action: _____

_____

* _____ *

a. The smashing of the flask symbolized the destruction of Jerusalem.
b. The smashing of the pot foretold the destruction of Jerusalem and emphasized God's determination to carry out the prophecy.

9. This episode is similar to another event in Jeremiah's ministry that we
have already studied.

a. Give the reference for that event: _____

b. Where did it take place? _____

c. What was Jeremiah's message? _____

_____

d. What was the reaction to Jeremiah's message? _____

* _____ *

a. Jer. 26; 7:1-8:3
b. At the entrance to the Temple
c. He prophesied the destruction of the Temple (like Shiloh).
d. The priests and prophets and people were angered and tried to have him
condemned to death.

10. Consider Jer. 19-20 as a whole and see if all of these paragraphs belong together in one section of the book of Jeremiah. List the paragraphs

that deal with the story of the broken flask. _____

* _____ *

Jer. 19:1-9, 10 - 13, 14-15; 20:1-6

11. We could include just these paragraphs. But there seems to be some relationship between Jer. 20:1-6 and the rest of the chapter. Look over these
paragraphs and find two links (repeated phrases or ideas) between them.

a. _____

_____

_____

b. _____

_____

a. First, you may or may not have noted that both Jer. 20:1-6 and Jer. 20:7-18 contain the idea of Jeremiah's humiliation. In v.2 he is beaten and put in the stocks as an object of public scorn. In v.7 he says, "I have become a laughingstock all the day."
b. You should have found the other link, the phrase "Terror on every side" which is found in v.3 and in v.10. Underline this phrase in your Bible.

12. These links do not mean that Jer. 20:7-18 comes to us from the broken flask incident. These words of Jeremiah probably form a separate piece of his collected prophecies. But these links do suggest that Jeremiah or some- one else deliberately attached the soliloquy to the broken flask story when the book was put together.

So we can group all of Jer. 19-20 together as a section in our outline of the book of Jeremiah. Make this indication in your outline, and write in the title for this section, "Broken Flask."

13. Examine the paragraphs before chapter 19 and after chapter 20. Explain

why they do not belong in this section. _____

_____

They do not form a part of the broken flask incident. This story evidently begins at Jer. 19:1, and a new section evidently begins at Jer. 21:1.

14. Go back to <u>Jer. 19:1-9</u> and look at some of the details.

Whom did Jeremiah take as witnesses of this acted parable? _____

Some of the elders and some of the senior priests.

15. Where did he perform the symbolic act? _____

In the valley of Ben-hinnom at the Potsherd Gate. This was a place where refuse was dumped.

16. Notice the name Topheth. Underline it each time it appears in this para-

graph and the following paragraphs. List the references. _____

* _____ *

Jer. 19: 6, 11, 13, 14

17. List the evils that were being practiced there, according to Jer. 19:4-5.

a. _____   c. _____

b. _____   d. _____
*   *

They were worshipping other gods, burning incense, building high places,
and sacrificing their sons as burnt offerings.

18. We have studied a similar passage in Jeremiah which tells of these

practices. Find the reference. _____
*   *

Jer. 7:30-31.

19. Jeremiah pronounces the Lord's judgment on them. List the coming events
of Jer. 19:6-9.

a. _____

b. _____

c. _____

d. _____
*   *

They will fall by the sword; the place will be called Valley of Slaughter;
their bodies will be left to the birds and beasts; the city will become a
horror; they will cannibalize each other because of the siege.

20. Which of these prophecies are mentioned in Jer. 7:32-34? _____

* _____ *

All but the last item.

21. Remember what Josiah had done to Topheth. _____

* _____ *

See 2 Kings 23:10

22. Now look at some of the details in Jer. 20:1-6.

Who was Pashhur? _____

* _____ *

He was a priest, the son of Immer, and he was chief officer of the Temple.

23. Is he the same Pashhur who is mentioned in Jer. 21:1? _____

* _____ *

No. Jer. 21:1 speaks of Pashhur, the son of Malchiah.

24. How long was Jeremiah kept in the stocks? _____
*   *

The text doesn't say exactly, just that he passed the night there.

25. Try to put yourself in Jeremiah's position and imagine the different kinds of suffering he went through that night in the stocks.

a. _____

b. _____

c. _____
*   *

Jeremiah must have suffered physically, psychologically or socially, and spiritually. It was painful to be held in one position hour after hour, and he probably was unable to sleep. The people probably scorned and laughed at him. And he must have agonized before the Lord (as in Jer. 20:7-18) about his humiliation.

26. The next morning Jeremiah has some harsh prophecies for Pashhur personally and for Jerusalem. What will happen to Pashhur?

a. _____

b. _____

c. _____

d. _____
*   *

a. He will be a terror to himself and his friends.
b. He will see his friends slaughtered.
c. He and his household will be taken to Babylon captives.
d. There they will die and be buried.

27. What will happen to Jerusalem and Judah?

a. _____

b. _____
*   *

a. They will be defeated by Babylon.
b. Their treasures will be taken to Babylon.

28. Note especially that Jeremiah gives Pashhur a new name. Interpret this

as a means of prophecy. _____

_____

_____

_____

*   *

We have said that the prophets' words did not just proclaim God's will or
describe what was going to happen. They believed that the words themselves
were instrumental in the fulfillment of God's will. And we said that a
prophetic act, such as the smashing of the earthen flask, carried this same
force. So when Jeremiah called Pashhur "Terror on Every Side," he was bringing to pass the terrors he mentioned in Jer. 20:4-6.

29. Every time you study a passage of the Bible you should think about the
significance of that passage for your life and ministry. Some passages will
be more applicable than others. What lessons do you find in the story of
the broken flask? (Do not include Jer. 20:7-18. We may consider this part
in a later lesson.)

a. _____

_____

b. _____

_____

c. _____

_____

30. In our study of Jer. 19-20 we have used several of the methods we have used in other lessons. We have tried to find out what the text has to tell us. We have studied the passage inductively. Review the steps we have used in this section by reading over the following list. If you do not understand one of these steps, underline it and go back and see what we did. If you still do not understand it, bring it up in your next class session.

a. We analyzed each paragraph, finding the main idea and a title.
b. We noted that the passage contains an acted parable and distinguished the action and the message.
c. We interpreted Jeremiah's symbolic action with a diagram.
d. We distinguished the material Jer. 20:7-18 from the rest of the passage and found how it is linked to Jer. 20:1-6.
e. We noted the reaction to Jeremiah's acted parable and asked why it was so violent.
f. We compared this incident with the Temple Sermon incident.
g. We identified Jer. 19-20 as a section of the book of Jeremiah.
h. We considered some of the details in Jer. 19:1-9 and 20:1-6.
i. We tried to imagine what this experience must have meant to Jeremiah.
j. We asked what lessons this passage has for us.

D. The Yoke-Bars Episode (Jeremiah 27-28)

In Jer. 27-28 we find another acted parable which is a dramatic episode in the life of the prophet Jeremiah. This time he prophesies to King Zedekiah and to the neighboring nations. And he comes into conflict with another prophet who contradicts him.

In this section you will study this incident from Jeremiah's ministry. Your primary objective is to learn how to study the Bible inductively and independently. Therefore, study this passage conscientiously, and make note of the methods which help you discover its meaning.

1. As a first step read through Jer. 27-28 and underline or mark historical information, names, and key passages. Note especially all references to the yoke bars.

2. Read through Jer. 27-28 again and analyze the main idea of each paragraph. Choose a title for each paragraph as we have done for each passage we have studied. And fill in your outline of the book of Jeremiah as you go. Do not skip this important step: it will help you study the text. (You will be asked to turn in your outline at the end of this course.)

3. Explain why all of the paragraphs of Jer. 27-28 belong together. _____

_____

* _____ *

Evidently they all deal with the same event, the Yoke-Bars Episode.

4. Explain the meaning of the yoke-bars in Jer. 27 using the following diagram.

The yoke-bars	The rule of Babylon
Were worn by Jeremiah	Must be accepted by the nations

5. Summarize Jeremiah's message in Jer. 27. _____

_____

*   *

Jeremiah announces to Judah and her neighbors that they must subject themselves to the rule of Babylon or perish.

6. Explain Hananiah's message and action in Jer. 28:1-4, 10-11.

a. His message: _____

_____

_____

b. His action: _____

*   *

a. The Lord has broken Babylon's yoke and within two years He will bring back Jeconiah and the exiles.
b. Hananiah dramatized this message by taking Jeremiah's yoke-bars and breaking them.

7. Summarize Jeremiah's response to Hananiah in Jer. 28:5-9. _____

_____

*   *

Jeremiah wishes that what Hananiah says might be true, but he notes that the ancient prophets prophesied war, not peace.

8. In Jer. 28:12-16 Jeremiah responds to Hananiah with forceful, figurative language. Analyze the figure of the iron yoke-bars.

| | |
| | |

*   *

As iron yoke-bars cannot be broken, so the rule of Babylon will not (yet) be thrown off.

9. Finally, Jeremiah pronounces a harsh judgment upon Hananiah.

a. Of what crime was Hananiah guilty? _____

b. What was his sentence? _____

c. How soon was this sentence carried out? _____

*   *

a. False prophecy
b. Death (see Deut. 18:20)
c. In two months. (Compare Jer. 28:17 with Jer. 28:1)

10. We have noted that all of the paragraphs of Jer. 27-28 belong together because they all deal with the Yoke-Bars Episode. Look now at Jer. 26 and 29 to see if any other paragraphs should be included in this section of the book of Jeremiah.

Explain why this section should include only Jer. 27 and 28. _____

_____

* _____ *

Jer. 26 and 29 refer to other events at other times. Jer. 27 and 28 form a separate section referring to the Yoke-Bars Episode.

11. Mark of Jer. 27-28 in your outline of the book of Jeremiah and put in the title for this section: "Yoke-Bars."

12. Consider some of the details in <u>Jer. 27:1-7.</u> First note when this event took place.

a. According to Jer. 27:1, when did the Yoke-Bars Episode occur? _____

_____

b. According to Jer. 28:1, when did it occur? _____

*   *
_____

Different versions give different information. Apparently there is conflic-ting evidence in the oldest manuscripts. The best conclusion seems to be, according to the commentaries, that it occurred in the fourth year of Zede-kiah.

13. If this event occurred in the fourth year of Zedekiah, we can place it

at the year _____ B.C. Mark it on your chronological chart with the

title, "Yoke-Bars Episode."

14. In this paragraph Jeremiah is told to speak directly to _____

*   *
_____

The envoys (ambassadors) of Edom, Moab, Ammon, Tyre, and Sidon.

15. Point out the general location of each of these nations in relation to Judah. Use your atlas or Bible dictionary.

a. Edom: <u>just south and southeast of Judah</u>_____

b. Moab: _____

c. Ammon: _____

d. Tyre: _____

e. Sidon: _____

16. Now use your imagination. Since the Battle of Carchemish in 605 B.C. Babylon has been extending its empire over this region. It is now 594 B.C. and the surrounding nations have sent envoys to King Zedekiah of Judah.

What do you think they were there to talk about? _____

_____

_____

*   *

Probably they were planning to rebel against Babylon. These nations were not traditionally friendly to each other. Only a common enemy would bring them together. And their enemy was Babylon.

17. How do you think they received Jeremiah's message? _____

*   *

I suppose they were angry with Jeremiah for contradicting their plans. Or perhaps they ignored him.

18. Note that Jeremiah calls Nebuchadnezzar the servant of the Lord. In

what sense is he God's servant? _____

*   *

Nebuchadnezzar was God's servant only as the instrument of His judgment.

19. Abraham, Moses, David, and Isaiah were called servants of the Lord. In

what sense were they God's servants (as distinct from Nebuchadnezzar)? _____

*   *

They were called into intimate relationship to God and sought to do His will.

20. What does Jer. 27:1-7 say to indicate that Nebuchadnezzar does not en-

joy a special relationship to the Lord? _____

*   *

V.7 says that Babylon, too, will be enslaved later.

21. It is easy to read that Jeremiah addressed the ambassadors gathered in Jerusalem, opposed their plans, and upheld the enemy. But try to imagine yourself in such a situation. Or think what it would be like to speak to an international congress in similar terms today.

Jeremiah was called to play an unusual role as God's spokesman to His people and to the nations.

Where is the first indication of that fact? _____

*   *

Jer. 1:4-10. The Lord called him to be a prophet to the nations.

22. Read over <u>Jer. 27:8-11</u>.

a. Who else was giving counsel to the nations besides Jeremiah? _____

_____

b. What was their advice? _____

c. Why do you think they gave this kind of advice? _____

* _____ *

The other prophets, diviners, dreamers, soothsayers, and sorcerers told
them not to serve Babylon. They probably gave this advice because it was
what the people wanted to hear.

23. Notice that this theme of the false prophets is repeated several times

in Jer. 27. List the references. _____

24. Read over <u>Jer. 27:12-15</u>. Jeremiah now gives his message to Zedekiah.
Once again use your imagination and remember Zedekiah's history.

a. What did Jeremiah tell Zedekiah to do? _____

_____

b. Why would this message be hard for Zedekiah to accept? _____

* _____ *

See 2 Kings 24:17, 2 Chron. 36:10. Zedekiah had been put on the throne by
Nebuchadnezzar. He had been Babylon's vassal. He would not be eager to
accept Jeremiah's message for that reason.

25. Read over <u>Jer. 27:16-22</u>. Jeremiah refers to King Jeconiah and an earlier exile.

a. Who was Jeconiah (give his other name)? _____

b. When was he taken exile (give the year)? _____

c. When did the Yoke-Bars Episode take place? _____

* _____ *

a. Jehoiachin
b. 598 B.C. (See your Chronological Chart)
c. 594 B.C. (four years later)

26. In this paragraph Jeremiah mentions the people and the treasures that were taken to Babylon in the first exile. Give the references for the rec-

ord of this exile in two other Old Testament books. _____

_____

27. Once again use your imagination. King Jeconiah and the nobles of Judah and Jerusalem have been taken into exile in Babylon. Many of the Temple and Palace treasures have been taken away, also.

a. How would the people respond to the false prophets' message? _____

_____

b. How would they respond to Jeremiah's message? _____

_____

Obviously, they would much rather hear the false prophets than Jeremiah. They might well be angered at his counsel.

28. In Jer. 28 the conflict between Jeremiah and the false prophets is in-tensified and personalized. Make a short outline of the steps or stages of this conflict.

a. Jer. 28:1-4   _____

b. Jer. 28:5-9   _____

c. Jer. 28:10-11 _____

d. Jer. 28:12-16 _____

e. Jer. 28:17   _____

29. There must have been a real crisis among the people as they listened to Jeremiah and Hananiah.

a. In whose name did Jeremiah speak? _____

b. In whose name did Hananiah speak? _____

30. Analyze carefully this debate and find out what is the proof of true

and false prophecy. _____

_____

_____

The ultimate proof of prophecy is what comes to pass. Jeremiah states this clearly in v.9.

31. This chapter contains proof that Jeremiah was a true prophet and Hananiah a false one. What is that proof? _____

* _____ *

Jeremiah said that Hananiah would die, and he did (v.17).

32. Write down at least one important lesson from Jer. 27-28 for the church

today. _____

_____

_____

_____

_____

Because this is such a dramatic story, you may want to prepare a sermon based on this passage.

E. Test (Jeremiah 18)

In this section you are asked to study Jer. 18 and be prepared for a brief test on this passage at your next class session. The best way to prepare for the test is to make a complete Inductive Study of the passage as a whole and paragraph by paragraph. Fill in your outline for this section and give the section a title.

Give special attention to Jer. 18:1-12. This is not an acted parable but it is very similar. Give your explanation of this passage, and be particularly careful in your interpretation of Jeremiah's message. Many have been mistaken in their understanding of Jeremiah's literary figures or parables. Find a contemporary application of this passage; it would be a good text for a sermon.

Work out an analysis of Jer. 18 in your notebook. You will be entirely on your own. Once again this is an opportunity to see whether you can do Inductive Bible Study independently. Remember that you will probably be tested on this passage at your next class session.

10

Jeremiah's Tragic Role

The book of Jeremiah is not a biography of the life of the prophet. But it does tell us far more about Jeremiah than we know about any other prophet. The book includes not only collections of his prophecies but also incidents from his ministry. It reveals not only what he said and did but also what he felt and what he suffered. At a time of greatest national disaster Jeremiah the Prophet was called to fulfill a tragic role of unfathomable depths. As he carried out that high calling as God's mouthpiece, he showed himself to be all too human.

In this lesson you will study several passages that expose Jeremiah's difficult role and his inner struggle. In order to understand these passages you will have to reflect on the historical background of the book and the message of Jeremiah, which we have analyzed previously. You will have to use your imagination and try to relive the terrible experiences of Jeremiah. And as you project yourself into Jeremiah's world and into his soul, you will gain invaluable insight into the role of God's messengers in our own day.

Your objectives in this lesson are to:

Define Jeremiah's role as the Lord's prophet in a time of judgment.

Experience and express his inner struggle.

Interpret his "Confessions."

Apply Jeremiah's experience to your own ministry.

A. Outline

Your assignment in this section is to go through Jer. 14-20 rapidly, making the usual paragraph analysis. Fill in your outline of the book of Jeremiah indicating the main idea and choosing a title for each paragraph. Also, underline unusual and important words and phrases, and try to identify groups of paragraphs or sections of the book. Look for structure.

As you read through these chapters, give special attention to Jeremiah's role and inward struggle. Mark for further study those passages which reveal Jeremiah's innermost thoughts and conflicts. You should have outlined Jer. 18-20 already in the previous lesson, but read through these chapters once again with this subject in mind.

B. The Great Drought (Jeremiah 14:1-15:4)

In this section you will work through Jer. 14:1-15:4, paragraph by paragraph. A drought is mentioned at the beginning of Jer. 14 as the occasion for the following prophecies. We do not know, however, how much of Jer. 14:1-15:4

is specifically related to the drought. It is even difficult to tell where this section of the book ends and another begins. As you go through this passage, look for indications of the drought and also of other circumstances such as war and destruction.

Throughout this section keep in mind especially the role that Jeremiah had to play. Notice who is speaking to whom in each paragraph. At times the Lord speaks to Judah, and at other times Judah speaks to the Lord. In both cases Jeremiah is the messenger who identifies himself with the one who is speaking. And in some of these paragraphs you will find a personal dialogue between the Lord and the prophet.

As you work through this section, notice the kinds of questions we are asking. As you read the text, see what questions come to your mind. Remember that your objective is not primarily to answer my questions. Your purpose is to learn how to study the Bible inductively.

1. Read carefully Jer. 14:1-6. Check what you have put in your outline for this paragraph. Underline in the text the words "concerning the drought."

Explain the significance of these words. _____

_____   _____

_____

* _____ *

They tell us the occasion or circumstances for the following prophecy as well as the topic of the following prophecy.

2. The prophecy itself begins at v. 2. Describe briefly what v. 2-6 contain. _____

_____

* _____ *

This is simply a description of the drought.

3. This description is an example of Jeremiah's literary skill, which we have noted throughout our study of his book. Read through v. 2-6 again and underline the different things he mentions, for example, "Judah,""her gates," "her people," "the cisterns," etc. Then fill in the following chart by listing these objects and Jeremiah's description of each one.

Object	Description

4. Why do you think the Lord (through Jeremiah) describes the drought in

so much detail and with such literary skill? _____

_____

_____

_____

_____

*   *

He could have said, "There is a great drought, and all Judah suffers for
lack of water." But this simple statement does not make us feel the impact
of the drought. Jeremiah's language helps us see and feel the effects of
the drought. We can imagine what it would be like if even the nobles could
not send their servants for water to drink. We can imagine the wild asses
panting on the dry, bare mountain tops. Apparently, the Lord (through Jeremiah) wanted to make his hearers feel the full impact of the drought.

5. Now answer the following questions. Be careful. The first, obvious answer may not be correct.

a. Who is speaking in Jer. 14:1-6? _____

b. To whom? _____

*   *

The Lord, through Jeremiah, is speaking to Judah.

6. Again we must ask ourselves why the Lord speaks to Judah about the drought. Surely the people know that there is a drought and that it is a

terrible thing. Explain. _____

_____

_____

* _____ *

Apparently the Lord speaks to Judah about the drought so that she will re-flect on her relationship to Him. Notice that in the following paragraph Judah responds by confessing her backslidings. The great drought symbo-lizes Judah's great apostasy, her spiritual drought.

7. Jeremiah often relates outward circumstances and the inner spiritual condition of his people. For example, how does Jeremiah interpret the com-

ing Babylonian invasion? _____

* _____ *

It is God's judgment on Judah for her apostasy.

8. Read Jer. 14:7-9. Check your analysis of this paragraph in your outline.

Who is speaking to whom in this paragraph? _____
*   *

Judah is speaking to the Lord, either directly or through Jeremiah.

9. Study carefully Judah's response to the Lord verse by verse. What does Judah say and what is her attitude?

a. v. 7 _____

b. v. 8 _____

c. v. 9 _____
*   *

a. In v. 7 Judah confesses her sins and asks for help.
b. In v. 8 Judah praises the Lord and challenges Him to act.
c. In v. 9 Judah almost insults the Lord and demands that He save her.

10. Underline the expressions which are used to describe the Lord in v. 8-9.

Are these complimentary? _____ List them here.

a. _____

b. _____

c. _____

d. _____

e. _____

f. _____

11. Read Jer. 14:10. Check your outline.

What is the Lord's response to Judah? _____

* _____ *

He does not accept her plea.

12. In Jer. 14:7-9 Judah confesses her sins and asks for help. Why does

the Lord reject Judah in v. 10? _____

_____

_____

* _____ *

Apparently the Lord does not consider Judah's confession to be a genuine
repentance. Judah's attitude was not one of humble repentance, as we have
noted. Judah demanded that the Lord save His people. So the Lord remembers
their sins and overlooks their words of repentance. He will punish them.

13. What lesson do you find in this passage for Christians today? _____

_____

_____

_____

14. People today often act just like Judah did. They only turn to God when
they face a personal crisis. They confess their sins and ask God to forgive
their unfaithfulness. And they expect Him to answer their requests. Mention
a specific situation or circumstance when we are likely to turn to God no

matter how far from Him we have been. _____

Many turn to God at a time of sickness, when out of a job, in time of war, when facing danger, before an examination, and especially at death.

15. Is it wrong to turn to God at times of personal crisis or national emergency? _____ What should our attitude be? _____

God calls us to Himself at all times, especially in times of special need. It is never wrong to turn to Him. But if we have been living far from God's will, we cannot come to Him demanding forgiveness and help. Our attitude can only be one of humble confession and repentance. We do not deserve His help. Remember the attitude of the prodigal son when he returned to his father (Luke 15:18-19, 21).

16. Read Jer. 14:11-12.

Who is speaking to whom in this paragraph? _____

The Lord is speaking to Jeremiah. In v. 10 the Lord speaks through Jeremiah to Judah. In v. 11-12 the form of speech is very similar, but this passage contains specific instructions for Jeremiah. In v. 13-16 the dialogue between the Lord and Jeremiah continues.

17. The Lord commands Jeremiah not to pray for his people. Give the reference for another passage, which we have studied, which gives the same command. _____

18. Think of the significance of these words for Jeremiah. In one sense they constitute a denial of his life-long mission.

a. What was Jeremiah's basic message to Judah from the beginning of his ministry? _____

b. What great warning did he give his people? _____

_____

c. What was his constant prayer? _____

* _____ *

a. Jeremiah constantly called his unfaithful apostate people to repentance.
b. He warned them of the coming destruction.
c. He must have prayed constantly that the Lord would save his people from
that terrible destruction.

19. In verse 12 the Lord says again that He will not hear the cry of Judah.
We have already seen that God wanted obedience more than sacrifices.

According to v.12 God will not accept Judah even though the people _____

_____

_____.

* _____ *

fast, pray, and offer burnt offerings and cereal offerings.

20. In v. 10 in response to their plea the Lord will _____.

In v. 12 He will _____.
* _____ *

Punish them.
Consume them by the sword, famine, and pestilence.

21. What hope, then, remains for Judah? _____
* _____ *

There is no hope.

22. Read over Jer. 14:13-16. Identify who is speaking to whom in this para-

graph. _____

* _____ *

In v. 13 Jeremiah speaks to the Lord and in v. 14-16 the Lord speaks to
Jeremiah.

23. In the light of what the Lord says in v. 11-12, explain why Jeremiah

brings up the matter of the false prophets in v. 13. _____

*   *

Apparently Jeremiah is still interceding for his people. He offers an excuse for their sinfulness and blames the false prophets.

24. What is the Lord's response? _____

*   *

He rejects Jeremiah's excuse and says that the false prophets and the people will perish.

25. What did the false prophets say to the people about the coming destruc-

tion? _____

_____

What did the Lord say would happen to them?_____

*   *

Sword and famine shall not come on this land.
By sword and famine shall those prophets and the people be consumed.

26. Remember our previous study of the false prophets. (Jer. 5:30-31).

a. Why did the other prophets prophesy such lies? _____

_____

b. Why are the people guilty as well as the prophets? _____

_____

*   *

a. Because the people wanted to hear those lies. (By the same token they
hated to hear Jeremiah's warnings of destruction.)
b. Because they asked (and perhaps paid) the prophets to prophesy lies.
They heard only what they wanted to hear.

27. Read Jer. 14:17-18. Who is speaking to whom in this paragraph? _____

*   *

The first introductory words indicate that the Lord tells Jeremiah to say these words to Judah. But perhaps we should read them as Jeremiah speaking to the Lord. In any case, Jeremiah is weeping over his people.

28. What is the situation described in this paragraph? Does it refer to the drought or to some other event? _____

_____

_____

* _____ *

From verse 12 on God links sword, famine, and disease. The famine in the city may be the result of the drought, an enemy invasion which has taken away her crops, a siege, or a combination of all three.

29. Read Jer. 14:19-22. Who is speaking to whom in this paragraph? _____

* _____ *

Judah is again appealing to the Lord, either directly or through Jeremiah.

30. What situation is mentioned in this paragraph? Does it refer to the drought or to some other event? _____

* _____ *

V. 22 mentions the need for rain, so this paragraph probably refers to the great drought.

31. On what basis does this prayer appeal to the Lord for help? Why should He come to Judah's aid? _____

_____

‖
Jeremiah acknowledges Judah's wickedness and sin against God both in his time and in former generations, but he pleads for mercy on the basis of God's honor. This is much like Moses' intercession for Israel when God was about to abandon her because of her sins. Jeremiah prays for God's help for the honor of His covenant, His name, and His throne.

32. Read <u>Jer. 15:1-4</u>. Who is speaking to whom in this paragraph? _____

* _____ *

The Lord is speaking to Jeremiah, giving him a message for Judah.

33. What is the Lord's reply to Judah's plea for help this time? _____

* _____ *

Once again the Lord rejects Judah with terrible words of judgment.

34. This paragraph makes two striking references to important historical
personalities of Israel's past. Why are Moses and Samuel referred to in

v. 1? _____

_____

* _____ *

Moses represents the law and Samuel was a judge and prophet. They were two
of Israel's greatest leaders, and they had both interceded with God for
the people.

35. Why is Manasseh mentioned in v. 4? What had he done in Jerusalem? _____

_____

_____

* _____ *

See 2 Kings 21:1-18, 2 Chron. 33:1-20. Manasseh is mentioned because he was
the most evil of Judah's kings. Judah is to be punished not only because of
Manasseh's sins but because the people have persisted in the sins exempli-
fied by Manasseh.

36. List the four kinds of destruction mentioned in v. 2.

a. _____   c. _____

b. _____   d. _____

37. List the kinds of destruction mentioned in v. 3.

a. _____   b. _____

c. _____   d. _____

38. Why does the Lord not respond to Judah's plea? Why does He answer her

with such violence? _____

_____

_____

* _____ *

Apparently the Lord considered Judah's confession superficial and her plea
presumptuous. She was only turning to the Lord because of her dire need at
the moment. So the Lord utterly rejected Judah and hurled at her these
words of terrifying destruction.

39. Once again consider Jeremiah's position as Judah's messenger before the
Lord and as the Lord's spokesman before Judah. Was his an easy task? What

kind of an experience was this for him personally? _____

_____

_____

* _____ *

It must have been a terrible ordeal for Jeremiah personally. He had called
his people to repentance year after year. Now, finally, they did turn to
the Lord, at least in appearance. But the Lord utterly rejected them. And
Jeremiah had to pronounce on them the deadly sentence of the Lord. And he
could not longer intercede on their behalf.

40. As a review of Jer. 14:1-15:4 fill in the following chart. In the first
column indicate who is speaking to whom. In the other column summarize the
content of the paragraph. You have already figured out this information.

The chart is on the following page.

14:1-6	Lord to Judah	Describes the drought
7-9		
10		
11-12		
13-16		
17-18		
19-22		
15:1-4		

C. Jeremiah's Anguish (Jeremiah 15:5-21)

Jer. 15:5-21 contains a variety of materials which are only superficially related to Jer. 14:1-15:4. It includes one of Jeremiah's "confessions" and an extraordinary "private oracle" which echoes some of the words of Jeremiah's call. The dialogue between the Lord and His prophet reaches an almost unbelievable intensity. Jeremiah expresses blasphemous thoughts, and his prophetic office itself is called into question.

As you study this passage, allow the text to speak to your life. Try to experience with Jeremiah the anguish of his calling as God's prophet in a time of great tragedy. And let his experience illumine your role as God's servant and messenger in our own day, which is also a time of great tragedy.

1. Read Jer. 15:5-9. Who is speaking to whom in this paragraph? _____

* _____ *

The Lord is speaking to Jerusalem or to Judah.

2. What is the topic of this paragraph? _____

_____

What situation does it refer to? _____

_____

What specific event does it refer to (give two possibilities)? _____

* _____ *

the destructuin of Jerusalue. It may refer to the fall of Jerusalem in 487 B.C. or to the defeat of Jerusalem in 498 B.C. See your Chronological Chart. The passage is similar to the Lamentations Jeremiah wrote after Jerusalem's fall.

3. Some Bible translators use the past tense in Jeremiah 15:5-9. Others use the future. In the Revised Standard Version it sounds as if Jerusalem had already fallen when Jer. 14:17-18 and 15:5-9 were written. However, Bible prophecy often uses the past tense to describe future events that God has determined to bring about. So we can't tell when these words were written.

Compare these passages in whatever versions you have.

4. Compare in the RSV the topic and tenses of Jer. 15:1-4 with those of Jer. 15:5-9._____

4. Compare in the RSV the topic and tenses of Jer. 15:1-4 with those of

Jer. 15:5-9._____

* _____ *

Tney both speak of destruction but 15:1-4 is still a warning of impending doom.

5. Write down the Lord's question in v. 5. _____

_____

What is the understood answer to this question? _____

* _____ *

Who will have pity on you, O Jerusalem?
No one. If the Lord has rejected His people, there is no pity.

6. Why does the Lord not have pity on Jerusalem? _____

* _____ *

In v. 6 the Lord repeats His often stated accusation against His people. They have rejected Him. It is only because they have rejected Him that He hno now rejected them.

7. Notice what the Lord has done to His people. Read through the paragraph again and circle the personal pronoun "I" each time it is repeated. Underline the phrases that describe what He has done to His people.

8. Describe Jeremiah's role in Jer. 15:5-9. _____

*

As prophet of the Lord, Jeremiah had to pronounce these awful words of judgment. He had to tell Jerusalem that her defeat was not just a victory for
her enemies but also the will and action of the Lord Himself. As a citizen
of Judah, Jeremiah had to experience the full tragedy of these words. His
people had been slaughtered, his friends and relatives destroyed, his nation and city defeated.

8. Read Jer. 15:10-12 in whatever versions you have. Translators disagree
on the meaning of the original and on paragraph divisions. Many versions
give only v. 10 as words of Jeremiah and have v. 11-14 as the reply of the
Lord in the following paragraph. In these versions v.11 is a promise of
protection for Jeremiah and the salvation of a remnant of Judah. V. 12
probably refers to Judah's defeat by the armies of the north.

9. Write a brief analysis of verse 10.

a. What is the topic? _____

_____

b. Why does Jeremiah say these things? _____

_____

*

a. Jeremiah speaks of his own role as "a man of strife and contention."
b. Apparently Jeremiah wants to complain to the Lord or at least express
the hardship he feels as a prophet at a time of national apostasy and judgment.

10. Explain the expression "Woe is me, my mother, that you bore me." _____

_____

_____

*

Obviously, Jeremiah feels that his life is so difficult and his ministry so useless that it would have been better not to be born. This is strong, almost suicidal language. Read Jer. 20:14-18.

11. In what sense was Jeremiah "a man of strife and contention"? _____

_____

*   *

_____

He was forced to play a role of constant accusation and judgment. As the Lord's prophet, he was sent to show his people their apostasy and to call them to repentance. But they refused to accept his message and turn to the Lord. So he had to announce the Lord's sentence of destruction upon them.

12. Explain the reference to loaning and borrowing in v. 10. _____

_____

_____

*   *

_____

This is a simple illustration of contention. If you loan people money, they resent you because they have to pay you back. If you borrow, they resent you because they have to get their money back from you. But, Jeremiah says, he hasn't loaned or borrowed, and they still resent him.

13. Explain v. 11 in your own words. _____

_____

_____

*   *

_____

Jeremiah says, Let their curses on me (v. 10) come true if I have not sought their well-being. He had tried to bring his people to repentance and save them from judgment and destruction. But they only rejected his message and cursed him for preaching it.

14. Does this ever happen today? Think of an illustration from everyday

life or from your experience in the church. _____

_____

_____

_____

_____

15. Read <u>Jer. 15:13-14</u>. Who is speaking to whom in this paragraph? _____

*   *

The Lord to Judah.

16. What is the topic of this paragraph? _____

*   *

The destruction and captivity of Judah.

17. What relationship can you see between Jeremiah's bitter complaint in

v. 10-12 and the Lord's answer in v. 15-18? _____ __

_____

* The Lord is not indifferent to Jeremiah's suffering or to Judah's treat-   *
ment of His messengers. His anger blazes. Compare 2 Chron. 36:15-21.
18. Read <u>Jer. 15:15-18</u>. Who is speaking to whom in this paragraph? _____

*   *

Jeremiah to the Lord.

19. What is the topic of this paragraph? _____

*   *

Jeremiah again speaks of the difficult role he has had to play.

20. What seems to be Jeremiah's purpose in this paragraph? _____

_____

*   *

He seems to complain of his sufferings so that the Lord will come to his aid.

21. Obviously this paragraph continues the thoughts expressed in _____ .
*   *

Jer. 15:10-16

22. We can consider Jer. 15:10-11, 15-18 as one of Jeremiah's "confessions."
List two characteristics which distinguish these verses from the rest of
Jeremiah's prophecies.

a. _____

b. _____
*   *

You should include or add the following:
a. Jeremiah speaks personally (in first person singular).
b. He expresses his inner struggle and feelings.

23. Read over v. 15-17 again and notice the strong feelings that Jeremiah
expresses.

a. What is his attitude toward his persecutors? _____

b. Is this a commendable attitude for a prophet? _____

c. Who are his persecutors? _____
*   *

a. Vengeance or hate or anger.
b. Certainly not.
c. They are Jeremiah's own people, who have rejected him.

24. What does Jeremiah's reference to "thy words" in v. 16 mean? _____

* _____   *

The prophecies he was given to proclaim.

25. What is Jeremiah's complaint in v. 17? _____

* _____   *

He was deprived of the normal pleasures of life and isolated from his people because of his calling.

26. What is Jeremiah's pain in v. 18? _____   _____

_____

_____

* _____   *

He is probably referring to the unrelenting responsibility of proclaiming
the coming judgment to an unrepentant people. He continues to preach that
terrible message, and the people continue to reject and reproach him. This
is like an open, festering wound which he has endured year after year.

27. Analyze Jeremiah's figure of a deceitful brook in v. 18.

A deceitful brook	The Lord
Is unreliable, dries up.	Is unreliable, fails to deliver Jeremiah

28. Here the Prophet Jeremiah approaches blasphemy, it seems to me. Of
course he does not <u>affirm</u> that the Lord <u>is</u> like a deceitful brook. He only
asks or suggests that He might be. But this is a miserable contrast to his
earlier concept of the Lord who had formed him in the womb and appointed
him to be a prophet to the nations (Jer. 1:5). Try to put yourself in Jere-

miah's position. Then write a short paragraph explaining v. 18. _____

_____

_____

_____

_____

_____

29. It seems Jeremiah in his bitterness has become almost as disrespectful
as his people toward the Lord. Compare his critical attitude toward the
Lord in v. 18 with Jer. 14:8,9. Does focusing on our own problems ever
make us bitter and critical toward God? Pray for anyone you know who has
this problem.

30. Remember, too, that Jeremiah had once referred to the Lord, not as "a
deceitful brook" but as "the fountain of living waters." Give the refer-

ence for this passage. _____

31. Can you think of a situation in which you and I might fall to the
depths of despair that Jeremiah experienced and speak to the Lord in terms

like v. 18? _____

_____

_____

_____

32. Do you think it was entirely bad that Jeremiah should give vent to his
feelings as he did in v. 15-18? Consider what the psychologists tell us
about our hostile feelings. Consider Rev. 3:15-19. Consider what follows

in Jer. 15:19-21. _____

_____

_____

33. Read Jer. 15:19-21. Who is speaking to whom in this passage? _____

_____

34. What is the Lord's response (v. 19) to Jeremiah's challenge (v.18)?

Put it in your own words. _____

_____

* _____ *

This is a call to repentance. The Lord does not answer Jeremiah's challenge.
He simply calls him back from his despair to his former obedience.

35. The Lord then offers to restore Jeremiah to his prophetic calling with
a simple, eloquent phrase. Copy that phrase here, then put beside it a
similar expression from Jer. 1:4-10.

Jer. 15:19-21	Jer. 1:4-10

*   *

You shall be as my mouth.   I have put my words in your mouth.

36. Explain these words: "They shall turn to you, but you shall not turn

to them." _____

_____

_____

* _____ *

Jeremiah should remain true to his calling and not become like the people.
In Jer. 15:18 Jeremiah had spoken like the people (Jer. 14:8-9), which was
worthless. If he would remain faithful, perhaps they would turn to him,
hear his message, and be saved.

37. In Rom. 12:2 Paul gives a similar exhortation. Write it down here. _____

_____

_____

38. In Jer. 15:20 the Lord gives Jeremiah a promise. But this is not a response to Jeremiah's hot demands in v. 18. Where have we seen these words

before? _____
*   *

Jer. 1:18-19. The Lord does not respond to Jeremiah's blasphemous challenge
in v. 18 but simply repeats the promise He had given Jeremiah when He first
called him.

39. Once again put yourself in Jeremiah's position as he hears these words
(v. 19-21). What do you think he felt?

What was his response? _____

_____

40. What evidence do we have that Jeremiah did repent and return to the

Lord? _____

_____

What would have happened if he had not responded to the Lord's calling in

v. 19-21? _____

Jeremiah must have repented and returned to the Lord because he continued to carry on his ministry as a prophet. This passage indicates that if he had not responded he would not have been able to serve as the mouth of the Lord.

41. What lesson for your own ministry do you find in this experience from

the life of Jeremiah? _____

_____

_____

_____

42. Jer. 15:5-21 probably has no direct relationship with the great drought (Jer. 14:1-15:4). There are several superficial links between the two passages, however. For example, 15:5-9 repeats the theme of destruction found in 14:17-18 and 15:1-4. We noted a similarity between 14:8-9 and 15:18. Jeremiah's intercession is mentioned in 14:11-16 and 15:11. Perhaps this is why Jer. 15:5-21 was located after Jer. 14:1-15:4 as the book of Jeremiah was compiled. Certainly the frustrating experience of Jeremiah at the time of the great drought provides an appropriate setting for his despondent rebellion. Mark off these two sections in your outline of the book of Jeremiah as follows:

a. Jer. 14:1-15:4 Great Drought.
b. Jer. 15:5-21 Jeremiah's Anguish.

D. More Confessions (Jeremiah 18:18-23; 20:7-18)

In this section you will study two more passages which reveal the struggle in Jeremiah's soul as he fulfills his tragic role as the Lord's prophet in a time of apostasy and destruction. Go through these "confessions" paragraph by paragraph and draw out their meaning as we have just done with Jer. 15:5-21. Use your imagination, but be sure to base your imagination on the text and on your understanding of the book of Jeremiah as a whole.

Use the following pages to work out your independent Inductive Study of Jer. 18:18-23 and Jer. 20:7-18. As you have done in other lessons, put down your questions as well as your conclusions in order to show how you have approached the text. This will give you material for a future class or Bible study or sermon. Ask questions which will bring out the meaning of the text, the experience of Jeremiah, and the application of Jeremiah's experience to your own ministry today. Look at the details and also the broader scope of the text. Use the methods which best help you interpret the text.

The study of these passages will help you in your analysis of Jeremiah's tragic role in the final section of this lesson. Also, you will be asked to report on your interpretation of these passages at the next class session. Still more important, you are testing your ability to do Inductive Bible Study on your own.

Jer. 18:18 _____

_____

_____

_____

_____

_____

_____

_____

Jer. 18:19-23 _____

_____

_____

_____

_____

_____

_____

_____

_____

_____

Jer. 20:7-12

_____

_____

_____

_____

_____

_____

_____

_____

_____

_____

_____

_____

_____

_____

Jer. 20:13 _____

_____

_____

_____

_____

_____

_____

_____

_____

Jer. 20:14-18 _____

Conclusions _____

_____

_____

_____

_____

_____

_____

_____

_____

_____

_____

_____

_____

_____

_____

_____

_____

_____

_____

_____

_____

_____

_____

E. Review and Summary

Although you have studied only a few chapters of the book of Jeremiah in
this course, you already know a lot about the prophet. In this lesson you
have studied several passages that reveal his strongest feelings and deepest tragedy. As you continue your Inductive Study of Jeremiah, you will
learn much more about the prophet's ministry and message.

In this last section of Lesson X you will bring together all the information
you have gathered about Jeremiah from the beginning of the course and especially in this lesson. Then you will be ready to write a summary on "Jeremiah, the Lord's Prophet in a Time of Judgment."

As usual, notice the procedure we are using. In the future you will want to
make summaries of other subjects in your Inductive Study of the Bible. You
may want to preach a series of sermons on Great Personalities of the Old
Testament, give a course of study on Great Pauline Doctrines, etc. So it
is important for you to learn how to summarize information and concepts
from relatively large sections of the Bible. And you will want to do this
inductively.

In this section you will not be able to confirm your answers to some of the
questions. Be sure to answer all the questions and be ready to discuss them
in class. Make a note of any problem you have and bring it up in class, too.

1. Write down, from memory, our definition of Inductive Bible Study. _____

_____

_____

* _____ *

Inductive Bible Study is an approach to Bible study that begins with the
Bible and studies it on its own terms.

2. Using the inductive approach, how should we summarize Jeremiah's role

as a prophet? _____

_____

_____

_____

_____

* _____ *

We should begin with the Bible, that is, with the book of Jeremiah. We should study the book to find out as much as we can about Jeremiah. Then we should bring together all this information as the book itself suggests. For example, we know that some sections are prophecies that Jeremiah gave to his people. Others are confessions of his own inner feelings. And others narrate what he did and what happened to him.

3. Mention at least one non-inductive way to summarize Jeremiah's role. _____

_____

_____

There are several procedures:
a. One way would be to find a summary in a commentary.
b. Another way would be to look in a Bible dictionary or in a book about the prophets or in a history of the Old Testament or in some other book.
c. Another way would be to use a sermon outline you have heard or Sunday School lesson materials.

4. The following steps will help you write a summary of Jeremiah's role based on an Inductive Study of the book of Jeremiah. We will consider the following information about Jeremiah, most of which we have already studied.

> I. His Personal Life
>
> II. His Message
>
> III. Incidents from His Ministry
>
> IV. His Inner Struggle

I. Jeremiah's Personal Life

5. First, read over Jer. 1:4-19, the call of Jeremiah. Remember your previous study of this passage. It gives us some of the basic concepts of his role. Summarize briefly these ideas paragraph by paragraph.

a. Jer. 1:4-10. _____

_____

_____

_____

_____

b. Jer. 1:11-12. _____

_____

_____

c. Jer. 1:13-16. _____

_____

_____

_____

d. Jer. 1:17-19. _____

_____

_____

_____

* _____ *

If necessary you may refer back to Lesson II. Be sure you have taken into
account not only the words of these paragraphs but also the Old Testament
concepts of the holy, powerful Lord, the efficacy of His word, and the role
of the prophets in proclaiming and fulfilling His will. And think of the
importance of the Lord's call, His sovereign presence, and His promises
during Jeremiah's ministry for 40 long, tragic years ending in the destruction of Jerusalem.

6. In order to check over your summary of Jeremiah's call, answer the following questions based on Jer. 1:4-19.

a. To whom was Jeremiah sent as a prophet? _____

_____

b. What were the two basic functions or objectives of Jeremiah's ministry? ___

_____

_____

_____

c. What circumstances prevailed in Judah at that time? _____

_____

_____

_____

d. What was the attitude of the people of Judah, including the political

and religious leaders, toward Jeremiah? _____

_____

e. What was the theological significance of the fall of Jerusalem at the

end of Jeremiah's ministry? _____

_____

_____

7. Read over <u>Jer. 11:18-23.</u> This is a passage which you have not yet studied. It contains an interesting and significant reference to Jeremiah's per-

sonal life. Write a brief summary of this passage. _____

_____

_____

_____

_____

8. In order to check over your summary of this passage, answer the following questions.

a. Who opposed Jeremiah, according to this passage? _____

_____

b. What special significance did Anathoth have for Jeremiah? _____

_____

c. What did these men try to do to Jeremiah? _____

_____

9. Read over Jer. 16:1-13. This is a passage which you have not studied in
detail. Write a summary of what this passage tells us of Jeremiah's role or

ministry._____

_____

_____

_____

_____

_____

10. In order to check your summary of this passage, answer the following
questions.

a. What limitation was placed on Jeremiah's personal life, according to

v. 1-4? _____

b. What further restrictions were placed on his life according to v. 5-9? ____

_____

_____

c. Explain the terrifying expression, "I will hurl you out of this land." ____

_____

_____

_____

II. Jeremiah's Message

11. Turn to **Jer. 2:1-4:4.** The overall subject of Jeremiah's message in this

collection of prophecies is _____.

12. We have already summarized Jeremiah's message in these prophecies. You
will be able to recall these four main points by reading through a few of
these paragraphs.

a. _____

b. _____

c. _____

d. _____

If necessary, you may refer back to Lesson V.

13. In Jer. 1:10 we noted that Jeremiah's message has two objectives, one negative and the other positive. According to your summary of Jeremiah's message in Jer. 2:1-4:4, what was the negative objective and what was the positive objective?

a. Negative: _____

b. Positive: _____

14. We made a study of Jeremiah's use of literary figures in Jer. 2:1-4:4. Make a list of some of the things to which he compares his people. (Note that some of the figures do not refer to Israel or Judah. List only those which do refer to Jeremiah's people).

a. _____   e. _____

b. _____   f. _____

c. _____   g. _____

d. _____   h. _____

15. Are these figures complimentary? Do you think the people were pleased at Jeremiah's message? How did they respond to his constant preaching

against their apostasy? _____

_____

16. Now look at Jer. 4:5-6:30. This section is a collection of prophecies which deal almost exclusively with one of the four main themes of Jeremiah's message. Perhaps these prophecies come from a later period in Jeremiah's ministry when Judah's political situation had become very critical. What

is the constant theme of these paragraphs? _____

_____

17. What is the title we have used for this section of the book of Jere-

miah? _____

18. Explain the following.

a. The enemy from the north. _____

_____

b. The enemy from within. _____

_____

c. The relationship between the enemy from the north and the enemy from

within: _____

_____

_____

* —— *

If necessary, you may refer back to Lesson VI.

19. In our study of Jer. 2:1-4:4 and 4:5-6:30 we noted that Jeremiah spoke
of three different kinds of evil being practiced by his people. List them.

a. _____

b. _____

c. _____

20. Throughout Jer. 4:5-6:30 Jeremiah describes again and again the awful
destruction which is coming upon Judah. How did the people respond to these
prophecies? Did they approve of Jeremiah's message? Why did Jeremiah call

himself "a man of strife and contention" (Jer. 15:10)? _____

_____

_____

_____

III. Incidents from Jeremiah's Ministry.

21. Turn to Jer. 7:1-8:3 and Jer. 26, the Temple Sermon. Write a brief sum-

mary of what happened to Jeremiah on that occasion. _____

_____

_____

_____

* —— *

If necessary, you may refer back to Lesson VII.

22. Answer the following questions based on the same passages, Jer. 7:1-8:3
and Jer. 26.

a. What did the people and the priests and the prophets try to do to Jeremiah after he preached this sermon? _____

_____

b. Why were they so angry with Jeremiah? What did they accuse him of? _____

_____

_____

_____

c. What was the purpose of Jeremiah's sermon? Was it for their own good that he preached? _____

_____

_____

d. How did Jeremiah defend himself against their accusations? _____

_____

_____

23. Explain the following phrases:

a. "The Temple of the Lord" (Jer. 7:4) _____

_____

b. "a den of robbers" (Jer. 7:11) _____

_____

c. "as I did to Shiloh" (Jer. 7:14) _____

_____

_____

24. Turn to the Broken Flask Episode, Jer. 19:1-20:6. Explain briefly the meaning and significance of this acted parable. _____

_____

_____

_____

*   _____   *

If necessary, you may refer back to Lesson IX, Section C. Remember particularly the concept people had of the prophets' words and actions at the time of Jeremiah.

25. Answer the following questions based on the same passage, Jer. 19:1-20:6.

a. What terrible evil was being practiced in Judah? _____

_____

b. What terrible judgment did Jeremiah pronounce upon them? _____

_____

c. What was the objective of this prophecy? Did it include any note of hope

or a call to repentance? _____

_____

_____

26. Who heard Jeremiah's message at the Potsherd Gate? _____

_____

Who heard his message at the court of the Temple? _____

_____

How do you think the leaders and the people reacted to this message?_____

_____

27. What did Pashhur, the Temple officer, do to Jeremiah? _____

_____

How did Jeremiah feel about this experience? (Use your imagination.) _____

_____

_____

_____

28. Turn to the Yoke-Bars Episode, Jer. 27-28. Summarize the meaning of
this acted parable. _____

_____

_____

_____

* _____ *

If necessary, you may refer back to Lesson IX, Section D.

29. Answer the following questions based on Jer. 27-28.

a. Who was Judah's greatest enemy at this time? _____

b. What was Jeremiah's counsel with regard to that enemy? _____

_____

c. What did the people and King Zedekiah think of Jeremiah's counsel? (Use
your imagination.) _____

_____

30. Here again Jeremiah comes into conflict with the other prophets.

a. What did the other prophets prophesy, according to Jer. 27? _____

_____

_____

b. What did Hananiah prophesy, according to Jer. 28? _____

_____

_____

c. What did the people and King Zedekiah think of these false prophecies?
(Use your imagination.) _____

_____

_____

31. Consider what Jeremiah must have felt when he encountered the Prophet Hananiah.

a. What did Hananiah say about Jeremiah's message? _____

_____

b. What did Hananiah do to Jeremiah's yoke-bars? _____

_____

c. Who witnessed the incident and heard Hananiah's prophecy? _____

_____

d. What did Jeremiah feel at that moment? (Use your imagination. And note

that Jeremiah did not reply to Hananiah until sometime later,) _____

_____

_____

_____

IV. Jeremiah's Inner Struggle.

32. Throughout our study we have noted that the book of Jeremiah describes a great deal about Jeremiah's role and reveals his inner feelings about his role as the Lord's prophet.

Remember briefly Jeremiah's call in Jer. 1:4-19. What was his first response when the Lord called him to be a prophet to the nations? What did he feel

about himself? _____

_____

_____

33. In Jer. 4:5-6:30 we noted three passages which describe Jeremiah's role in very difficult and tragic terms. Explain briefly each of these references.

a. Jer. 5:14 _____

_____

b. Jer. 6:11 _____

_____

c. Jer. 6:27 _____

_____

34. No doubt Jeremiah's feelings toward himself and toward his people and toward the Lord changed and contradicted themselves many times as he watched the destruction of his people. Explain briefly his feelings expressed

in Jer. 4:19-22. _____

_____

_____

_____

35. In this lesson we studied Jeremiah's prophecies at the time of the great drought, Jer. 14:1-15:4. Summarize Jeremiah's role in this section.

_____

_____

_____

_____

36. The following questions are based on the same passage.

a. When the people confessed their sins and prayed to the Lord for help,

what did He answer them? _____

_____

b. Jeremiah interceded for his people and tried to blame the false prophets for their continued apostasy. But what did the Lord command Jeremiah specifically? _____

_____

37. Finally, we studied Jeremiah's confessions in three passages, Jer. 15:10-18, Jer. 18:18-23, and Jer. 20:7-18. Summarize briefly the deep feelings that Jeremiah expressed in these passages:

a. Toward himself and his role: _____

_____

_____

b. Toward his people: _____

_____

_____

c. Toward the Lord: _____

_____

_____

38. These are terrible, despicable, blasphemous things for any man to say.
It is almost unbelievable that these feelings were expressed by a prophet
of the Lord. Explain in your own words why Jeremiah fell to such depths

of tragedy and horror. _____

_____

_____

_____

* _____ *

Your explanation should reflect your understanding of the book of Jeremiah
as a whole up to this point. Note that we cannot and should not justify
Jeremiah's feelings and expressions. But we can and should try to understand them and learn from them.

39. The outstanding fact that comes out of our study of Jeremiah's inner
struggle is not his weakness and his failure. The remarkable thing is that
he kept on serving the Lord, year after year, even through the final siege
and destruction and deportation of the city of Jerusalem. That is why his
prophecies and experiences are recorded for us, even these terrible words.

What did Jeremiah have to do in order to continue as the Lord's prophet? _____

_____

_____

With what words did the Lord renew His call to Jeremiah? _____

_____

_____

What promise did the Lord renew at this time? _____

_____
*   *

See Jer. 15:19-21.

40. There is no time now to write out your summary on "Jeremiah, the Lord's
Prophet in a Time of Judgment." In this section, however, you have gathered
enough material to write such a summary. You have also reviewed much of
Lessons I-X. Refer back to this section in the future when you want to
review your study of Jeremiah's tragic role.

11

Important Events in the Life of Jeremiah
(Jeremiah 21-29)

In the previous lesson you studied Jeremiah's role as the Lord's prophet in a time of judgment. You reviewed his call, his message, and some incidents from his ministry. Most of all you tried to analyze Jeremiah's concept of himself as the Lord's prophet and his inner struggle.

In this lesson you will read through several chapters of the book of Jeremiah which describe important events in the life of Jeremiah. As a prophet he not only preached in the Temple and in the streets of Jerusalem. He not only proclaimed his message to the people and to the religious leaders of the nation. And his message was not just a call to spiritual and moral renewal. Jeremiah counseled the kings of Judah. He spoke to his own people, and to the nations. He proclaimed the Lord's will for the heart of men, for the life of His people, and for the course of history.

As you study these passages consider the wider scope of Jeremiah's ministry. Look at the implications of his message for the rulers of his people. And see if there is any application of his experience for us today.

Your objectives in this lesson are to:

Identify important events and collections of prophecies in Jer. 21-29.

Locate these events on your chronological chart.

Summarize Jeremiah's message in each section.

A. Jeremiah 21

Read through Jer. 21, keeping in mind the objectives we have just listed for this lesson. Underline any historical references, for example, dates, names of kings, descriptions of what was happening, any countries that are mentioned. This will help you identify the important events in Jeremiah's life and locate them on your chronological chart.

As you read through each paragraph, notice any other details that should be explained and look for the main ideas. Fill in your outline of the book of Jeremiah for this passage as you have done previously for each section we have studied. As you put down the main idea and a title for each paragraph, you are summarizing Jeremiah's message.

Do not go on to the following questions until you have completed the previous tasks.

1. One of the first steps in identifying an event is to give it a date. For example, we know that the first deportation under Nebuchadnezzar took place in 598 B.C. and that Jerusalem was destroyed in 587 B.C.

When you are studying a passage in Jeremiah which describes an important event, try to give it a date, also. Sometimes the passage tells exactly

what year it refers to. In other cases you can figure out more or less when
it took place. But in some cases you cannot tell what year or even what
period it refers to.

a. Does Jer. 21 give an exact date? _____

b. Does it indicate a general date or period of history? _____

_____

c. What clues as to date have you found in this chapter? _____

* _____ *

a. No.
b. Yes. It refers to Zedekiah's reign, which took place 598-587 B.C.
c. In addition to the references to Zedekiah you should have noted the Babylonian siege, which is mentioned in v. 4 and 9.

2. This chapter refers to the Babylonian siege of Jerusalem when Zedekiah

was king. So we can give it a date between _____ B.C. and _____ B.C.

(See your chronological chart.)

3. Once you have identified a passage like this with a date or with a specific event, you can look for further information about that event. This
will help you understand the background of the passage, and it may help
you interpret specific details of the passage.

Where in the Bible can you find more information about the Babylonian siege?
Give three references.

a. _____

b. _____

c. _____

* _____ *

Probably the three most important passages are:
a. Jer. 52:4-27
b. 2 Kings 25:1-26
c. 2 Chronicles 36:17-21

4. Where outside the Bible can you find more imformation about the Babylo-

nian siege? _____

* _____ *

There are many possibilities. Probably the most useful sources are books on the history of Israel and the Old Testament.

5. You now know that Jer. 21 refers to a certain period, 589-587 B.C., and to a specific event, the Babylonian siege. And you know where to find additional information about that event.

Look at the text again and see if it specifies the occasion or the reason for these prophecies.

a. To whom does Jeremiah say these words? _____

b. Why does Jeremiah speak to them? _____

_____

c. What is the topic of his message? _____

* _____ *

a. Pashhur the son of Malchiah and Zephaniah the priest.
b. Because they are sent by King Zedekiah to ask for his counsel.
c. The Lord's will regarding the Babylonian siege.

6. Is this Pashhur the same person as the Pashhur mentioned in Jer. 20? How

can you tell? _____

_____

* _____ *

They are evidently two different people, because Jer. 20:1 refers to Pashhur the son of Immer and Jer. 21:1 refers to Pashhur the son of Malchiah.

7. Look up the following names in your concordance and write down the information you find and the references.

a. Pashhur son of Malchiah: _____

_____

_____

b. Zephaniah the priest: _____

_____

_____

* ─── *

a. Pashhur is mentioned in Jer. 38 as one of the princes of Judah who condemned Jeremiah to death and who threw him into a cistern.
b. Zephaniah is mentioned in 2 Kings 25:18, Jer. 29:25, 29; 37:3; 52:24.
Apparently he was not hostile to Jeremiah. He was killed by Nebuchadnezzar
at Riblah after the fall of Jerusalem.

8. Explain who are the Chaldeans. If in doubt, consult a Bible dictionary.

_____

_____

_____

9. As you study this passage, consider the historic importance of the event
and the dramatic elements of the story, the background information that you
have and use your imagination.

a. Who is inquiring of the Lord? _____

b. What has been his attitude toward the Lord? _____

_____

c. What is his attitude as he makes this request? _____

_____

d. What answer does he want from Jeremiah? _____

_____

e. What power does he have over Jeremiah? _____

* ─── *

a. King Zedekiah.
b. He was an evil king, disobedient to the Lord.
c. He is very conciliatory, praising the Lord to gain His favor.
d. He wants Jeremiah to say that Jerusalem will be spared.
e. He can have Jeremiah put to death, as in Jer. 38.

10. Think of Jeremiah's position as the Lord's prophet and at the same time
as a citizen of Jerusalem.

a. What was Jeremiah's reply about Nebuchadnezzar and the Chaledeans? _____

_____

_____

b. What was Jeremiah's message regarding King Zedekiah? _____

_____

c. What was Jeremiah's advice to the people of Jerusalem? _____

_____

d. What was the political situation at that time? _____

_____

e. In the light of this situation, how would Jeremiah's message to Zedekiah

and his advice to the people be taken? _____

* _____ *

a. The Lord would fight with the enemy against Jerusalem and destroy her.
b. Zedekiah and his followers would be defeated and destroyed mercilessly.
c. They should abandon the city and surrender to the enemy.
d. It was war time. The city was surrounded by the enemy.
e. This was treason. In most countries a man who spoke this way would be
silenced immediately.

11. It would be interesting to know King Zedekiah's reaction when his emis-
saries returned from their interview with Jeremiah.

a. What does the text tell us about Zedekiah's response? _____

b. What do you think was his reaction? _____

* _____ *

The text tells us nothing. But we can imagine that he was angry with Jeremiah because of his terrible prophecies.

12. Remember that the book of Jeremiah is not arranged in chronological
order. It does not tell the complete, chronological story of Jeremiah's life
and ministry. We have found collections of prophetic sayings in some sections. In others we have found rather long descriptions of incidents in the
life of Jeremiah. We have noted personal, inner expressions from the soul
of Jeremiah. And often we have seen that different kinds of materials are
mixed together: prophetic sayings, incidents, and confessions.

Now look at Jer. 21 and analyze what it contains.

a. Give the reference for the part that refers specifically to the

story of King Zedekiah's inquiry._____

b. What does the rest of the chapter contain?_____

_____

c. In what way is this material different from the first part of the chapter?

_____

_____

d. It may be that the second part of the chapter comes from a different time

in Jeremiah's ministry. If so, why was it placed here?_____

_____

*   *
_____

a.Jer. 21:1-10. Although v. 8-10 does not mention Zedekiah, it does refer
to the siege of the Chaldeans.
b. These are prophetic sayings addressed "to the house of the king of Judah."
c. It does not mention Zedekiah or the siege or any specific incident. And
it is poetry, in contrast to Jer. 1:1-10.
d. Look for similarity of theme and for other links. For example, both Jer.
21:1-10 and 11-14 contain prophecies for the kings of Judah. And the expression "I myself will fight against you" in v. 5 is very similar to the
phrase "I am against you" in v. 13.

13. Review the steps we have taken in our study of Jer. 21. These steps
may be useful as you study other, similar passages in the book of Jeremiah.
Go back to the beginning of this section of the lesson and write down the
steps we have followed.

a. We read through the chapter, underlining historical references._____

b. _____

c. _____

d. _____

e. _____

f. _____

g. _____

B. Jeremiah 22-23

Read through Jer. 22-23 as you did the previous chapter. See if this passage or part of it refers to a specific event in the life of Jeremiah. Underline historical references that will help you identify or relate these prophecies to specific kings, periods, and events.

As you go through Jer. 22-23, pick out the main idea and a title for each paragraph and write this information in your outline. Underline words and phrases in the text that will help you find the structure and define Jeremiah's message in this part of the book.

The following questions are based on the previous steps. Therefore do not try to answer them until you have completed the above assignment. We will only be able to consider certain general aspects and some of the details of this passage because it is rather long.

1. In your reading of Jer. 22-23, did you find any specific event from the life of Jeremiah? Do any of these paragraphs describe Jeremiah's encounter with specific people as in Jer. 21:1-10? What kind of material do Chapters

22 and 23 contain? _____

_____

* _____ *

No specific event is mentioned. These chapters contain collections of Jeremiah's prophecies.

2. Certain kings of Judah are mentioned. List these kings and give references for the paragraphs which deal with each one.

a. _____

b. _____

c. _____

3. Be sure you have identified these kings. All of them have other names. List them again and give their alternate names and put down the dates for each one's reign.

a. _____

b. _____

c. _____

*   *

See your chronological chart. You may also refer back to Lesson III, A. And
you may refer to 2 Kings and 2 Chron. And you may consult a Bible dictionary.

4. This information will help you relate at least two of these prophecies
to specific periods and specific events.

a. Jer. 22:11-12 refers to what event? _____

_____

b. Jer. 22:24-30 refers to what event? _____

*   *

_____

a. King Jehoahaz (Shallum) was deposed and taken captive to Egypt in 609 B.C.
b. King Jehoiachin (Coniah, Jeconiah) was deposed and taken captive to Babylon in 598 B.C.

5. Most of Jer. 22-23 contains collections of Jeremiah's prophecies. As you
worked through these chapters you should have noted the repetition of certain topics. And you should have noted that this whole passage is divided
into two parts. The first part is a collection of prophecies about one subject. The second part is a collection of prophecies about another subject.

Look over the key words and phrases you have underlined in the text. And
read over your outline for Jer. 22-23. Then write down the references and
the topics for the two sections.

a. _____

b. _____

*   *

a. Prophecies concerning the kings of Judah, Jer. 22:1-23:8.
b. Prophecies concerning the false prophets, Jer. 23:9-40.

6. If you have not done so previously glance rapidly over these sections
and underline all the references to the kings of Judah and the prophets.
These references show clearly the paragraph groupings we have defined.

In Jer. 22:20-23 and Jer. 23:1-4 the kings are referred to as _____.

7. In order to complete our analysis of structure here, we should compare
the material in Jer. 22-23 with the paragraphs that precede and follow
these chapters. Refer back to Jer. 21 and look ahead at Jer. 24.

a. Where does the collection of prophecies concerning the kings of Judah

begin? _____

b. Where does it end? _____

c. Where does the collection of prophecies concerning the false prophets

begin? _____

d. Where does it end? _____
*   *

a. Jer. 21:11. Do not include Jer. 21:1-10 because it is a separate, complete story of a specific event.
b. Jer. 23:8.
c. Jer. 23:9.
d. Jer. 23:40.

8. Now identify these two sections on your outline of the book of Jeremiah,
and mark off Jer. 21:1-10 as a separate section as follows:

a. Jer. 21:1-10   "Zedekiah's Inquiry
b. Jer. 21:11-23:8   "Concerning Kings of Judah"
c. Jer. 23:9-40   "Concerning False Prophets"

Be sure you know how to put this information in your outline. And keep it
up to date. You may be required to show your outline at any class session.
And your outline will be graded at the end of the course. This is one of
the most useful steps in Inductive Bible Study, so it is very important
that each student work out his outline as he goes through these lessons.
For the same reason, ask for further explanations in class if you do not
understand how we have made this analysis.

9. Write a summary of Jeremiah's prophecies concerning the kings of Judah.

List only the main ideas in Jer. 21:11-23:8. _____

_____

_____

_____

_____
*   *

Your summary should include these basic themes:
a. The Lord exhorts them to do justice and righteousness.
b. He warns them of destruction because of their injustices and idolatry.
c. Judah will be destroyed and her people exiled but a remnant shall return.

10. Write down Jeremiah's specific prophecies concerning the following:

a. Shallum _____

b. Jehoiakin _____

c. Coniah _____

11. Explain the significance of Jer. 23:5-6. _____

_____

_____

_____

* _____ *

This is one of the few messianic prophecies in the book of Jeremiah. In contrast to the present evil kings who lead astray the people and deliver them
into the hands of their enemies, a true descendant of David will one day
rule over Judah, wisely, justly, and righteously. We believe that Jesus
Christ is the fulfillment of this prophecy.

12. Cite other passages in Jeremiah and elsewhere that repeat the messianic

theme of the Branch of David. _____

* _____ *

See Jer. 33:15, Is. 4:2; 11:1, Zech. 3:8; 6:12

13. Write a summary of Jeremiah's prophecies concerning the false prophets.

List only the main ideas of Jer. 23:9-40. _____

_____

_____

_____

_____

_____

_____

_____

14. List the specific evils which the prophets were practicing, according to this passage.

a. _____

b. _____

c. _____

d. _____

*   *

a. They prophesied by Baal.
b. They committed adultery.
c. They filled the people with false hope at a time of judgment.
d. They prophesied lies, claiming that their messages were from the Lord.

15. Explain, as we have done elsewhere, why the prophets told the people

that no evil would come upon them. _____

_____

16. Explain why this was a terrible thing to do. _____

_____

_____

*   *

These lies perverted the Lord's real message of judgment and gave the people false hope when they should have been called to repentance. If they had repented, perhaps they could have been saved from the coming destruction.

17. List two or three other passages which we have studied where Jeremiah

prophesies concerning the false prophets. _____

_____

18. No doubt these prophets were Jeremiah's bitterest enemies throughout his ministry. Explain why it was especially hard for Jeremiah to deal with

the other prophets. _____

_____

*   *

Probably his greatest difficulty stemmed from the fact that these prophets,
like Jeremiah, claimed that their prophecies were from the Lord. But they
contradicted Jeremiah. And their messages pleased the people whereas his
prophecies were very unpleasant.

19. What is the final proof of true prophecy over against false prophecy?

_____

*   _____   *

We noted in an earlier lesson that the final proof is that which comes to
pass.

20. What judgment did Jeremiah prophesy against the false prophets? _____

_____

_____

*   _____   *

The Lord will bring evil upon them (v. 12). He will feed them poison (v. 15).
He will oppose them (v. 30-32) and cast them off (v. 33-40).

C. Jeremiah 24-25

Read through Jer. 24-25 as you did in sections A and B of this lesson. See
what events are referred to in these chapters. Underline references to dates,
kings, and specific events.

Work out your outline for these chapters. Analyze the main idea and write a
title for each paragraph. Then try to identify groups of paragraphs or sections of the book.

When you have completed these steps go on to the following questions. As
always, notice the kinds of questions that are raised as you study the text.
In the following section of this lesson you will have the opportunity of
studying a similar passage on your own.

1. What important events or dates are reported in Jer. 24-25? Give the references and dates for these events.

a. _____

b. _____

*   _____   *

a. Jer. 24:1 refers to the exile of King Jeconiah.
b. Jer. 25:1-3 refers to the fourth year of King Jehoiakim which was the
first year of Nebuchadnezzar, the 23rd year of Jeremiah's ministry.

2. Consider Jer. 24:1. Give Jeconiah's other name and the date of his exile.

* _____ *

Jehoiachin.   598 B.C.

3. Consider Jer. 25:1-3. Give the dates of Jehoiakim's reign and calculate

the date of this prophecy. _____
*   *

Jehoiakim reigned from 609 to 598 B.C. Jer. 25 refers to the year 605 B.C.

4. What great event took place at about the time Jeremiah prophesied the

words found in Jer. 25? Check your chronological chart. _____

* _____ *

The Battle of Carchemish.

5. You now have two important dates which indicate the historical background
of these prophecies of Jeremiah. On the basis of these historical references,
divide Jer. 24-25 into two sections. Give the reference for each section.

a. _____

b. _____
*   *

a. Jer. 24:1-10
b. Jer. 25:1-38

6. Look over Jer. 24:1-10.

a. Does this passage seem to be a unit? Do the paragraphs all belong to-

gether in a section? _____

b. What is the main topic of this section? What is Jeremiah's message in

Jer. 24:1-10 about? _____

_____

c. How is this topic related to the historical reference at the beginning

(Jer. 24:1)? _____

_____

d. Write a brief (three or four words) title for this section, Jer. 24:1-10.

* _____ *

a. Yes.
b. This section presents Jeremiah's vision of the two baskets of figs, which
contains a message about the exile.
c. The message of Jer. 24:1-10 refers directly to the historical event, the
exile of Jehoiachin, which is mentioned in v. 1. In other words, Jer. 24:1
is an introduction to the vision of the two baskets of figs.
d. A possible title: "Two Baskets of Figs."

7. Analyze the figure of the baskets of figs. Use one diagram for the good
figs and the other for the bad figs.

8. Write a brief summary of Jeremiah's message in Jer. 24. _____

_____

_____

_____

_____

9. Now look over Jer. 25:1-38.

a. Does this passage seem to be one unit? Do all these paragraphs seem to

belong together in one section? _____

_____

b. What is the main topic of this section? What is Jeremiah's message about in Jer. 25:1-38? _____

_____

c. How is this topic related to the historical reference at the beginning

(Jer. 25:1)? _____

_____

_____

_____

_____

d. Write a brief (three or four words) title for this section. _____

* _____ *

a. It is difficult to tell how much of Jer. 25:1-38 originally referred to
Jeremiah's prophecies in the fourth year of Jehoiakim. But these paragraphs
do seem to be grouped together.
b. These prophecies are mainly about Babylon and the nations.
c. There is a very interesting relationship between the historical reference in Jer. 25:1 and the prophecies of this chapter. We have noted that
the Battle of Carchemish took place at about this time. At that battle
Babylonia defeated Egypt and became the dominant empire in the Near East,
including Judah and the surrounding nations. So Jeremiah's prophecies
about Babylonia and the nations are very appropriately related to this
historical reference.
d. A possible title: "Babylon and the Nations."

10. In order to compare Jeremiah's message here with his message elsewhere
in the book, write down the summary which we made in our study of Jer. 2:1-
4:4. The overall theme is "Israel's Apostasy." List the main ideas of Jeremiah's message in that section.

a. _____

b. _____

c. _____

d. _____
*   *

Check your answer by referring back to Lesson V.

11. Now analyze Jeremiah's message in each of the paragraphs of Chapter 25.
Indicate first to whom the prophecy is directed (Judah or the nations). Then
note which of the above ideas is expressed.

1-7	to Judah	Judah's call to repentance
8-14		
15-16		
17-26		
27		
28-29		
30-31		
32		
33-38		

12. How is the first paragraph, Jer. 25:1-7, different from the rest of

the chapter? _____

_____

_____

* _____ *

It is the only paragraph that contains a call to repentance. The rest of
the chapter speaks of judgment. Also, it is the only paragraph addressed
exclusively to Judah. The other paragraphs are addressed to Judah and the
nations or just to the nations.

13. Note the reference to the enemy from the north in Jer. 25:9. You will
recall that this theme appears repeatedly from the beginning of the book
of Jeremiah.

a. What is the first reference to the enemy from the north? _____

b. On what occasion, apparently, did Jeremiah receive that first prophecy

about the enemy from the north? _____

c. What section of the book of Jeremiah which we have studied includes several references to the enemy from the north? _____

d. What is the title of that section? _____

_____

e. What nation is the principal enemy from the north, according to Jer. 25:9?

_____

f. In what year did this nation become a major enemy or threat to Judah?

_____
*   *

a. Jer. 1:13-16   d. "The Enemy from the North and the Enemy
b. His call.   from Within"
c. Jer. 4:5-6:30   e. Babylonia
                                f. 605 B.C. - at the Battle of Carchemish

14. Look up the location of Judah and Babylonia on a map.

a. In what direction is Babylon from Jerusalem? _____

b. Why is Babylon called the enemy from the north? _____

_____

_____
*   *

a. To the east.
b. As we noted in Lesson III, Babylonia would not invade Judah straight
across the Arabian Desert. She would go up the Euphrates Valley and then
down on Judah from the north.

15. Look up Carchemish on the map.

a. In what direction is Carchemish from Jerusalem? _____

b. After what event did Babylon begin to invade Judah? _____

_____
*   *

a. To the north.
b. After the Battle of Carchemish.

16. Where in the book of Jeremiah is the Battle of Carchemish mentioned

specifically? _____ (See a concordance)

What date does that passage give for the Battle? _____

How does that date compare with the date for Jer. 25? _____
*   *

Jer. 46:2
The fourth year of Jehoiakim.
It is the same date.

17. Both Jer. 25:1 and Jer. 25:9 refer to Nebuchadnezzar (a variant spel-
ling of Nebuchadrezzar) as the king of Babylon. In what year did Nebuchad-

nezzar become king of Babylon? _____
*   *

605 B.C. Note that Jer. 25:1 mentions that the fourth year of Jehoiakim
was the first year of Nebuchadnezzar.

18. Consult a Bible dictionary to check the date when Nebuchadnezzar became king.

What year does the dictionary give? _____

Did he become king before or after the Battle of Carchemish? _____

19. Jer. 25 refers to the year _____ B.C. The Battle of Carchemish took

place in the year _____ B.C. Nebuchadnezzar became king of Babylon in

the year _____ B.C.
*   *

All three should be marked 605 B.C.

20. Summarize Jeremiah's prophecies in Jer. 25:8-14 concerning:

a. Judah: _____

_____

_____

b. The nations: _____

_____

_____

c. Babylon: _____

21. Of particular interest is Jeremiah's prophecy concerning the 70 years
of Babylonian ascendancy. Probably the number was originally intended as a
round number. Nevertheless it turned out to be remarkably accurate, for
Babylon was defeated in 539 B.C. by Persia.

a. One way to calculate the period of Babylonian dominance is to begin with
the fall of Nineveh (Assyria) and end with the fall of Babylon. Put down

these two dates and indicate the length of this period. _____

b. Another way is to begin with the Battle of Carchemish (when Egypt was
defeated) and end with the fall of Babylon. Put down these two dates and

indicate the length of this period. _____

22. Note the phrase "everything written in this book" in v. 13. At some
later date you should make a further study of the technical problems surrounding Jer. 25:12-14. Following is a brief summary of some of the Old
Testament scholars' comments.

As the text stands now, the threat of v. 13 is against Babylonia. However
there are signs of considerable change in v. 12-14, particularly in the
ancient Septuagint (Greek) version, which predates our Hebrew version.

The Septuagint omits all references to Nebuchadnezzar and Babylon in
Jer. 25:1-12 and ends this discourse with the phrase "everything written
in this book." It then omits v. 14 and inserts all of Jer. 46-51, the
prophecies concerning the nations.

Perhaps the original version was much briefer, and the threat in v. 13 was
against Judah. The phrase "everything written in this book" would refer to
the prophecies underlying Jer. 1-25.

23. Jer. 25:15-38 contains prophecies concerning the nations. We will consider only v. 15-28.

Analyze the figure of the cup of wine.

24. Summarize Jeremiah's message in Jer. 25:15-28. _____

_____

_____

_____

_____

25. Underline in the text the names of the nations about whom Jeremiah
prophesies in Jer. 25:15-28.

26. Consider Jeremiah's role in this passage as the Lord's prophet.

a. From the beginning of his ministry Jeremiah was called to be a prophet

to _____.

b. As a prophet of the Lord he was called not only to proclaim the word of

the Lord but also to _____

_____.

c. In Jer. 25:15-28 he was commanded not just to tell the nations about the

Lord's wrath but to _____

_____.

d. This simple man from the tiny village of Anathoth thus played a major

role at one of the major turning points of history when _____

_____

_____

* _____. *

a. the nations
b. be the Lord's instrument in carrying out His will.
c. take the cup of the wine of the wrath and make them drink it.
d. the Babylonian Empire gained the ascendancy over Egypt and extended its
rule from the Persian Gulf to the Sinai Peninsula.

D. Jeremiah 29

In this section your assignment is to study Jer. 29 on your own. Analyze
this chapter as we have analyzed the other passages in this lesson. Work
out your outline. Note all historical references, and place these prophecies in their historical context. Underline and explain difficult and important words and phrases. Summarize Jeremiah's message. Consider Jeremiah's
role as he proclaimed these prophecies and lived these experiences.

Put down on notebook paper all your questions as well as the information
you are able to uncover. This will help you follow a careful, inductive
procedure. In so far as is possible lay out your steps in logical order so
that you can evaluate your work later. Finally, see if the material you
develop would provide a good basis for a class discussion or small group
Bible study.

This assignment should be added to your Jeremiah notebook. Lesson IX. E,
(Jer. 18) should have been added to your notebook as well.

E. Summary

In the previous sections of this lesson you studied Jer. 21-25 and 29. In
Lesson VII you studied Jer. 26, and in Lesson IX you studied Jer. 27-28. In
this final section of Lesson XI you will summarize the content and composi-
tion of Jer. 21-29. And you will review the methods used in this lesson.

1. Turn to Jer. 21-29 in your Bible. It would be impossible to remember the
entire content and it is not necessary. But even with your Bible in front
of you it is difficult to tell exactly what these chapters contain.

Now look at your outline of the book of Jeremiah. What is the purpose of
this outline? What does it tell you, for example, about Jer. 21-29?

_____

_____

_____

_____

It summarizes the content. It tells briefly and concisely what the author
of the book has to say. It gives the main idea of Jer. 21-29, for example.
And it shows how this material is organized.

2. What two levels of structure do you have in your outline of Jer. 21-29.

a. _____

b. _____
*   *

a. Paragraphs
b. Sections

3. Why is it necessary to outline the sections as well as the paragraphs?

How many paragraphs are there in Jer. 21-29? _____

   _____

   _____

* _____ *

Jer. 21-29 contains 55 paragraphs. You need to group these paragraphs into
sections in order to have a shorter, clearer summary of the content. No one
can look at or think about 55 ideas or titles at one time. But it is easy
to consider five or ten ideas or titles.

4. How many sections does Jer. 21-29 contain? _____

List these sections, giving the references and titles.

a. _____

b. _____

c. _____

d. _____

e. _____

f. _____

g. _____

h. _____

These references and titles give a clear, brief summary of the content of
Jer. 21-29, even though this is a rather long portion of the book of Jeremiah.

We have given this lesson a title, "Important Events in the Life of Jeremiah."
But we have not said that Jer. 21-29 is a division of the book of Jeremiah.
The overall structure of the book will be discussed in a later lesson.

5. One of the characteristics of Jer. 21-29 is that it contains sections which describe important events in Jeremiah's life and ministry. How did

we identify these events? _____

_____

* _____ *

We looked for historical references which give the date or period or the occasion of Jeremiah's prophecies. In other words these sections tell the story of a specific event when Jeremiah prophesied a specific message.

6. Make a summary of the historical information in Jer. 21-29, using the following chart. In the first column put the date of each section, if the text indicates when it occurred. In the second column put down the events which are referred to in the text. If no date or event is mentioned, leave that section blank.

Date Jer. 29 at the beginning of the siege. Put Jer. 24 and 29 at the beginning of Jeremiah's exile. And remember that we decided to use the fourth year of Zedekiah as the date for Jer. 27-28.

21:1-10		
21:11-23:8		
23:9-40		
24		
25		
26		
27-28		
29		

* *

You should be able to fill in this chart simply by referring to the text and your chronological chart. You may also look back at the earlier sections of this lesson. Be sure you complete the chart. (Only Jer 21:11-23:8 and Jer. 23:9-40 should be left blank.) You may be tested on this at your next class session.

7. What is the significance of this historical information? Why do we study

the historical references in Jer. 21-29? _____

_____

_____

_____

* _____ *

This information enables us to understand the text, to see the significance
of Jeremiah's message. For example, we can interpret Jer. 21:1-10 better
because we know about the Babylonian siege. We see the importance of Jeremiah's message in Jer. 25 as we relate those prophecies to the Battle of
Carchemish, etc.

8. At the beginning of this course we said that one of the beginning steps
in Inductive Bible Study is to look for the historical background of the
book.

Explain why we look for the historical background as we begin an Inductive

Bible Study. _____

_____

* _____ *

The reason we gave in Lesson III is this: We look for the historical background in order to study the book on its own terms, to see it as it really
is.

9. The historical background helps us understand and interpret a book or a
passage correctly. It helps us find the meaning and importance of the text.
And it sometimes helps us see how the book was put together.

Look over your chart at #6 above again. It reveals at least two things about
the structure of the book of Jeremiah. Write down your observations, then
compare them with mine.

a. _____

_____

b. _____

* _____ *

a. The most obvious fact is that the book of Jeremiah is not organized or
structured in chronological order.

b. Nevertheless, it is significant that so much of Jer. 21-29 is tied to its historical context by specific references.

10. Our first observation is about the chronological order. Six of the eight sections of Jer. 21-29 are dated. List these six sections now in chronological order. Put down the reference and date of each section.

a. _____   _____

b. _____   _____

c. _____   _____

d. _____   _____

e. _____   _____

f. _____   _____

Two sections have the same date, of course. It doesn't matter which order you use for those two sections.

11. The second observation is simply to note that much of Jer. 21-29 is dated and related to the historical events of Jeremiah's day. This is significant because it helps us interpret the prophecies that are attached to these references. It also is significant because it tells us something about the structure of the book of Jeremiah.

Go back quickly through the previous chapters of Jeremiah and look for other historical references. Think over the passages in Jeremiah which we studied in Lessons I-X.

Are the prophetic materials in Jer. 1-20 dated? Or is this a distinctive characteristic of Jer. 21-29? What does this observation tell us about the

structure of Jeremiah? _____

_____

_____

_____

* ___   _____   _____ *

We can assume that Jer. 1:4-19 comes at the beginning of Jeremiah's ministry in 627 B.C. But no specific date or event is mentioned. Jer. 14:1-15:4 is related to a drought. But we do not know the date of that drought.

The historical references really begin at Jer. 21. And apparently the materials in Jer. 21-29 were grouped together at least in part because of these historical references. Certainly we will want to keep this observation in mind as we look for the overall structure of the book of Jeremiah.

12. If you have not already done so, make a note of the historical references of Jer. 21-29 on your outline in the column marked "Special Details." For example, for Jer. 21:3-7 put "Chaldeans besieging," and repeat this phrase at Jer. 21:8-10. For Jer. 22:11-12 put "King Shallum," for Jer. 22:18-19 put "King Jehoiakim," and for Jer. 22:24-30 put "King Coniah." For Jer. 24:1-3 put "Exile Jeconiah." Etc.

13. Now locate these dated passages on your chronological chart. Use the line marked "Jeremiah's Ministry." But be sure you put these references on the "Jeremiah's Ministry" line at the points exactly opposite or parallel to the events they refer to on the other lines. Put down just the six dated sections of Jer. 21-29 (by section, not by paragraph).

14. Throughout our study of Jer. 21-29 we have made very little contemporary application of Jeremiah's message. We have been interested primarily in the relationship of Jeremiah's prophecies to their historical references and background. But we should ask what significance these prophecies and these events have for us today. We should note what lessons or concepts are important for our teaching and preaching.

Zedekiah's Inquiry, Jer. 21:1-10

a. Summarize Jeremiah's message to Zedekiah. _____

_____

_____

b. Find a contemporary application from this message or from this experience.

_____

_____

_____

_____

You will have to work out your own interpretation. This is only a sample.
a. The Lord will fight with the Chaldeans against Zedekiah and his people.
b. The Lord may judge and punish people today if they turn to Him only in time of need.

15. Concerning the Kings of Judah, Jer. 21:11-23:8

a. Summarize Jeremiah's message. _____

b. Find a contemporary application. _____

_____

_____

16. Concerning the False Prophets, Jer. 23:9-40

a. Summarize Jeremiah's message. _____

_____

_____

b. Find a contemporary application. _____

_____

_____

17. Two Baskets of Figs, Jer. 24

a. Jeremiah's message. _____

_____

_____

b. A contemporary application. _____

_____

_____

18. Babylon and the Nations, Jer. 25

a. Jeremiah's message. _____

_____

_____

b. A contemporary application. _____

_____

_____

19. <u>Letter to the Exiles, Jer. 29</u>

a. Jeremiah's message. _____

_____

_____

b. A contemporary application. _____

_____

_____

20. Finally list the most important methods we have used in this lesson.
Most of these methods are referred to in this final section. None of them
is really new. But it is useful to review the steps we have taken.

a. _____

_____

b. _____

_____

c. _____

_____

d. _____

_____

e. _____

_____

f. _____

* _____ *

a. Outline the passages paragraph by paragraph (main idea, title).
b. Underline the historical references and explain their significance with
the help of other sources and your knowledge of the historical background.
c. Note and explain other special details, figures, phrases, terms.
d. Summarize the message.
e. Relate each passage with other passages, noting similarities and differences, and find the larger structure or units of the book.
f. Look for important lessons or concepts for your own ministry.

The important thing is to see how we were able to discover the structure, historical background, and message of Jer. 21-29, and to be able to find the structure, historical background, and message of other passages in the future. Your objective in this is not to memorize a list of ready-made rules or techniques of Bible study. Your purpose is to gain skills that will enable you to discover the meaning of the text.

12

The Fall of Jerusalem

Jeremiah's ministry reached its tragic climax at the fall of Jerusalem in
587 B.C. In this lesson you will study several passages from the book of Jeremiah that tell us about Jeremiah's prophetic mission and message during the
final siege, when the city was destroyed, and on into the succeeding events.
You will see what happened to Judah, and you will interpret the historical
and theological significance of those events in Jeremiah's prophecies, and
you will consider what happened to Jeremiah in those final, terrible years
of his ministry.

As in the previous lesson, you will cover a large amount of material. So you
will not be able to analyze all the details in the text. In Inductive Study
you will at times want to consider a very brief passage in great detail. And
at times you will want to survey a large passage. Both kinds of study can be
useful as long as you are careful to begin with the text and study it on its
own terms.

Before you go on to the following exercises, write out your own objectives
for this lesson.

_____

_____

_____

_____

_____

A. Survey of Jeremiah 30-45

In order to study the fall of Jerusalem you need to find the passages that
deal with the fall. One way to find these passages is to read rapidly through
the text. You could also use your concordance. But there may be some passages
that refer to the fall of Jerusalem which do not contain the key words you
would look under in the concordance.

The story of the fall of Jerusalem begins with two years of Babylonian siege,
as we noted in Lesson III. And it does not end with the burning of the city.
We need to know what happened to King Zedekiah and his government and what
happened to the remnant in Jerusalem. And we want to see how Jeremiah ended
his ministry.

1. Your assignment in this section is to read rapidly through Jer. 30-45 and
find out what you can about these events. You will use some of the methods
we applied in Lesson XI. Do not attempt to analyze each paragraph in your outline because that would take too long. Just underline in the text the impor-

tant information and the main ideas. Then make a survey of this information
and these ideas using the following chart of Jer. 30-45 You need not read
through Jer. 46-51 because, as we have noted already, these chapters contain
prophecies concerning the nations. You will study Jer. 52 in a later lesson.

Look for the following as you read through Jer. 30-45.
a. Historical information.
b. Events in the life of Jeremiah.
c. The main ideas and key phrases in Jeremiah's message.
d. Special details that need further explanation.
Put only the essential information in the following chart. Note especially
the passages that deal with the fall of Jerusalem. In later sections of this
lesson you will study these passages in some detail.

2.	Chapter	Historical Information	Events in the Life of Jeremiah Jeremiah's Message
	30		
	31		
	32		
	33		
	34		
	35		
	36		
	37		

38		
39		
40		
41		
42		
43		
44		
45		

3. Now you should be able to identify the chapters in Jer. 30-45 which deal with the siege and fall of Jerusalem, etc.

a. First, list those chapters which are collections of prophecies which do not provide historical information. _____

b. Now list those chapters which contain historical information but which are related to a different period of Jeremiah's ministry. _____

c. List here the chapters that refer to the Babylonian siege previous to the breach in the wall of Jerusalem. _____

d. Now indicate which chapter describes the actual fall of Jerusalem. _____

e. Finally, put down the chapters which tell what happened to the remnant

after Jerusalem was sacked and her people deported. _____

The chapters that interest us in this lesson are the ones you have listed at
c, d, and e.

4. Locate the dated chapters on your chronological chart.

5. As you study these chapters in this lesson put the historical information
on your outline of the book of Jeremiah in the column marked "Special Details."

B. Jeremiah 32-34

This section is an Inductive Study of Jer. 32-34 similar to other previous lessons. Since this is a rather long passage, it will not be possible to discuss
all the details.

As you work through this material, note the steps which are used and the kinds
of questions which are asked. In the following Sections C and D you will prepare your own Inductive Study on Jer. 37-39 and Jer. 41-44.

1. Read over Jer. 32. Work out your outline for this section, indicating the
main idea and writing a title for each paragraph.

2. Give the date and explain the historical background for this passage. _____

_____

_____

_____

3. Describe the specific situation of Jeremiah at this time. _____

_____

_____

_____

4. Make note of the details of Jeremiah's imprisonment.

a. Who had imprisoned Jeremiah? _____

b. Where was he being held? _____

c. What was the accusation against him? _____

_____

5. Explain the relationship between what happened to Jeremiah and what was

happening to the city. _____

_____

_____

_____

* _____ *

Since Jerusalem was at war and under siege, Jeremiah's statements about his
people and about King Zedekiah and about the enemy could be considered highly treasonous. Jeremiah's words could demoralize the people and their
army; so Zedekiah treated him as a dangerous man and had him locked up.

6. This was obviously not the only occasion on which Jeremiah uttered treasonous words about the political situation. List two other similar passages that
we have already studied in which he speaks to Zedekiah about his coming defeat.

a. _____   b. _____

7. The greater part of Jer. 32 is about another one of Jeremiah's acted para-

bles. Explain what is an acted parable. _____

_____

* _____ *

You may refer back to Lesson IX.

8. What did Jeremiah do? _____

_____

b. What did this action symbolize? _____

* _____ *

The text itself gives the interpretation. See Jer. 32:15, 42-44.

9. Demonstrate your interpretation of this acted parable by completing the following diagram.

Jeremiah purchased land in Anathoth by right of inheritance.	The Lord promised to restore His people to their land.
Although it was in Babylonian hands.	Although they were about to be delivered to the Chaldeans.

10. Explain the following details, using your Bible and a concordance only.

a. What was "the right of redemption"? _____

_____

_____

b. What significance did Anathoth have for Jeremiah? _____

_____

c. Who was Baruch? Why did Jeremiah give him the deed? _____

_____

_____

* _____ *

a. See Lev. 25:25. The law stated that when a man had to sell his land, the closest relative had the right and the duty to buy or "redeem" it.
b. It was Jeremiah's home town.
c. See Jer. 36. Baruch was Jeremiah's scribe or secretary. He would naturally take care of Jeremiah's legal documents.

11. Consider this business transaction in the light of the political situation.

a. Why do you think Hanamel was eager to sell this land? _____

_____

b. What attitude toward the transaction does Jeremiah reveal in Jer. 32:16-

25? _____

* _____ *

a. It may be that Hanamel was poor and needed money. More likely, he and
the other members of Jeremiah's family were eager to sell out because the
Babylonians had already occupied Anathoth.
b. Apparently Jeremiah was doubtful of the wisdom of buying the land. Note
especially v. 25.

12. Explain the significance of Jeremiah's purchase as a prophetic act. _____

_____

_____

_____

* _____ *

Jeremiah's purchase dramatizes and makes unforgettable God's promise to
bring back a remnant and resettle the land. The purchase is a sign and
seal of the will of the Lord. It also demonstrates Jeremiah's faith in
God's promise and must have encouraged others to trust and have hope
during their exile. Just as the prophecy of destruction had been fulfilled, so would be the prophecy of restoration.
13. Go on to Jer. 33. Work out your outline for this section, indicating
the main idea and writing a title for each paragraph.

14 Give the approximate date and explain the historical background of this

passage. _____

_____

* _____ *

It is the same situation as Jer. 32, perhaps a few months later. See #2
above.

15. Describe Jeremiah's specific situation in this chapter. _____

_____

16. Summarize Jeremiah's message in Jer. 33. _____

_____

_____

17. Compare this message with his message in the previous chapter. Is it similar or different? _____

_____

18. Compare this message of restoration and hope with Jeremiah's message in Jer. 30-31. _____

_____

19. Compare Jeremiah's message in Jer. 30-33 with his message in the other passages we have studied in Jer. 1-29. _____

_____

_____

20. Make a list of the main ideas of Jeremiah's message in Jer. 1-29. We first made this analysis in our study of Jer. 2:1-4:4, "Israel's Apostasy." Then add the theme of hope and restoration as point "e".

a. _____

b. _____

c. _____

d. _____

e. _____

Check your summary by referring back to Lesson V, D, 30.

21. Note that the idea of restoration and a future hope is almost totally absent from Jer. 1-29. And yet in Jer. 30-33 it is the dominant note of Jeremiah's prophecies.

How would you explain this phenomenon? _____

_____

_____

_____

22. One explanation is that the prophecies dealing with this theme were put together in this part of the book deliberately either by Jeremiah or by someone else.

Another explanation arises from the historical background of Jeremiah's ministry.

a. What was the political situation when the prophecies of hope and restoration were given, as far as we know? _____

_____

b. What was the political situation when the prophecies of warning and repentance were given? _____

* _____ *

a. Chapters 30-31 are not dated. But Chapters 32-33 refer to the time of siege and destruction.
b. Chapters 1-29 generally refer to the period previous to the siege and destruction.

23. Consider what kind of message was appropriate and necessary from these different historical perspectives.

a. What did Judah need to hear when the destruction was still in the future?

_____

_____

b. What did Judah need to hear when the destruction was upon them? _____

_____

_____

* _____ *

a. When the destruction was still in the future Judah needed to be warned about the Lord's judgment and called to repentance. It was not appropriate or necessary to speak to them at length about the future restoration. In fact, this might have weakened Jeremiah's message of judgment and repentance.

b. When destruction was upon them, on the other hand, they needed a message of hope. They needed to know that the destruction was God's righteous judgment on their apostasy, but they also needed urgently a word from the Lord to keep them from complete despair.

24. Look through Jer. 33 and make a list of the different things that the Lord promised to do for Judah in the restoration. Be specific.

a. _____

b. _____

c. _____

d. _____

e. _____

f. _____

g. _____

h. _____

25. Note the reference to "a righteous Branch to spring forth for David" in v. 15.

a. Where have we seen this expression before? _____

b. What does it mean? _____

_____

_____

See Lesson XI, B, 11.

26. Explain the reference to "my covenant with the day and my covenant with

the night" in v. 20, 25. _____

_____

_____

This is a comparison like a literary figure. Just as night and day are
fixed by God's unchanging natural law, so Judah's future is secured by God's
unchanging covenant.

27. Read over Jer. 34. Work out your outline for this section, indicating
the main idea and writing a title for each paragraph.

28. Give the approximate date and explain the historical background of this

passage. _____

_____

_____

_____

29. Notice how serious Judah's plight had become.

a. Who was fighting against Jerusalem? _____

_____

b. Who was fighting with Jerusalem? _____

* _____ *

a. Nebuchadnezzar, all his army, and all the kingdoms under the Babylonian
Empire (v.1).
b. Only two other fortified cities of Judah remained, Lachish and Azekah (v.7).

30. But notice, too, v. 21. What was happening at that particular period? ____

_____

_____

_____

31. The Babylonian army had momentarily withdrawn from the siege of Jerusalem. Why? Try to recall another passage which you have read recently which
will explain this phenomenon.

a. Reference: _____

b. Explanation of the Babylonian withdrawal: _____

* _____ *

See. Jer. 37:5

32. Now notice the specific circumstances of the prophecies in this chapter, first in Jer. 34:1-5.

a. To whom does Jeremiah speak in Jer. 34:1-5? _____

b. Find another similar passage which we have studied in which Jeremiah

counsels Zedekiah about the Babylonian siege. _____

*   *

a. King Zedekiah
b. Jer. 21:1-10

33. Summarize Jeremiah's message to Zedekiah in Jer. 34:1-5. _____

_____

_____

_____

34. What incident provoked Jeremiah's prophecies in Jer. 34:8-22? _____

_____

_____

_____

* _____ *

Zedekiah had proclaimed liberty to all the Hebrew slaves in Jerusalem. Then the owners took back their slaves, which broke the king's word and also an ancient law.

35. One of the intriguing things about Inductive Bible Study is the way in which you can unlock the meaning and explanations that are hidden right in the text. There are at least two such cases in Jer. 34:8-22.

Explain first why Zedekiah freed the slaves.

a. What was the religious reason? _____

_____

_____

b. What was the political reason? _____

_____

c. Which one of these was the real reason? _____

d. Explain how you know which was the real reason? _____

_____

*   *

a. v. 15. Zedekiah wanted to gain favor with the Lord, so he repented of
his evil ways, and as proof of his repentance he released the slaves in
keeping with the law.
b. In time of siege the army needed to use every man available. It was con-
venient, even expedient to release the slaves and use them as soldiers.
c. Obviously the political reason was the real reason, and the religious
reason was only pretense.
d. The proof is in the fact that the king and the people reversed their decision and took back their slaves as soon as circumstances changed.

36. Now explain why Zedekiah and the people took back their slaves. The se-

cret is in the political situation described in the text itself. _____

_____

_____

*   *

v. 21. The siege was lifted. The city was no longer in immediate danger.
The slaves were no longer needed for the defense of the city. So Zedekiah
and the people broke their covenant.

37. What does this reversal show about their repentance? _____

_____

*   *

It was obviously false, a pretense to gain the Lord's favor and to meet a
political crisis.

38. What lesson do you find in this experience for us today in the ministry?

Does this kind of thing happen in our congregations? _____

_____

_____

_____

_____

*   _____   *

People often repent at a time of personal crisis, but sometimes that repentance is only a matter of convenience or need. And when the crisis passes, they return to their old ways and forget their repentance and their promises.

39. Summarize Jeremiah's message in Jer. 34:8-22. _____

_____

_____

_____

_____

40. Explain the following details from this paragraph.

a. Find the reference for the law regarding the release of Hebrew slaves in

Deuteronomy. _____

b. Find in Genesis an example of the covenant ceremony mentioned in v. 18.

_____

a. Deut. 15:1, 12
b. Gen. 15:7-17

41. In order to conclude your study of Jer. 32-34, define the overall structure of this portion of the book.

a. First, consider the historical background of these three chapters. Do

they all belong to the same period of Jeremiah's ministry? _____

b. What political situation do they refer to? _____

_____

c. Second, consider the specific events or circumstances of Jer. 32-34. Note that each section begins with an editorial introduction. How should this

passage be divided, according to these introductions? _____

_____

_____

d. Third, consider the dominant themes of Jeremiah's message in Jer. 32-34.

What is his main emphasis in Jer. 32? _____

In Jer. 33? _____

In Jer. 34? _____

e. With regard to theme Jer. 32-33 can be grouped with _____.
(See your survey of Jer. 30-45 at #A, 2 above.)

f. With regard to theme Jer. 34 can be grouped with _____.
(See your survey of Jer. 30-45.)

*   *

a. Yes.
b. Jerusalem under the Babylonian siege, 589-587 B.C.
c. Jer 32, Jer 33, 34. Each chapter is one complete unit or section. Jer. 34 can be divided v. 1-7 and v. 8-22.
d. Jer. 32: Future restoration; Jer. 33: Future restoration; Jer. 34: Imminent destruction or judgment.
e. Jer. 30-31.
f. Jer. 37-38.

C. Jeremiah 37-39

Your assignment in this section is to make an Inductive Study of Jer. 37-39. Analyze these three chapters, using the methods you consider most helpful in uncovering and interpreting the text. You may follow the steps we have just used in our study of Jer. 32-34 and in other lessons. And you may use other methods. Be sure you find the historical information in Jer. 37-39, and summarize the basic ideas of Jeremiah's message in each paragraph and in each section.

Prepare your Inductive Study of Jer. 37-39 as a lesson, with questions and exercises, as we have done in this course. Put down not only the questions but also the answers, so that you will have all the information you need to teach this lesson. Keep in mind that you will need to use the results of this study in the final section of this lesson, which deals with the historical and theological significance of the fall of Jerusalem. And you may be examined over this portion of the text in your next class session.

Use notebook paper to make notes, to work out your questions, etc., and
put these pages in your Jeremiah notebook. You will probably want to change
the order of the steps or questions after you have completed your Inductive
Study of Jer. 37-39. Just change the numbering or make a list at the end.

D. Jeremiah 40-44

Your assignment in this section is similar to the previous section. Make an
Inductive Study of Jer. 40-44. Prepare your study in the form of a lesson
which you can use in your teaching ministry.

It would be impossible in the time available to study all the details of
these five chapters. Just work on the essential information and ideas.
Since this portion of the text contains a series of events, you will probably want to work out a chart or a list showing the references and the sequence of these events.

Work out your lesson again on notebook paper to put in the notebook. You
will probably want to teach this lesson. So write down clear instructions
for your students, and plan the questions and exercises in logical order,
step by step.

E. The Historical and Theological Significance of the Fall

In Inductive Bible Study we look at details of information, such as the historical references and the literary figures. And we study ideas or concepts,
such as the covenant relationship between the Lord and His people. We analyze
words and phrases, paragraphs, sections, and major divisions.

In Lesson X you studied "Jeremiah's Tragic Role." In that case you examined
in detail four passages which are closely related to the subject. Then you
reviewed rapidly a large amount of material on the book of Jeremiah which
you had studied previously in order to see what it reveals about the same
subject.

In Lesson XII you have been studying several chapters of the book of Jeremiah that deal with the fall of Jerusalem. You have found a lot of information about that event and about the preceding and succeeding events. And
you have summarized Jeremiah's message in each paragraph and in each section or chapter. You can recall other information and concepts related to
the fall of Jerusalem from the previous lessons. Now it is time to bring
together all this information and all these ideas. You need to see how all
these pieces fit together - how different events, ideas, experiences, passages are related to each other. Then you will have a general picture of the
historical and theological significance of the fall of Jerusalem. This general picture will increase your understanding of Jeremiah's message, his
ministry, and his book as a whole. And it will increase your understanding
of particular passages in the book.

In another lesson you will study in greater detail how to carry out this
kind of Biblical investigation. It is an important part of Inductive Bible
Study, since it begins with the text and helps us to understand the text
on its own terms. At this point Inductive Bible Study becomes Biblical
theology.

The Historical Significance of the Fall of Jerusalem

1. We have noted that the fall of Jerusalem is referred to often throughout
the book of Jeremiah. Sometimes it is mentioned specifically, at other times
indirectly.

a. Give the reference for the first mention of the fall. _____

b. What important, specific information does this passage give us about the

* fall? _____   *

a. Jer. 1:3
b. The date of the fall, the 11th year of Zedekiah, that is, 587 B.C.

2. This first reference to the fall of Jerusalem is important not just because of this information. It is especially significant because it estab-
lishes a definite relationship between the event of the fall and the book
of Jeremiah and the ministry of Jeremiah.

a. What is the importance of the passage Jer. 1:1-3 in the structure of the

book? _____

_____

b. What, then, is the relationship between the fall of Jerusalem and the

book of Jeremiah? _____

_____

c. What does this passage say specifically about the ministry of Jeremiah?

_____

_____

_____

d. What, then, is the relationship between the fall of Jerusalem and the

ministry of Jeremiah? _____

---

*   *

a. Jer. 1:1-3 is the introduction to the book. It gives the historical background of the book.
b. The book deals with the period which ended at the fall of Jerusalem.
c. Jeremiah's ministry lasted from the 13th year of Josiah until the fall
of Jerusalem in the 11th year of Zedekiah.
d. The fall was the climax of Jeremiah's ministry, the fulfillment of his
prophecies, his vindication as God's prophet, the punishment of his persecutors, and the end of his ministry to Judah as a nation.

3. According to what you have studied in Jer. 40-44, does the book of Jere-

miah cover only the period ending at the fall of Jerusalem? _____

Did Jeremiah's ministry end immediately when Jerusalem fell? _____

What did he do after the fall? _____

---

*

Obviously, the book of Jeremiah deals with the period leading up to the fall
and also with events immediately after the fall. Jeremiah continued his ministry for months and probably for a few years after the fall. He stayed with
the remnant in Jerusalem, was taken by them against his will to Egypt, and   *
there uttered his last prophecies. He was probably still in Jerusalem when
he composed the five dirges, songs of mourning over the destruction of the
city, that we have in Lamentations. These songs perpetuated his ministry
as the people sang the acknowledgement of their guilt, pleas for forgiveness, and expressions of trust in God.

4. On the basis of this historical introduction to the book of Jeremiah,
Jer. 1:1-3, we turned to the Old Testament sources that describe the period.

List the other two Old Testament books. _____
*   *

2 Kings and 2 Chronicles

5. With additional information from 2 Kings and 2 Chronicles we were able
to make a simple map of the political situation during Jeremiah's ministry.
This map shows the power struggle between the three great empires of the

period, and it shows Judah's strategic geographic location between these
great enemies. It reveals the historical significance of the fall of Jerusalem.

Draw the map in the following space. You should be able to do it from memory. When you have finished turn to the copy of the map in your notebook
(or in the appendix to this manual) to make sure you have included all the
important information.

6. With the help of your map you can make some important observations about
the fall of Jerusalem.

a. Explain briefly Judah's geographical position. _____

_____

_____

_____

b. What empire threatened Judah's existence during the first part of Jere-

miah's ministry? _____

c. What significance did the Battle of Carchemish have for Judah? _____

_____

_____

_____

_____

d. What nation destroyed Jerusalem? _____ In what year? _____

*   *

a. Judah was on the invasion route between Egypt on the southwest and Assyria and Babylonia on the north and east. (She was bounded on the west by the Mediterranean and on the east by the Arabian Desert.)
b. Egypt.
c. Since Egypt was defeated, Babylonia became the new dominant threat to Judah's existence. (Therefore Judah looked to Egypt for help in Zedekiah's time, instead of considering her an enemy. And for the same reason the remnant in Judah after the fall fled to Egypt.)
d. Babylonia   In 587 B.C.

7. Turn now to your chronological chart. There you have almost all of the information which is included in your map of the world power struggle. And it contains much additional information drawn from many passages of the book of Jeremiah. Note first some of the historical events in the life of Judah.

a. When did Babylonia first attack Judah and enter Jerusalem? _____

b. Who was taken into exile on that occasion? _____

_____

c. When did the final Babylonian siege of Jerusalem begin? _____

d. What passages of the book of Jeremiah tell about the final siege of Jerusalem? _____

e. What passage describes the actual fall of Jerusalem? _____

*   *

a. 598 B.C.
b. King Jehoiachin and many nobles and artisans.
c. 589 B.C.
d. Jer. 21:1-10, Jer. 32-34, Jer. 37-38.
e. Jer. 39

8. In our study of Jer. 21-45 we noted again and again that Jeremiah gave King Zedekiah and his people very definite advice with regard to the Babylonian invasion, advice which could well be interpreted as treason.

a. What was Jeremiah's advice? _____

_____

b. Why was this treasonous? _____

* _____ *

a. Judah should surrender to Babylonia.
b. This was a time of war. To advocate surrender in a time of war, against the will of the government, is treason.

9. But Jeremiah's counsel was based on the will of the Lord. And it was based on a realistic analysis of the political situation.

a. Ever since the Battle of Carchemish the future of Judah as a nation was

in the hands of _____.

b. King Zedekiah himself was put on the throne by _____.

c. What did Zedekiah attempt to do in 594, according to Jer. 27? _____

_____

_____

d. Naturally Babylonia would not allow any rebellion by the tiny subject

kingdom of Judah. Who then was sent against Jerusalem, according to Jer. 34?

* _____ *

a. Babylonia
b. Nebuchadnezzar
c. He was apparently making plans with Edom, Moab, Ammon, Tyre and Sidon to rebel against Babylonia.
d. Nebuchadnezzar and all his army and all the kingdoms under his rule.

10. The end was inevitable. The enemy forces were overwhelming. The fall of Jerusalem was catastrophic. We know what happened then to the city, the Temple, the walls, the rulers, the people, and Jeremiah himself. (You should have listed this information in your Inductive Study of Jer. 39.)

We are interested not only in what happened, but also in the historical significance of what happened. Consider, for example, the first time the Wright brothers flew their tiny airplane for several hundred yards. That event by itself was of very little importance. But it takes on enormous historical significance when we look at it as the beginning of the air age.

State briefly what was the historical significance of the following aspects of the fall of Jerusalem.

a. The burning of the city and the breaking down of her walls. _____

_____

_____

_____

b. The destruction of the Temple. _____

_____

_____

_____

c. The deportation of all but a few people to Babylon. _____

_____

_____

_____

d. The naming of a governor to replace the king in Jerusalem. _____

_____

_____

* _____ *

a. Without her walls Jerusalem would be defenseless and without her capital and her other fortified cities Judah was no longer a nation.
b. The destruction of the Temple meant the end of the system of sacrifices and feast days. The Old Testament religion had to change radically or vanish.
c. Normally deportation meant slavery and probable extinction. Only by an extraordinary turn of events could a people expect to be restored to their land.

d. Judah's independence as a nation was finished. Even those few who remained were to be ruled by a governor appointed by Babylonia.

11. The people of Judah certainly knew the seriousness of their plight.
They could remember what had happened to the Northern Kingdom, Israel.

a. When was Israel destroyed? _____ By whom? _____

b. What happened to her people? _____

c. Were the ten tribes of Israel ever restored to their land? _____

d. Where are the lost tribes of Israel today? _____

*   *

a. 722 B.C.   By Assyria.
b. They were killed or deported.
c. No
d. Nothing remains of them.

12. Summarize in your own words the historical significance of the fall of

Jerusalem. _____

_____

_____

_____

_____

_____

_____

_____

The Theological Significance of the Fall of Jerusalem

13. The fall of Jerusalem was not only the most significant event that occurred during Jeremiah's ministry. It was also, as we have noted, one of
the central themes of his message throughout his ministry.

a. Give the reference for the first time the Lord spoke to Jeremiah about

the fall. _____

b. What is the importance of this passage? _____

_____

_____

_____

c. What is the theological significance of the fall according to this pas-

sage? _____

_____

* _____ *

a. Jer. 1:13-16
b. This passage is part of the section on "The Call of Jeremiah." It reveals
to us not just one of Jeremiah's prophecies but a message which he was to
proclaim throughout his ministry.
c. The fall was an act of God's judgment on His people for all their wickedness.

14. It should be clear even from this one passage that the fall of Jerusalem was not only an event of great historical significance but also a
theme of great theological significance. What do we mean by the expres-

sion "theological significance"? _____

_____

* _____ *

It reveals something about God, His will, His intervention.

15. In a sense all of history is theologically significant. We see God's
hand especially as He guides His people down through history. His will and
His intervention are even evident in our own lives.

What does the fall of Jerusalem reveal about God, according to Jeremiah's

prophecies? _____

_____

* _____ *

Obviously it was God's judgment on His people for their apostasy. But much
more was implied in the fall, which we will consider later.

16. Consider Jeremiah's message as a whole, and see how the fall of Jerusalem is related to that message. We first made a summary of Jeremiah's message in our study of Jer. 2:1-4:4. And we have referred back to that summary several times to see if it changes through the book. In our study of Jer. 30-45 we added an additional basic point to the summary. Write out the summary once again as a review. And mark the point that is most directly related to the fall of Jerusalem.

a. _____

b. _____

c. _____

d. _____

e. _____
*   *

If you need to check your answer, refer to B, 20 above.

17. One of the major points in Jeremiah's message was the warning of God's judgment upon His people for their apostasy. But this summary is not a list of isolated themes. Jeremiah faced one major problem and he preached one basic message.

What was that problem? _____
*   *

Judah's apostasy.

18. Write a paragraph showing that Jeremiah preached one basic message. Explain what is the relationship between the five major ideas or themes in

his prophecies. _____

_____

_____

_____

_____

_____

_____

_____

_____
*   *

God had established a special covenant relationship with His people. But they were unfaithful to Him. So He had to call them to repentance. Since they did not repent He warned them of judgment. Then when judgment came, He told them of a future hope and restoration.

19. Obviously the theme of judgment was an essential, integral part of Jeremiah's message. And in some sections of the book it is practically the only theme. List two or three sections which speak almost entirely of judgment.

_____

* _____ *

See your outline.

20. The fall of Jerusalem thus came as the final act of God's judgment on His unfaithful people. They should not have been surprised. They had no excuse. They should have been ready. For Jeremiah had warned them, pleaded with them, wept over them, and fought with them for 40 years, before the fall came.

What was the spiritual and moral condition of Judah and her rulers and her

religious leaders when God's judgment finally overtook them? _____

* _____ *

They were still practicing idolatry, injustices, and false alliances.

21. So the fall of Jerusalem was not a disaster for God, even though it was a catastrophe for Judah. It had important, positive theological significance. It teaches something important about God and His people.

a. What does the fall teach about God? _____

_____

_____

b. What does it teach us about His people? _____

_____

* _____ *

a. The fall teaches us that God is holy and powerful and that His will must be done.

b. It teaches us that God's people must be faithful to Him or they will suffer His judgment.

22. The fall of Jerusalem was, then, a vindication of God and a judgment
of His sinful people. This leads us to a further conclusion. Follow carefully the reasoning in these questions:

a. If God had been defeated as well as His people by the fall of Jerusalem,

what hope was there for Judah in the future? _____

b. Since God had willed that Jerusalem should fall into the hands of Baby-

lonia, was He capable of restoring His people in the future? _____

c. As long as Judah remained in her rebellious, apostate condition, was

there any hope that she would serve the Lord? _____

d. Once Judah had been utterly destroyed, what was her only hope for life

and restoration? _____
*   *

a. None   c. No
b. Yes   d. God's intervention.

23. As you continue to reason along this line, you begin to see that the
fall of Jerusalem had tremendous theological significance. It stands beside
the deliverance of Israel from Egypt as one of the great redemptive acts of
God.

a. What passages in Jeremiah indicate that there was a future hope beyond

the fall of Jerusalem and the exile? _____

_____

b. What promises did the Lord give His people through Jeremiah? _____

_____

_____

_____

c. Would this hope have been possible without the fall? Explain. _____

_____

*

a. Jer. 30-33 contains the most notable collection of prophecies about the future hope. There are, however, other passages.
b. A return to the Lord, restoration, a new descendant of David, a new covenant, prosperity, etc.
c. No. The future hope required a radical change in the heart and life of the people. So they had to go through this terrible judgment first.

24. This theme of judgment and restoration is very similar to one of the

central themes of the New Testament. What is that New Testament concept? _____

*

Death and resurrection. Or life through death. Christ had to die to bring new, eternal life to mankind. The believer passes through a death to self and finds life in Christ.

25. This theological understanding of the fall of Jerusalem throws new light on all of Jeremiah's ministry. Now all of his failures become part of a new victory. And although he went through great suffering, he led the way to a new beginning.

Refer back to Jer. 1:10 and give a new interpretation of the two dimensions of Jeremiah's calling.

a. "To pluck up and to break down, to destroy and to overthrow" _____

b. "To build and to plant" _____

*

Note that these two dimensions are inseparable. Jeremiah was the prophet of doom who led the way to a future hope. He announced judgment, but that judgment was necessary for a future redemption.

13

The Structure of the Book of Jeremiah

From the beginning of this course we have said that it is important to look for the structure of the book. But we have also said that the book of Jeremiah does not have a clear, simple structure. In this lesson we will bring together some of the observations we have made about the structure of this book, and we will try to identify the major divisions of the book.

It is interesting to note that the book of Jeremiah itself tells us, at least in part, how Jeremiah's prophecies were collected and written down. You will study this information in detail in Jer. 36 and 45. Then you will read an explanation of how the book of Jeremiah was put together.

Your objectives in this lesson are:

Explain the importance of structure.

Make an overall outline of the book of Jeremiah.

Review the structural elements in the book.

Consider how the book of Jeremiah was put together.

Remember that your primary concern in this course is to learn how to study the books of the Bible inductively. One of the beginning steps in Inductive Bible Study is to look for structure. The analysis of structure is important not only at the beginning but throughout Inductive Study of a book. Therefore be sure you understand the significance of structure, and be sure you know how to look for structure.

A. The Importance of Structure

In Lessons I and IV you began your study of the structure of the book of Jeremiah. You learned a definition of structure, and you looked at several different levels of structure. Throughout this course you have looked for the structure of the book of Jeremiah at these different levels.

In this section you will review the basic concept of structure and consider the importance of studying structure in Inductive Bible Study. Then in the following sections you will bring together your observations and conclusions about the structure of the book of Jeremiah.

1. First write down a definition of structure. Include in your definition the ideas we put down in our definition of structure in Lesson IV. That definition is made up of two examples and four characteristics.

The structure of a book is _____

413

_____

_____

_____

_____

_____

The structure of a book is its skeleton or outline. It is made up of several parts or divisions. These parts may be hidden, but we know they are there.
They are tied together to form a central idea or plot or story. The structure holds the book together, gives it meaning, and enables it to teach us
something.

2. In order to remember this definition, take it apart. Note the examples
and characteristics. List the two examples first.

The structure of a book is like:

a. _____

b. _____
_____

a. The structure of a book is like the skeleton of an animal.
b. It is like an outline or a drawing for a painting.

3. Now list the four characteristics of the structure of a book.

a. _____

b. _____

c. _____

d. _____

_____

a. It is made up of several parts or divisions.
b. These parts may be hidden, but we know they are there.
c. They are tied together to form a central idea or plot or story.
d. The structure holds the book together, gives it meaning, and enables it
to teach us something.

4. This definition reveals why we should study the structure of a book.
Write in your own words two or three reasons for studying structure.

_____

_____

_____

_____

5. We shall analyze here three important reasons for studying structure.
There may be other good reasons. You should remember at least these three.

> 1. In order to find the central ideas or message.
> 2. In order to see the relationships between the differ-
>   ent parts.
> 3. In order to be able to review the contents and to
>   find specific passages.

6. These three reasons apply not only to the study of the overall structure
of a book but also to the study of any passage. If you are studying a paragraph, you need to find the central idea, the relationships between the
parts, etc. If you are studying a larger section or division you need to
do the same thing. So the study of structure is important for all levels.

In Lesson IV we listed six levels of structure. Put them down here.

a. _____   d. _____

b. _____   e. _____

c. _____   f. _____

a. words   d. paragraphs
b. phrases   e. sections
c. sentences   f. divisions

7. The first reason for studying the structure of a passage or book is <u>to
find the central idea or message.</u>

For example, you looked for the main idea of each paragraph in Jer. 2:1-4:4.
You discovered that these paragraphs contain four basic ideas. List them
here.

a. _____

b. _____

c. _____

d. _____

*   *

a. Israel's special relationship to the Lord.
b. Israel's unfaithfulness to the Lord.
c. Israel's judgment.
d. Israel's call to repentance.

8. These four basic ideas in Jer. 2:1-4:4 fit together as one message. We
summarized this message in the title we gave to this section of the book,

which is _____.

*   *

Israel's (or Judah's) Apostasy

9. As we studied other sections of the book of Jeremiah, we continued to
look for the main ideas in each paragraph and in each group of paragraphs.
In a later section we noted that Jeremiah's message included an additional
basic idea.

a. What is that new basic idea? _____

b. In what chapters or sections is this idea dominant? _____

*   *

a. A future restoration or hope.
b. Jer. 30-33

10. As we study a book like Jeremiah we look for the main ideas, and this
helps us find the structure. We look for the structure, and this helps us
find the message. The structure is a summary of the main ideas.

Another word for structure is _____.

*   *

summary

11. In a book like Jeremiah we cannot simply find the main idea or the main
ideas in each paragraph. We need to group the paragraphs which have the
same basic ideas into sections and the sections into divisions. Only then
will we have a clear idea of the structure and message of the book. Why?

_____

_____

_____

*   *

There is a simple reason. The book contains so many paragraphs that we cannot possibly think of all of them at once. So we group together those paragraphs that have the same basic ideas.

12. Paragraphs that have the same basic ideas are grouped into _____.

Sections that have the same basic ideas are grouped into _____.

*   *

sections   divisions

13. A paragraph is a unit of one or more sentences grouped together around
the same basic idea or ideas.

What is a section? _____

* _____ *

A section is a group of paragraphs with the same basic idea or ideas.

14. What is a division? _____

* _____ *

A division is a group of sections with the same basic idea or ideas.

15. In our study of the first chapter of Jeremiah, for example, we grouped
Jer. 1:4-10 and Jer. 1:11-12 and Jer. 1:13-16 and Jer. 1:17-19 in one sec-

tion. Why? _____

_____

* _____ *

Because these four paragraphs all tell something about Jeremiah's call.
They are all related to the same experience or the same basic idea.

16. We left Jer. 1:1-3 as a separate unit. Why? _____

_____

* _____ *

Because it is unique. The paragraphs that follow Jer. 1:1-3 do not contain
the same kind of information or the same basic idea.

17. Beginning at Jer. 4:5 we found a series of paragraphs dealing with the same basic idea and we grouped them together.

a. Give the reference for this section: _____

b. Give the title for this section: _____

_____

*   *

a. Jer. 4:5-6:30
b. "The Enemy from the North and the Enemy from Within"

18. If you continue with your study of the book of Jeremiah this way, analyzing the main idea in each paragraph and grouping the paragraphs with the same basic ideas into sections, you will eventually have an excellent summary of the contents of the book. You will know what is the central message.

List here the references and titles for the first five sections of the book of Jeremiah. You may copy this information from your outline of the book. Consider Jer. 1:1-3 as the first section. Notice how this list gives you a clear idea of the contents and message of the book of Jeremiah.

a. _____

b. _____

c. _____

d. _____

e. _____

19. We have just considered the first reason for studying structure: in order to find or summarize the central ideas or message of a passage or a book.

The second reason for studying structure is <u>to see the relationships between the different parts.</u>

Look at the following series of words from Jer. 1:5.

    "Nations prophet the I a you to appointed"

As they stand, these words do not make sense. They lack order or structure. You cannot understand the meaning or message of this important group of words until you understand the right relationships between them. Write them

in the correct order. _____

*   *

"I appointed you a prophet to the nations."

20. The same principle applies to all the different levels of structure. Words fit together to form phrases, phrases to form sentences, sentences to form paragraphs, paragraphs to form sections, sections to form divisions, and divisions to form a book.

In our study of the book of Jeremiah we have been able to find the structure and analyze relationships on several levels.

a. What levels have we analyzed? _____

_____

b. What levels have we not yet found? _____
*   *

a. Words, phrases, sentences, paragraphs, sections.
b. Divisions (the book as a whole)

21. The study of structure is at times very difficult. Sometimes it is difficult because the structure is very complicated or unclear. Sometimes we find materials that are grouped together with only superficial links or even with no apparent connection.

Would you say that the overall structure of the book of Jeremiah is clear

or unclear? _____

*   *
_____

The experts are able to find major divisions and sections. But they generally admit that the book as a whole does not have a clear structure. It is almost as puzzling as the jumbled group of words we made out of Jer. 1:5 above.

22. Although the book of Jeremiah as a whole does not have a clear structure, we still need to study the relationships between the different passages. In fact, since it does not have a definite order, it may be even more important to find these hidden relationships.

First, remember that there are different kinds of structure. When you study a passage or a book you have to find out what kind of structure it has.

For example, if you see that the paragraphs are grouped around certain top-

ics, you can say it has a _____ structure. If you find that

the paragraphs or sections are placed in the order of time of occurrence

you can say it has a _____ structure.
*   *

topical   chronological

23. You may find that a book has several different kinds of structure. List
five different kinds of structure, including the two types you have mentioned above.

a. _____   d. _____

b. _____   e. _____

c. _____

*   *

These are the types of structure we mentioned in Lesson IV: topical, chronological, biographical, geographical, and logical (or theological).

24. Now consider the book of Jeremiah in terms of these different types of
structure.

a. Are some of the passages grouped together topically? _____

b. Are the dated passages in chronological order? _____

c. Are there some biographical passages? _____

d. Are some sections identified geographically? _____

e. Is there a logical order from one section to the next throughout the

book? _____

*   *

a. Yes   b. No   c. Yes   d. Yes   e. No

25. We must recognize once again that the book as a whole is remarkably un-
structured. The passages have not been arranged in a careful, meaningful
order.

We now have some clues for our understanding the relationships between passages. Some paragraphs are grouped together topically. Some sections are
dated and related to historical events, although they are not in chronological order. Some passages describe experiences in the life of Jeremiah.

We have said that it is necessary to see the relationships between the parts
in order to understand a passage or a book. How then can we fit together
the jumbled pieces of the book of Jeremiah? We have already done this to
some extent. Explain how the following methods help us see the relationships between different passages in the book of Jeremiah.

a. Political map of the time of Jeremiah: _____

_____

_____

_____

_____

_____

b. Chronological chart of the time of Jeremiah: _____

_____

_____

_____

_____

_____

c. Summary of Jeremiah's message: _____

_____

_____

_____

_____

_____

d. Analysis of Jeremiah's experience: _____

_____

_____

_____

_____

* _____

These methods do not show us the order or structure of the book as we now
have it. But they do reveal important relationships between passages. And
these relationships are essential to our understanding of the passages them-

selves and the book as a whole.

a. The political map shows how many passages are related to the major events of Jeremiah's time. For example, there are many references to the enemy from the North and the destruction of Judah, the siege and fall of Jerusalem, the exile, etc. When we relate these passages to the historical background, we can see how they are related to each other.

b. The chronological chart also helps us see the relationships between these passages by relating them to the historical background. And it puts some of these passages in exact chronological order. This chronological structure comes from Inductive Study of the book, although the book as it stands does not have a chronological structure.

c. The summary of Jeremiah's message also helps us see important relationships between passages. For example, we noted that the concept of the covenant (Israel's special relationship to God) underlies the words of judgment and the call to repentance. In fact all of Jeremiah's prophecies must be understood in terms of the Lord's covenant with His people. Therefore as we summarize Jeremiah's message we see a unity and a structure in the book, even though on the surface the book seems to lack structure and unity.

d. Our analysis of Jeremiah's experience (especially in Lesson X) enabled us to see relationships between many passages. Some of these passages are almost meaningless until we relate them to the prophet's outward struggle with his people and his inner struggle with the Lord and with himself. And this analysis is essential to our understanding of the book as a whole.

26. We have considered two reasons for studying structure. The first reason is to find or summarize the central ideas or message. The second reason is to see the relationships between the different parts.

The third reason for studying structure is <u>to be able to review the contents and to find specific passages.</u>

For example, you may not read or study Jeremiah for a long period of time. You will forget the outline and much of the contents. What will be the best

way to refresh your mind when you turn to Jeremiah again? _____

* _____   *

Just read over your outline.

27. Or, you may not discontinue your study of Jeremiah. And you want to preach a sermon on the figure of the cup of the Lord's wrath. How will you find that

passage? _____
*   *

Just look through your outline.

28. Of course you could review the book of Jeremiah by reading it over. And
you can find any passage by looking in the text itself. But this method is

not very efficient. Why? _____

* _____ *

It takes too long. In just a few minutes you can read through your outline
or find a passage in your outline. But it would take hours to read through
the book of Jeremiah.

29. So we have three basic reasons for studying the structure of a passage
or of a book like Jeremiah. See if you can now list these three reasons
from memory.

a. _____

b. _____

c. _____

*   *

See # 26 above.

30. These three reasons indicate how important the study of structure is --
at all levels. And they indicate why the study of structure is an important
part of Inductive Bible Study.

a. What is the basic principle of Inductive Bible Study? _____

_____

b. Why is the study of structure a necessary part of Inductive Bible Study?

_____

_____

c. How do we study structure in Inductive Bible Study? _____

* _____ *

a. Begin with the Bible and study it on its own terms.
b. We need to understand the structure of a book in order to see it on its
own terms.
c. We find the structure by studying the text itself.

B. Outline of the Book of Jeremiah

The book of Jeremiah, as it now stands, does not have a clear, overall structure. It is an anthology, a collection of prophecies and narratives, thrown loosely together. This is the first observation or conclusion we can make about its structure.

Nevertheless, there are some important, positive features about the structure of the book of Jeremiah. We shall now bring together from earlier lessons some of our observations about the overall structure. And we shall try to form an outline of the book.

1. An outline of a book is like an outline of a face or an object. As we noted in Lesson IV, a painter draws a simple sketch or outline of the object he is going to paint before he paints it. The outline just defines the size and shape of the object. Then he adds the details, color, shadows, etc.

What is the outline of a book? What does it do? _____

_____

_____

*   *

The outline of a book is a summary of its major divisions and sections and paragraphs. It defines the overall structure of the book.

2. An outline not only summarizes the contents of the book. It also shows how the different parts are related. Look over the following outline of the book of Romans.

```
    I. Introduction - Rom. 1:1-17
   II. Doctrinal Teachings - Rom. 1:18-11:36
        A. The Condemnation of Man - Rom. 1:18-3:20
        B. Justification by Faith - Rom. 3:21-4:25
        C. Reconciliation in Christ - Rom. 5
        D. Dead to Sin; Alive in Christ - Rom. 6
        E. The Liberation of Man - Rom. 7
        F. Life in the Spirit - Rom. 8
        G. The Gospel and the Jews - Rom. 9-11
  III. Practical Exhortations - Rom. 12:1-15:13
   IV. Conclusion - Rom. 15:14-16:27
```

In this outline there are _____ major divisions. The second division contains _____ sections. The paragraphs are not listed.

*   *

4   7

3. Explain briefly the relationships between the different parts of the book of Romans as they are presented in the above outline.

a. How is Division I related to the other divisions? _____

_____

_____

b. How is Division II related to Section C? _____

_____

_____

c. How is Section A related to Section B? _____

_____

* _____ *

If you look at the references in this outline, you can explain the relationships this way:
a. Division I is separate from all the other divisions and parallel to them. It does not include them, nor is it included within any other divisions of the book.
b. Division II includes Section C along with all the other sections. That is, Section C is one part of Division II.
c. Section A and Section B are two separate, parallel parts of Division II.

If you look at the titles in the outline, you can explain the references this way:
a. Division I is the introduction to the whole book of Romans. It is not an introduction to one part of the book.
b. Division II is a series of doctrinal teachings. Reconciliation in Christ is one of those teachings.
c. Sections A and B are two doctrinal teachings in a series.

4. Turn to your outline of the book of Jeremiah. This outline also gives a summary of the paragraphs, sections, and divisions and shows the relationships between them.

a. How does the outline show the groups of paragraphs (sections)? _____

_____

_____

b. How will you group sections into divisions? _____

_____

* _____ *

a. A heavy line marks the beginning and end of each section. The paragraphs
are joined by a bracket. And the section has a reference and a title.
b. You may set off the divisions by marking a double line at beginning and
end. Then make a bracket joining the sections that belong together. And
give each division a reference and a title.

5. You already know what is the first major division of the book of Jeremiah. It is Jer. 1:1-3. Of course this is a very short passage, really, on-

ly a paragraph. Why then is it set off as a major division? _____

_____

_____

* _____ *

Jer. 1:1-3 must be set off from the other divisions because it is an introduction to the whole book. It cannot be part of a section or of another division. Therefore it should be considered one of the major divisions or at
least parallel to and separate from the other divisions.

6. Now consider Jer. 52.

a. What does this chapter contain? _____

_____

_____

b. Where else in the Old Testament is this information given? _____

_____

c. What do the previous chapters contain?_____

_____

d. What special characteristic sets off Jer. 52 from the rest of the book?

* _____ *

a. Jer. 52 contains historical information about King Zedekiah, the fall of
Jerusalem, the three deportations, and King Jehoiachin in exile.
b. 2 Kings and 2 Chronicles.
c. Jer. 52 is different from the previous chapters, which contain prophecies
concerning the nations.
d. Jer. 51:64 indicates that the words of Jeremiah end there. That means
that Jer. 52 is an appendix added by someone else.

7. Mark off Jer. 52 in your outline as a major division. The title that is
usually given to this division is "Historical Appendix."

8. By setting off Jer. 52 as a division, we indicate that it is parallel

to _____ and related to _____

* _____. *

the other divisions   the rest of the book

9. In Lesson XI we mentioned briefly that Jer. 46-51 is a collection of
prophecies concerning the nations. In the early Septuagint Greek version
of the Old Testament this whole passage is placed after Jer. 25:13. Apparently, therefore, this is a major division of the book of Jeremiah.

Mark off Jer. 46-51 as a division of the book of Jeremiah and give it the
following title: "Prophecies to the Nations."

10. Now read rapidly through Jer. 46-51 and underline the names of the nations about which these prophecies are given. Then list the nations here
and give the references for the prophecies concerning each one.

a. _____   _____

b. _____   _____

c. _____   _____

d. _____   _____

e. _____   _____

f. _____   _____

g. _____   _____

h. _____   _____

i. _____   _____

11. Now mark off these <u>sections</u> in your outline of the book of Jeremiah. Put in the lines, brackets, titles, and references.

12. Another important group of passages that we have discovered is the one that contains a strong emphasis on the future hope and restoration of Judah. This theme is found in isolated passages in other parts of the book. But apparently most of Jeremiah's prophecies were collected in these chapters.

Give the reference: _____
*   *

Jer. 30-33.

13. Jer. 30-33 is usually called the "Book of Consolation" because of its message of hope. The rest of the book speaks mostly of judgment. Mark off this group of passages in your outline as a major division.

14. Jer. 34-45 contains a series of narratives. Look over your survey of these chapters in Lesson XII, A. Although several of these chapters seem to

be out of place, most of them deal with _____.
*   *

See Lesson XII, A.

15. Set off Jer. 34-45 in your outline as a major division and give it the following title: "The Fall of Jerusalem."

16. Remember that several chapters of Jer. 34-45 do not refer to the fall of Jerusalem. The dates of these chapters should be marked in your outline in the column marked "Special Details."

List the chapters here. _____
*   *

Jer. 35, 36, 45.

17. It is especially difficult to know how to divide up Jer. 1-29. Following the introduction (Jer. 1:1-3) we find a long series of Jeremiah's prophecies. We have studied "The Call of Jeremiah" (Jer. 1:4-19), the collection of prophecies concerning "Israel's Apostasy" (Jer. 2:1-4:4), another collection of prophecies of judgment, "The Enemy from the North and the Enemy from Within" (Jer. 4:5-6:30), and "The Temple Sermon" (Jer. 7:1-8:3). Other similar prophecies follow in Chapters 8-10.

There is only one reference to time (Jer. 3:6) in these prophecies. They are a mixed collection with regard to topic and also with regard to date. Nevertheless they seem to represent in general the earlier half of Jeremiah's ministry.

Mark on your outline Jer. 1:4-10:25 as a major division, and give it the title "Earlier Prophecies."

18. Beginning in Chapter 11 and running through Chapter 20, we have noted several personal experiences of Jeremiah. Chapter 11 indicates that men from Jeremiah's home village, Anathoth, sought his life. Jer. 13:1-11 is one of Jeremiah's acted parables, "The Linen Waistcloth Episode." Jer. 14:1-15:4 presents Jeremiah's prophecies and intercessions at the time of "The Great Drought." Jer. 19:1-20:6 presents another acted parable, "The Broken Flask Episode," and his subsequent night in the stocks.

Intertwined with these incidents from Jeremiah's ministry in Jer. 11-20 we found a series of passages called "confessions" (Jer. 11:18-20; 12:1-6; 15:10-21; 17:14-18; 18:18-23; 20:7-18). These confessions are striking expressions of Jeremiah's inner struggle as the Lord's prophet in a time of judgment.

Mark off Jer. 11-20 as a major division of the book of Jeremiah with the title, "Judgment of Judah and Anguish of Jeremiah."

19. The remaining chapters, Jer. 21-29, form another major division. We studied these chapters in Lesson XI. They deal with important events in the life of the prophet, in which he is in direct conflict with the rulers and prophets of Judah. In Jer. 21:1-10 King Zedekiah asks for Jeremiah's counsel concerning the Babylonian siege. Then follows a section of prophecies concerning the kings of Judah (Jer. 21:11-23:8), and another section concerning the false prophets (Jer. 23:9-40). Chapter 24 presents Jeremiah's vision of the two baskets of figs, concerning King Jehoiachin and the exiles on the one hand and King Zedekiah and the remnant in Judah on the other. Chapter 25, in the crucial year 605 B.C., gives Jeremiah's prophecies concerning Babylon's rule over the nations. Chapter 26 is the story of Jeremiah's bold Temple Sermon and his subsequent trial. Jer. 27-28 presents another of Jeremiah's acted parables, "The Yoke-Bars Episode." Apparently King Zedekiah and several neighboring rulers were plotting to throw off Babylonian rule, but Jeremiah challenged them, referring to King Nebuchadnezzar as the Lord's servant sent to rule over the nations. Finally, Jer. 29 contains Jeremiah's message to those who were in exile with King Jehoiachin.

Identify in your outline Jer. 21-29 as a major division. Give it a title like "Jeremiah and the Leaders of Judah."

19 Now list the references and titles of the eight major divisions of the book of Jeremiah. Be sure these divisions are all clearly marked in your outline of the book of Jeremiah. You may also want to include this list separately in your notebook for Jeremiah, because it gives you a rapid survey of the contents of the book. You will not be asked to memorize this list.

a. _____

b. _____

c. _____

d. _____

e. _____

f. _____

g. _____

h. _____

20. This overall outline of the book of Jeremiah is only provisional. As you continue to study the book, you may want to change it.

Remember, too, that this outline only represents the structure of the book of Jeremiah as it now stands. We have said that the book is an anthology of prophecies and narratives from the ministry of the Prophet Jeremiah. This anthology contains several groups or collections of materials related in some sections to definite topics, linked in other sections rather superficially, and gathered almost haphazardly in other sections.

Therefore, we cannot say that the overall structure contributes greatly to our understanding of the message of the book, the mind of the author, or even the life of Jeremiah. Really, the present structure, because it is so puzzling, hinders our understanding of Jeremiah, his ministry, and his message.

On the other hand, we have been able to relate the different passages of the book to structures which are not apparent in the order of the book itself. The historical background, the experience of the prophet, and his message can be studied and structured by using the information in the book itself. (See A.25 above.) The individual passages, when related to these structures, take on tremendous significance. And then we are able to understand the ministry and message of Jeremiah.

Later in this lesson you will consider how Jeremiah's prophecies and experiences were recorded and how the book of Jeremiah was formed over a long period of time.

C. Structural Elements

You now have an outline of the overall structure indicating the major divisions of the Jeremiah anthology which we call the book of Jeremiah. You have analyzed the structure of several sections of the text in previous lessons. And you have studied structural elements in smaller passages.

In this section you will consider further some of the details of the text which have to do with structure. You will never have time to consider all the pertinent details, but you should always be on the lookout for further clues to the structure and meaning of the text.

1. Turn to the opening words of the book of Jeremiah. Try to imagine what the original text looked like, when the book of Jeremiah was first put together. It had no chapters and verses, no paragraphs, no punctuation, no spaces between words. It was written by hand in Hebrew with all the letters run together. And in Hebrew at that time they used no vowels. Look over the following line to get an idea of what the original text was like.

THWRDSFJRMHTHSNFHLKHFTHPRSTSWHWRNNTHTH

Now see if you can decipher that line by adding vowels and separating the words. It is taken from a passage in Jeremiah that you have read many times.

_____

* _____ *

"The words of Jeremiah, the son of Hilkiah, of the priests who were in Anathoth."

2. Another thing we should note about the original text is that it did not include titles as most of our modern versions do - at the beginning, at the top of each page, sometimes at the beginning of each section or division.

Pretend that the title at the beginning of the book of Jeremiah is not there. Look at Jer. 1:1. Is there a word or a phrase there that could be considered

the original title of the book? _____

Write down the words that probably formed the original title of the book of

Jeremiah. _____
*   *

Yes.   "The Words of Jeremiah."

3. When we pick up a book to read it, the first thing we do is read the

title. Why? _____
*   *

To see what it is about.

4. When you turn to a book of the Bible to read it inductively, one of the

first things you should do is look for a title. Where should you look? _____

* _____
                                                                          *

Look in the text itself. Do not depend on the title given in your Bible because that one was added by someone else. Inductive Bible Study begins with
the original text and studies it on its own terms.

5. Different books have many different kinds of titles. Serious, non-fiction
books usually have titles that tell us what the book is about.

Explain the significance of the title "The Words of Jeremiah." Does this

title tell what the book contains? _____

* _____
                                                                          *

This is a very appropriate title. It tells what the book contains - the
words or prophecies of Jeremiah.

6. At the top of the first page of your outline of the book of Jeremiah
there is a short line. Write on that line the title we have just discovered
at the beginning of the original text of the book.

7. Another important structural element in the book of Jeremiah is the presence of editorial comments throughout the book. Jer. 1:1-3, for example,
does not contain prophecies; it is an introduction that explains the historical background of Jeremiah's prophecies. Jer. 1:4, likewise, is an explanation about the following words of Jeremiah. In v. 5-10 there are other
brief editorial links.

Write here the editorial phrases in Jer. 1:5-10. _____

_____

_____

* _____
                                                                          *

Then I said.   But the Lord said to me.   Then the Lord put forth His hand
and touched my mouth; and the Lord said to me.

8. Some of these editorial comments, like Jer. 1:1-3, give us historical background. Others, like the often repeated expression, "The word of the Lord came to me saying," distinguish prophecies from narrative or editorial comments and show us where a new prophecy begins.
We studied very carefully the editorial statements in Jer. 21-29. Look over these chapters once again and explain the importance of the editorial comments at the beginning of most of these chapters. _____

_____

_____

Chapters 21, 24, 25, 26, 27, 28, and 29 begin with editorial statements that explain the historical background of the prophecies.

9. Explain the importance of the editorial statements in Jer. 46-51. _____

_____

_____

_____

These statements indicate whom these prophecies concern, that is, the different nations. They introduce each section. In this way they reveal the structure and message of Jer. 46-51.

10. Explain the importance of Jer. 46:1. _____

_____

_____

_____

This is an editorial statement. It introduces the whole division of prophecies (Jer. 46-51) and tells what this division contains (prophecies "concerning the nations").

11. Explain the importance of the editorial statement at the end of Jer. 51:64.

_____

_____

_____

_____

This statement indicates that all of Jeremiah's prophecies end at this point and that Jer. 52 is an appendix written by someone else.

12. We noted earlier that Jer. 52 is an "Historical Appendix." And we have just noted that it was not written by Jeremiah. What does Jer. 52 contri-

bute to our understanding of the book? _____

_____

* _____ *

Like the "Introduction" (Jer. 1:1-3), the "Historical Appendix" (Jer. 52) gives us important background information about the history of Jeremiah's time.

13. Note the three deportations mentioned in Jer. 52:28-32. If you have not already done so, calculate the date for these three deportations. Use 605 B.C. as the date Nebuchadnezzar became King of Babylonia.

a. The first deportation was in the _____ year of Nebuchadnezzar, _____ B.C.

b. The second deportation was in the _____ year of Nebuchadnezzar, _____ B.C.

c. The third deportation was in the _____ year of Nebuchadnezzar, _____ B.C.
*   *

If you have trouble figuring out these dates, go back and review Lesson III.

14. Mark these deportations on your chronological chart on the line for international events.

15. Another important structural element comes to light in the editorial comments scattered throughout the book of Jeremiah. You may have noticed that sometimes Jeremiah is referred to in the first person ("I," "me") and at times he is referred to in the third person ("Jeremiah," "Jeremiah the prophet"). These references are important because they may indicate who created these editorial comments.

a. Who created the statement "The word of the Lord came to me"? _____

_____

b. Who created the statement "The word of the Lord came to Jeremiah"? _____

* _____ *

a. Jeremiah himself   b. Another person

16. If you study all of the editorial statements in terms of their references to Jeremiah, you will have another clue to the structure of the book.
It has been observed, for example, that most of the cases in Jer. 1-20 use
the first person ("I," "me"). In Jer. 21-52, in contrast, most of the editorial statements use the third person "Jeremiah," "Jeremiah the prophet."

Glance through your Bible and underline some of these editorial references
to Jeremiah.

a. How is Jeremiah referred to (first person or third person) in Jer. 1-20?

_____

b. How is Jeremiah referred to in Jer. 21-52? _____

17. Another important structural element is the presence of different types
of material. You have probably noticed that parts of the book of Jeremiah
are written as poetry and parts as prose. In most modern versions poetic
passages are arranged line by line, with special indentations, etc.

If your Bible does distinguish poetry from prose, glance through the major
divisions of the book of Jeremiah and see if some divisions contain only
one kind or another. If your Bible does not make this distinction, do not
try to answer the following questions.

In the following spaces put down "all poetry," "mostly poetry," "all prose,"
"mostly prose," "equally prose and poetry."

a. Jer. 1:4-10:25 _____

b. Jer. 11-20 _____

c. Jer. 34-45 _____

d. Jer. 46-51 _____
*   *

a. Jer. 1:4-10:25 Mostly poetry
b. Jer. 11-20 Equally prose and poetry
c. Jer. 34-45 All prose
d. Jer. 46-51 Mostly poetry

18. In the analysis of literary types, we find some grouping of poetic
passages and prose passages, but this is not a dominant feature in the
structure of the book.

We should note that there are three major types of material, not just two:

                    1. Poetic sayings
                    2. Biographical prose
                    3. Prose discourses

There is not sufficient space to analyze these types of material here, but
you should be aware of them. Perhaps you will be able to carry on this analysis in your study of the book of Jeremiah in the future.

Likewise, we have not studied Hebrew poetry and Jeremiah's use of it. This
is important, but we do not have time to go into it here. Perhaps you will
be able to do this in the future on your own or in another course.

18. Another element in the structure of the book of Jeremiah is the presence
of links between passages. We have noted this factor a number of times. It
is related to the fact that many passages are grouped together topically.
But at times the links between passages are only very superficial.

We noted, for example, the relationship between Jer. 18 and Jer. 19.

a. What is the link between these two passages? _____

_____

b. Is the message basically the same in both passages? _____

*   _____   *

a. They are probably linked together because they both mention something
about the potter.
b. No. Jer. 18 is a call to repentance. Jer. 19, on the contrary, is a message of inevitable, hopeless judgment.

19. We noted two links between Jer. 20:1-6 and Jer. 20:7-18. These two passages are not inappropriately joined together. But the links are in themselves rather superficial. List the two links.

a. _____

b. _____
*   *

a. "Terror on every side" - see Jer. 20:3 and Jer. 20:10.
b. The reference to the stocks in v. 2 seems to find an echo in v. 7.

20. As you continue your study of the book of Jeremiah you will find many
similar links.

What is the significance of these links? _____

_____

*   _____   *

These links are clues to the present structure of the book. They help explain how different passages were grouped together. They do not, however, contribute greatly to our understanding of the ministry and message of Jeremiah.

21. As a final structural element, we should mention once again that there are evidences of topical, chronological, biographical, and logical arrangement in the book of Jeremiah.

a. Mention two major divisions (besides Jer. 1:1-3 and Jer. 52) that are

topical groupings of passages. _____

b. Find a series of chapters that are in good chronological order. _____

_____

c. What major division contains many biographical insights? _____

d. Mention two key passages that are located in important, logical order. ____

* _____ *

a. Jer. 30-33 and Jer. 46-51   c. Jer. 11-20
b. Jer. 37-44   d. Jer. 1:1-3 and Jer. 1:4-10

22. Following is a list of the structural elements we have noted in this section. As you continue your study of the book of Jeremiah you will want to pursue some of these factors further and add other elements. You will want to continue your study of structure at all levels (from words and phrases to sections and divisions) in order to understand more clearly Jeremiah's message and his ministry. You need not memorize this list. But refer back to it when you study the structure of the book of Jeremiah.

```
1. The original title of the book.
2. Editorial comments in the text.
3. The personal references to Jeremiah.
4. The three different types of material: poetic say-
   ings, biographical prose, and prose discourses.
5. Links between passages.
6. Topical, chronological, biographical, and logical
   arrangement.
```

D. How Jeremiah's Prophecies Were Recorded (Jeremiah 36, 45)

In Lesson XII you read through Jer. 30-45. But you did not make a detailed study of Jer. 36 and Jer. 45. That lesson was concerned with the fall of Jerusalem. And these two chapters, 36 and 45, do not deal with the time of the fall. They deal with an earlier period in Jeremiah's ministry. And they

give us important insight into the writing of the book of Jeremiah. So you
will study Jer. 36 and 45 at this time.

Once again you will test your ability to do Inductive Study independently.
Study these passages as you have done previously. Work out your outline
for these two passages, analyzing each paragraph. Then write down the important questions that come to your mind as you explore the text. And work
out your answers to these questions. Use notebook paper and keep this material in your notebook. You may be asked to turn in this assignment at the
next class session and you may want to use it in a Bible study or in a Sunday school class.

Pay special attention to the information about how Jeremiah's prophecies
were written down. Use your imagination and your reasoning ability. Ask
yourself, for instance, what we can say about the accuracy and dependabili-
ty of these writings. Locate these passages on your chronological chart and
explain what was happening at that time.

Do your work carefully. You may be quizzed on this material at your next
class session.

E. How the Book of Jeremiah Was Put Together

This final section of Lesson XIII is different from any assignment you have
had in this course. You are asked simply to read through the following paragraphs.

Through Inductive Study you have learned a great deal about the structure
and the message of the book of Jeremiah. And you have found definite information about how Jeremiah's prophecies were recorded. But you have also
seen that the structure of the book is very puzzling. This is due in part
to the nature of the material and in part to the way it was compiled.

What follows is an attempt to explain how the book of Jeremiah was put together. In itself it is not an Inductive Study of the book of Jeremiah. But
these observations and suggestions are based on our previous Inductive Study.
At this point each student of Jeremiah should follow his own path of reasoning. The Bible itself does not explicitly describe the history of these materials, though it does provide many clues. Therefore read these paragraphs
with a critical mind, consider the opinions of others, and draw your own
conclusions.

Our starting point in analyzing the history of the formation of the book
of Jeremiah is to recognize that it is an anthology containing prophecies
and narratives related to the prophet Jeremiah. This material covers a
period of 40 years or more. How would you organize it? Some anthologies
give an author's works in the order in which they were written. Others
place them in topical order. But the very nature of the material makes
a closely knit structure impossible.

Several of the books of the Bible (such as the Psalms and Proverbs) were compiled long after they had been written. This is probably true to some extent of Jeremiah too. Jeremiah and his secretary Baruch evidently compiled part of it. The final compilation, however, seems to have been at a much later date. The fact that the order of the materials is not the same in the Septuagint (Greek) version and the early Hebrew version suggests that the final compilation was at a late date.

We must remember that the Old Testament prophets preached their messages. They did not, by and large, publish them. Some, at least, had disciples or schools of followers who memorized their prophecies and repeated them and passed them on from one generation to the next. We know that in those days books were few and that vast amounts of literature were passed on orally.

We must remember, too, that the period during and following Jeremiah's ministry was chaotic. With the total destruction of Jerusalem, the deportation of her leaders and many of her people to Babylonia, and later the departure of the remnant to Egypt, it is surprising that any of Jeremiah's prophecies and deeds remain at all.

Yet our study of the book of Jeremiah goes a long way to show how and why these records were preserved. You discovered in Jer. 36 and 45 several important data. Jeremiah did set down in writing many of his prophecies. He had a secretary, Baruch, who wrote down at least some of these prophecies at the prophet's dictation. Jeremiah may have dictated these prophecies from memory or with the help of notes he himself had written. We know that on one occasion in 605-604 B.C. he dictated systematically his prophecies from the previous 23 years of his ministry. Other passages (see Jer. 29:1; 51:60) mention other writings of Jeremiah. And it is likely that Baruch continued to serve as Jeremiah's secretary through the remaining years of his ministry.

Another important clue that we have noted in this lesson is the presence of editorial comments. In Chapters 1-20 these are largely in the first person, as though created by the prophet himself. But from Chapters 21 through 52 they are largely in the third person, indicating that someone else had a hand in forming these materials. This was probably Baruch. It seems likely that Baruch not only took down Jeremiah's dictation, but also kept a record of the important events in the life of Jeremiah and his people.

This would explain the major groupings of materials that we have found. Jeremiah and Baruch probably gathered various materials together on more than one occasion and put them down with editorial comments. And others may have done the same thing. These collections or anthologies probably circulated for some time before they were finally incorporated into the book of Jeremiah as we now have it. For example, Jer. 30-33 and Jer. 46-51 may have been separate books.

At the same time allowance should be made for oral transmission of some of these materials, for this was largely the way the prophetic traditions were carried on. This would account for the loosely structured nature of some parts of the book today. These oral materials were written down years later, grouped together, and given editorial introductions and comments. The commentators point out linguistic and historical arguments for suggesting that some of these materials reflect a later setting. The text itself (Jer. 52:31) refers to an event that occurred "in the thirty-seventh year of the captivity of Jehoiachin," which is 26 years after the fall of Jerusalem.

Nevertheless the evidence we have already cited, especially the facts presented in Jer. 36 and 45, indicates overwhelmingly that the contents of the book of Jeremiah are authentic and trustworthy. In spite of the chaos of the times the words of Jeremiah have been preserved faithfully for 2600 years. Through memory and dictation and a gradual process of accumulation, these amazing records have come to us. In spite of its very difficult structure, the book of Jeremiah stands among the Old Testament Prophets as a true and invaluable testimony of "The Lord's Prophet in a Time of Judgment."

Finally, we should add an important theological explanation of why and how these materials were preserved and later became part of the Old Testament canon. We recognize, of course, the hand of God not only in Jeremiah's ministry but also in the preservation of these records. But this is only a very general and a very superficial statement. There is much more to be said. In Lesson XII we analyzed the historical and theological significance of the fall of Jerusalem. In that analysis it became evident that Jeremiah's prophecies played a singular role in Judah's faith and history. That nation should have ceased to exist with the destruction of her cities and the deportation of her people. Her religion should have died with the destruction of the Temple, the termination of the sacrificial rites, the exiling of her divinely annointed kings, and the discreditation of the vast majority of her prophets. But Jeremiah's prophecies, the very words that condemned Judah and foretold her terrible destruction, proclaimed that Judah's Lord was not defeated. They revealed that His will was not thwarted but rather fulfilled in those cataclysmic events. And that same Lord who judged His people so completely in 587 B.C. had promised, through His prophet Jeremiah, a future restoration, a future hope, a new covenant.

So the prophecies of Jeremiah, which had been so completely rejected by the people and rulers and prophets of Judah before 587, became after 587 the most important legacy of their past history and future hope. They would be preserved at all cost and through every upheaval as the foundation of Judah's renewed religious faith. They remain to this day as the primary bridge across the terrible chasm in the history of the people of God in the Old Testament at the time of the fall of Jerusalem.

14

The Theology of the Book of Jeremiah

We study the Bible for many reasons. Those who practice regular Bible reading and prayer find edification and instruction for their lives each day. Those who preach and teach in their churches find the basic material for their sermons and lessons in the Bible. All who study the Bible seriously find in it an unlimited store of insights and inspiration for their understanding of God and of His will for man.

As we come to the conclusion of our course of Inductive Study of Jeremiah, we should naturally ask ourselves what benefits we can derive from the book of Jeremiah. As our comprehension of this book grows and our ability to interpret its pages increases, we will find that it becomes more and more meaningful for our ministry and for our own lives. If we use the book of Jeremiah in our daily Bible reading, we will now find far more insights and practical lessons than we did previously. We are much more equipped to preach and teach from Jeremiah passages. And we probably will find that our understanding of God and His will for man has been profoundly affected by our encounter with the Prophet Jeremiah.

In this lesson you will study this last factor, the significance of the book of Jeremiah for our understanding of God and His will. You will try to define some of the basic concepts of Jeremiah's theology. You will relate these concepts to the thinking of other books of the Bible. And you will consider their significance for your own message and ministry. This is the process for the formation of Biblical theology.

Your objectives in this lesson are to:

Summarize Jeremiah's message.

Define his concept of the covenant, religion, and social justice.

Learn some basic steps in the formation of Biblical theology.

A. Basic Steps

In this section you will consider some basic steps for theological studies in the book of Jeremiah. You will see once again that it is important to use the inductive approach. In the following sections of this lesson you will apply the inductive approach as you study certain theological concepts in the book of Jeremiah.

1. In our analysis of the theology of the book of Jeremiah we want to follow the basic approach of Inductive Bible Study. Write out once again our definition of Inductive Bible Study. _____

_____

See Lesson I, A, 14. You should be able to write this definition from memory.

2. An Inductive Study of the theology of the book of Jeremiah should begin

with _____ and study it on _____.

the Bible (the book of Jeremiah)   its own terms

3. Obviously, if we are to define the theology of the book of Jeremiah, we should begin with the book of Jeremiah. But how do we begin with the book of Jeremiah? Once again we can refer back to the beginning steps for Inductive Bible Study, which you learned in the early lessons of this course. List these three steps.

a. _____

b. _____

c. _____

a. Find out what kind of literature it is.
b. Find out something about its historical background.
c. Look for the structure.

4. See if these three steps are necessary in an Inductive Study of the theology of the book of Jeremiah.

a. In order to interpret the theology of the book of Jeremiah, do you have

to know what kind of literature it is? _____

b. In order to interpret the theology of the book of Jeremiah, do you have

to know something about its historical background? _____

c. In order to interpret the theology of the book of Jeremiah, do you have

to look for the structure of the book? _____

a.b.c. Yes.

5. Just think what would happen if you tried to state the theology of the book of Jeremiah without taking into account these three factors.

a. Would you be able to understand messages like Jeremiah's "confessions" if you did not know that this book is an anthology of prophetic literature? _____

b. Would you be able to interpret the many references to destruction in this

book without some understanding of the major historical events of that per-

iod? _____

c. Would you be able to explain the concept of judgment in the book of Jere-

miah without finding the structure of Jeremiah's message as a whole? _____
*   *

a.b.c. No.

6. We can see readily that the inductive approach is absolutely essential to
any legitimate interpretation of the book of Jeremiah or the theology of the
book of Jeremiah. And yet many people fail to take even these three basic
steps.

Consider, for example, the preacher who wants to preach a sermon about sexual immorality. He finds the reference to harlotry in Jer. 3:1-5 and bases
his sermon on this text. Is this a legitimate interpretation of Jeremiah's

theology? Explain. _____

_____

* _____ *

This preacher has neither understood Jeremiah's basic message nor his use of
figurative language. In Jer. 3:1-5 he is not talking about sexual immorality;
he refers to harlotry as a literary figure for Judah's infidelity to the Lord,
Judah's idolatry.

7. Take, as another example, the case of the theologian who is writing a book
of systematic theology. He has chosen a list of doctrines, and he goes through
the Bible pulling out passages that refer to each of these doctrines. Is this

an inductive approach? What danger is there in this method? _____

_____

_____   _____

* _____ *

This is not an inductive approach. The danger is that this theologian will
quote passages from Jeremiah and other books without adequate attention to
the three factors we have mentioned above. He is likely to misinterpret or
distort the original meaning of the text.

8. Whether we are just reading the Bible for our own edification, preaching a sermon, or writing a theological text, we should apply the basic insights of Inductive Bible Study.

Another expression of this rule is found in the well-known saying:

"Text out of context is pretext."

Explain the meaning of this saying. _____

_____

_____

* _____ *

This saying means that you have to understand the context of a passage before you can interpret its meaning.

9. What, then, is the context of a passage or text? _____

_____

* _____ *

Most people would say that "context" refers to the verses that precede the passage and the verses that follow the passage. But it means much more than this.

10. Every passage should be interpreted in context. It should be studied in its own setting. This means we have to understand the passage not just in the context of the nearby verses and paragraphs but in its broader context. We find the broader context by taking the three basic steps of Inductive Bible Study, which we have listed above. List these steps once again and notice how they help us understand the broader context of any passage in the book of Jeremiah.

a. _____

b. _____

c. _____

* _____ *

See #3 above.

11. Later in this lesson you will analyze several of the principal theological concepts of the book of Jeremiah. Each of these concepts should be studied not just as an isolated idea, but in relation to what? _____

_____

_____

* _____ *

The same three factors you have just listed: the kind of literature, the historical background, and the structure of the book.

12. Up to now we have been careful to speak of the theology of the book of Jeremiah, not the theology of Jeremiah. In the previous lesson, however, we noted that the book of Jeremiah as we now have it does not reveal a clear, overall structure. Although other men, notably Baruch, had a hand in recording and gathering these materials, they did not impose their own thoughts on these materials. Therefore the theological concepts we find in the book are essentially the theology of Jeremiah.

List the principal ideas of Jeremiah's message. Four of these ideas we found throughout Jeremiah's prophecies, beginning in Jer. 2:1-4:4. The fifth is not so prevalent; it appears primarily in Jer. 30-33. State these ideas concisely and as completely as you can.

a. _____

_____

b. _____

_____

c. _____

_____

d. _____

_____

e. _____

* _____ *

a. Judah has had a special covenant relationship with God.
b. Judah has been unfaithful to God, following other gods, trusting in false alliances, and carrying on injustices.
c. Judah shall be judged and destroyed by God because of her evil ways.
d. Judah is called to repent and return to God.
e. Judah, though destroyed and exiled, shall be restored one day by God.

13. This message must be interpreted as the expression of a certain kind of literature. State briefly what kind of literature the book of Jeremiah con-

tains. _____

_____

_____

_____

* _____ *

Your answer should include these elements:
a. This book contains prophecies. It is an anthology of the prophecies and deeds of the prophet Jeremiah.
b. Prophecy is the proclamation of God's will for a particular time in history.
c. It is also instrumental in the fulfillment of God's will.

14. The second thing we have to know about the book of Jeremiah and the message of Jeremiah is the historical background. State briefly the historical

background of Jeremiah's message. _____

_____

_____

_____

_____

_____

_____

_____

_____

_____

_____

_____

* _____ *

Your answer should include these elements:
a. Jeremiah prophesied during the last 40 years of Judah and during the siege, fall, and deportation of the people of Jerusalem.
b. His people were practicing idolatry, making alliances with other nations, committing moral and social injustices, with the approval of their rulers, priests, and prophets.
c. Egypt exercised hegemony over Judah in Jeremiah's early years. From 605 onward, however, Babylonia extended its empire over the whole region east of the Mediterranean, including Judah.
d. Although Jeremiah counselled submission to Nebuchadnezzar, King Zedekiah tried to break away, bringing on final destruction in 587 B.C.

15. The third factor we need to know about the book of Jeremiah is its structure. We have discovered, however, that the book of Jeremiah does not have a meaningful structure. We have to depend on hidden structures. List the three hidden structures which enable us to relate the different passages to each other and find unity in the book as a whole.

a. _____

b. _____

c. _____

a. The historical background (a chronological structure).
b. The experience of the prophet (a biographical structure).
c. The summary of his message (a topical, logical structure).

16. Note particularly the summary of Jeremiah's message. It is not merely a list of ideas. The five main ideas which we have listed are interrelated. They must be interpreted in relation to each other.

What is the basic idea that underlies the other four ideas? _____

The covenant relationship.

17. Explain how the covenant concept is related to the following in Jeremiah's prophecies.

a. Judah's apostasy: _____

_____

_____

b. God's judgment: _____

_____

_____

c. The call to repentance: _____

_____

d. The future restoration: _____

_____

* _____ *

a. Because Judah has been given this special relationship to the Lord, she
is not free to follow after other gods. Therefore the Lord exposes her unfaithfulness as apostasy, harlotry, and idolatry.
b. Because Judah has broken her commitment to the Lord, He will judge her.
c. Because Judah has been the Lord's people, He calls her back to Himself.
d. Because Judah has been covenanted to God and this covenant has been broken, the Lord promises a future restoration and a new covenant.

18. Explain the relationship between God's word of judgment and His call to

repentance in Jeremiah's prophecies. _____

_____

_____

* _____ *

The relationship is reciprocal and alternative. If Judah repents, God will
not destroy His people. When Judah shows that she will not repent even after many years of pleading, judgment becomes inevitable.

19. Explain the relationship between God's judgment and the future restora-

tion in Jeremiah's prophecies. _____

_____

* _____ *

There is a logical sequence: first judgment, then restoration. Because Judah is so obstinately rebellious, she can be brought into a new relationship
to God only through a time of terrible judgment.

20. In conclusion, Inductive Study of the theology of Jeremiah must consider:

> 1. The kind of literature the book contains.
> 2. The historical background of the period.
> 3. The hidden structures: the chronological structure,
>   the biographical structure, and the structure of
>   Jeremiah's message.

B. Jeremiah's Concept of the Covenant

In this section you will investigate Jeremiah's concept of the covenant between the Lord and His people. Then you will briefly analyze the concept of
the covenant in other books of the Bible. Finally you will consider the significance of the covenant in our own day.

1. One way to begin our analysis of Jeremiah's concept of the covenant is to
refer to the passages we have already studied. Mention at least one passage

which we have studied which presents the idea of the covenant. _____

* _____ *

The first and one of the most prominent messages is Jer. 2:1-3.

2. This approach is a good one, because it takes you to passages which you
have already analyzed inductively, in context. But it has certain shortcom-

ings. Mention one. _____

* _____ *

One problem with this approach is that you probably haven't studied all the
passages dealing with the covenant. Or you may not remember all the references to the covenant.

3. Another way to begin our analysis of the covenant in the book of Jeremiah would be to look in a concordance. List all the references to the word

"covenant" in Jeremiah in your concordance. _____

_____

* _____ *

If you have a complete concordance, you should have 22 references. Notice
that most of the occurrences are found in Chapters 11 and 31-34.

4. This is a good approach, also, because it takes you immediately to a
large number of passages that refer to the covenant. But this method also

has shortcomings. Mention one. _____

_____

_____

* _____ *

One danger in using a concordance is that you are tempted to take passages
out of context, without making a careful analysis of the background of each
one. Another shortcoming is that you still might miss many important passages that present the covenant concept but do not use the word "covenant."
These passages would not be listed in the concordance under the word "covenant."

5. A third approach is to look for the covenant concept in the summary or
structure of Jeremiah's message. This is the approach we recommended in the

previous section of this lesson. Why did we recommend this approach? _____

_____

_____

* _____ *

We said that each theological concept should be studied on its own terms,
in context, not as an isolated idea. Therefore each idea must be understood
in relation to Jeremiah's other ideas and in relation to his message as a
whole.

6. Here we will use all three approaches.

First read over Jer. 2:1-3 and write a summary of Jeremiah's concept of the

covenant here. _____

_____

_____

_____

_____

* _____ *

Your answer should include these points:
a. Jeremiah, like other prophets, used the marriage figure to describe the special relationship between the Lord and His people. He refers back to the wilderness wanderings as an ideal time.
b. Israel's response is one of love (devotion) and obedience (following).
c. The Lord protected Israel.

7. Now turn to Jer. 11:1-17. We have not yet studied this passage. But we have just noted that it mentions the covenant several times. Read through this passage and underline the phrases that contain the word "covenant."

Then read through Jer. 11:1-17 again. This time underline with one color the phrases which indicate what the Lord has done and will do for and to His people. Underline with another color the phrases which indicate what the people should have done and have done in response to the Lord.

8. Analyze the significance of the covenant by listing first the phrases that tell what the Lord did for His people.

a. "I brought them out of the land of Egypt." _____

b. _____

c. _____

9. Now list the phrases that indicate how Israel or Judah should have responded to the Lord.

a. _____

b. _____

10. Now list the phrases that show how the people did in fact respond to the Lord.

a. "They did not obey or incline their ear." _____

b. _____

c. _____

d. _____

e. _____

f. _____

11. Finally, put down the phrases that tell what the Lord will do to His people because of their unfaithfulness.

a. "I am bringing evil upon them." _____

b. _____

c. _____

d. _____

12. Now summarize in your own words Jeremiah's concept of the covenant in

Jer. 11:1-17. _____

_____

_____

_____

_____

_____

_____

* _____ *

These seem to me to be the essential elements in Jeremiah's concept of the
covenant in Jer. 11:1-17.
a. God took the initiative by bringing Israel out of Egypt, offering to be
her God, and giving her a land.
b. Israel in turn was to obey God and be His people.
c. Israel broke this agreement. She disobeyed God, turned to her previous
evil ways, and went after other gods.
d. Therefore God will bring evil upon Israel.

13. We have reviewed one of the covenant passages from our previous study,
Jer. 2:1-3. And we have analyzed rapidly another passage which mentions the
word covenant four times, Jer. 11:1-17. It is evident that both of these
passages present the covenant as a special, mutual relationship between God
and Israel or Judah.

Now consider once again the place of the covenant concept in Jeremiah's message as a whole. List the five basic ideas of Jeremiah's message as we did
in the previous section of this lesson.

a. _____

b. _____

c. _____

d. _____

e. _____
*   *

See A. 12 above.

14. We noted in the previous section that these basic ideas are all inter-
related and that one concept underlies all the other ideas. What is this ba-

sic underlying concept? _____
*   *

The covenant.

15. Both the importance of the covenant concept and its meaning in the book
of Jeremiah are quite evident. But we should be careful to remember the historical context of this concept in the time of Jeremiah, as a return to earlier foundations, and as a projection into the future.

First, consider the importance of the covenant in the life of Judah during
Jeremiah's ministry.

a. Which of the five kings of Judah remembered the covenant and tried to

keep the covenant? _____

b. What was the general response of the people toward the covenant during

Jeremiah's ministry? _____

c. What was the attitude of the priests and prophets toward the covenant?

_____
*   *

a. Josiah only.
b. They were unfaithful, apostate, disobedient.
c. Apparently they encouraged the people in their apostasy.

16. Look up the record of Josiah's reign and find out what he did about the
covenant.

a. Give the references for our best Old Testament sources. _____

_____

b. What covenant was discovered during the reign of Josiah? _____

_____

c. What did he do about the covenant? _____

_____

d. This was in the _____ year of his reign, which was the year _____ B.C.,

which was the _____ year of Jeremiah's ministry.

*   *

a. 2 Kings 23:1-3, 2 Chronicles 34:29-33.
b. The Mosaic covenant, found in the books of the law.
c. He made a new covenant to keep the Mosaic covenant - and all the people
joined in.
d. 18th   622 B.C.   5th. (Be sure this event is marked
on your chronological chart.)

17. Now turn back to Jer. 11:1-17. Note that the Lord tells Jeremiah to proclaim "the words of this covenant." Which covenant does this passage refer

to? What is the relationship between this passage and Josiah's reform? _____

_____

_____

_____

*   *

These questions are still being discussed by the experts. You will have to
draw your own conclusions. It does seem likely, though, that Jer. 11:1-17
refers to Josiah's covenant in 2 Kings 23:1-3. Jeremiah probably supported
Josiah's reforms because they were in keeping with his own message.

18. We do not know how closely Jeremiah was related to Josiah's reforms. But
we know that Jeremiah's message and Josiah's reforms both called the people
back to the covenant made between God and Israel at Sinai at the time of
Moses. And we know that Josiah's reforms took place during the ministry of
Jeremiah. So we must consider that Josiah's covenant and his reforms are
part of the historical background of the book of Jeremiah. And we should
look for possible mention or hints of Josiah's reforms in the book of Jeremiah.

Earlier in this course we noted that one passage, Jer. 3:6-10, is dated during Josiah's reign. Read over this paragraph carefully. See if it contains
any reference to Josiah's reforms. Put down any pertinent information or

possible interpretation about those reforms. _____

_____

_____
_____
_____
_____

* _____ *

It seems likely that v. 10 refers to Josiah's reforms: "Judah did not return to me with her whole heart, but in pretense." Apparently Jeremiah considered Josiah's reforms to be only superficial. And he was right. Under
the following kings the people returned to their pagan, idolatrous practices.

19. We have now related Jeremiah's concept of the covenant with Josiah's
covenant, which is an important factor in the historical background of Jeremiah's ministry.

We have noted, too, that both Jeremiah and Josiah refer back to the Mosaic
covenant.

a. Where is the Mosaic covenant described in the Old Testament? _____

_____

b. What are the basic concepts of the Mosaic covenant? _____

_____
_____
_____

* _____ *

a. Exod. 19-20 is the most prominent among many passages. Read it over.
b. The basic concepts are the same as Jeremiah's:
      a) God took the initiative by bringing Israel out of Egypt and offer-
         ing to be her God.
      b) Israel in turn was to obey God and be His people.

20. Look in your concordance to see how often the word "covenant" appears
in the Old Testament. We do not have time to study more of these passages.
It is obvious that the idea of the covenant is one of the most important
concepts of the Old Testament.

Which of the Old Testament prophets use the term "covenant"? _____

_____
_____

21. One of the fascinating passages in the book of Jeremiah is Jer. 31:31-34.
Here Jeremiah projects the concept of the covenant into the future.

First note that Jeremiah refers to two covenants in this passage.

a. The first covenant is _____.

b. The second covenant is _____.

*   *

a. The Mosaic Covenant or the Covenant at Sinai.
b. A new future covenant.

22. Now notice that Jeremiah makes a contrast between the old covenant and

the new covenant. What is the basic difference? _____

_____

*   _____   *

The new covenant, unlike the old, will be written on their hearts, and all
will know the Lord.

23. There are three important aspects that distinguish the new covenant, according to Jer. 31:31-34. List these three characteristics.

a. _____

b. _____

c. _____

*   *

a. The Lord will write His law upon their hearts.
b. All the people will know the Lord.
c. He will forgive their sins.

24. Explain the first characteristic. What does he mean when he says, "I will

put my law within them, and I will write it upon their hearts"? _____

_____

_____

_____

*   _____   *

The basic concept here is one of will. Under the new covenant the people will not merely be subject to an external law (the Ten Commandments, the sacrifices, feast days, etc.). They will have a new heart, a new will united to the Lord's will, an internal law that will respond spontaneously.

25. This concept of the new covenant is perhaps the high point of Jeremiah's theology. It is one of the greatest promises of the Old Testament. And it was born at the time of Judah's deepest tragedy.

The concept of the new covenant projects us into the New Testament.

a. On what occasion did Jesus Himself refer to the new covenant? _____

_____

b. Give the references for this occasion. _____

_____

c. How did the new covenant come into being? _____

* _____ *

a. At the Last Supper.
b. Mark 14:22-25, Matt. 26:26-29, Luke 22:14-23, 1 Cor. 23-32.
c. By the sacrifice of Jesus, who gave Himself in order to establish a new relationship between God and man.

26. List once again the three characteristics of the new covenant, according to Jer. 31:31-34. Have they become true for the followers of Jesus Christ?

a. _____

b. _____

c. _____
* *

See #23 above.

27.How do men experience the new covenant today? Write down your concept

of the new covenant. _____

_____

_____

_____

28. We should make note of the vast importance of the covenant concept in the Bible and of Jeremiah's contribution to our understanding of the covenant concept.

One of the most obvious statements of the two covenants is found in the division of the Bible into two parts.

a. What is another name for the Old Testament? _____

b. What is another name for the New Testament? _____

*   *

a. The Old Covenant.
b. The New Covenant.
"Testament" is another way of saying "Covenant."

29. We could carry on our study of the covenant concept in the book of Jeremiah, the rest of the Old Testament, the New Testament, through the history of Christianity, and today. You should some day investigate this most important concept more thoroughly. Certainly you will be on the lookout for further passages and further insights as you do further Inductive Bible Study. And perhaps you will preach on this subject more than once, particularly when you celebrate the Lord's Supper.

30. As a final assignment in this section, think back over the steps we followed in our study of the covenant concept. This review may be helpful as you think about making other studies in Biblical theology in the future.

---

a. First, we used three different approaches to find and analyze key passages.
  1. Refer to passages that you have studied that present the concept.
  2. Look up relevant passages in a concordance under a key word.
  3. Study the concept in relation to the summary or structure of the book's message.
b. Second, we referred to the historical background of the concept and found other references to the concept in other books of the Bible.
  1. At the time it was expressed by the author.
  2. In a previous period, to which the author refers.
  3. In the future, which the author foretold.
c. Third, we considered briefly the significance of the concept for us today.
  1. In our understanding of the Bible as a whole.
  2. In our preaching.
  3. In our own lives.

C. Jeremiah's Concept of Religion

In this section you will study another important concept in the theology of the book of Jeremiah, the concept of religion. You will work out this study on your own. You may follow the steps which we used in our study of the covenant and which are listed at the end of the previous section. You should analyze primarily Jeremiah's concept of religion, but then go on and consider the concept of religion in other parts of the Bible, including the New Testament.

Here are some suggestions. Remember that we studied the popular concept of the Temple and the matter of sacrifices in Jer. 7:1-8:3. Remember, too, that Jeremiah attacked the religious leaders of his time in passages like Jer. 2:8; 3:30-31; 14:13-16; 23:9-40. And on more than one occasion he was in direct conflict with them, e.g. Jer. 20:1-6; 26:7-9; 28:5-17. As you study these or other passages, ask yourself, What was Jeremiah's concept of true religion? What did God want of His people? As you relate Jeremiah's concept of religion to the historical background, you may want to mention again Josiah's reforms. In any case you should refer to the moral corruption and apostasy of his day. And you will find that the word "heart" is prominent in Jeremiah's prophecies and in his concept of religion. Finally, you will want to compare Jeremiah's concept of religion with the New Testament concept of religion. And this will lead you toward some important applications of the Biblical concept of religion in our own lives and in our ministries today.

Write out all the steps you take in this theological investigation. Prepare both questions and answers, as you have done on other occasions, so that you will be able to use this material in a Bible study or a Sunday School class. Use notebook paper and keep this lesson in your notebook. You may be asked to turn in this assignment at your next class session.

D. Jeremiah's Concept of Social Justice

One of the vital concerns of our time is the problem of social justice. And the book of Jeremiah deals directly with the problem. Therefore we will use this opportunity to investigate Jeremiah's concept of social justice.

We have chosen this topic for several reasons. In the first place, Jeremiah speaks boldly and repeatedly about the evils of his day. And he himself became seriously involved in national and international politics. In the second place, many people today in all parts of the world have criticized the churches for their participation in the social concerns on the one hand or for their non-participation on the other hand. Finally, we have chosen this topic because it challenges us to see things in the Bible that we may not have seen before. Inductive Bible Study should do just that. In fact, if all our Bible studies merely confirm what we already believe, we may be in grave danger of imposing our ideas on the Bible rather than letting the Bible speak to us.

The purpose of the following questions is not to impose one point of view but to stimulate your thinking. We have insisted throughout this course that Inductive Study begins with the Bible and studies it, in so far as is possible, on its own terms. So you should not depend on others' interpretation of the Bible. Look at it anew and openly each time you turn to its pages.

1. One of the many passages in the book of Jeremiah that deal with social justice is Jer. 5:20-29, which we have already studied. Read Jer. 5:20-29 once again. If you have not already done so underline the phrases that describe particular evil practices. Jeremiah uses figurative language here, so explain what he means in your own words.

a. What evil does Jeremiah describe in v. 26? _____

_____

_____

b. What evil does Jeremiah describe in v. 27? _____

_____

_____

c. What evil does Jeremiah describe in v. 28? _____

_____

_____

a. Apparently he is speaking about fraudulent or legitimate business dealings that take advantage of the people.
b. Again he speaks of economic practices that permit some to become rich at the expense of the poor.
c. These men exploit the poor and the fatherless instead of defending them and looking out for their needs.

2. Why do these things happen? What is the root of these abuses? _____

_____

See v. 23. The people have an evil heart. They have rebelled against the Lord.

3. How does the Lord look upon these practices? What will He do to these

men? _____

---

*   *

The Lord considers these practices to be sins, worthy of punishment.

4. Another passage which we have studied and which condemns these social injustices is Jer. 7:1-15. Read through this passage and note the evils that
are mentioned. Here the social sins and religious sins (idolatry) are listed
together.

a. What social sins are mentioned in v. 5-7? _____

_____

b. What social sins are mentioned in v. 8-15? _____

---

*   *

a. Oppression of the alien, the fatherless and the widow, shedding innocent
blood.
b. Stealing, murder, adultery, swearing falsely.

5. Is there any indication that the religious sins are more serious than the
social sins or that the social sins are more serious than the religious sins?

---

*   *

No.

6. What does the Lord require of those who do these things? What is His com-

mandment in this passage? _____

_____

---

*   *

They must repent. He says to them, "Amend your ways and your doings." "Execute justice with one another."

7. What is the Lord's warning to those who do not change their ways? _____

_____

---

*   *

He will send destruction; He will destroy the Temple.

8. You will remember from our previous study of this passage that the people were still going to the Temple to worship God. Jeremiah calls the Temple "a den of robbers."

a. Why does Jeremiah refer to the Temple as a den of robbers? _____

_____

_____

b. Of what value is Temple worship for these people, according to Jeremiah?

* _____ *

a. The people were committing social and religious sins and still running to God for protection and blessing.
b. This kind of worship is useless pretense because of their disobedience.

9. Look up the words "justice" and "judgment" in your concordance and read through the lists for the book of Jeremiah. These references provide more material for your study of Jeremiah's concept of social justice.

a. What did the Lord demand of the kings of Judah, according to Jer. 22:1-7? ˌ

_____

_____

_____

b. What did He promise them if they obeyed His Word? _____

_____

c. What did He promise them if they disobeyed His word? _____

* _____ *

a. "Do justice and righteousness, and deliver from the hand of the oppressor him who has been robbed. And do no wrong or violence to the alien, the fatherless, and the widow, nor shed innocent blood in this place."
b. They shall continue to rule.
c. They shall be destroyed.

10. In Jer. 22:13-17 we find further warnings about social justice. Underline in the text the specific evil practices. Then list them here. _____

_____

* —— *

Forced, unpaid labor, material pretense, dishonest gain, shedding innocent blood, oppression and violence.

11. Note that in both Jer. 22:1-7 and Jer. 22:13-17 Jeremiah the Prophet speaks out against the sins of the rulers of Judah. He not only points out their evil practices. He challenges their right to rule.

Explain how Jeremiah challenges the political structure of his day. _____

——

* —— *

He warns them that if they do not obey the Lord and practice justice they will be destroyed.

12. Jer. 21:11-23:8 is, you will remember, a collection of prophecies concerning the kings of Judah. Read through this whole section and underline all references to justice. Later we will consider the meaning of this concept for us today. It is important to note that Jeremiah not only exhorted individuals to practice social justice but also challenged the power structures of his day.

13. We have briefly consulted several passages in the book of Jeremiah that deal with the problem of social justice. We reviewed passages which we had studied previously, and we used a concordance.

Now consider the importance of this concept in Jeremiah's message as a whole. List the five main ideas of Jeremiah's message.

a. _____

b. _____

c. _____

d. _____

e. _____

* —— *

See A. 12, above.

14. Now explain how the concept of social justice is directly related to each one of these five main ideas of Jeremiah's message.

a. The covenant relationship: _____

_____

_____

b. Judah's apostasy: _____

_____

_____

c. God's judgment: _____

_____

_____

d. The call to repentance: _____

_____

_____

e. The future restoration: _____

_____

* _____ *

a. In the covenant relationship Judah was expected to do God's will and
practice social justice. See Jer. 34:13-15.
b. Judah's apostasy was manifested not only in idolatry but also in unjust
practices among the rulers and the people. See Jer. 7:1-15.
c. God threatened to judge and destroy Judah because of these evil practices. See Jer. 22:5-7.
d. Judah was called to repent of these evil deeds, to amend these social
evils. See Jer. 7:3, 5.
e. The future restoration implied the establishment of justice and righteousness. See Jer. 23:5-6.

15. When we look at Jeremiah's concept of social justice in terms of the
main ideas of his message, it takes on tremendous significance. These prophecies about evil social practices are not idle exhortations. They are not
warnings to be taken lightly. They are not minor exhortations. Social justice is a major factor in the covenant relationship between God and His
people. In fact, as we saw clearly in Jer. 7:1-15, religion without social
justice is utterly unacceptable to the Lord.

16. We will now consider Jeremiah's concept of social justice in its historical context - past, present, and future.

First, explain how we know that unjust practices were widespread at the time

of Jeremiah's ministry. _____

_____

* _____ *

The fact that Jeremiah attacked these practices so frequently is a strong
indication that they were widespread at that time. If this were not a major
national problem, he would not have bothered to fight against it.

17. Now we must ask whether the people and rulers of Jeremiah's day recognized that their covenant relationship with God required them to practice
justice. Jer. 34:8-22 gives us an example of a social evil.

a. What evil practice is dealt with here? _____

b. What was the basis for this demand for justice? _____

_____

c. Why did Zedekiah decide to reform this evil? _____

_____

* _____ *

a. Slavery (among the Hebrews themselves)
b. The Mosaic covenant (See Jer. 34:13-14)
c. Apparently Jerusalem was under siege and Zedekiah thought that he might
gain God's favor (and deliverance from the enemy) by eradicating this evil
practice in fulfillment of the covenant.

18. This particular passage refers back to the Mosaic covenant. And as we
consider Jeremiah's concept of social justice in general we must turn back
to previous teachings of social justice in the history of Israel.

Turn to the Ten Commandments in Ex. 20. These commandments are a summary of
the Mosaic covenant.

a. Which of these commandments are directly related to social justice? _____

_____

b. Which of these social commandments were being broken in Jeremiah's day?

a. Commandments 5 through 10, that is, more than half.
b. Murder, adultery, robbery, lying, covetousness.

19. See if you can find at least one reference to each of these evils in Jeremiah's prophecies.

a. Murder _____

b. Adultery _____

c. Robbery _____

d. Lying _____

e. Covetousness _____

20. See if you can find in the books of the Mosaic law references to the following evils mentioned by Jeremiah.

a. Oppression of the alien _____

b. Mistreatment of orphans and widows _____

c. Unjust gain _____

21. It is evident that social justice was an important concept in Jeremiah's day and that this concept goes back to the Mosaic covenant.

Jeremiah also projected the concept of social justice into the future. Turn now to Jer. 23:5-6.

a. What will be the characteristic of the new age? _____

_____

b. How will this come to pass? _____

a. Justice and righteousness.
b. Through the Branch of David (the Messiah).

22. Turn also to the promise of a new covenant in Jer. 31:31-34.

a. What will be the characteristics of the people under the new covenant?

_____

_____

b. Which of these characteristics include the idea of social justice? _____

* _____ *

a. God's law will be written on their hearts; they will know the Lord; their
sins will be forgiven.
b. All three. As we analyzed the five points of Jeremiah's message we noted
that social justice is an essential part of the covenant relationship.

23. Now consider briefly the New Testament concept of social justice.

a. Find a passage that indicates that Jesus' purpose was to fulfill the com-

mandments of the old covenant. _____

b. Find a passage that indicates that Jesus considered both obedience to God

and concern for our fellow men to be essential. _____

c. Find a passage that indicates that worship without social justice is

worthless. _____
*   *

You need not have the same references. The following are outstanding examples of these concepts. Look them up if you have not already done so.
a. Matt. 5:17-48. (In the Sermon on the Mount)
b. Mark 12:28-34 (The Greatest Commandments)
c. Matt. 25:31-46 (The Parable of the Sheep and the Goats)

24. There are differences of opinion as to whether Jesus challenged the power structures of His day. Certainly He refused to become a Zealot and lead
an uprising against the Roman occupation forces (John 6:15). He understood
His own mission in terms of the Suffering Servant (Mark 10:45). He subjected
Himself to an unjust crucifixion at the hands of the Roman authorities.

Jesus did, nevertheless, challenge the religious authorities of His day. He
used His strongest language to condemn the scribes and pharisees. He threw
out the money changers in the Temple, bringing on the wrath of the priests
and scribes. The Herodians, too, sought to destroy Him. The leaders of the
Jews were the ones who brought Him to His terrible death on the cross.

An important passage that may lead you to further research on this issue is found at Mark 12:13-17. Consider the following questions for possible discussion in class.
a. What is our responsibility to Caesar?
b. What is our responsibility to God?
c. Which takes priority, our responsibility to Caesar or our responsibility to God?
d. May our loyalty to God lead us to oppose Caesar?
e. May our concern for social justice lead us to oppose the power structure?

25. Another key passage is Luke 4:16-30. It is set at the beginning of Jesus' ministry, and it has been considered the keynote address of His ministry. Read over these verses and note especially the quotation from Isaiah. And think over, but do not write down, your answers to these questions.

a. What does it mean "to proclaim release to the captives"?
b. What does it mean "to set at liberty those who are oppressed"?

26. You have made an initial study of Jeremiah's concept of social justice. You have briefly related his concept with the Mosaic covenant and with Jesus' teachings and mission. You are probably not yet ready to enter into the contemporary debate over social justice. But you should begin to face these issues, and this in turn will cause you to study the Biblical concept of social justice more seriously and more carefully in the future.

Ask yourself these questions. You are not asked to write out your answers.

a. Were there social injustices in Jeremiah's day?
b. Did Jeremiah oppose these social injustices?
c. Did Jeremiah challenge the kings of Judah and warn them of God's judgment for their social injustices?
d. Were these kings and the people of Judah in fact destroyed because of their social injustices and because of their religious apostasy?
e. Are there social injustices in our own day?
f. Are we fighting against these social injustices?
g. Should we challenge the government authorities and warn them of God's judgment for their social injustices?
h. Will our societies and our governments be destroyed because of their social injustices and because of their rebellion against God?

E. Biblical Theology

At the beginning of this lesson we stated that one of your objectives is to learn some basic steps in the formation of Biblical theology. You have now studied three important theological concepts in the book of Jeremiah. In this final section we will review the steps we have been using. These steps will serve as guidelines for the formation of Biblical theology.

1. First, a definition:

> Biblical theology is the inductive analysis of the mes-
> sage of the Bible.

2. There are different ways of defining Biblical theology, but we will insist here that Biblical theology must be <u>inductive</u>.

This means that Biblical theology begins _____ and

analyzes the Bible on _____.

with the Bible   its own terms

3. The Biblical theologican recognizes that the Bible is not one book by one
author but many books by many different authors. Therefore he must begin by

analyzing the theology of _____.

each book or each author

4. The systematic theologian works differently. He usually forms the major
ideas of the whole Bible into one system of thought, his own theological
system.

a. Is this an inductive approach to the theology of the Bible? _____

b. Explain your answer. _____

_____

_____

a. No.
b. This approach does not study the theology of the Bible on its own terms,
by books, as several systems of thought by different authors.

5. The Biblical theologian studies the theology of each author of the Bible
in context. How does he do this? Remember the basic steps we have been using
throughout our Inductive Study of the book of Jeremiah.

a. _____

b. _____

c. _____

a. He finds out what kind of literature it is.

b. He looks for the historical background.
c. He looks for the structure of the book or the message of the book.

6. Once the Biblical theologian has analyzed the theology of one book, he can relate that author's theology to the theology of other books of the Bible. But he does not do this the same way as the systematic theologian.

How can the Biblical theologian relate the theology of one Biblical author

with other parts of the Bible using the inductive approach? _____

_____

_____

* _____ *

See how the author himself refers to other parts of the Bible, and see how other books refer to this author's ideas. This is what we did in our study of the theology of the book of Jeremiah. This is an inductive approach because it relates different books of the Bible on their own terms.

7. After studying Jeremiah's concept of the covenant we turned to the con-

cept of the covenant in _____ .
*   *

Exodus and in the gospels.

8. After studying Jeremiah's concept of social justice we turned to _____

* _____ *

The concept of social justice in the Mosaic laws and in the teachings of Jesus.

9. When the Biblical theologian wants to study the theology of one book he has to know three things about that book. What are they?

a. _____

b. _____

c. _____
*   *

a. The kind of literature it is.
b. The historical background of the book.
c. The structure of the book.

10. Why does the Biblical theologian study the kind of literature, the historical background, and the structure of the book as well as the theology of

the book? _____

_____

* _____ *

Because he wants to study the theology of the book on its own terms. He
wants to study the theology of the book in its proper context.

11. If the Biblical theologian wants to study one theological concept in a
book, he studies these same three basic steps. He must know something about:

a. _____

b. _____

c. _____
* *

See #9 above.

12. Even if the Biblical theologian wants to study just one theological concept in a book, he needs to consider the message of the book as a whole. He

needs to know all the main ideas of the book. Why? _____

_____

_____

* _____ *

Each concept should be studied in relation to the other ideas of the book
and in relation to the message of the book as a whole. This is how to study
that concept in its context, on its own terms, inductively.

13. Each idea or theological concept in a book is part of the book's _____

* _____. *

message or its system of thought.

14. Although each book of the Bible is independent, the Biblical theologian
studies one book's theology in relation to other parts of the Bible. Why?

Because the different books of the Bible refer to each other. They are inter-related.

15. In this lesson you have studied three important theological concepts in the book of Jeremiah. List them.

a. _____

b. _____

c. _____

16. Your analysis of these concepts was largely based on the previous lessons. In other words you already knew a lot about the book of Jeremiah, before you analyzed its theology.

In your analysis of the covenant concept, the concept of religion, and the concept of social justice in the book of Jeremiah, how did you find appropriate passages? List three ways to find and analyze key passages.

a. _____

b. _____

c. _____

See B.30 above.

17. After analyzing several key passages on each theological concept in the book of Jeremiah you referred to the broad historical background of that concept. You referred to three different periods of history. List them.

a. _____

b. _____

c. _____

See B. 30 above.

18. First, you found and analyzed key passages on the theological concept in the book of Jeremiah. Second, you studied the broad historical background of that concept. (at that time, in the past, and in the future) by referring to different parts of the Bible.

Finally, you considered the significance of the concept for us today. List three ways in which Biblical theology can be useful for us.

a. _____

b. _____

c. _____
*   *

See B. 30 above. You may have additional ones.

19. Now summarize the process we have just reviewed for the study of Biblical theology. List the three main steps we used in our analysis of theological concepts in the book of Jeremiah.

a. _____

b. _____

_____

c. _____
*   *

a. Find and analyze key passages in the book.
b. Refer to the historical background of the concept (at that time, in the past, and in the future) by referring to other parts of the Bible.
c. Consider the significance of the concept for us today.

20. These are very simple guidelines for the formation of Biblical theology. You have analyzed some important theological concepts in the book of Jeremiah. And you have learned some basic steps which can be applied to other theological studies in the book of Jeremiah and in other books. In other courses you will learn more about how to study Biblical theology.

Write down once again our definition of Biblical theology. _____

_____

_____

*   *

See #1 above.

15

Inductive Bible Study

In the Introduction to this course you were invited to take an excursion into the land of Inductive Bible Study. Your final destination was defined first: to learn how to study and use the Bible in your own life and ministry. In order to get to that destination you looked at a road map, which listed a number of intermediate stops or objectives. The road which has taken you through these intermediate steps toward your destination has been the Inductive Study of the book of Jeremiah. You could have taken other roads, by studying the book of Isaiah, for example, and this would have led you to the same goal, although the scenery would have been somewhat different. Now that you have arrived at your destination, you should be able to take many other roads, such as the study of Ezekiel, Amos, and Micah. And you should move along these roads much faster than you have traveled in the past. At the beginning you were just learning how to drive, and you had to be guided carefully. Now you are an experienced driver and can go ahead entirely on your own.

This final lesson is a check-up. It has been prepared to help you go over many of the terms and concepts and methods you have been using. It should help you clarify in your own mind and define what is Inductive Bible Study. It should help you see whether you have in fact reached your final destination and can study the books of the Bible inductively on your own.

Your objectives in this lesson are to:

Clarify your understanding of Inductive Bible Study.

Review some methods for studying a passage.

Review some methods for studying a book like Jeremiah.

List some practical ways for applying Inductive Bible Study.

Test your ability.

A. Definition and Understanding

One thing you should be able to do is to write a definition of Inductive Bible Study. Another thing is to understand and to be able to explain what is Inductive Bible Study. And you should not confuse these two things. Be sure you can do both.

1. First, write out the definition of Inductive Bible Study which we have

been using. _____

_____

* _____ *

Inductive Bible Study is an approach to Bible study that begins with the Bible and studies it on its own terms.

2. It is important to remember this definition of Inductive Bible Study. But it is far more important to understand what it means and to be able to explain it.

a. What is the value of being able to define Inductive Bible Study? _____

_____

_____

b. What is the value of understanding what is Inductive Bible Study? _____

_____

_____

c. What is the value of being able to explain what it is? _____

_____

_____

a. The definition itself is of little value. It is just a label, which is useless unless you know what it means.
b. If you understand what Inductive Bible Study is, you can study the books of the Bible and find out what they have to say. This is tremendously important for your life and ministry.
c. If you can explain what is Inductive Bible Study, you can teach someone else how to study the Bible. This is tremendously important for his life and ministry.

3. Note that Inductive Bible Study is an approach to Bible Study. We did not say that it is a method. See if you know what is the difference between an approach and a method. Identify each of the following phrases as an approach or a method.

a. A way of looking at the Bible and finding out what it contains: _____

b. A technique for finding certain things in the Bible: _____

a. An approach
b. A method

4. An approach is a way of looking at the Bible and finding out what it contains. Methods are techniques for finding certain things in the Bible.

a. Does the inductive approach use methods? _____

b. How does the inductive approach decide what methods to use? _____

_____

* _____ *

a. Yes.
b. The inductive approach looks at the text first, then chooses or invents
methods which will explain what is in the text on its own terms.

5. There is always a danger that the methods we use in our study of the Bible
will not interpret the text on its own terms. We may find in the Bible what
we want to find there rather than what the text really means. Mention a spe-

cific case of this problem. _____

_____

_____

* _____ *

We noted in Lesson XIV the case of the preacher who used Jer. 3:1-5 as a
text for a sermon on sexual immorality, which is not the real meaning of
that text. This kind of misinterpretation happens all the time.

6. The methods we use in our study of the Bible should always be based on an
inductive approach. If we struggle always to study the text on its own terms,
then various methods and techniques can be extremely useful.

How can we study the text on its own terms? What is an inductive approach?
List the three beginning steps we recommended at the beginning of this course.

a. _____

b. _____

c. _____
*   *

a. Find out what kind of literature it is.
b. Look for the historical background of the book.
c. Analyze the structure of the book.

7. These three beginning steps are not just beginning steps. They are basic
steps for Inductive Bible Study, from beginning to end. We used these same
steps in our study of the theology of the book of Jeremiah. What is the

purpose of these three steps? _____

*   *

To help us study the text on its own terms.

8. How can we study the Bible on its own terms? By studying each passage and each concept <u>in context</u>. Explain what this means. _____

_____

_____

*   *

Your answer should refer to the three basic steps listed at #6 above.

9. How can we study the Bible on its own terms? By finding out <u>what the author intended</u>. Explain what this means. _____

_____

_____

*   *

Again, your answer should refer to the three basic steps listed at #6 above.

10. Here are three different ways of saying the same thing. These are three similar definitions of Inductive Bible Study.

> a. Study the Bible on its own terms.
> b. Study the text in context.
> c. Find out what the author meant to say.

All three of these definitions require us to take the same three basic steps.

> a. Find out what kind of literature it is.
> b. Look for the historical background.
> c. Analyze the structure.

11. The third definition of Inductive Bible Study listed above is: Find out what the author meant to say or intended. We have not used this definition before now because it requires further explanation. Inductive Study seeks to find out what the author meant to say. But in some cases we must recognize more than one stage in the formation of a book. In those cases Inductive Study seeks to find out the intention of the author and also the intention of the person or persons who edited the book.

In our study of the book of Jeremiah we dealt with this factor.

a. Who is the author of the prophecies contained in the book of Jeremiah?

_____

b. Who probably composed the editorial comments of Jer. 1-20? _____

_____

c. Who probably composed the editorial comments of Jer. 21-52? _____

d. Did Jeremiah himself write or dictate Chapter 52? _____

*   *

a. God. He gave them through Jeremiah.
b. Jeremiah, dictating to Baruch. (The first person singular is used most
frequently.)
c. Baruch. (The third person singular is used most frequently.)
d. No. (See Jer. 51:64)

12. In Lesson XIV we noted that the structure of the book of Jeremiah as we
have received it is very weak. And we suggested that this lack of structure
tells us something important about the formation of the book.

a. It indicates that Jeremiah himself did not put the book together. How

does the lack of structure show this? _____

_____

_____

b. The lack of structure also indicates that the person or people who finally gathered these collections of prophecies and narratives together did not

impose their own ideas on the book. How does it show us this? _____

_____

*   *

a. Jeremiah was aware of the sequence and relationship between the prophecies. He would probably have put them together more systematically in
either topical or chronological order.
b. If the final editors had wanted to express their own ideas, they would
have organized the materials in some definite order so as to express those
ideas.

13. In your Inductive Study of the Gospels you will have to take into account at least two levels of meaning or intention. The Gospels contain the

words and deeds of Jesus. These materials were gathered and arranged differently by each author. And the authors added editorial comment. Therefore we
have to study:

a. The intention of _____.

b. The intention of _____.
*   *

a.b. Jesus and the authors of the Gospels. Some scholars add a third factor
or level: the influence of the oral tradition between the time of Jesus and
the time of the writing of the Gospels.

14. This explanation has taken us away from our definition of Inductive Bible Study. List again the three ways of explaining how we study the Bible
or a passage inductively.

a. _____

b. _____

c. _____
*   *

a. Study it on its own terms.
b. Study the text in context.
c. Find out what the author intended.

15. Now let's compare Inductive Bible Study with other kinds of research and
technology. Sometimes illustrations from other fields are useful in helping
us to understand and explain what we are talking about.

This first example points out the importance of technical training. Look at
the radio. It is a common instrument of life today. We take it for granted.
It is the simplest thing in the world to turn on a radio and listen to it.
And it is fairly easy to learn how to tune in on different radio stations.

But what happens if something goes wrong with your radio? If you open it up
and look at the insides, you are helpless; you could never fix it. If you
start poking around with tools, you might do some damage. And if you take
it apart, you will never get it back together again.

If you take your radio to a radio technician, on the other hand, he can open
it up, look at the diagram, locate the problem, fix it, and put the radio
back together again with no trouble at all. He knows how the radio works,
how the wires, transistors or tubes and other parts fit together. He knows
what tools to use. He is trained to do his job.

See how many parallels you can find between Inductive Bible Study and radio
repair work.

a. The Bible is easy to read and understand, like turning on a radio.

_____

b. It is easy to learn how to find the different books of the Bible, like

tuning in to different radio·stations.

c. _____

_____

d. _____

_____

e. _____

_____

f. _____

_____

There are many possible points of comparison or parallels. Just remember how
you used to read through the book of Jeremiah. Wasn't it rather like the insides of a radio, impossible to decipher? But now you can understand the
meaning of almost every paragraph. You can see how the different passages
are related to the hidden structures of the book. Your political map, chronological chart, and outline are like the radio technician's diagram. You have
many other methods or tools which you can use now as you continue to study
the book of Jeremiah and other books of the Bible. You are becoming a technician skilled in Inductive Bible Study.

16. Here is another illustration. It shows the importance of using your reasoning ability and of looking out for the unexpected. Read through the following story and figure out the answer to the riddle. And ask yourself how
this example is like Inductive Bible Study.

The story is told of a man and his son, who were riding on a motorcycle at
high speed. They crashed. The man was killed instantly, and his son's head
was badly injured. They rushed him to a hospital and called the best brain
surgeon in the city to operate on the boy's head. The famous surgeon went
immediately to the hospital. On seeing the patient the surgeon refused to
operate for personal reasons. The injured boy was the surgeon's own son.

a. Who was the surgeon? _____

b. Why was this a surprise answer? _____

_____

_____

c. Does this happen in Inductive Bible Study? _____

d. See if you can give an example. _____

_____

_____

*   *

a. The surgeon was the boy's mother.
b. Everyone thinks the surgeon is a man, but the boy's father is dead. Since they expect one answer they fail to look for the other logical answer.
c. Yes.
d. Jer. 1:1-3 says that Jeremiah prophesied during the reigns of three kings of Judah. But we discovered that he prophesied during the reigns of five kings of Judah. This is a surprising thing, but there is a very simple explanation. Do you remember what it is?

17. As you have worked through the book of Jeremiah, you may have felt that much of your time was spent going through certain routines. The next illustration emphasizes the necessity of patient, methodical observation in Inductive Bible Study.

This is the way a scientist has to work most of the time. Think of the biologist looking for a cure for a disease. He tries different kinds of chemicals, perhaps 50,000 different combinations, one by one, day after day, year after year, and even then he may fail. Or think of the geologist searching for mineral deposits. He studies thousands of rock samples, miles of topography, hundreds of drillings. But only rarely does he find anything valuable.

Inductive Bible Study, too, requires patient observation. Mention some routine methods we used repeatedly in our study of the book of Jeremiah.

a. _____

b. _____

c. _____

*   *

One important routine is the analysis of the main idea in each paragraph. Another is to write a title for each paragraph. Another is to look for special details in the text. Another is to try to group paragraphs into sections and sections into divisions. Another is to interpret each literary figure. Another is to explain each name and place mentioned in the text. Another is to consider the meaning of each phrase.

18. These methods of routine observation may be tedious and slow to begin with. But later they become fairly automatic. The following example illustrates the importance of practice.

Inductive Bible Study is like learning to ride a bicycle. At first you have to be very careful to keep your balance, push on the pedals, and watch out where you are headed. Someone may have to go along beside you and hold onto you and keep telling you what to do. But after a few days' practice you can move right along by yourself without particularly worrying about balance, pumping, and obstacles.

a. What help did you receive as you began your study of the book of Jeremiah?

_____

b. What help do you need now? _____

_____

c. Why the difference between how you began and how you can operate now? _____

* _____ *

a. At first you were led along slowly step by step.
b. Now you should be able to study the Bible inductively all by yourself.
c. You have had enough practice now to be on your own.

19. The following illustration comes from the arts. It shows the importance of imagination.

Consider the great paintings of the French Impressionists. If you look up close at one of these pictures you will see that it is not drawn very exactly. It is not like a photograph at all. It may even look crude or unrealistic. But when you stand back and gaze at the picture, you get a very definite feeling, a strong impression. You experience something that a photograph could never convey to you, something that is more real than a photograph. You can imagine that scene or object as if it were part of your own experience.

a. Mention something about the book of Jeremiah that is like a rough impressionist painting. _____

_____

b. Mention something about the book of Jeremiah that you have been able to experience by using your imagination. _____

---

a. You might have mentioned the rough, almost haphazard structure of the book of Jeremiah.

b. Perhaps you have been able to identify yourself with the Prophet Jeremiah at the moment of his call, or during his conflicts with the leaders of his people or in his inner anguish or in his fearless preaching.

20. Another illustration reveals <u>the sense of commitment to the object</u> in Inductive Bible Study. Here we turn to the philosophy of science.

A well known theologian has pointed out that the essential approach to any science must be determined by the nature of the object. If you wish to study plants you must observe what they are like and analyze them in their own environment. If you wish to study the stars you must develop the kinds of instruments and the techniques which will allow you to observe them and explain their movements. If you wish to study psychology, you must deal with people and allow them to show you how they think and feel. If you wish to know about God, you must depend upon Him to reveal Himself to you, you must go to Him on His terms, you must be reconciled to Him. In all of these fields the investigator is committed to the object of study.

Explain Inductive Bible Study in these terms. In what ways is our approach

to the Bible determined by the Bible itself? _____

_____

_____

_____

_____

_____

_____

_____

_____

_____

_____

You may have mentioned the three basic steps we have used throughout our Inductive Study of the book of Jeremiah. In order to study the Bible on its
own terms we have to consider what kind of literature we are looking at,
what is its historical background, and what is the structure of the material.
And much more could be said. At a lower level we need to consider the language and grammar of the text to be reasonably certain that we understand
it as it was originally intended. At the upper level, we need to go into
Biblical theology to be reasonably certain that we understand each concept
in relation to the message of each author and to the Bible as a whole. And
since the Bible deals with God's special relationship with His people down
through history, we can only expect to understand its message if we identify
ourselves with His people in response to Him.

In all of these dimensions Inductive Bible Study is a science. We are scien-
tists to the degree in which our analysis of the Bible is determined by the
nature of the Bible itself.

21. Finally, Inductive Bible Study motivates the Bible student through the
joy of discovery.

For some time I have felt that Bible study should be as fascinating as reading a mystery novel. These novels catch the attention of the reader from
the very first page by telling him a crime has occurred or is about to happen. Then page after page the author presents the clues and challenges the
reader to unravel the mystery of that crime. The reader's interest rises
steadily as he picks up these clues and tries to fit them together. Only
at the very end does the author allow the reader to see the whole picture
and discover the true story.

See if you can see some similarities between Inductive Bible Study and reading a mystery novel.

a. Mention at least one way in which Inductive Bible Study is like reading

a mystery novel. _____

_____

_____

b. Show how other kinds of Bible study take away the joy of discovery. _____

_____

_____

* _____ *

a. Inductive Bible Study is like reading a mystery novel because you have
the joy of discovering for yourself the message of the book. You study
the details (clues) and gradually fit them together and finally see the
full significance of the book as a whole.
b. Other kinds of Bible study usually take away the joy of discovery. They
find all the clues and fit them together for you. They give you the outline
of the book, the historical background, and the message. You aren't moti-
vated to study the Bible yourself.

22. Following is a listing of the illustrations we have used to explain what
is Inductive Bible Study. You are not supposed to memorize this list. But
it may be useful to you when you want to explain or teach Inductive Bible
Study to someone else.

	Examples	Lessons
a.	The radio technician	The importance of technical training
b.	The brain surgeon	The importance of using reason and of look-ing for the unexpected
c.	Scientists	The necessity of patient, methodical obser-vation
d.	Learning to ride a bicycle	The importance of practice
e.	The French Impressionists	The importance of imagination
f.	The philosophy of science	The sense of commitment to the object
g.	The mystery novel	The joy of discovery

Write out once again the definition of Inductive Bible Study. Then read over
the list of examples above and see if they help explain what this definition

means. _____

_____

_____

_____

B. Some Useful Methods for Studying a Passage

We have said that Inductive Bible Study is not a method but an approach to
Bible study. But we have also said that this approach to Bible study uses
many methods. And we have used many different methods in our analysis of
the book of Jeremiah.

In this section you will review some of the methods we have used in this course. Remember that these methods are valid only in so far as they serve the basic purpose of Inductive Bible Study: to study the Bible on its own terms. Remember, too, that these methods are only suggestions; you should constantly look for new and better methods.

In this section you will review methods that are useful for studying specific texts. In the following section you will review methods that are useful for analyzing larger passages and books.

1. Rather than discuss these methods abstractly, we will look at a passage and see how certain methods help us understand what that passage has to say.

Turn to Jer. 10:1-16 and read it over two or three times. This is the first step in studying any passage: read the text carefully.

2. Usually we are careless when we read the Bible. We don't really observe what is in the text, even if we read it over two or three times. And if we read a very long passage, it is difficult to remember what it contains.

What is your impression of the main ideas of Jer. 10:1-16? Write down the two principal concepts that are repeated many times in this passage.

a. _____

b. _____ *

*

a. The idols are no gods; they are useless.
b. The Lord is the true God, the king of the nations, creator of the earth.

3. The first step in studying a passage is, we have said, to read the text carefully.

A second possible step is to _____

_____ *

*

Identify the main ideas of the passage.

4. Once you have a general impression of what a passage contains, you can go through the text again and point out each reference to the central idea or ideas.

Go through Jer. 10:1-16 once again. Underline all the phrases that describe the false gods with one color. And underline the phrases that describe the true God with another color.

5. A possible third step in studying a passage is _____

_____. *

*

To underline the phrases that describe the main ideas.

6. In our study of the book of Jeremiah we have noted that the most important unit of the text is the paragraph. We have spent much of our time analyzing the text paragraph by paragraph.

How many paragraphs does Jer. 10:1-16 (RSV) contain? _____

four

7. What is a paragraph? _____

_____

A paragraph is one or more sentences grouped together around one basic idea.

8. A paragraph is only one level of structure. In Jeremiah we have studied six different levels of structure. List them here.

a. _____   d. _____

b. _____   e. _____

c. _____   f. _____

a. Words   d. Paragraphs
b. Phrases   e. Sections
c. Sentences   f. Divisions

9. In our analysis of each paragraph we look for three things. What are they?

a. _____

b. _____

c. _____

a. The main idea
b. A title
c. Special details

10. There are many possible ways of writing paragraph titles. Explain the

system we have used. _____

_____

Choose four words or less from the text itself.

11. We suggested that these titles should have certain characteristics in order to help us remember what each paragraph contains. List these characteristics.

a. _____

b. _____

c. _____
*   *

a. They should <u>represent</u> the content of the paragraph.
b. They should <u>distinguish</u> this paragraph from other paragraphs.
c. They should convey the most <u>important</u> idea or information of the paragraph.
If you wish to review the explanation of paragraph titles, turn to Lesson IV, D.

12. Analyze the paragraphs of Jer. 10:1-16. Figure out the main idea of each paragraph and write a title for each paragraph. Put this information in your outline of the book of Jeremiah.

13. We have now mentioned four steps or methods for the study of a passage. List them here.

a. _____

b. _____

c. _____

d. _____
*   *

a. Read the text carefully.
b. Identify the main ideas of the passage.
c. Underline in the text the phrases that describe the main ideas.
d. Analyze the paragraphs; put down the main ideas, titles, and special details.

14. We have not consistently noted in our outline of the book of Jeremiah special details that appear in some paragraphs. Mention some kinds of details

that we have noted. _____

_____

_____

* _____ *

We put down key phrases like "From the North" in Jer. 4:5-6:30.
We put down the historical references in Jer. 30-45.
You may have noted important literary figures.
You may have noted Jeremiah's confessions.

15. Remember that the outline we have used in our study of the book of Jeremiah is only one of many possible ways of making an outline. When you study
another book you may want to make a different kind of outline.

If you study the book of Mark, for example, you will notice that many paragraphs have geographical information and almost all the paragraphs deal with
the public, the disciples, or the enemies of Jesus. Both the geographical
information and the information about the people are important factors in
the analysis of each paragraph. And they are important in the analysis of
the structure of the book. How could you include this information in your

outline of the book of Mark? _____

_____

* _____ *

One way would be to add one column for geographical information and another
column for information about the people.

16. Another necessary process in Inductive Study of a passage like Jer. 10:
1-16 is to explain all the important words and phrases in the text, paragraph by paragraph. We will not consider many details in Jer. 10:1-16 because our purpose here is primarily to review the methods we have been using
in our study of the book of Jeremiah.

One item that should be explained is the literary figure in v. 5. Draw a
diagram and analyze the meaning of this literary figure.

*   *

Scarecrows in a cucumber field	Idols
Cannot speak, walk, do good or evil	Cannot speak, walk, do good or evil

17. In order to review this way of analyzing literary figures, fill in the following diagram with the four questions you ask yourself as you interpret each figure.

*   *

| 1. What object is used as a literary figure? | 2. What does this object represent? |
| 3. What particular characteristic of the object is emphasized? | 4. What message does this characteristic express? |

18. Often names of places and people which are not very familiar appear in the text. Note the names Tarshish and Uphaz in v. 9. What do you recommend

that a Bible student do in these cases? _____

*   *

Normally he should look up these names in a concordance, a Bible dictionary, or an atlas.

19. The information that you find as you investigate these names is sometimes important. But at times it is unimportant with regard to the message of the passage.

a. Look up Tarshish and Uphaz. Where were they located? _____

_____

b. Does this information contribute greatly to your understanding of this

passage? _____

*   *

a. Tarshish is in Spain; Uphaz is unknown.
b. No

20. There is an interesting footnote at v. 11 in some versions. The footnote indicates that this verse is in Aramaic. Look up the term "Aramaic" in your Bible dictionary.

a. What books in the Old Testament contain some Aramaic language? _____

_____

b. Where is Aram? _____

*   *

a. Genesis, Ezra, Jeremiah, Daniel
b. Generally where Syria is today.

21. In v. 16 we find the phrase "the Lord of hosts." Explain what this means.

_____

_____

* _____   *

Look in your Bible dictionary under "hosts."

22. "The Lord of hosts" is a phrase which we read often in the Bible and which
is common to us. But perhaps many people in our churches do not really know
what it means.

a. Did you know what it meant before you looked it up in the dictionary? _____

b. Do most of the members of your congregation know what it means? _____

23. We have only explained a few of the details in Jer. 10:1-16. But our
purpose has been to review some of the methods you can use as you go through
a passage like this. It is very important to analyze well known and unknown
words, names, phrases and literary figures as you study the text paragraph
by paragraph.

After going through the paragraphs in this way you may want to look at the
passage as a whole again. There may be a key word or phrase or idea that is
repeated. Or you may want to define more carefully the way in which these
paragraphs are grouped together.

One interesting aspect of Jer. 10:1-16 is its presentation of different
names for God. Make a list of these names with the corresponding references.

a. _____

b. _____

c. _____

d. _____

e. _____

f. _____

24. Also, it is interesting to note the contrast that this passage makes between the true God and the false gods. In order to gain a fuller appreciation of this contrast make a list of the phrases that describe the true God
and another list of the phrases that describe the false gods.

The false gods	The true God

25. Now write a summary of the message of Jer. 10:1-16. _____

_____

_____

_____

_____

_____

* _____ *

You should have emphasized these two main ideas.
a. The false gods are worthless images made by men. They shall perish.
b. The Lord is the living and true God, creator and ruler of the earth, Israel's Lord. He is everlasting.

26. What is the purpose of these words of prophecy? Why does the prophet make

this striking contrast between the false gods and the true God? _____

_____

_____

* _____ *

Obviously, his purpose is to get the people to reject the false gods and
turn to the true God. He is calling them to repentance and obedience.

27. The linguistic experts say that this passage has a complex history and
probably comes from a later period. We have noted that v. 11 is in Aramaic.
Nevertheless Jer. 10:1-16 contains a clear, powerful, and timeless message.
Men of every age need to be called back from their idols to the living and
true God.

a. What were the false gods of Judah at the time of Jeremiah? _____

_____

b. What were the false gods of the Pharisees at the time of Jesus? _____

_____

c. What were the false gods of the Roman Catholic Church at the time of Mar-

tin Luther? _____

_____

d. What are the false gods of the Protestant churches today? _____

_____

* _____ *

a. Judah had borrowed pagan deities and images from her neighbors.
b. The pharisees made false gods out of their laws and customs and piety.
c. The Catholic Church made images and relics of the saints and promised
salvation by works and indulgences.
d. Anything that takes the place of God in our lives is a false god, an idol.
It may be worldly ambition, material possessions, or even religious pretense.

28. Jer. 10:1-16 would make an excellent text for a sermon. Following the procedure we have used in this course, make a brief outline of the main points for a sermon.

A. _____

    1. _____

    2. _____

B. _____

    1. _____

    2. _____

Points A and B should refer to the false gods and the true God (in either order). Points 1 and 2 under each main point should refer to Jeremiah's time and our own situation today. See Lesson VIII if you need to review the steps in sermon outline preparation.

29. Jer. 10:1-16 is so effective because it shows how foolish it is to worship idols. Your congregation will be able to see that clearly.

In your sermon you will have to explain how we worship other, more sophisticated things today. And you will have to point out that this is just as foolish as worshipping wooden idols.

a. Mention one particular modern idol. _____

b. Explain how men worship that idol. _____

_____

_____

c. Point out why it is foolish to worship that idol. _____

_____

_____

30. We have reviewed rapidly some useful methods for the study of a short passage, using Jer. 10:1-16 as an example. Read over the list of methods we have mentioned in this review. You are not asked to memorize this list. But if you are given a passage to study, you should be able to find and use the methods that would help you discover the meaning of that passage.

a. Read the text carefully.
b. Identify the main ideas of the passage.
c. Underline in the text the phrases that describe the main ideas.

d. Analyze the paragraphs; put down the main ideas, titles, and special
details.
e. Explain all important words and phrases, paragraph by passage.
f. Look at the passage as a whole and pull out key words or phrases that
show how the paragraphs are grouped together.
g. Write a summary of the message of the paragraph.
h. State the purpose of the passage.
i. See if the passage and its message can be applied to our situation.
j. If the passage is appropriate, make a sermon outline.

C. Some Useful Methods for Studying a Book

In this section you will review some of the methods we have used in our study
of the book of Jeremiah as a whole. If you do not remember clearly how to
apply these methods, you may turn back to the earlier lessons where they are
discussed more fully.

1. At the beginning of our study of the book of Jeremiah we asked the question: How should we begin? In answer to that question we recommended three
beginning steps for Inductive Bible Study. List them here.

a. _____

b. _____

c. _____
*   *

a. Find out what kind of literature it is.
b. Find out something about the historical background.
c. Look for the structure of the book.

2. We said that these three steps are essential to Inductive Bible Study.

Explain why. _____

_____

_____

_____

_____
*   *

They help you study the book on its own terms. In other words you have to
know what kind of literature it is so that you can interpret it correctly.
You need to know what period of history it comes from and what situation it
refers to. You need to see how the book is organized in order to understand
its message.

3. These three factors (the kind of literature, the historical background, and the structure) should be studied inductively.

How? _____

* _____ *

By beginning with the text and studying it on its own terms.

4. Later in the course we found that these same three factors were impor-
tant throughout our study of the book of Jeremiah. In Inductive Bible Study every passage and every section of the book must be studied in its own con-

text. What does this mean? _____

_____

* _____ *

This context means the particular kind of literature, the historical background, and the structure of the book. That is, the same three factors.

5. Finally, we defined Biblical theology as the inductive analysis of the message of the Bible. And when we investigated the theology of the book of Jeremiah, we had to refer back to the same three basic factors (the kind of literature, the historical background, and the structure of the book). Why

are these three factors essential to the study of Biblical theology? _____

_____

_____

* _____ *

Because Biblical theology is inductive. We must study each theological con-
cept in the context of each book (its nature, historical background, and overall structure). Only then will we understand that concept on its own terms.

6. We already knew that the book of Jeremiah was a prophetical book. But we investigated the nature of prophetical literature by studying the book of Jeremiah itself.

List several indications (some are quite obvious) that the book of Jeremiah is a prophetical book.

a. _____

_____

b. _____

_____

c. _____

_____

d. _____

* _____ *

a. The introduction (Jer. 1:1-3) states that the book contains the word of the Lord through Jeremiah.
b. Jeremiah is called to be a prophet (Jer. 1:4-19), and he is called a prophet.
c. Throughout the book phrases like "the word of the Lord" are repeated frequently.
d. The book is a collection of prophecies and deeds of Jeremiah the Prophet.

7. On the basis of your analysis of the book of Jeremiah define the following terms.

a. Prophet: _____

_____

_____

b. Prophecy: _____

_____

* _____ *

a. A prophet is a man called to proclaim God's word and His will at a particular time in history.
b. Prophecies are proclamations of God's word and His will at a particular time in history.

8. On the basis of your study of the book of Jeremiah answer the following questions.

a. Does a prophet simply tell what is God's will or does he actually set

God's will in motion? _____

b. Does a prophet speak primarily about God's will for his own period of his-

tory or about the distant future? _____

c. What is the final proof of true prophecy over against false prophecy? _____

_____

d. Why do false prophets prophesy falsely? _____

_____

a. He actually sets God's will in motion.
b. He speaks primarily about his own period of history.
c. The final proof is the fulfillment of the prophecy.
d. In the book of Jeremiah we found that the false prophets prophesied what the people wanted to hear.

9. What were the two dimensions of Jeremiah's message and ministry, according to Jer. 1:4-10? Explain each one briefly.

a. _____

_____

_____

b. _____

_____

_____

See v. 10.
a. To destroy - Jeremiah pronounced God's judgment on Judah's apostasy and announced the coming destruction.
b. To plant - Jeremiah called his people to repentance. And when destruction came upon them, he proclaimed a future restoration.

10. Mention two important and effective methods Jeremiah used to communicate his message.

a. _____

b. _____

The most outstanding ones are:
a. His use of literary figures.
b. His acted parables.

11. Throughout the book of Jeremiah we read that Jeremiah faced many enemies
among his own people and among the rulers of his people. Why did they fight

against Jeremiah? _____

_____

* _____ *

They were rebelling against God, and they did not want to repent. And when
Jeremiah warned them of the coming destruction, they were angry.

12. List three specific events in which Jeremiah was threatened or abused
by his enemies.

a. _____

b. _____

* c. _____ *

Some of the most notable events were: The Temple Sermon episode (Jer. 26),
the Broken Flask episode (Jer. 19-20), the Two Scrolls episode (Jer. 36),
the Yoke Bars episode (Jer. 27-28), the Miry Cistern episode (Jer. 38).

13. We noted that the Prophet Jeremiah suffered not only outward conflicts,
with his enemies but also inner anguish. He reveals profound and awful feelings in some of his discourses.

a. What do we call these passages? _____

* b. List some references. _____ *

a. Jeremiah's Confessions.
b. Jer. 11:18-20; 12:1-6; 15:10-21; 17:14-18; 18:18-23; 20:7-18.

14. What feelings does Jeremiah express in these confessions....

a. toward his enemies? _____

b. toward himself? _____

* c. toward God? _____ *

a. Vengeance and anger.
b. Strife and despair of his very life.
c. Complaint and doubt, blasphemy.

15. In spite of all his struggles Jeremiah carried on his ministry for 40 years as "the Lord's prophet in a time of judgment." Explain how Jeremiah

was able to continue prophesying year after year. _____

_____

_____

*   _____   *

It seems to me that the secret lies in Jeremiah's call (Jer. 1:4-19). He had a profound concept of God's power and holiness. He believed that the Lord Himself had chosen him to be His prophet to the nations. And the Lord promised to be with him and deliver him.

16. We have just reviewed the first basic factor in Inductive Bible Study. You must find out what kind of literature you are studying. Jeremiah is a prophetical book, and we have referred to its prophetic nature many times throughout this course.

Following is a list of methods we used in our study of the book of Jeremiah. These methods arose out of our study of the text itself. They may be helpful in studying other prophetical books. But the important thing to do in Inductive Bible Study is to find out what kind of literature you are studying and develop methods that will help you understand the text.

a. We noted that the book of Jeremiah is known as a prophetical book.
b. We looked in the book itself to find indications that it is a prophetical book.
c. On the basis of our analysis of the text we defined the term "prophet" and "prophecy."
d. We answered a number of questions about the nature of prophecy on the basis of our analysis of the text.
e. We analyzed the two dimensions of Jeremiah's ministry mentioned first in Jer. 1:10.
f. We studied Jeremiah's use of literary figures and acted parables.
g. We asked why Jeremiah's people and their rulers opposed him.
h. We studied a number of events in which Jeremiah was threatened or abused.
i. We studied his inner anguish expressed in his confessions.
j. We noted that Jeremiah's call was a profound experience that sustained him during 40 difficult years of ministry as "the Lord's prophet at a time of judgment."

17. The second basic factor in Inductive Bible Study is the historical background. Why is it especially important to keep in mind the historical back-

ground when you are studying a prophetical book? _____

_____

* _____ *

Because prophecy is the proclamation of God's will <u>at a particular time in history</u>. You must know something about the historical background of a prophetical book in order to study it on its own terms.

18. We found that the Bible itself contains a great deal of information about the historical background of the book of Jeremiah. List the most important passages. _____

* _____ *

Jer. 1:1-3, Jer. 52, 2 Kings 22-25, 2 Chron. 34-36.

19. We also found that it was necessary to organize this historical information. What methods did we use to arrange this historical information?

a. _____

b. _____
* _____ *

a. Political map of the time of Jeremiah.
b. Chronological chart of the time of Jeremiah.

20. Why was it necessary to organize the historical information in these ways? _____

* _____ *

It is impossible to see the significance of the information unless it is arranged geographically and chronologically.

21. Our starting point was Jer. 1:1-3. Read over this passage and explain

how we figured out the dates for Jeremiah's ministry. _____

_____

_____

_____

See Lesson III, A if you need to review the calculations for the dates of the kings of Judah and Jeremiah's ministry.

22. Then we turned to 2 Kings 22-25 and 2 Chron. 34-36 to complete our information about the kings of Judah. There, too, we found information about the power struggle which was going on between the three great world empires at that time. This information has been important for our understanding of the book of Jeremiah.

Name the three great empires. _____

Assyria, Egypt, Babylonia

23. We discovered that there were four major international events which profoundly affected the history of Judah during Jeremiah's ministry. You were asked to remember the dates and the significance of these events. See if you can write down the dates from memory.

a. The fall of Nineveh _____

b. The battle of Megiddo _____

c. The battle of Carchemish _____

d. The fall of Jerusalem _____

a. 612 B.C.   b. 609 B.C.   c. 605 B.C.   d. 587 B.C.

24. Now explain the significance of these events by sketching quickly a political map of the time of Jeremiah. Locate the three major world empires and the four places mentioned above with the dates of these events. Show the invasion routes between the major empires by means of arrows.

You will find the box for the map on the next page.

See Appendix A.1. You should be able to sketch this map from memory.

25. This map has been very useful throughout our study of the book of Jeremiah. It gives us a picture of the world power struggle that was going on
at that time. And it shows clearly Judah's position in relation to that
struggle. It reveals the significance of Jeremiah's ministry in general and
of his message in specific passages.

a. Jeremiah constantly warned the people of the peril from the north. At

the beginning of his ministry the great empire to the north was _____,

but during the latter half of his ministry the great empire to the north was

_____.

b. Toward the end of his ministry, Jeremiah advised his people and the   ·
rulers to submit to the rule of Babylon. How did the rulers view this

advice? _____   What kind of advice was it? _____.

a. Assyria   Babylonia
b. As treason.   Good advice.

26. In order to complete our picture of the historical background of the book of Jeremiah we made a chronological chart of the period. What is a chronological chart? _____

_____

_____

*   *

A chronological chart is a time diagram showing historical events and periods in the order in which they happened.

27. Draw a chronological chart showing the ministry of Jeremiah, the reigns of the five kings of Judah, and the four major international events of the period. This is practice for the final exam, so see if you can make the chart with the help of your Bible only.

*   *

See Appendix A 2.

28. This chronological chart has been very useful throughout our study of the book of Jeremiah. Explain how we have used it. _____

_____

_____

_____

_____

*   *

When we found dated passages, we located them on the chronological chart.
This enabled us to put many prophecies and events of Jeremiah's ministry
in their proper historical context. And we have been able to understand
much more clearly the historical background of the book of Jeremiah as a
whole.

29. In Lesson XII we studied Jer. 32-34, 37-44 and the fall of Jerusalem.
Explain briefly the historical and theological significance of that disas-

trous event. _____

_____

_____

_____

_____

* _____ *

See Lesson XII, E.

30. The historical background is a basic factor in Inductive Bible Study.
In our study of the book of Jeremiah one of our beginning steps was to look
for the historical background. As we continued to study the book we realized
that it was necessary to refer constantly to the historical background.

In this process we made use of several methods. Read over the following list
to see if you understand how to use these methods.

a. We looked for historical information in the book of Jeremiah and in other
parts of the Bible.
b. We found that it was necessary to organize this historical information.
c. We calculated the dates of Jeremiah's ministry on the basis of Jer. 1:1-3.
d. We found important information about the three world empires in 2 Kings
and 2 Chron.
e. We memorized the dates of four major international events: the fall of
Nineveh, the battle of Megiddo, the battle of Carchemish, and the fall of
Jerusalem.
f. On the basis of the previous information we made a political map of the
time of Jeremiah.
g. We also made a chronological chart of the period.
h. We referred back to the political map and chronological chart frequently
for orientation of specific passages and of the book of Jeremiah as a whole.

31. The third basic factor in Inductive Bible Study is structure. One of the
beginning steps in the study of a book like Jeremiah is to look for its
structure. Not only at the beginning but throughout the process of Inductive Bible Study structure is important. In the analysis of a brief passage

or a long one it is important to find its structure. And when a book does not have a clear overall structure, you have to look for the hidden structures.

Why do we study structure in Inductive Bible Study? _____

_____

_____

_____

*   *

Earlier we mentioned three reasons:
a. In order to find the central ideas or message.
b. In order to see relationships between the different parts or ideas.
c. In order to help you review the contents and find specific passages.

32. Write out a definition of structure. Try to remember the definition we

used earlier. _____

_____

_____

_____

_____

_____

*   *

See Lesson XIII, A, 1.

33. List the six <u>levels</u> of structure found in a book like Jeremiah.

a. _____   d. _____

b. _____   e. _____

c. _____   f. _____
*   *

See Lesson XIII, A, 6.

34. List five different <u>kinds</u> of structure.

a. _____   d. _____

b. _____   e. _____

c. _____

See Lesson XIII, A, 23.

35. In Lesson XIII you made an extensive study of structure in the book of Jeremiah. Therefore we will list here some of the methods we have used. You should now know how to use these methods. Above all, you should know how to look for structure inductively.

a. We made a summary of Jeremiah's message (five main ideas) and noted the relationships between these ideas.
b. We grouped paragraphs into sections by finding the main idea in each paragraph.
c. We made an overall outline of the book of Jeremiah by grouping the sections into divisions.
d. Since the overall structure of the book of Jeremiah is very weak, we turned to the following hidden structures:
    1. The historical background.
    2. The experience of the prophet.
    3. The summary of Jeremiah's message.
e. We noted many other structural elements in the book of Jeremiah:
    1. The original title of the book (Jer. 1:1).
    2. Editorial comments in the text.
    3. The personal references to Jeremiah.
    4. The three different types of material: poetic sayings, biographical prose, and prose discourses.
    5. Links between passages.
    6. Topical, chronological, biographical, and logical arrangement.
f. We studied how Jeremiah's prophecies were recorded (Jer. 36, 45).
g. We made a study of how the book of Jeremiah was put together.

D. Practical Application

In this course we have suggested several ways in which you can apply what you have learned about the book of Jeremiah in your life and ministry. We will review those suggestions and extend the lists of specific applications.

There are at least two important reasons why we should look for practical applications of Inductive Bible Study. In the first place, it is hard work. It takes time and discipline. And very few people will go to all that trouble unless they find that it does help them in their daily life and ministry. In the second place, Inductive Bible Study is not worth doing unless it does contribute in significant ways to your life and ministry. It can be

very exciting and it can be an interesting academic pursuit. But its real
value is that it enables you to understand and communicate God's word.

1. First, read over the following suggestions. See if Inductive Bible Study
can help you significantly in these areas. And see if these applications
are important enough to make you continue doing Inductive Bible Study on
your own. Now is the time to decide. Before you leave this course you should
decide to make Inductive Bible Study a part of your life and ministry, or
you may never do so. And this course will have failed.

> 1. Devotional reading and study.
> 2. Sermon preparation.
> 3. Lessons for Sunday school and other programs.
> 4. Formation of Biblical theology.
> 5. Other special uses.

2. The first suggestion is that you use Inductive Study in your <u>daily devotional Bible reading</u>. Think over the methods and tools we have been review-
ing in this lesson. Then write down a plan for your own future devotional
Bible reading and study. Indicate clearly which methods or tools you would

like to continue using. _____

_____

_____

_____

_____

_____

_____

I would especially recommend three methods and one tool.
a. First ask God to apply the passage to your own life. Pray about it and
act accordingly as He shows you His will for you.
b. Look for the spiritual and practical applications of the passage for
your congregation and community. Pray about these.
c. As you read through a book like Jeremiah, work out an outline of it.
At least analyze the main idea of each paragraph and choose a title for
it. Even if you don't figure out all the sections for a complete outline,
you will have a significant record of what you have read.
d. Keep a notebook. At first you may not know what to put in it. But if
you have it available during your devotional reading and study, your
notebook can become a real treasure store of God's messages to you and
material for your ministry. You can keep in it your outlines of the books
you study and outlines and notes for sermons and lessons.

3. The second suggestion is to use Inductive Bible Study in sermon preparation. If you do carry on Inductive Bible Study regularly as part of your daily devotions or as part of your daily study program, you will be building a constant supply of preaching material. And if you do preach regularly, there is no better way to get the necessary sermon material.

Think over the methods we have used in this course and pick out the ones you would like to continue using in the future as you prepare sermon outlines.

_____

_____

_____

_____

_____

You may want to turn back to Lesson VIII now or later to review the methods for sermon outline preparation which are presented there. The steps for preparing sermon outlines are listed also in the Appendix, and you have prepared already in this course five sermon outlines based on texts from the book of Jeremiah. Keep these outlines along with other preliminary notes in your notebook on the book of Jeremiah.

4. You may want to prepare a series of sermons based on the book of Jeremiah. This series could be used at regular worship services. And later you could use them at special conferences or retreats.

Think how many sermon outlines you could develop out of your Inductive Study of the book of Jeremiah. Extend the following lists of texts and titles for possible sermons.

Important experiences in the life of the Prophet Jeremiah:

a. Jer. 1:4-10   "The Call of Jeremiah"

b. Jer. 26; 7:1-15   "The Temple Sermon"

c. Jer. 15:10-21   "Confessions of a Prophet"

d. _____   _____

e. _____   _____

f. _____   _____

g. _____   _____

h. _____   _____

Jeremiah's acted parables:

a. Jer. 13:1-11 _____   "The Linen Waistcloth Episode" _____

b. Jer. 19:1-20:6 _____   "The Broken Flask Episode" _____

c. _____   _____

d. _____   _____

e. _____   _____

Literary figures from the book of Jeremiah:

a. Jer. 1:11-12 _____   "The Sprouting Rod" _____

b. Jer. 1:13-16 _____   "The Boiling Pot" _____

c. Jer. 2:1-3 _____   "The Devoted Bride" _____

d. Jer. 2:12-13 _____   "Broken Cisterns" _____

e. Jer. 3:1-5 _____   "The Insatiable Harlot" _____

f. Jer. 10:1-16 _____   "Scarecrows in a Cucumber Field" _____

g. _____   _____

h. _____   _____

i. _____   _____

j. _____   _____

k. _____   _____

l. _____   _____

m. _____   _____

n. _____   _____

o. _____   _____

Historic events at the time of Jeremiah:

a. Jer. 25, 46 _____   "The Battle of Carchemish" _____

b. Jer. 39 _____   "The Fall of Jerusalem" _____

c. _Jer. 29_____   _"A Letter to the Exiles"_____

d. _____   _____

e. _____   _____

f. _____   _____

g. _____   _____

5. The third suggestion for the practical application of Inductive Bible
Study is this: Use these materials in teaching Sunday school lessons or in
other classes.

You have studied many passages in the book of Jeremiah, answering questions
and using various methods. And you have prepared a number of lessons based
on passages in Jeremiah. How would you like to use these materials?

_____

_____

_____

_____

_____

_____

_____

_____

_____

_____

Here are some possibilities:
a. Try teaching some of these Jeremiah lessons in a Sunday school class or
some other class. You may have to adapt or simplify the materials for your
students. And you will be able to improve the materials on the basis of
your experience with them. Don't answer the questions for them. Help them
to discover the joys of Inductive Bible Study.
b. You may want to use a more informal approach in small groups interested
in Bible study. Your role would be to raise questions and get them to raise
questions about the text.
c. Someday you may find a group of people interested in taking this course.
You could be the teacher, and they could use this same material. Or you
could use some other course.

d. The lists of passages and topics for sermons which you have just completed could be developed into lessons rather than sermon outlines. In fact
you could work out a sermon outline with your students at the end of each
lesson.
e. You may want to change the format of one of your weekly church services
so that the members will participate in the Bible study rather than listen
to another sermon. Just develop the methods and questions that will help
them find out what the text has to say and what it means for us today.

6. The fourth suggestion is to apply Inductive Bible Study in <u>the formation
of Biblical theology</u>.

In Lesson XIV you studied several theological concepts in the book of Jeremiah. And you learned some basic steps in Biblical theology. What practical

application could Biblical theology have in your ministry? _____

_____

_____

_____

_____

_____

* _____ *

Perhaps Biblical theology does not seem to be very practical. It is not like
sermon outlines or lesson plans, which can be used directly. But behind all
that you do in your ministry -- teaching, preaching, counseling, administra-
tion, etc. -- lies your theology or philosophy of life. The concepts that
make up your theology or philosophy of life should be based on the Bible.
The formation of Biblical theology is the best way to ground your theology
or philosophy of life in the Bible. And Biblical theology is the inductive
analysis of the message of the Bible.

7. You have investigated three theological concepts in the book of Jeremiah.
You should study these three concepts further. And you may want to study
other theological concepts in the book of Jeremiah. Add to the following
list. And note how important these concepts are for your own theology and
philosophy of life.

a. __The covenant_____

b. __Religion_____

c. __Social justice_____

d. _____

e. _____

f. _____

g. _____

8. The final suggestion in this section is to find <u>other special uses</u> for Inductive Bible Study.

Use your imagination. What could you do with the insights you have drawn from your Inductive Study of the book of Jeremiah? What other uses would you suggest besides the ones we have mentioned? What are some different ways of expressing the tragic experiences and poetic expressions and inci-

sive proclamations of Jeremiah? _____

_____

_____

_____

_____

_____

_____

_____

*   *

Here are some suggestions:
a. Try writing a poem about Jeremiah. Or, if you teach a class on Jeremiah, ask your students to write a poem about Jeremiah.
b. Prepare a play. It could be primarily historical and tell the story of Jeremiah's ministry. Or it could be a modern interpretation and tell what Jeremiah would do if he were alive today.
c. Select a series of readings from the book of Jeremiah. His language is poetic and dramatic, and his message is powerful. You could give a whole sermon by quoting Jeremiah's prophecies without commentary. Or a gifted person could develop a full evening program of readings from the book of Jeremiah.
d. Do a painting or a series of sketches from the life and ministry of Jeremiah. Or make a collection of famous artists' interpretations of Jeremiah the Prophet.

e. Prepare a large wall-size map and a large wall-size chronological chart of the time of Jeremiah as we suggested earlier in this course. This would be a good project for a Sunday school class.

9. We have considered five major suggestions for the practical application of our Inductive Study of the book of Jeremiah. As you study other books of the Bible you will probably discover other ways of applying the results of Inductive Study in your life and ministry.

Read over these five suggestions and check the ones which you hope to carry out. This is just for your own benefit. But remember that if you don't find some very significant ways to apply Inductive Bible Study you won't want to work at it and you probably won't do it at all.

1. Devotional reading and study _____

2. Sermon preparation _____

3. Lessons for Sunday school and other

   programs _____

4. Formation of Biblical theology _____

5. Other special uses _____

10. Here is one final, practical suggestion. Before you finish this course, organize your Jeremiah notebook. Be sure you have all the materials from the appendix of this workbook. Set up a section for sermon outlines and another for lesson materials. The outline of the book of Jeremiah will be a section by itself. Decide what other materials you want to include.

On the basis of your experience with this Jeremiah notebook you may want to start notebooks on other books of the Bible as you continue your own Inductive Bible Study. If you keep this up over the years, you will become a real student of the Bible and you will have an abundance of material for your own guidance and for your ministry to others.

E. Final Examination

Most courses end with a final examination. At your next class session you will probably have to take a final examination on this course. In this lesson you have reviewed the course in order to prepare yourself for the final examination.

But let's ask ourselves what is the purpose of a final examination. Most people think of exams as judgment day. Other students approach their examinations with fear and trembling. The professor grades their examinations as a judge gives out sentences. With this last, tense, disagreeable experience the course ends. And all that has been learned can be forgotten.

516 15:E   Lesson XV: INDUCTIVE BIBLE STUDY

We have tried to avoid that concept of final examinations. The important
thing is not for your professor to judge your work in this course. But
there are two important things that we need to find out. First, you need
to see if you have achieved what you set out to do in this course. And
second, your professor needs to see if this course has achieved what it
set out to do.

Throughout this course we have talked about objectives. At the very beginning we listed a number of specific goals. And we stated that your main
purpose in this course is to learn how to study and use the Bible. That, we
have assumed, has been your primary objective, and it has been the primary
objective of this course.

Therefore the final examination in this course has been designed to evaluate
our achievement -- your achievement and the course's achievement -- of this
primary objective. The purpose of this exam is to enable you to see if you
can do Inductive Bible Study on your own. At the same time it will show
your professor if this programmed workbook can teach Inductive Bible Study.
In other words, you are being tested, and this workbook is being tested. If
you have not learned how to do Inductive Bible Study, this course should be
changed.

1. The first part of the final examination will test what you have learned
about the book of Jeremiah. Our main purpose has not been to teach what
the book of Jeremiah contains. But we have used this book of the Bible as a
case study, an experiment. So you will be asked to answer some questions
about the book of Jeremiah.

Turn back to the introduction to this book. Read over the list of objectives.
This will tell you what kind of questions you will be asked about the book
of Jeremiah. This part of the examination contains no surprises, because
you have known what to expect from the very beginning of the course.

Note that there is very little information that you need to memorize. There
are three or four dates, which you know already, and a simple map. The rest
of the questions will deal with basic concepts and skills which you have
studied extensively.

You will be able to use your Bible in all three parts of this examination.
It would be foolish to test you without the Bible when our purpose has been
to teach you how to use the Bible.

2. The second part of the final examination will test your ability to analyze a brief passage of the Bible. It may be a passage from the book of
Jeremiah. Or it may be a passage from another Old Testament prophet. The
important thing is to see if you can study the text inductively on your own.

You should know how to look at the passage on its own terms, find out what
is the context. You should be able to choose and use methods that will help
you analyze the meaning of the passage. (You have practiced using many

methods in your study of passages in Jeremiah, and you reviewed some of
those methods in Section B of this lesson.) Finally, you should know how to
apply that passage in your own life and ministry.

You will be given a text. You will make your analysis of that text. You will
explain how you worked out your Inductive Study of that text step by step.
And you will prepare a sermon outline or a lesson based on that text. In
other words you will go through the process of Inductive Bible Study just
as you would in your ministry day by day. If you can do it for an exam, you
will be able to do it for your ministry. If you cannot do it on an exam,
you are probably not prepared to do it in your ministry.

3. The third part of the final examination will test your ability to analyze a book of the Bible. Since you have already made a study of the book
of Jeremiah, you will be asked to begin an Inductive Study of some other
book, probably another prophetical book of the Old Testament.

You should know how to do an Inductive Study of a book like Jeremiah. You
should know what beginning steps to take. And you should be able to choose
and use methods that will help you study that book on its own terms. (You
have used many methods in your study of the book of Jeremiah, and you reviewed some of those methods in Section C of this lesson.)

You will be asked to begin an Inductive Study of a book. Since you will
have only a little time, you will only be able to take the basic beginning
steps. You will be asked to explain these steps and methods. In other words
you will begin the process of Inductive Bible Study as you would in your
ministry day by day, year after year.

4. If you have studied faithfully the lessons in this course, you are probably already prepared for the final examination. You do not need to study
any more. if you have not done the previous work conscientiously, you probably are not ready for the final examination. And you won't be able to prepare for it now by studying just a few hours. You may have to go back
through the previous lessons all over again. That is because you are being
tested primarily on your ability to do Inductive Bible Study, not on information you have memorized.

If you have studied conscientiously this course and are now ready for the
final examination, you are also ready to carry out Inductive Bible Study on
your own in your daily ministry. That has been our primary goal. Let me encourage you to go on beyond the examination to the real test: Inductive
Bible Study for personal growth and fruitful ministry. Now, while your experiment with the book of Jeremiah is fresh in your mind, is the time to
get started on your own. If you don't do it now, you probably never will.
So make your decision now.

Also, if you have the opportunity, take other courses in Inductive Bible
Study. Study one of the historical books or a poetical book from the Old

Testament, a gospel or an epistle from the New Testament. But don't let
these courses take the place of your own independent study. In fact, it will
be much more important and valuable for you to study a book on your own than
it will be to take another course.

Appendices

NOTE:

Pages A.9 through A.25 are perforated for easy removal and punched so that they can be stored in a three-ring Jeremiah notebook.

Pages A.4-A.8 must be developed on separate notebook paper.

Pages A.1 and A.2 will have to be removed carefully with a knife. We could have perforated these sheets only by doing so for another 32 pages.

Political Map of the time of Jeremiah

Chronological Chart of the Time of Jeremiah

Steps for Preparing Sermon Outlines

1. Choose a Text.
    a. Does it have an important application to the life of your congre-
       gation?
    b. Is it interesting?
    c. Is it a manageable unit?

2. State the Purpose of Your Sermon.
    a. Is it similar to the purpose expressed in the text?
    b. Is it personal?
    c. Is it clear and definite?

3. Write a Summary of the Content of the Passage.
    a. Is it complete?
    b. Is it in order?
    c. Is it brief?

4. Give Your Sermon a Title.
    a. Does it represent the content of the sermon?
    b. Is it attractive?
    c. Is it concise?

5. Make the Outline Itself.
    a. Does it have some kind of order?
    b. Does it express the message of the text?
    c. Does it apply that message to our lives?

6. Write Out the Introduction and Conclusion of the Sermon.
    a. Do they arouse interest in the topic of the sermon?
    b. Do they focus attention on the purpose of the sermon?
    c. Do they relate the sermon to the lives of the listeners?

Text: _Jeremiah 1:4-10_

Title: _____

Purpose: _____

_____

NOTE: PLEASE USE THIS MODEL FOR EACH OF
THE FIVE SERMON OUTLINES YOU ARE TO PREPARE:

Summary: _____

Page A4:   Jeremiah 1:4-10
Page A5:   Jeremiah 2:12-13
Page A6:   Jeremiah 5:22-23
Page A7:   Jeremiah 7:1-15
Page A8:   Jeremiah 13:1-11

_____

_____

_____

_____

Outline

Introduction: _____

_____

_____

I. _____

    A. _____

    B. _____

II. _____

    A. _____

    B. _____

III. _____

    A. _____

    B. _____

IV. _____

    A. _____

    B. _____

Conclusion: _____

_____

Outline of the Book of Jeremiah

Division	Section	Paragraph	Paragraph Title — Josiah, Jehoiakim, Zedekiah	Main Idea — Historical Background of the Books	Special Details
Intro-duction -:1-3	Call of Jeremiah 1:4-19	1: 1-3			
		4-10			
		11-12			
		13-16			
		17-19			
		2: 1-3			
		4-8			
		9-13			
		14-19			
		20-25			
		26-32			
		33-37			
		3: 1-5			
		6-10			
		11-14			
		15-20			
		21-23			
		24-25			
		4: 1-4			
		5-8			

Division	Section	Paragraph	Paragraph Title	Main Idea	Special Details
		9-10			
		11-18			
		19-22			
		23-28			
		29-31			
		5: 1-3			
		4-5			
		6			
		7-9			
		10-13			
		14-17			
		18-19			
		20-29			
		30-31			
		6: 1-5			
		6-8			
		9-15			
		16-21			
		22-26			
		27-30			
		7: 1-4			
		5-7			

A.11

Division	Section	Paragraph	Paragraph Title	Main Idea	Special Details
		8-15			
		16-20			
		21-26			
		27-29			
		30-34			
		8: 1-3			
		4-7			
		8-13			
		14-17			
		18-21			
		22-6			
		9: 7-9			
		10-11			
		12-16			
		17-19			
		20-22			
		23-24			
		25-26			
		10: 1-5			
		6-10			
		11			
		12-16			

Division	Section	Paragraph	Paragraph Title	Main Idea	Special Details
		17-18			
		19-21			
		22			
		23-24			
		25			
		11: 1-5			
		6-8			
		9-13			
		14-17			
		18-20			
		21-23			
		12: 1-4			
		5-6			
		7-13			
		14-17			
		13: 1-7			
		8-11			
		12-14			
		15-17			
		18-19			
		20-27			
		14: 1-6			

Division	Section	Paragraph	Paragraph Title	Main Idea	Special Details
		7-9			
		10			
		11-12			
		13-16			
		17-18			
		19-22			
		15: 1-4			
		5-9			
		10-12			
		13-14			
		15-18			
		19-21			
		16: 1-4			
		5-9			
		10-13			
		14-15			
		16-18			
		19-20			
		21			
		17: 1-4			
		5-6			
		7-8			

A.14

Division	Section	Paragraph	Paragraph Title	Main Idea	Special Details
		9-10			
		11			
		12-13			
		14-18			
		19-23			
		24-27			
		18: 1-4			
		5-11			
		12			
		13-17			
		18			
		19-23			
		19: 1-9			
		10-13			
		14-15			
		20: 1-6			
		7-12			
		13			
		14-18			
		21: 1-2			
		3-7			
		8-10			

Division	Section	Paragraph	Paragraph Title	Main Idea	Special Details
		11-12			
		13-14			
		22: 1-7			
		8-9			
		10			
		11-12			
		13-17			
		18-19			
		20-23			
		24-30			
		23: 1-4			
		5-6			
		7-8			
		9-15			
		16-17			
		18-20			
		21-22			
		23-32			
		33-40			
		24: 1-3			
		4-7			
		8-10			

Division	Section	Paragraph	Paragraph Title	Main Idea	Special Details
		25: 1-7			
		8-14			
		15-16			
		17-26			
		27			
		28-29			
		30-31			
		32			
		33-38			
		26: 1-6			
		7-9			
		10-11			
		12-15			
		16-19			
		20-23			
		24			
		27: 1-7			
		8-11			
		12-15			
		16-22			
		28: 1-4			
		5-9			

A.17

Division	Section	Paragraph	Paragraph Title	Main Idea	Special Details
		10-11			
		12-16			
		17			
		29: 1-9			
		10-14			
		15-23			
		24-28			
		29-32			
		30: 1-3			
		4-7			
		8-9			
		10-11			
		12-17			
		18-22			
		23-24			
		31: 1-6			
		7-9			
		10-14			
		15			
		16-20			
		21-22			

Division	Section	Paragraph	Paragraph Title	Main Idea	Special Details
		23-25			
		26			
		27-30			
		31-34			
		35-36			
		37			
		38-40			
		32: 1-5			
		6-8			
		9-15			
		16-25			
		26-35			
		36-41			
		42-44			
		33: 1-9			
		10-11			
		12-13			
		14-16			
		17-18			
		19-22			
		23-26			
		34: 1-5			

Division	Section	Paragraph	Paragraph Title	Main Idea	Special Details
		6-7			
		8-22			
		35: 1-11			
		12-17			
		18-19			
		36: 1-3			
		4-8			
		9-10			
		11-19			
		20-26			
		27-31			
		32			
		37: 1-2			
		3-5			
		6-10			
		11-15			
		16-21			
		38: 1-6			
		7-13			
		14-16			
		17-23			
		24-28			

A.20

Division	Section	Paragraph	Paragraph Title	Main Idea	Special Details
		39: 1-10			
		11-14			
		15-18			
		40: 1-6			
		7-12			
		13-16			
		41: 1-3			
		4-8			
		9-10			
		11-18			
		42: 1-6			
		7-17			
		18-22			
		43: 1-7			
		8-13			
		44: 1-10			
		11-14			
		15-19			
		20-23			
		24-30			
		45: 1-5			
		46: 1			

Division	Section	Paragraph	Paragraph Title	Main Idea	Special Details
		2-6			
		7-12			
		13-17			
		18-19			
		20-21			
		22-24			
		25-26			
		27-28			
		47: 1-7			
		48: 1-2			
		3-8			
		9			
		10			
		11-13			
		14-17			
		18-20			
		21-25			
		26-27			
		28-33			
		34-36			
		37-44			
		45-47			

Division	Section	Paragraph	Paragraph Title	Main Idea	Special Details
		49: 1-2			
		3-6			
		7-11			
		12-16			
		17-22			
		23-27			
		28-30			
		31-33			
		34			
		35-38			
		39			
		50: 1-3			
		4-5			
		6-7			
		8-10			
		11-16			
		17-20			
		21-27			
		28			
		29-30			
		31-32			
		33-34			

A.23

Division	Section	Paragraph	Paragraph Title	Main Idea	Special Details
		35–38			
		39–40			
		41–42			
		43			
		44–46			
		51: 1–5			
		6–10			
		11–14			
		15–19			
		20–23			
		24			
		25–26			
		27–33			
		34–37			
		38–40			
		41–44			
		45–46			
		47–49			
		50–51			
		52–53			
		54–57			
		58			